Linguistics and Semiotics in Music

Contemporary Music Studies

A series of books edited by Nigel Osborne, University of Edinburgh, UK

Volume 1
Charles Koechlin (1867–1950) His Life and Works
Robert Orledge

Volume 2
Pierre Boulez – A World of Harmony
Lev Koblyakov

Volume 3
Bruno Maderna
Raymond Fearn

Volume 4
What's the Matter with Today's Experimental Music? Organized Sound Too Rarely Heard
Leigh Landy

Volume 5
Linguistics and Semiotics in Music
Raymond Monelle

Additional volumes in preparation:

Hanns Eisler
David Blake

Stefan Wolpe
Austin Clarkson

The Other Webern
Christopher Hailey

New Music Notation: A Handbook
Rosemary Dunn

Cage and the Human Tightrope
David Revill

Italian Opera Music Theatre
Since 1945
Raymond Fearn

The Toneclock
Peter Schat

Edison Denisov
Yuri Kholopov and Valeria Tsenova

Soviet Film Music
A Historical Perspective
Tatanya Yegorova

Music, Myth and Nature
The Dolphins of Arion
François-Bernard Mâche

This book is part of a series. The publisher will accept continuation orders which may be cancelled at any time and which provide for automatic billing and shipping of each title in the series upon publication. Please write for details.

Linguistics and Semiotics in Music

Raymond Monelle
University of Edinburgh, UK

Copyright © 1992 by Harwood Academic Publishers

First published 1992 by Harwood Academic Publishers

Transferred to digital printing 2002
by Routledge, 11 New Fetter Lane, London EC4P 4EE

Routledge is an imprint of the Taylor & Francis Group

Cover photo:
Girl playing the Kithara.
Reproduced by kind permission of the Musée du Louvre AGR.
© Photo R.M.N.

Library of Congress Cataloging-in-Publication Data
Monelle, Raymond, 1937-
    Linguistics and semiotics in music / Raymond Monelle.
        p.   cm. -- (Contemporary music studies ; v. 5)
    Includes bibliographical references and index.
    ISBN 3-7186-5208-0 (hard). -- ISBN 3-7186-5209-9 (soft)
    1. Music--Semiotics. 2. Linguistics. I. Title. II. Series.
ML3838.M69 1991
   780'.14--dc20   91-33172
                                                                            CIP
                                                                            MN

No part of this book may be reproduced or utilized in any form or by any means, electronic or mechanical, including photocopying and recording, or by any information storage or retrieval system, without permission in writing from the publisher.

To Cathy and Julia

CONTENTS

Introduction to the Series   xi
Preface   xiii
Copyright Acknowledgements   xv

1. Introduction: Music and Meaning
   - 1.1. The changing views of musical meaning   1
   - 1.2. Alternative views of meaning   13
   - 1.3. Semiotics as radical theory   21
   - 1.4. Linguistics and semiotics   24
   - 1.5. The emergence of music semiotics   27

2. Linguistic and Structuralist Theory, from Saussure to Piaget
   - 2.1. Philology and linguistics   32
   - 2.2. Saussure   32
   - 2.3. The Prague school: Pertinence and opposition   35
   - 2.4. American linguistics   39
   - 2.5. Hjelmslev's 'glossematics'   43
   - 2.6. Chomsky: Transformation and generation   47
   - 2.7. The linguistic emphasis   52
   - 2.8. The coming of structuralism   53

3. Metalanguage, Segmentation and Repetition
   - 3.1. The problem of musical segmentation   59
   - 3.2. Syntagmatic repetition and segmentation   65
   - 3.3. Duplication in the music of Debussy   69
   - 3.4. Segmentation based on logic   74
   - 3.5. A 'machine' for discovering paradigms   80
   - 3.6. The problems of segmentation   88

4. The Analysis of the Neutral Level
   - 4.1. The neutral level   90
   - 4.2. Paradigmatic analysis   94
   - 4.3. A paradigmatic analysis of Debussy's *Syrinx*   100
   - 4.4. Varèse's *Density 21.5*   108

4.5.	Formative repetition in themes by Debussy	115
4.6.	The semiotics of analysis	120
4.7.	Analysis of music or theory of music?	124

5. Transformation and Generation

5.1.	Chomsky's generative grammar	127
5.2.	The contribution of Bernstein	127
5.3.	Embedding and left-branching	131
5.4.	Deep structure and transformation in jazz	134
5.5.	Lerdahl and Jackendoff: generative analysis	135
5.6.	The computer analysis of chorales	146
5.7.	Generating music by rule	149
5.8.	Generation of tunes by computer	153
5.9.	John Blacking on musical competence	155
5.10.	A glance back at Chomsky	158

6. Linguistics and World Music

6.1.	Studies based on phonemics, phonology and pure structuralism	162
6.2.	Studies based on generative theory and semantics	172
6.3.	Meaning in ethnic musics	187
6.4.	The boundaries of semiotic studies	190

7. Icon, Index and Symbol

7.1.	The semiotic theory of C S Peirce	193
7.2.	The limitations of iconism	200
7.3.	Expression as icon	203
7.4.	Wilson Coker on icon and index	204
7.5.	'Formal iconism'	206
7.6.	Music as indexical sign	209
7.7.	Rheme, legisign and sinsign in music	214

8. Semantics and Narrative Grammar

8.1.	Music and semantics	220
8.2.	The historicity of semantic accounts	220
8.3.	Grammar and design in Beethoven	221
8.4.	Topic, rhetoric and structure in Classical music	226
8.5.	Structural semantics	232
8.6.	Lexeme and context in the *Tristan* Prelude	236
8.7.	Semic systems	242
8.8.	Narrative grammar	244
8.9.	Myth and music	251
8.10.	Narrative patterns in instrumental music	258

       8.11. The semiotic square   264
       8.12. Markedness theory   268
       8.13. The formal nature of semantic analysis   272

9. The Theory of Intonation
       9.1. The music of speech   274
       9.2. Asafiev's *Musical Form as Process*   274
       9.3. Intonation in popular song   279
       9.4. Two Scottish singers   284
       9.5. Kojak and Abba   285
       9.6. The piano music of Liszt   294
       9.7. The art of intoned meaning   303

10. Deconstruction and Allegory
       10.1. Deconstruction and *Différance*   304
       10.2. Deconstructive criticism   308
       10.3. Some errors   315
       10.4. Deconstruction and music theory   316
       10.5. The myth of unity   320
       10.6. The implications of deconstruction   321

11. Epilogue   324

Bibliography   328

Index of persons   343

Introduction to the Series

The rapid expansion and diversification of contemporary music is explored in this international series of books for contemporary musicians. Leading experts and practitioners present composition today in all aspects - its techniques, aesthetics and technology, and its relationships with other disciplines and currents of thought - as well as using the series to communicate actual musical materials.

The series also features monographs on significant twentieth-century composers not extensively documented in the existing literature.

NIGEL OSBORNE

PREFACE

What is music semiotics? It is a question semiologists are often asked, and unfortunately there is no quick answer. If you try to explain the many sides of this study to the casual enquirer, he has usually lost interest long before you get through the half of it.

Nor has there been a single book you could send people to; the various applications to music of linguistic and semiotic ideas have resulted in an extensive spread of analytical and theoretical studies which are contained in articles, books and conference papers in many languages. Although there have been works with names like *Introduction to the Semiotics of Music* (Stefani 1976), *Semiotics of Music* (Schneider 1980) and *Outline of Musical Semantics* (Karbusicky 1986), there has so far been no simple 'layman's guide' to the whole subject; most scholars are committed to their own particular approach, and assume a familiarity with technical and philosophical language. The most important treatise is Nattiez's *Foundations of a Semiotics of Music*; the indefinite article in the title reveals that this is one man's view, and in any case, certain new approaches have been proposed since the publication of this work in 1975.

The present book is intended to satisfy the enquirer who is more than casual - in fact, to introduce the educated musician to the whole field of music semiotics. Linguistic and semiotic terms are explained and certain typographic habits of the linguist - the placing of an expression or sign-vehicle between oblique lines, or the use of 'guillemets' to indicate items of content - are avoided. Naturally, some areas have been stressed more than others; the omission of certain important studies does not necessarily imply disrespect. Drawing together the many aspects of musical semiotics is like rounding up a flock of particularly wayward sheep; alas, some have got away from the present shepherd.

The temptation has been resisted to branch into related subjects; the sociology and cognitive psychology of music are scarcely touched on, and the extensive writing on computers in music has been no more than mentioned. Thus, outstanding figures like Ivo

Supicic, Christopher Longuet-Higgins, John Sloboda and Otto Laske are either ignored or given merely a glance.

I wish to thank the Faculty of Music of the University of Edinburgh for giving me a term's leave to finish this project. Two distinguished friends, Professor Nigel Osborne and Professor Eero Tarasti, performed the incomparable service of reading the original draft in its entirety and offering valuable suggestions; my warm thanks to them. I must thank also, for their help and encouragement in various ways, Dr Craig Ayrey, Dr Peter Cooke, Steve Dowers, Professor Jonathan Dunsby, Bruce Gittings, Catherine Gray, Dr Robert Hatten, Dr Sandor Hervey, Professor David Lidov, Steve Mackenzie, Professor Jean-Jacques Nattiez, Peter Nelson, Robert Samuels, Dr Philip Tagg, and the late Professor James Thorne. The final preparation of copy would have been impossible without the help of my daughters, the dedicatees, who also compiled the index.

It goes without saying that this book's virtues are largely due to the above persons. Its faults are all mine; but since the censure of a man's self is oblique praise, as Johnson said, I will keep quiet about that.

Raymond Monelle
Edinburgh

Copyright Acknowledgements

I am grateful to the following publishers, editors and authors for permission to use copyright graphic material.
The American Anthropological Association, for figures 6.4, 6.5, 6.6 and 6.7; the American Musicological Society, for figures 3.6, 3.7 and 3.8; Basil Blackwell Publishers Ltd and the Editor, *Music Analysis*, for figures 4.13, 4.14, 4.15, 4.16 and 4.17; Bocu Music Limited, for figures 9.12a, 9.13a and 9.13g; Christian Bourgois Editeur, for figure 4.22 and the diagrams on pp. 170 and 193; Cambridge University Press, for figures 9.1, 9.2, 9.3, 9.4, 9.5, 9.6 and 9.7; Armand Colin Editeur, for figure 7.1; CPP/Belwin/International Music Publications, for figures 7.3 and 9.11f; Elsevier Science Publishers BV, the Editor, *Cognition* and Professor J E F Sundberg, for figures 5.23, 5.24, 5.25 and 5.26; EMI United Partnership/International Music Publications, for figures 9.10b and 9.13f; Harper-Collins Publishers Ltd, for figure 7.2; Harvard University Press, for figures 5.1, 5.2, 5.3 and 5.4; Harvester Wheatsheaf (Simon and Schuster International Group) for figure 2.1; the Editor, *International Review of the Aesthetics and Sociology of Music*, for figure 8.37; the Editor, *Journal of Music Theory*, for figures 5.21, 5.22, 6.8, 6.9, 6.10, 6.11, 6.12, 6.13, 6.14 and 6.15; MCA Music Publishing and Music Sales Limited, for figure 9.9a; MIT Press, for figures 5.10, 5.11, 5.12, 5.13, 5.14, 5.15, 5.16, 5.17, 5.18, 5.19 and 5.20; Professor Jean-Jacques Nattiez and the University of Montreal, for figures 3.3, 3.4, 4.18, 4.19, 4.20, 4.21 and 5.27; Florian Noetzel Verlag, for the table on p. 171; Penguin Books Ltd, for figure 2.4 and the chart on p. 82; the Managing Editor, *Perspectives of New Music*, for figure 6.3; Frances Pinter (Publishers), for figure 8.25; Princeton University Press, for figures 8.5 and 8.8; the School of Scottish Studies, University of Edinburgh, for figures 9.8b and 9.8c; Editions du Seuil, for figures 3.1, 3.11 and 3.12; Dr Philip Tagg, for figures 9.9, 9.10, 9.11, 9.12 and 9.13; Professor Eero Tarasti, for figures 8.31 and 8.37; the University of Texas Press, Austin, for figures 5.5, 5.6, 5.7, 5.9 and 5.29; Union Générale d'Editions, for figures 4.2, 4.3, 4.4, 4.5, 4.6, 4.7, 4.8, 4.9, 4.10, 4.11 and 4.12; and Warner/Chappell Music, Scandinavia AB, for figure 9.13b.

Rather more than half of the music examples were type-set by Words and Music, 9 Malvern Villas, Durham DH1 2JP. I am grateful to them.

1

INTRODUCTION: MUSIC AND MEANING

1.1. The changing views of musical meaning

1.1.1. Semiotics is the theory of signs, from the Greek word for sign, σημειον. Since music seems meaningful - it is more, apparently, than its physical sounds - many have taken it to be a sign. Gino Stefani goes so far as to say it 'does not need demonstrating' that music is a sign (Stefani 1974, 280).

When educated musicians inquire about semiotics, they often ask, 'Has it anything to do with Deryck Cooke's *The Language of Music?*' Others wish to know if it is related to the established theories of musical signification: the ideas of imitation, expression, symbolism. Things would be easy if one could simply reply in the negative. But in fact, all of these traditions have semiotic ingredients; the best introduction to semiotics is not to discard every familiar view of musical communication, but to review the intellectual traditions of the modern world and show how they relate to the disciplines of semiotics.

In the first part of this chapter, therefore, the various views of music, from the eighteenth century to the writings of Langer and Cooke, are examined to bring out their semiotic content. It will become clear that, while each tradition bears obvious relations to semiotic theory, there is a missing ingredient: the rigorous and explicit scientificity of the modern study. This is its hallmark. Each of the past writings has been no more than critical speculation.

Still, if you are not interested in the roots and lineage of music semiotics, you should go on to Chapter 2. The present chapter is a sort of bridge passage or modulation from the diverse world of traditional intellectuality to the bracing atmosphere of semiotic science.

1.1.2. The eighteenth-century theory of imitation, with its roots in Aristotle; its derivative, the idea of expression; the symbolic theory of Susanne Langer, and Deryck Cooke's lexicon of emotion - none of these approaches could be called semiotic, though some of them are perhaps pre-semiotic. The first two were often confused in the eighteenth century; much of the so-called *Affektenlehre*, indeed, is based on this confusion. For example, André Morellet, in his book *De l'Expression en Musique et de l'Imitation dans les Arts* of 1771, makes no attempt to distinguish the two.

> I regard as synonymous, at least in the present question, the terms *express* and *depict* (which perhaps are always so); and as all depiction is imitation, to ask if music has expression, and in what the expression consists, is to ask if music imitates, and how (Lippman 1986, 269).

Writers were troubled, however, by the apparent stress on musical onomatopoea which came with imitation theory. The imitation of 'the glidings, murmurings, tossings, roarings, and other accidents of water', and of 'the voice of some animals, but chiefly that of singing birds' (from James Harris, *A Discourse on Music, Painting, and Poetry*, 1744), seemed only a marginal part of the function of music. The business of music was not imitation but expression.

> Musical imitation is greatly below that of painting, and... at best it is but an imperfect thing...
> As to the efficacy therefore of music, it must be derived from another source, than imitation. It remains, therefore, that these things be explained. Now, in order to do this, it is first to be observed, that there are various affections, which may be raised by the power of music. There are sounds to make us cheerful, or sad; martial, or tender; and so of almost every other affection, which we feel (Harris 1765, 69 and 95-96).

Charles Avison (in *An Essay on Musical Expression*, 1752), finds the grosser kind of imitation an enemy to true expression, in fact.

> And, as dissonance and shocking sounds cannot be called musical expression; so neither do I think, can mere imitation of several other things be entitled to this name... Thus the gradual rising or falling of the notes in a long succession, is often used to denote ascent or descent, broken intervals, to denote an interrupted motion, a number of quick divisions, to describe swiftness or flying... Now all these I should choose to style imitation, rather than expression; because, it seems to me, that their tendency is rather to fix the hearer's attention on the similitude between the sounds and the things which they describe, and thereby to excite a reflex act of the understanding, than to affect the heart and raise the passions of the soul.

Introduction

> For the sake of a forced and... an unmeaning imitation, [the composer] neglects both air and harmony, on which alone true musical expression can be founded... Music as an imitative art has very confined powers... Imitation is only so far of use in music, as when it aids the expression (Avison 1752, 57-59).

When it came to explaining the expressivity of music, writers were divided. French theorists favoured the idea that music reproduced the tone of voice and gestures of a person moved by passion. Charles Batteux, who wrote the standard text on imitation (*Les Beaux Arts réduits à un Même Principe*, 1743) saw music as an 'imitation of feeling or of the passions'; there are three means of 'expressing ideas or feelings', namely, *parole, ton* and *geste*.

> Speech expresses passion only by means of the ideas to which the feelings are linked, as if by reflection. Musical sound and gesture reach the heart directly without any deviation. In a word, speech is a language of institution, which men made to communicate their ideas more distinctly: gestures and musical sounds are like the dictionary of simple nature; they contain a language which we all know at birth, and which we use to declare everything related to the needs and the preservation of our being: also it is lively, terse, energetic. What better foundation for the arts whose object is to move the soul, than a language whose expressions are more those of all humanity than of particular men! (Batteux 1746, 254-255)

Rousseau (in the *Essai sur l'Origine des Langues* of 1753) adds to this the idea that music originated from the stress and rhythm of natural speech. In ancient Greek, speech rhythm was nearer to melody than is the case in modern languages, and the sound of the language was more directly an expression of the feelings of the speaker.

> With the first voices were formed the first articulations or the first sounds, according to the various types of passion which dictated them. Anger arouses menacing cries articulated by the tongue and palate; but the voice of tenderness is gentler, it is the glottis that modifies it, and this voice becomes a tone; only its accents are more rare, the inflections more or less sharp, according to the feeling that is joined to it. Thus cadence and sounds are born with syllables; passion makes all the organs speak, and endows voices with all their lustre; thus verse, song, speech have a common origin.

This is to suggest that all human utterances are fundamentally expressive of feeling, and that with the decline of languages through the stress on 'logical argumentation' (Neubauer 1986, 98) the rhythmic and melodic aspects of expression passed into music. Nevertheless, Rousseau persisted in regarding music as an imitative art - imitative not of the movements of nature, but of the sound of passionate speech.

> By imitating the inflexions of the voice, melody expresses the complaints, the cries of pain or joy, the menaces and the groans; all the vocal signs of passion are at its disposal. It imitates the accents in languages and the linguistic turns that certain movements of the soul create in every idiom; it speaks instead of merely imitating, and its inarticulate but quick, ardent, and impassioned language has a hundred times more energy than the word itself (quoted by Neubauer, 1986, 100).

Some writers distrusted the speculative view that music imitated the speech-tones of a lost, emotionally heightened language. Perhaps there is some inner movement of the 'nerves' or 'spirits' which music imitates, thought Daniel Webb.

> There is just reason to presume, that the passions, according to their several natures, do produce certain proper and distinctive motions in the most refined and subtle parts of the human body... I shall take advantage of the received opinion touching this matter, and assign the functions in question to the nerves and spirits. We are then to take it for granted, that the mind, under particular affections, excites certain vibrations in the nerves, and impresses certain movements on the animal spirits.
>
> I shall suppose, that it is in the nature of music to excite similar vibrations, to communicate similar movements to the nerves and spirits. For, if music owes its being to motion, and if passion cannot well be conceived to exist without it, we have a right to conclude, that the agreement of music with passion can have no other origin than a coincidence of movements' (Webb 1769. 5-7).

In evoking the passions music is much less detailed, however, than painting can be in portraying the visual aspects of reality. There are really just four broad classes of feeling which music can depict, 'distinguished by their accords with the passion of pride, sorrow, anger, and love'. Music makes up for this deficiency by being an art of expression as well as imitation; while painting and sculpture are merely imitative arts, 'music acts in the double character of an art of impression as well as of imitation'.

Finally, expression took over decisively from imitation as the received theory of musical meaning. It was expected that performers feel and experience the passions which they convey: 'Since a musician cannot move unless he is moved, he must be able to project himself into all the affects which he wants to arouse in the listeners; he makes them understand his passions and moves them thereby best to sympathy' (C P E Bach in the *Versuch über die wahre*

Art, das Clavier zu spielen, 1753, quoted by Neubauer, 1986, 157-158). Johann Gottfried Herder placed expression even before sensual pleasure; he considered that 'expressions of passion, in irregular, bold, powerful accents of feelings' came earlier in music's development than the desire to please (in the *Critische Wäldchen*) and in the *Adrastea* he condemned 'painting objects instead of expressing emotions'.

It should be noted that neither of these views - that music imitates nature, or that it expresses feeling - is current today. Modern expression theory departs from the assumption that an emotion, felt by the composer, is transmitted to the listener. Music is a *presentation* of feeling rather than a direct expression; we should say, according to Peter Kivy, that music is 'expressive of sadness' rather than that it merely 'expresses' sadness (Kivy 1980, 23). 'In other words, the affect of sadness is not a result of music but a quality we ascribe to it' (Neubauer 1986, 151).

Eighteenth-century views of musical meaning are, in fact, much nearer to semiotic theory than the Romantic views that succeeded them. The sign that signifies by resembling its object (the imitative view), and the sign that is in natural contiguity with its object (the expressive view), are classes recognised by the semiotic theory of Peirce (see below, Chapter 7). But the old views can only be described as proto-semiotic; they are, first of all, not rigorously logical and inductive; and secondly they make no attempt to describe the *workings* or *mechanism* of musical signification, but merely generalise about its principles. Semiotics tends to concentrate on pattern rather than content, to seek out structure rather than to interpret meanings. The eighteenth century was mainly concerned with the setting of words to music; writers sometimes affirmed that music without words 'signifies nothing' (Rousseau on 'Sonata' in the *Encyclopédie*) or is 'only noise' (D'Alembert in the 'Discours Préliminaire' to the same work). They were therefore chiefly interested in the specific emotional expression and content of music, so that it could be aptly fitted to its text. Such a concern is not characteristic of modern theory.

1.1.3. The nineteenth-century view of musical signification occupied a different part of the intellectual universe. The new generation of writers was convinced that music conveyed a special kind of feeling, or at least that it revealed a special order and significance within the world of feeling. Schopenhauer's aesthetics was a new kind of Platonism; music was able to bypass the representation of real feelings and get in touch with their inner essences. The meaning of music, in philosophical terms, was transcendent; it was something not accessible to ordinary experience.

> [Music] does not express this or that particular joy, but anxiety, pain, horror, jubilation, happiness, contentment in themselves, to a certain extent in the abstract, unaccompanied by any incidentals and thus by any self-interest. And yet we understand them completely in this quintessential form... Music expresses only the quintessence of life and its happenings, not those happenings themselves, the details of which thus do not always affect it (Schopenhauer, *Die Welt als Wille und Vorstellung*, in Le Huray and Day 1981, 328).

Like Schopenhauer, Hegel believed music to be an art of emotion. Just as inarticulate cries are direct expressions of the soul, so is music the art of the inner consciousness (*Kunst der Innerlichkeit*). The inner consciousness may, indeed, express itself in words; but music communicates with it on a deeper level, that of emotion, 'the self-extending subjectivity of the ego'. Though emotion, in real life, usually attaches itself to some content or other, 'it still leaves this content confined within the ego unconnected with anything external and is not thereby formally connected with it. In this way, emotion always remains only the outward covering of the content. It is this field in which music operates' (Hegel, *Ästhetik*, in Le Huray and Day, 344).

Emotion, then, is the living trace of *Innerlichkeit*, and in its purest form is not connected with any object or content. Music proceeds from, and communicates with, that inner consciousness; its 'meaning' is thus prior to anything that can be put into words.

Since music somehow escaped involvement in the messy affairs of life to present feelings in a pristine state, it was considered to have a moral purity and strength - a notion the Greeks would have found congenial. Anton Friedrich Thibaut thought that music represented 'all states of sensation, of emotion and of the passions, but poetically, and thus not such that they are presented in a decadent state, but in all force and purity' (Thibaut 1861 [1826], 110).

Contemporary with these philosophical voices were the Romantic writers, who suggested a different kind of transcendence in music, based on mystical notions rather than intellectual ones. The unhappy consequences of shifting musical meaning into the area of the transcendent are even more apparent here. Wackenroder simply shrouds music in mystification; for E T A Hoffmann, the emotions of music are fragments of some elemental and overmastering emotion. Nothing could be further from a semiotic tone.

> Music is the breath of the spiritual in its highest form, its finest manifestation, the invisible stream as it were from which the soul draws sustenance for its deepest dreams. Music engulfs the human spirit. It means both everything and nothing. It is a finer and perhaps subtler medium than language (W H Wackenroder, *Phantasien über die Kunst für Freunde der Kunst*, in Le Huray and Day 1981, 250).
>
> Is not music the mysterious language of a more distant spiritual realm whose wonderful accents strike a responsive chord within us, and awaken a higher and more intense life? All passions, armed glitteringly and splendidly, fight with each other and dissolve in an unutterable yearning which fills our breast... [Music] unlocks for man an unknown realm, a world which has nothing in common with outward existence, a world in which he renounces every distinct feeling... All tone-painting which violates this inborn essence of music is to be rejected (E T A Hoffmann, quoted by Brown, 1968, 19).

This sort of obscurantism was popular throughout the nineteenth century; it has left us with a suspicion of any sort of cool or scientific theorizing about music. Even in our own time, speculative writing has gravitated towards the ineffable and the hidden. The greatest music aesthetician of the twentieth century, Susanne Langer, while she abjures any idea of transcendence, nevertheless favours a view of symbolism based on the idea of *sentience*, the content of which cannot be named or put into words. One cannot help thinking of Hegel's *Innerlichkeit*.

There is a tension in Langer's work, however, resulting from a debt to her teacher Alfred North Whitehead. Whitehead had this to say of symbolism:

> The human mind is functioning symbolically when some components of its experience elicit consciousness, beliefs, emotions, and usages, respecting other components of its experience (from *Symbolism, its Meaning and Effect*, 1927).

The climate of this statement is positivistic and anti-transcendent; both symbol and meaning are 'components of experience' and are thus, presumably, accessible apart from the symbol-function. But the assumption of the Romantic writers was that the signification of an artistic symbol was transcendent and available only through art. A linguistic symbol - a word or phrase - is a good example of Whitehead's kind, on the other hand; both the phonological and the semantic component can be known apart from the linguistic function. When one hears an object named in an unknown language, both the idea of the object and the sound of the word are 'components of experience'; only the connection is lacking.

Langer, then, has to show that both music and its meaning are accessible to ordinary experience. Her view of musical symbolism is worked out in *Philosophy in a New Key* (1942), and extended to all the arts in the later *Feeling and Form* (1953). It is based on the notion of 'significant form', which Langer gets from Clive Bell's important book *Art* (1914).

> It is useless to go to a picture gallery (said Bell) in search of expression; you must go in search of Significant Form.

Music, thinks Langer, is not an embodiment of emotion but the 'expression of an idea'; and thus it is a symbol, for symbols are defined as related to ideas of things, not to things themselves. It is not, however, a conventional symbol; it is a symbol by virtue of being 'felt as a quality' rather than 'recognized as a function'. This is accounted for by its 'logical similarity to the forms of human feeling':

> Forms of growth and of attenuation, flowing and stowing, conflict and resolution, speed, arrest, terrific excitement, calm, or subtle activation and dreamy lapses - not joy and sorrow perhaps, but the poignancy of either and both - the greatness and brevity and eternal passing of everything vitally felt (1953, 27).

All these things add up to the 'logical form of sentience'. This cannot be put into words; however, this does not imply that it is unavailable to ordinary knowledge. 'It seems particularly hard for our literal minds to grasp the idea that anything can be known which cannot be named'. Music is described as a 'tonal analogue of emotive life'.

> Our interest in music arises from its intimate relation to the all-important life of feeling, whatever that relation may be. [The function of music is] not the symptomatic expression of feelings that beset the composer but a symbolic expression of the forms of sentience as he understands them. It bespeaks his imagination of feelings rather than his own emotional state, and expresses what he knows about the so-called 'inner life'; and this may exceed his personal case, because music is a symbolic form to him through which he may learn as well as utter ideas of human sensibility (Langer 1953, 28).

Introduction

Langer is extremely wary of any suggestion that the 'forms of sentience' are some kind of transcendence. Her disciple, Gordon Epperson, rushes in where she feared to tread. The musical symbol, he says, gives 'a more meaningful configuration to the vagaries of experience' (Epperson 1967, 290). If experience becomes 'more meaningful' when it is incorporated into art, then some extra signification must be added, and this can only be transcendent.

Apparently, music's mode of signifying, for Langer, is based on the same congruence with the movement of the 'nerves' or 'spirits' that was suggested by Daniel Webb. But her added contribution is crucial. Music supplies some information or perception about the life of emotion, which gives it order and intelligibility; it turns into the 'forms of sentience'. It is hard to see how this order could be apprehended or communicated apart from music. This makes the musician an important member of society, with an educational and prophetic function; 'an enlightened society usually has some means, public or private, to support its artists, because their work is regarded as a spiritual triumph and a claim to greatness for the whole tribe' (1953, 28).

The order introduced into emotional life by music is a transcendent order. The significance of Clive Bell's 'significant form' was clearly meant to be transcendent; Bell did not think that the insights of art could be known by any other means. So transcendence was built into Langer's system from the start, and Epperson was right in concluding from this that music spoke of something 'more meaningful' than experience.

Such notions are neither related to semiotics, nor capable of discussion in semiotic terms. Idealist metaphysics, on which most aesthetic writing has been based since 1800, is a speculative concern beyond the reach of scientific theory. If music has no other meaning than a transcendent one, then semiotics has nothing to say. Where idealist aesthetics formulates a philosophy of music, semiotics merely tries to encompass a theory of music.

1.1.4. As a counterbalance to the many theories of musical expression and communication, there are a few writers who deny absolutely that music has any meaning at all. Hanslick's *Vom musikalisch-Schönen* comes to mind as an apparent rebuttal of the whole idea that music is a sign. 'The essence of music is sound and motion'; music is like an 'arabesque' or a 'kaleidoscope' which, if it expresses anything, conveys 'musical ideas' only. Any attempt to make music into a signifying system like language merely destroys the life of music; 'the innate beauty of form [is] annihilated in pursuit of the phantom "meaning"'.

It is true that Hanslick meant to base music aesthetics on a theory of beauty (and thus on a transcendent notion) rather than an expression theory. He is surprisingly ready, however, to admit the emotional power of music.

> Every real work of art appeals to our emotional faculty in some way... Far be it from us to underrate the deep emotions which music awakens from their slumber, or the feelings of joy or sadness which our minds dreamily experience... Music operates on our emotional faculty with greater intenseness and rapidity than the product of any other art.

Hanslick is even quite old-fashioned in finding that music can imitate natural phenomena: 'the falling of snow, the fluttering of birds, and the rising of the sun can be painted musically only, by producing auditory impressions which are dynamically related to those phenomena'.

One purpose of music aesthetics, writes Hanslick, is not to describe the emotions expressed by music, but to describe the process whereby music (as opposed to other arts) goes about expressing them. 'Everything depends upon the specific *modus operandi* by means of which music evokes such feelings.' While Hanslick does not really achieve this goal, getting bogged down eventually in pseudo-physiological accounts of 'nerves' and 'ganglia', his observation is truly acute and is in tune with the spirit of semiotics. The semiologist, like Hanslick, is more interested in the *system* of signification than the material signified; he sees systems as empty webs of relations, 'without positive terms' (the phrase is Saussure's, but it sets the theme for all structuralist study).

Music cannot express specific emotions like love or anger because these imply life-situations which have to be described in words.

> What part of the feelings, then, can music represent, if not the subject involved in them?
> Only their dynamic properties. It may reproduce the motion accompanying psychical action, according to its momentum: speed, slowness, strength, weakness, increasing and decreasing intensity. But motion is only one of the concomitants of feeling, not the feeling itself. It is a popular fallacy to suppose that the descriptive power of music is sufficiently qualified by saying that, although incapable of representing the subject of a feeling, it may represent the feeling itself - not the object of love, but the 'feeling of love'. In reality, however, music can do neither. It cannot reproduce the feeling of love, but only the element of motion, and this may

occur in any other feeling just as well as in love, and in no case is it the distinctive feature (Hanslick 1891, 37-38).

There is little attempt to show in what respect emotion has 'dynamic properties'. The phrase 'psychical action' suggests that Hanslick follows Daniel Webb in thinking that affections 'impress certain movements on the animal spirits'; that there is an inner quality of movement that characterises each emotion. If this is a correct inference, then Hanslick is an exceedingly old-fashioned exponent of imitation theory.

While he admits that music stimulates and expresses feelings, Hanslick recommends that music aesthetics be founded on the quality of beauty which we attribute to music. This quality is connected with the abstract play of shapes and patterns, not with expressive features. In spite of this, he has important advice for music semiologists: study the manner of signification, not the matter signified.

1.1.5. Let us now approach the study of musical signification that is, perhaps, best known to people today. The philosophical and theoretical content of Deryck Cooke's *The Language of Music* is slight, but this book has appealed to many readers as a revelation of expressive meaning in music. The programme Cooke sets himself is at once semiotically oriented and quite at odds with semiotics.

> The task facing us is to discover exactly how music functions as a language, to establish the terms of its vocabulary, and to explain how these terms may legitimately be said to express the emotions they appear to.

The study of 'how music functions', as Hanslick saw, is a proper pursuit for the theorist. But Cooke never really considers the manner of functioning of musical expression; when he approaches the problem he becomes confused about the nature of language itself.

> Is the traditional language of music... a genuine emotional language, whose terms actually possess the inherent power to awaken certain definite emotions in the listener, or is it a collection of formulae attached by habit over a long period to certain verbally explicit emotions in masses, operas and songs, which produce in the listener a series of conditioned reflexes?

Language itself, however, is precisely that collection of formulae established by tradition - 'arbitrary signs', the linguist would say -

which Cooke rejects. If music is an inherent language, based on natural correspondences between sounds and meanings, then it is what semiologists would call an *indexical sign* rather than a language. Much of Cooke's discussion of expressive value uses the ideas of tension and resolution, suggesting the sympathy of movements between music and feeling, envisaged by Hanslick and Daniel Webb. The central thesis of this book adheres to a particularly naive form of expression theory.

The discovery of the 'terms of the vocabulary', however, occupies most of Cooke's time and effort. He is, in fact, chiefly concerned with the description of connotations rather than the system of signifying; this book is a lexicon of musical significations.

Of the pattern 'ascending 5-1-(2)-3 (minor)', for example (the figures are degrees of the diatonic scale), he has the following to say:

> If the major version of 5-1-3 stresses joy pure and simple, by aiming at the major third, the minor version expresses pure tragedy, by aiming at the minor third. And to move upward firmly and decisively from the lower dominant, via the tonic, to the minor third, gives a strong feeling of courage, in that it boldly acknowledges the existence of tragedy and springs onward (upward) into the thick of it, as composers have realized (Cooke 1959, 124-125).

This is illustrated with fragments of melody by Morley, Schütz, Purcell, Handel, Mozart, Schubert, Wagner, Berlioz, Mussorgsky, Verdi, Debussy, Delius, Stravinsky and others.

In some respects Cooke approaches his material in a characteristically semiotic way. He segments musical utterances according to meaning (according to pertinence, the linguist would say), and then constructs paradigms - fields of similar terms which occur throughout the work and throughout the language, and persistently carry similar meanings. He is not concerned with metaphysical speculation. Perhaps his 'basic terms' could be thought of as *morphemes* in the linguistic sense, or even *musemes*, a term used by Charles Seeger and Philip Tagg to mean a musical morpheme. They even resemble the 'vocabulary of intonations' which Boris Asafiev envisaged as the key to music, especially as Cooke occasionally cites themes from popular music (see Chapter 9, below, on Asafiev and Tagg).

Asafiev believed, however, that a system of intonations defined a particular musical culture; for him, there is no question of *natural* signification in music. The chief thrust of the Russian writer was to show that great music is embedded in the whole musical scene of its time, and that masterpieces are made up of the same bricks that build folksong and popular tunes. By situating his 'terms' on the side of nature rather than culture (in the structuralist dichotomy of Lévi-Strauss) Cooke departed fundamentally from semiotic theory.

It must be admitted, however, that the gravest criticism of Cooke's work can be levelled at Asafiev and Tagg also. There is a tendency - pronounced in Cooke, implied in Asafiev - to take a view of meaning which is outmoded and naive.

1.2. *Alternative views of meaning*

1.2.1. Let us now progress one step nearer to semiotics itself. Much of the writing on musical signification is vitiated by a naive view of meaning, the *referential* or *denotative* view; many of the difficulties are reduced, or at least change their nature, when we consider the extensive writings on this concept by linguists and logicians.

The referential view of meaning - the one-to-one or this-means-that view - was the starting point for British semiotic theory. John Locke's *Essay Concerning Human Understanding* dominated logical and semiotic thought for a century after its publication in 1690. In this work words are defined as the 'sensible signs of ideas'. Most ideas are abstract or general, so a word is not strictly speaking a sign of an object but of an 'essence', which is the 'bond between particular things'. 'Every distinct abstract idea is a distinct essence' (Locke 1964, 269), and thus words are the names of essences.

This kind of thinking is peculiarly unfruitful when applied to music, and it sets many problems when applied to language, too. If a word is the name for an idea that reveals the bond between a number of similar objects, as when *table* proclaims the common features of all particular tables, then what kind of idea or essence is named in words like 'should', 'realise' and 'with'?

1.2.2. Saussure's distinction of the 'signifier' and 'signified', which is discussed in the next chapter, seems to resemble Locke's analysis of referential meaning (though in fact Saussure's emphasis is quite different). Music is clearly not referential, and for this reason the whole idea of signification in music, and the suggestion that music is a language, are rejected by some of the most sophisticated modern writers. The notion of the signified, thinks Célestin Deliège, makes little sense in music.

> All the force is retained by the signifier which... transforms itself into mental images which it alone can release... To define the meaning of a musical work is an insurmountable task: every relation is pertinent and the possible number is probably infinite (Deliège 1987, 255).

The description of music in linguistic terms is considered by Karbusicky to be an 'exaggerated metaphor' (Karbusicky 1987b, 431). Musical signification is thus 'in reality a sub-metaphor'. Even when a musical element has apparently a clear denotative meaning, 'the symbolic quality is generally faintly defined'; for example, the imitation of a cuckoo seems to mean an object in the external world, but the figure is merely the interval of a third; its purely musical status is that of a structural element, and as such it is on equal terms with other structural intervals in the work. When the Soviet writer Medusevskij defines the signification of the dominant ninth on C as 'attesting to the presence of F major tonality or the proximity of the tonic', he is just misappropriating function as meaning. 'Music is very rarely reduced to being the vehicle of a signification,' says François-Bernard Mâche; 'it is enough that it has a sense but more like that of the water of a river than a syllogism' (Mâche 1969, 587; the French word *sens* also means 'direction').

Roland Harweg goes further than this: language and music are entirely different in nature. Language is 'nothing but the world's representational repetition through signs'. A linguistic expression simply stands for something in the world, which it momentarily replaces. Language need not be manifested in sound: 'it is irrelevant whether the entities that designate are sounds, written symbols, symbols of the morse code, or flag signals'. Music is 'not a significational/representational institution as is language... Language and music, in view of their immanent function, i.e. their very nature, cannot be compared at all' (Harweg 1968, 273). In the opposition language/world, music is on the side of the world, like 'sunsets and motor races'.

1.2.3. The Lockean view of signification was already being criticised in the eighteenth century; Edmund Burke, for example, said that the 'common effect' of words was not their 'raising of ideas of things' (in *A Philosophical Enquiry into the Origin of our Ideas of the Sublime and Beautiful*, 1757, quoted in Barry, 1987, 18).

The Lockean view is scarcely acceptable today. Nevertheless, it underlies the concept of referential meaning, which is still one of the acknowledged types. The contemporary linguistic writer John

Introduction

Lyons typifies referential meaning as 'the relation which holds between expressions of a language ('names' and 'predicates') and observable 'things' or 'qualities'... to which they refer or which they *denote*' (Lyons 1963, 53; my italics). This introduces into the discussion another important distinction, for referential meaning is evidently *denotative* meaning.

Denotation is distinguished from *Connotation*. It is the primary meaning of a term or expression, even if for practical purposes the meaning is rather different, or quite other, in a given circumstance. The penumbra of implied meanings generated by situation or context is called *connotation*, then. This may modify or even contradict the primary, face-value meaning; in practice, connotation is at least as important as denotation. G K Chesterton's cabby, coming to the end of a cul-de-sac in an unfamiliar part of London, exclaimed, 'This'll be all right!' The connotative, and real meaning was, 'This is no good at all.'

It has been said that musical meaning is entirely connotative, since no 'literal' meaning can be ascribed to musical terms. Each musical motive or fragment relies on context for its signification, and a single note can have no signification at all.

This simple inference is blocked by modern semiotic theory, however. Umberto Eco refers to Hjelsmlev in attacking the traditional view of denotation and connotation.

> The difference... is not (as many authors maintain) the difference between 'univocal' and 'vague' signification, or between 'referential' and 'emotional' communication, and so on. What constitutes a connotation as such is the connotative code which establishes it; the characteristic of a connotative code is the fact that the further signification conventionally relies on a primary one (Eco 1979, 55).

Hjelmslev showed that the expression plane of a connotative semiotic was itself another semiotic, expression plane and content plane together.

Thus, when I write 'yours sincerely' on a letter, my denotation is to signify, fictionally, that I am devotedly at the service of my correspondent, and (also fictionally) that this is not a fiction. Connotatively, I state that the letter is reaching a courteous conclusion. My courteous meaning is yielded, not merely by the formula of words but also by their fictional signification.

Figure 1.1.

CONNOTATION	
Expression	Content
Expression | **Content**	

DENOTATION

Music appears to have denotative meaning when some natural sound is imitated, or when a quotation from some other work or style is presented: a fanfare, horn call or shepherd's pipe. There is seldom a question of denotative meaning alone, however, as there can be in language. Karbusicky observes that the sound of the cuckoo, which presumably denotes the bird, can also signify, 'Spring is here!' In another context it can symbolise the whole of nature (in Mahler's First Symphony, for example); again, it can project an inner spiritual state, as in Beethoven's 'Pastoral' Symphony (the composer wrote, 'More an expression of feeling than a portrayal') (Karbusicky 1986, 61). In the 'Coucou au fond du bois' from Saint-Saens's *Carnaval des Animaux* the cuckoo becomes the voice of mockery. There is nothing in music, then, to resemble the linguistic expression 'cuckoo' which, as it stands, has denotative meaning only.

But language, like music, contains expressions entirely dependent on context for their meaning; expressions which have no denotative meaning in the ordinary sense. Roman Jakobson called these *shifters*. Personal pronouns are the most obvious example; clearly the meaning of 'I' changes according to the speaker. Musical expressions can be said to have this kind of meaning. The minor triad on E, in Smetana's *Vltava*, is the tonic chord, a primary element in an expression of simple majesty, tinged with sadness. In the chords of Brünnhilde's awakening in Siegfried, it is followed by a chord of C major and forms a serene, glowing cadence. The same chord, in different simultaneous contexts, could be part of the dominant ninth in D or the added sixth in G.

There is, of course, plenty of music with connotative meaning (emotional or illustrative); works which lack such meaning seem to lack denotative meaning also (the 'Forty Eight' Preludes and Fugues of Bach are often cited as an example). Yet music never seems meaningless. This suggests that denotation

Introduction

might have quite a different character in music, as I suggest below in Chapter 8.

1.2.4. The work of the Prague functionalists in the thirties revealed that language is a medium of communication as well as a bearer of signification. The 'meaning' of language - indeed, its being said to have meaning at all - varies according to its function in a given discourse. The denotative or referential function is only one of many.

It has become common to speak of the 'semiotics of signification' and the 'semiotics of communication'. For Eco, semiotics studies 'all cultural processes as processes of communication'. Luis Prieto entitles his first two chapters (in *Pertinence et Pratique*) 'Sémiologie de la communication' and 'Sémiologie de la connotation' (Prieto 1975). If there is indeed a division between the two approaches, then clearly the semiotics of communication is more suited to music; but Eco stresses that the two views are interdependent, and that all processes of communication 'would seem to be permitted by an underlying system of significations' (Eco 1979, 8).

Jakobson points out that speech events involve six factors. An addresser speaks to an addressee, using some medium of contact, audible speech, direct or by telephone, visual signs, writing or printing, gestures, or whatever. He conveys a message, which is framed in some code or other - language, probably, if the medium is oral. The whole event has a context, a human or intellectual world in which the participants exist and to which the message may refer (this account from Jakobson 1960).

```
                    context
                    message
addresser ------------------------ addressee
                    contact
                     code
```

The semiotics of signification examines the message and the context, expecting to find the whole meaning therein. But in fact, the real significance of an act of communication may lie chiefly in one of the other factors. For this reason, certain communicative events seem to have very little 'meaning' in the ordinary sense, and others, though meaningful, have meanings which are difficult to describe or isolate. Poetry and music, apparently, come into the latter group.

In most acts of communication, one of the six factors is primary. The function of the whole communication may then be described. If the *addresser* is predominant - if the speaker merely wishes to express himself, regardless of the means, or of the effect on a listener - then the communication is *emotive*. If his intention is directly to affect the behaviour of the addressee (as in a command or an official notice like 'Keep off the grass') the function is *conative*. If the stress is on *context*, then the message will seem to have a direct reference and importance, related to the circumstances of the participants; the function is *referential*. The emphasis on the *contact* produces a *phatic* utterance, which merely establishes or confirms the medium of communication itself, as when we say 'Hello!' on the telephone or make small talk in order merely to acknowledge the existence of communication. Communication about the *code* is called *metalingual*; all grammatical, linguistic and indeed semiotic discourse is of this type, language-about-language. And finally, if the *message* itself is the focus of interest, regardless of its direct relevance to our present circumstances or the actual situation of the speaker or hearer, then the function is *poetic*.

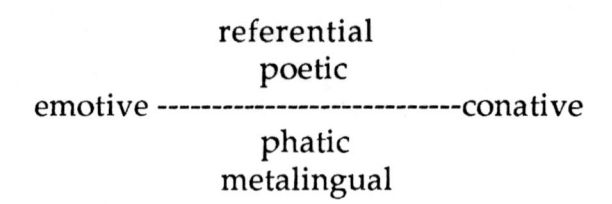

```
                     referential
                      poetic
      emotive ----------------------------conative
                       phatic
                     metalingual
```

From this analysis it is clear that language does not always refer to something beyond itself. The distinction of signifier and signified is chiefly relevant to the referential function of language; it is much harder to say what is 'meant' when somebody greets us with 'Good morning!' or when we read a poem. Nevertheless, both of these expressions are meaningful.

Music usually has a poetic function, of course. But it can also be emotive, as C P E Bach suggested when he required the performer to 'project himself into all the affects which he wants to arouse in the listeners', or when Sherlock Holmes released his inner tensions with cocaine and violin playing. It can be conative, when the bugle call 'reveille' commands soldiers to rise from their beds. It can even be phatic, when the *Cuckoo Waltz*, or some such tune, is played by a telephone on hold.

It is doubtful, however, that music can function metalingually or referentially. Hans Keller's 'functional analyses' of music, in

Introduction

which no word was spoken but structural affinities were demonstrated with bits of specially-composed material, might seem to use music in a metalingual manner, if it were not for their dependence on a whole tradition of verbal commentary. The referential or denotative function, as has been already stressed, is almost always problematic. Eco refers to 'trumpet signals in the army' as having 'explicit denotative value' (Eco 1976, 11) but these signals are primarily conative, as already suggested.

In fact, the referential function, which Locke considered to be the true function of semiosis and Deryck Cooke tried to graft on to music, is probably the least characteristic of the tonal art. Prejudice against the semiotic view of music is usually caused by the naive impression that all meaning is referential. Yet reference and denotation are often absent, even in language.

1.2.5. Something that is meaningful, but has no obvious meaning, is bound to suggest the deconstructionist idea of the *open* or *empty* sign. Indeed, two seminal deconstructionist texts are concerned with Rousseau's comments on music in the *Essai sur l'Origine des Langues*.

The disregard for 'positive terms' or 'real content' which always characterised structuralist semiotics led eventually to the suggestion that signs point fundamentally to a void. All historical views of meaning embraced a myth of presence, believing that within signification there was something real, some aspect of Being, some guarantee that man was at home in a universe of innocent and lucid expression. In views of language this led to a prejudice against writing, in which the speaker and listener appear to be absent; how can there be a 'presence' when the signification lies, unuttered and unread, on the page of a book?

According to Jacques Derrida in *De la Grammatologie* (1967) Rousseau 'opposed speech to writing as presence to absence and liberty to servitude... Writing takes the status of a tragic fatality come to prey upon natural innocence, interrupting the golden age of the present and full speech' (quoted in Neubauer 1986, 86-87). Yet Rousseau is even suspicious of the 'presence' that we sense in speech, 'of the illusion of presence within a speech believed to be transparent and innocent. It is toward a praise of silence that the myth of full presence... is then carried' (Derrida, quoted by Neubauer, 86).

In spite of these insights, Rousseau's theory of art is based on imitation; he imagines that there is something real, something with a habitation and name at the heart of signification.

> [Art] 'paints' the passions. The metaphor that transforms song into painting can force the inwardness of its power into the outwardness of space only under the aegis of the concept of imitation, shared alike by music and painting. Whatever their differences, music and painting both are duplications, representations (Derrida, quoted by Barry 1987, 9).

Paul de Man takes Derrida to task over this basic issue. Rousseau is impressed with the power of music, and de Man suggests that there is a counter-text in the *Essai*, a theory of signification based not on expression or imitation but on the empty play of signs, of which music is the best example. The philosopher's conviction that music is superior to painting is explained

> in terms of a value-system which is structural rather than substantial: music is called superior to painting despite and even because of its lack of substance (Paul de Man, Blindness and Insight, 1971, quoted by Barry, 9).

Music, in fact, is a tissue of relations only. A single note has no meaning. Musical sounds are 'empty characters, meaningless arbitrary signs that acquire significance only within a structure that man imposes on the infinite continuum of sounds' (Neubauer, 87). In support of this, de Man quotes a passage from Rousseau's *Essai*.

> For us, all sounds are relative and distinguished only in comparisons. No sound possesses by itself absolute properties that would allow us to identify it; only with respect to another sound is it high or low, loud or soft. By itself it has none of these properties. In a harmonic system, a sound is nothing on a natural basis. It is neither tonic, nor dominant, harmonic or fundamental. All these properties exist as relationships only, and since the entire system can be shifted from bass to treble, each sound changes according to its rank and place as the system changes in degree.

The musical sign is empty, not because of its impotence in referring to real objects, but because meaning is itself fundamentally empty; the sign points beyond itself, only to reveal a void. This is sharply reflected when music, an art of sound, represents silence, sleep and death, which are its opposites.

> The musician has the great advantage of knowing how to paint things one cannot hear; the greatest wonder of this art which can only be

Introduction

effective though motion is its ability to shape images of rest. Dream, calmness of night, solitude and even silence enter into the tableaux of music (Rousseau, quoted by Neubauer, 88).

The sort of consciousness revealed by music 'does not result from the absence of something, but consists of the presence of a nothingness' (de Man, quoted by Barry, 11). The almost ludicrous pursuit of musical meaning which we observe in aesthetic writings is thereby explained. Meaning is not to be found in the emotions of the composer or performer, or in the reactions of the listener, because these emotions are not real emotions. It is not to be found in the fabric of the music, because meaning has to be *attributed* to music. It is not to be found in the imitation of anything in nature, or in psychological or neurological sympathies. It is not, in fact, to be found anywhere; it is *absent*.

1.3. Semiotics as radical theory

1.3.1. It has been remarked that semiotics offers no philosophy of music; it proposes a *theory* of music. Although the tradition of structuralism, which is intimately linked with linguistics and semiotics, is shadowed by philosophical and political overtones, most of the approaches described in this book have no moral, metaphysical or ontological implications. 'Musical theory' is a long-established discipline; it is the repository of technical language, standard forms, techniques of analysis which lies behind every description of music in words. The semiotics of music is merely an alternative theory, which attempts to replace the views of established tradition with systems and approaches which are more radically scientific and logical, more comprehensive, more universal.

The need for such a radical theory may not be apparent to the ordinary musician. However, the ethnomusicologist, working as a member of the anthropological team, found that his methods and technical language were unscientific and quite unequal to coping with unfamiliar musical styles. His colleagues, especially the linguists, had worked out powerful general theories which permitted the analysis of strange languages and cultures; but musicology was unreformed, still the heir to medieval and Renaissance speculation and to the ideas of Rameau.

> Ethnomusicology is an anomaly in the twentieth century; we have ignored the philosophical and scientific discoveries of the last hundred

years, and we continue to use descriptive methods which, if they were known about, would fill a well-trained linguist or anthropologist with horror (Norma McLeod, quoted in Nattiez 1975, 89-90).

Terms like 'phrase', 'interval', 'scale' proved to be misleading when applied to ethnic music. In response to this problem, some investigators have proposed an 'ethnotheory', based on the native informant's theory of his own culture. But this, like the established theory of Western music, would be no more than a feature of the culture under review; 'the metamusical and ethnotheoretic discourse of our informants is only one of the possible documents that allow us to understand the whole musical fact'. Linguistic theory is not based on ethnotheoretical information; it is scientific and general.

1.3.2. Nevertheless, there is a muddy stream of opposition to pure theory which flows through the study of the humanities, especially in Great Britain. It is felt that all criticism, all analysis and description of the arts must be sensitive to the unique qualities of each work, and that theory is a combination of self-indulgent hot air and clandestine propaganda.

> What I now want to show is that the extension of [the scientific] model to the interpretation and judgement of literature, music and the arts, is factitious. Here the concept of theory and the theoretical, in any responsible sense, is either a self-flattering delusion or a misappropriation from the domain of the sciences. It represents a basic confusion, an "error of categories" as it is called in classical logic and metaphysics. To invoke and put forward a 'theory of criticism', a 'theoretical poetics and hermeneutic' in reference to the signifying forms of the textual and the aesthetic, in anything but the most scrupulously avowed metaphorical or mimetic sense, is to 'translate', to 'be translated' in the suspect, profoundly comical mode in which Bottom is "translated" in A Midsummer Night's Dream (George Steiner, 1989, 72).

It hardly needs saying that this kind of prejudice arises from a wish to defend the entrenched (and therefore unrevealed) canons of Western criticism, with their overtones of evaluative decree and normative prescription. Within every heuristics there lies a theory; an unwillingness to discuss it must be met with some suspicion. The outstanding feature of Western critical theory has been an exclusiveness or elitism, the very spirit which has filled our curricula with the study of one fraction of the music of one fraction of the world's cultures. This 'sensitivity' to the 'immediacy' of

Introduction

artistic experience, when applied to the arts of Africa or Asia, is merely ethnocentrism.

1.3.3. Traditional critical theory, expressed or otherwise, is not a basis for observing the art of a given culture; it is part of that culture itself. Naturally, the ideology of a society is embodied in its art, and equally in its criticism. The real structures of artistic and cultural life are not revealed by heuristic models, which just reflect the sort of preconceptions which we are taught to bring to aesthetic study.

> If real structures are to be discovered and their internal determinations revealed, it must be recognized that structures are distinct from models, in construction, logical status and purpose. As customarily conceived, a model is a heuristic device to simplify reality by expressing it in terms of a limited number of variables... or to deal with an unknown process by attributing to it a form known to operate elsewhere (Glucksmann 1974, 152).

Clearly, the real structures of art and society can never be revealed by traditional means, because tradition is committed to the preservation of these structures. Theory can only be based on deductive and inductive logic, on empirical observation and exhaustive study. We must make the '"epistemological break" that marks the transition from lived ideology to genuine theoretical knowledge' (Norris 1989, 306).

1.3.4. A vital objection to traditional theory is its normative quality. Viewed in a certain light, modern thought has been distinguished less by its empirical character, associated with the natural sciences, than its denial of the normative tendency, its deep suspicion of the desire to prescribe what should be, which is as characteristic of the social and human sciences as of physics and biology.

> Let us consider the concept of normative science in its relation to that of theoretical science. The laws of the first of these sciences, it is usually said, proclaim what should be, even though it is not so, and could not be so, in the given instance; the laws of the second, on the other hand, proclaim purely and simply what is (Husserl, *Les Recherches Logiques*, quoted in Sebag, 1964, 11).

Although normative science was historically first, the theoretical form is logically primary; you cannot say 'a soldier should be brave' without a theory of the 'good soldier'.

All the characteristic movements of the twentieth century have dissociated themselves from the normative. Freud's analytical psychology makes no distinction of right or wrong thinking, except to distinguish the healthy from the morbid. Durkheim describes elementary forms in the structure of society; he does not say what makes a good or bad society. Saussure shows that usage must be studied in seeking out the workings of a language; he does not speak of correct or incorrect language, except to discuss simple misunderstandings like the child's invention of 'viendre' for 'venir' (Saussure 1974, 168).

In politics and cultural studies, Lucien Sebag finds that Marxism and Structuralism represent the authentic theoretical sciences, 'the first being understood as a comprehensive theory of the social phenomenon, the second as the proper method of bringing to light the intelligibility of all things human' (Sebag 1964, 13-14). All study, whether in the exact sciences or in human studies, is dependent on theory. There is no information without observation, and observation is based on theory; it cannot yield theory since it is dependent on theory for its very methods of working. Without theory there is no physical reality to measure, and without the measurement, objective and disinterested, of reality our conclusions will merely embody the secret desire to manipulate the world for our own ideological interests.

1.4. Linguistics and semiotics

1.4.1. Semiotic study is related to familiar and established ways of thinking, but also essentially different. Like the imitation and expression theories of the eighteenth century, it is concerned with the idea of musical meaning, but not necessarily with meaning in any ordinary sense. Like Deryck Cooke, the semiologist is interested in the distinct meaningful fragments which can be found in music, but unlike him without any wish to interpret them.

Rigorously scientific, semiotics offers a new and radical theory as the basis for analysis and criticism. It is time now to observe its origins and historical development in the twentieth century.

Most historical accounts of structural semiotics find the fountainhead of the study in a famous passage from Saussure's *Cours de Linguistique Générale,* dating from the beginning of the century.

> A science that studies the life of signs within society is conceivable; it would be part of social psychology and consequently of general psychology; I shall call it semiology (Saussure 1974, 16).

There has been some controversy about the primacy of linguistics. Linguistics may have been the first to change from a speculative to a scientific study, but language is clearly just one of many systems of signs; semiotics is logically prior to linguistics. Saussure himself saw linguistics as 'only a part of the general science of semiology', and Jean Molino deplores the error of believing 'that language constitutes the model for all symbolic phenomena' (Molino 1975, 45).

However, in another place Saussure suggested that 'linguistics can become the master pattern for all branches of semiology although language is only one particular semiological system' (Saussure 1974, 68). Roland Barthes agrees with this, finding language embedded in everything.

> It is far from certain that in the social life of today there are to be found any extensive systems of signs outside human language. Semiology has so far concerned itself with codes of no more than slight interest, such as the Highway Code; the moment we go on to systems where the sociological significance is more than superficial, we are at once confronted with language. It is true that objects, images and patterns of behaviour can signify, and do so on a large scale, but never autonomously; every semiological system has its linguistic admixture (Barthes 1968, 9-10).

Sandor Hervey summarises the two alternative views.

> (a) Linguistics is the 'parent' discipline of semiotics; it has the more 'inclusive' theory...
> (b) Semiotics is the meta-discipline of which linguistics is a sub-discipline... linguistic notions are merely specialised semiotic notions (Hervey 1982, 5).

As a matter of fact, many enterprises in music semiotics have been based on linguistic theory. This is so much the case, that this book has had to cover a Wittgensteinian family of studies, some explicitly semiotic but not based on linguistics (like the sign-taxonomy of Peirce), some derived from linguistics but not avowedly semiotic (the generative analysis of Lerdahl and Jackendoff, for instance), some both linguistic and semiotic (the distributional analysis of Nattiez). Yet all of these efforts are joined by a common search for explicit and logically grounded theory, whether based on linguistic methods or not.

The disciplines of linguistics are so important to any study of semiotics that a whole chapter has herein been devoted to their history. In Chapter 2, below, references to music will be found to be sparse; an exposition of the various ventures in music semiotics is then able to follow without too much further groundwork.

1.4.2. It will be noticed that the science is sometimes called 'semiotics', sometimes 'semiology'. Another word derived from Greek σημειον will appear often in these pages: *semantics*.

The first of these terms, semiotics (or at least semiotic, without the S), is an established philosophical word. It is used by Locke and was common in the eighteenth century. J H Lambert named the second volume of his *Neues Organon* (1764) 'Semiotik oder Lehre von der Bezeichnung der Gedanken und Dinge' (Semiotics, or theory of the signification of thoughts and things). Since the American philosopher C S Peirce continued this tradition of nomenclature and called his sign-theory a 'semiotic', this term has tended to refer to the American, logic-based branch of the study.

'Semiology' is merely a translation of Saussure's term *sémiologie*, which dates only from 1893 (Karbusicky 1986, 12). Much of the linguistics-derived writing on semiotics has been in French, even though some of it (notably Nattiez's theory of paradigmatic analysis) is actually derived from American rather than French linguistics. With the founding of the International Association for Semiotic Studies in 1969, it was agreed that the term 'semiology' should be abandoned. French writers have continued to use it, however, even as a synonym for 'semiotics'. Its chief virtue seems to lie in its derivative, 'semiologist', which is surely to be preferred to 'semiotician', though one sometimes hears the latter. It has even been suggested that 'semiotics' be reserved for the logical study, based on Peirce, 'semiology' for the approach derived from linguistics. No such distinction is made in the present work, in which 'semiotics' and 'semiologist' are always preferred to 'semiology' and 'semiotician'.

There have been other terms which have flickered on the horizon. Mattheson writes in the *Vollkommene Kapellmeister* (1739) of 'Semeiographie'. Peirce's correspondent, Victoria, Lady Welby, called her sign-theory 'Significs' (in *What is Meaning? Studies in the Development of Significance*, 1903).

'Semantics' is another neologism, invented by Michel Bréal, who described his *Essai de Sémantique* (1904) as 'a simple introduction to the science which I have proposed to call

Semantics'. This was a 'science of significations', chiefly concerned with the way words change their meaning, extending, narrowing or shifting their original significations; it was thus distinct from phonetics and phonology, which concern themselves with the structures of linguistic sound. Karbusicky (1986, 17) gives definitions of the terms which have survived to describe the two branches of the subject.

> Semiotics ('theory of signs'): theory of human communication with the help of signs, which traces especially the factors of sign-morphology and the establishment of sign-systems: the essential logic and categories of its elaboration in basic relations (relations according to means, object and interpretant), its practical operation.
> Semantics ('theory of meaning'): theory of the conditions, psychological, anthropological, social-historical, cultural and aesthetic, which traces the processuality of the creation of meaning, its metamorphosis and dissolution.

Other terms have appeared. Karbusicky suggests that *Semasiology* be used for the whole science of signification, including the studies both of signifier and signified, while *Onomasiology* researches into its practical manifestation in particular signs. He admits, however, that all these terms are more often used fairly loosely.

1.5. *The emergence of music semiotics*

1.5.1. Music semiotics was born in the fifties and sixties and has taken many forms since then. A survey of the subject will reveal not a single developing discipline but a collection of varied and unrelated programmes. It is the same picture as one finds in general semiotics, according to Nattiez; rather than a single study called 'semiology', 'you have to speak of semiologies, or more precisely of possible semiological projects' (Nattiez 1975, 19).

One can divide the numerous approaches into two main trends, which might be called 'hard semiotics' and 'soft semiotics'. Tarasti speaks of the 'nominalists' and 'realists' among music semiologists. Originally it was envisaged that a rigorous scientific theory based on phonemics and distributionalism would wholly supersede traditional heuristics. When this golden age failed to dawn, attention was turned to transformational grammar and to semantics, making way for more intuitive studies.[1]

The idea of using linguistic methods in musicology was proposed in 1958 by the distinguished ethnomusicologist Bruno Nettl. He recommended that analysts of music first define the corpus which they intend to study. They should then ascertain the phonemic units; this work should follow distributional principles, which are not dependent on meaning, since meaning is so hard to define in music.

> The problem of meaning is not essential in that branch of descriptive linguistics with which we are concerned. The identification and distribution of elements, rather, is its task (Nettl 1958, 37).

This leads to the discerning of 'pitch phonemes', 'rhythmic phonemes', 'harmony phonemes', 'structure phonemes' and so on. Nettl shows how different phenomena may be considered equivalent - *allophones* - in various styles. The sixth and seventh degrees of the melodic minor scale each have two forms; certain rhythms in an Arapaho song, intervals in a piece by Krenek, or phrases and sections in Arab lute music, are understood as structurally identical. However, distributional laws can never be deduced from musical data; finally, one has only statistics.

William Bright echoed Nettl's insight, adding that separate *performances* of the same piece are like allophones since, with all their differences, they are considered equivalent. He sketched with particular clarity the evolution of a musical phonemics.

> If we find that, within a specified environment, two different events (whether single notes, or longer sequences) are accepted as equivalent or equally correct, then we may consider them as variants of a single musical 'phoneme' (or 'morpheme', or other unit), and thus determine the inventory of such basic units for each musical culture of the world (Bright 1963, 31).

In the event, the only successful phonemic analyses have appeared in quite marginal fields: in Kaeppler's brilliant analysis of Tongan dance (Kaeppler 1972) and Chandola's study of Indian drumming (Chandola 1977).

The comprehensive working out of a musical phonemics seemed to await only a definition of pertinence in music. When

---

[1] *Phonemics, distributionalism, transformational grammar.* These and other linguistic terms will be fully explained in the next chapter.

this proved difficult, Nicolas Ruwet suggested a means of applying distributionalism without necessarily requiring such a definition. He was impressed with the feature of *repetition*, varied and unvaried, which is the basis of Western musical form. After an article (1962) in which he showed the subtle implications of repetition in the works of Debussy, he compiled a coherent system for the distributional analysis of music (Ruwet 1966). This became the basis of Nattiez's theory of 'paradigmatic analysis', expounded chiefly in the *Fondements d'une Sémiologie de la Musique* (1975).

The tough theoretical stance of those days was typified by Gino Stefani, who proclaimed that the musical text must first be defined, apart from its production and perception (Stefani 1974), so that a specifically musicological study may be conducted, based on the 'principle of immanence'. This recalls the rigorous theoretical position of the linguist Louis Hjelmslev.

It will then be found that, on all levels, music can be viewed as signifier and signified. Semiotic study will proceed on strictly formal grounds, regardless of the signified, observing only the *syntactic* part of music. The investigator may then proceed to a *metascience*, a science-of-science, elaborating a systematic metalanguage of analysis and a *critical semiology* which analyses and assesses all the existing analyses. By making our criteria fully explicit, we may progress from traditional analogic language to formal symbols and finally to digital operations. Our analysis may then be tested by reconstitution - by allowing the analysis to generate the music again.

This kind of rigorous scientific approach, which turned its back on any idea of musical semantics or discernible musical meaning, dominated music semiotics in the seventies. It suffered a setback when Ruwet, who had been one of its instigators, denounced Nattiez's paradigmatic methods in a notorious article (Ruwet 1975). Nattiez was said to be 'an empiricist, a positivist' who failed to realise that theory has no basis in experiment; it is intuitive. Ruwet condemned the 'relativism' and 'behaviourism' which led, in Nattiez's analyses, to such meagre results. The progress of musical semiotics has been retarded by a desire for irrefutability, 'just as those who imposed the neo-Bloomfieldian approach have long prevented linguistics from seriously attacking semantic problems'.

At the same time, another linguistic tradition - the transformational-generative grammar of Chomsky - had impressed some musicians, particularly ethnomusicologists. There were a number of studies of ethnic music based on this principle. In addition, a similarity was realised between Chomskyan 'deep structure' and Schenker's idea of the *Hintergrund* and *Mittelgrund* of a musical event. This led eventually to the generative analytical theory of Lerdahl and Jackendoff (1983).

1.5.2. There were other influences. The semiotics of C S Peirce, dating from the turn of the century, seemed relevant to music because Peirce placed *iconic* and *indexical* signs alongside the linguistic variety which he called *symbolic*. This meant that many things, both in nature and culture, could be considered signs by virtue of their similarity to other things, or their habitual association or contiguity with their objects. The 'arbitrary' nature of linguistic signs was difficult to envisage in music.

The Soviet composer and critic Boris Asafiev, during the siege of Leningrad, wrote an inspired and highly speculative book, declaring that every musical gesture was meaningful and that music must be classified according to signification rather than syntax. Music is made up of *intonations*, drawn from a vocabulary that is universally understood in the given society; even the greatest music has its roots in the popular consciousness. Asafiev's influence has been chiefly felt in Eastern Europe, in the work of scholars like Vladimir Zak, József Ujfalussy and Jaroslav Jiránek.

The tendency to look for meanings in music - the turn away from distributionalism and 'nominalism' - was furthered by certain ideas of the anthropologist Claude Lévi-Strauss. He demonstrated the affinity between music and myth, suggesting that mythical 'themes' are presented, counterpointed and recapitulated like the themes of a fugue or - in one famous analysis - like the theme of Ravel's Bolero. The musical work is 'a myth coded in sounds instead of words' (Lévi-Strauss 1981, 659).

This overtly semantic view of music inspired Eero Tarasti, a Finnish scholar who had worked in Paris with the linguist A J Greimas, to examine the survival of mythical structures in Western music (Tarasti 1979), and to apply to music Greimas's theories of *semeanalysis* and *narrative grammar*. Music is viewed unreservedly as a semantic continuum and Tarasti even speaks of *thymic* analysis, from the Greek word for 'passion'; analysis is conducted according to the tensions, goals, accomplishments, frustrations of musical 'actors'. Other writers have adapted the ideas of Greimas in different ways (for example Stoianova 1987, Monelle 1991a, 1991b).

Introduction

The idea of musical semantics has become respectable. Célestin Deliège and Vladimir Karbusicky have dealt with this subject at length. A fresh look at vocal music has thus been possible (for example, Noske 1977, Dalmonte 1987). Other streams have flowed into the semantic analysis of music; markedness theory, in the writings of Robert Hatten, and the development of Eco's notion of 'cultural unit' in the writings of Ingmar Bengtsson and Peter Faltin, summarised by Schneider (1980).

The world of music semiotics is now a broad one, but its claim to supersede conventional theory has been laid aside. Finally, semiotics has come to mean 'any scientific description' of music (Ruwet 1975, 33), and its insights have been extremely various. The terminological precision, the declaration of explicit criteria and the clear distinction of categories remain as guiding principles, but heuristic intuition is no longer despised. The world of 'hard semiotics' was tough and polemic. The new, softer world is more fruitful, more fallible, more exciting.

2

LINGUISTIC AND STRUCTURALIST THEORY, FROM SAUSSURE TO PIAGET

2.1. Philology and Linguistics

2.1.1. It would be difficult to understand the methodology and technical language of semiotics without a grasp of the main traditions in linguistics, and the whole theory of structuralism which grew therefrom. Ideas like the *syntagm* and *paradigm*, the conception of *synchronic* versus *diachronic* analysis, *transformation* and *generation* are parts of the essential method of semiotics, and must be approached through linguistics.

2.1.2. The study of language in the nineteenth century was mainly concerned with *comparative philology*. This was essentially a historical study and it owed its origin largely to a realization that Latin and Greek, clearly related to each other, were also related to Sanskrit, and that behind the three languages lay a lost original language which was called 'Indo-European'. A consideration of grammar and phonology made possible the drawing-up of family trees of languages, which were thus classified into groups.
    All linguistic questions were approached from the historical standpoint. In the case of word-meanings this led to an emphasis on etymology, and here one of the dangers of the philological approach can be observed. A word form or usage that does not take account of history may be considered 'incorrect'. For example, the common spelling *extrovert* is sometimes condemned because of the Latin background of the word, the very uncommon *extravert* being preferred. This attitude is clearly normative.

2.2. Saussure

2.2.1. The Swiss linguist Ferdinand de Saussure brought about a linguistic revolution by dividing the historical view of language, which he called *diachronic,* from the view of language as a self-consistent system viewed at one moment of time, called *synchronic*. The speakers of a language may not know about its history but they are conversant with the structure of the language as it exists at this moment. Saussure did not publish his ideas, but notes were taken from his lectures at the University of Geneva from 1906 to 1911 and these were published after his death in 1915 as the *Cours de Linguistique Générale*.

2.2.2. Language, considered in the here and now, manifests itself in two ways. It is a performance, something that is reborn in every utterance of a native speaker, and this Saussure called 'speech' (*parole*). But no speaker could make up utterances without knowledge of an abstract structure or system which is unseen and unheard and can never be fully described, the 'language' (*langue*). Conversely, a language which never manifests itself in speech (writing was considered merely a kind of encoded speech) is unthinkable; it is only in speech-utterances that the abstract relationships of language realize themselves.

2.2.3. Thus every linguistic phenomenon - for example, a single word - can be viewed, so to speak, in its 'horizontal' and 'vertical' aspects, called *syntagmatic* and *paradigmatic*. On the syntagmatic level a word has possibilities of relation to other words: for example the word *key*, being a common noun, may be preceded by an article and followed by a verb, as in the sentence 'The key changes'. In a given utterance the particular chosen possibilities of relation are always manifested *in presentia*, that is, they can be actually observed.

2.2.4. Paradigmatic relations, on the other hand, are always *in absentia*; for the word *key* to be meaningful it must be perceptibly different from *ski* or *keys*, from *sea* and *tea* and *fee*, and from *car*, *cow* and *queue*. Even so, there is a considerable range of pronunciations which will still be heard as 'key'. Not only is *key* related to words that sound similar because of paradigmatic relations of the phonemes that make it up (*k* and *t* are distinct in English) but the word itself can be opposed to other words like *mode*, *time* and *tonality* because of greater or lesser differences of meaning. All these oppositions are necessary to the meaning and function of the word: it is important that *key* does not mean *mode*, and much musicology would have to be rewritten if the words were synonymous. But we do not actually say 'not-mode' when we say 'key'; 'not-mode' is implied or contained within 'key', and this is perfectly understood by the user of the language - in this case musical technical language.

2.2.5. Every word or other linguistic element is at once a 'sound-image' or 'signifier' (*signifiant*) and a concept (*signifié*). This dichotomy of signifier and signified is fundamental to Saussurean linguistics and to most semiotic theory. The combination of signifier and signified - a word plus its meaning, for example - is called a 'sign'(*signe*).

2.2.6. There is a certain pathos in Saussure's account of the irrevocable separation of *signifiant* and *signifié* which is later echoed in Lévi-Strauss's view of culture. Signifier and signified live in an everlasting *apartheid*, essentially together yet always apart, which Saussure expressed in a memorable simile.

> Language can... be compared with a sheet of paper: thought is the front and sound the back; one cannot cut the front without cutting the back at the same time; likewise in language, one can neither divide sound from thought nor thought from sound (Saussure 1974, 113).

Just as the signified is not a thing but the idea of a thing, so the signifier is not the 'material substance' of a word - the sound it makes - but its position within the system of the language, the sum of its syntagmatic and paradigmatic features. Language is defined as 'a system of signs that express ideas', both signs and ideas being understood categories of relations.

> In language there are only differences *without positive terms*. Whether we take the signified or the signifier, language has neither ideas nor sounds that existed before the linguistic system, but only conceptual and phonic differences that have issued from the system. The idea or phonic substance that a sign contains is of less importance than the other signs that surround it (120).

2.2.7. Linguistic signs are therefore *arbitrary*. There is no intrinsic reason for the word *tree* to stand for the arboraceous vegetable; it does not look like or sound like a tree. Any other sound would do just as well, and indeed some persons call this thing *arbre* or *Baum*. The relation between the sound 'tree' and the idea of a tree is not a necessary relation; it is merely part of the structure of the English language.

2.3. The Prague School: pertinence and opposition

2.3.1. Saussurean phonology was elaborated and completed by the so-called Prague School in the late 1920s and early 1930s, notably N Trubetzkoy whose *Principles of Phonology* became the standard exposition of Prague theories, and Roman Jakobson, who later moved to America and unified the two main linguistic movements, European and American.

2.3.2. Saussure seemed to regard the *phoneme* - the minimal unit of phonology - as a natural articulatory event, but it came to be realised that some events are not felt or heard by the native speaker while others, though in reality different, are considered identical. Phonology is not therefore the same as phonetics; the mere sound continuum of a language cannot reveal the phonemes - the intervention of a native informant must be sought.

For example, in English the initial consonant of *leap* and the final consonant of *peel* are considered to be the same sound. In many English dialects, however, including 'Received Pronunciation', they are very different. The *l* of *leap* is called a 'clear l' and is pronounced with the tip of the tongue just behind the upper teeth and the centre of the tongue very close to the roof of the mouth. The *l* of *peel* is called a 'dark l', made with the centre of the tongue well away from the roof of the mouth. If, however, we pronounce *leap* with a dark l or *peel* with a clear l, no change of meaning is heard: 'We get the same word with a slightly odd accent' (Crystal 1971, 177). In English the opposition clear l/dark l does not govern meaning.

However, the sounds are differently distributed in the language, clear l occurring before a vowel and dark l at the end of a word after a vowel, or before a consonant. The opposition is not *pertinent*; the two sounds are not separate phonemes, but *allophones* of the same phoneme, and their distribution is complementary throughout the language, there being no position in which *either* clear l or dark l could occur.

Let us consider, however, the sounds *l* and *r* in *leap* and *reap*. Notice two things: first, their distribution is not complementary, for in these two words they occur in the same position before a vowel. Second, the words *leap* and *reap* are not the same; the change of sound has caused a change of meaning. The opposition l/r is pertinent in English and these sounds are separate phonemes.

If we consult other languages we find that the nodes of distinction are not the same; phonemic groups are differently organized. For example, in Russian the case with clear l and dark l is similar to that with *l* and *r* in English; the two sounds can occur in identical positions, but they always cause a change of meaning. The word ЛЮК ('lik' with clear l) means the hatch of a ship; while ЛЧК ('lik' with dark l) means 'onion'. In Russian, then, clear l and dark l are separate phonemes.

On the other hand, surprisingly to English speakers, in Korean *l* and *r* are allophones of a single phoneme. Native speakers of Korean find great difficulty in hearing or articulating the difference between these sounds, just as English speakers seldom notice the difference between clear l and dark l. A Korean tends to confuse words like *leap* and *reap*.

2.3.3. The phoneme, then, is not a real unit of articulation or sound, but 'an abstract, functional concept - the smallest distinctive unit operating within the network of structural relationships which constitutes the sound-system of a language' (Crystal 1971, 179, from which most of this account is taken). In a sense, any sound can be an allophone of any phoneme, provided the native speaker understands it to lie in the same structural position; the physical experience of the sound is not important. In this respect the Prague writers maintained Saussure's view of language as an abstract system in which 'there are only differences'.

2.3.4. The opposition clear l/dark l is clearly *binary*. The sound 'clear l' can obviously be opposed to other sounds, but always in other respects.

Thus the whole sound system of a language can be reduced to a small number of binary oppositions. For example, in French the phonemes *d* and *t* are opposed on the axis voiced/unvoiced. Both *d* and *t* are sounded in the *mouth*, however; the sound of *d* changes if the nasal cavity is opened - it then becomes *n*. The phonemes *d* and *n* are thus opposed on the axis oral/nasal. The sound of *d* is made, furthermore, with the tongue against the roots of the upper teeth. If the articulation is made by the lips the sound *b* results. These sounds are thus divided on the axis dental/labial. In pronouncing *d* the tongue *occludes* the air-flow, that is, it cuts it off altogether for a moment. If the closure is not complete but the air-flow is only *constricted* we have the sound *z*. The structural position of the phoneme *d* in French is the result of a whole network of binary oppositions (Figure 2.1).

Now, Jakobson argues that the entire consonant system of French can be understood in terms of only five binary oppositions (the one missing from the above account is 'centrifugal/centripetal') (Jakobson 1978, chapter 5). This is why the infant, confronted with the dozens of different sounds that occur in French, is nevertheless able to learn the language with comparative ease.

Figure 2.1.

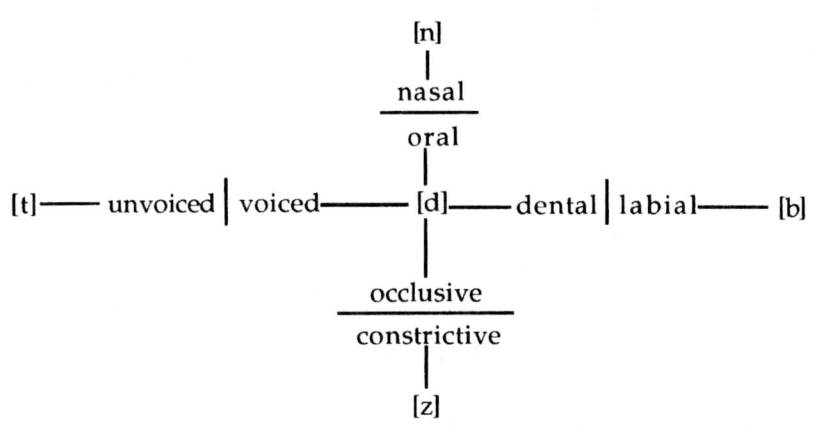

```
                          [n]
                           |
                         nasal
                         ─────
                         oral
                           |
[t] ── unvoiced | voiced ──── [d] ── dental | labial ── [b]
                           |
                       occlusive
                       ─────────
                      constrictive
                           |
                          [z]
```

2.3.5. The phoneme, in itself, has no meaning, but it determines meaning. The smallest unit *meaningful in itself*, that is, the smallest unit of *grammatical* analysis (as opposed to phonological) is called the *morpheme*. The morpheme is somewhat like a 'word', but some words are made up of several morphemes, like *upbow*, *bowing* and *bowed*, all of which clearly contain the morpheme *bow* but add other morphemes to it, or *unpedalled* which contains three morphemes.

Conversely a single morpheme may require more than one word: 'out of town' contains only two morphemes. Some morphemes are 'bound', in that they only occur with other morphemes (like *-ing* and *-ed* in *bowing* and *bowed*). Like a phoneme, a morpheme may have several different realisations in the language. In the words *strings*, *bridges* and *nuts* the morpheme of plural number is represented by z, ez and s respectively. These are called *allomorphs* of this morpheme, on the analogy of 'allophones'.

2.3.6. An adjunct of the concept of the morpheme is the setting up of that *double articulation* in the process of signification which

Lévi-Strauss considered essential. Because of its supposed absence he condemned serial music (Lévi-Strauss 1970, 23-26). The morpheme is the smallest meaningful sound, but there could be no morphemes without phonemes; the phoneme is the smallest distinctive sound (speaking for the moment, for the sake of simplicity, of 'sounds' instead of structural units). The language is thus articulated on two interdependent levels.

2.3.7. These lists of allophones and allomorphs make it clear that the distinctions which can be observed in nature - for example, in language viewed phonetically - are much more numerous than those chosen to be pertinent by a particular language. This is true throughout human culture, and for this reason Kenneth Pike coined the terms *emic* and *etic* (derived from 'phonemic' and 'phonetic') to mean *cultural* and *natural*. This distinction is fundamental to structuralism; it might be called the distinguishing feature of a truly structural analysis.

2.3.8. Can music, or a particular musical style, be analysed as an abstract structure of binary oppositions? The word *museme* has been employed by some writers, sometimes to mean a musical phoneme (Charles Seeger; see below, pp. 74-80), sometimes a musical morpheme (Philip Tagg; see below, pp. 285-294). Musicians usually tend to think that the unit has some kind of natural existence and can be isolated merely by an examination of the material. This was Saussure's view of the linguistic phoneme, but it has been rejected by linguists, the definition of the phoneme being based on pertinence. But it has proved very difficult to define a concept of musical pertinence.

    Nevertheless it is very easy to state certain traditional musical ideas in structuralist terms. Rameau's method of harmonic analysis, for example, appears to present the inversions of the triad somewhat like allophones, distinguished not by their 'meaning' but by their possibilities of combination. This is endorsed by the existence of musical styles in which only the harmonies, and not their inversions, are distinguished - like ukulele music - and of styles in which all triads are in root position, like American Country. The diatonic triads can be viewed as harmonic phonemes and can be classified according to four binary oppositions. The tonic chord is *final*, other chords *non-final*. Of the non-final chords the dominant and submediant commonly lead to tonic cadences and so are *centripetal*. The subdominant, supertonic and mediant harmonies are associated with progression and development; they are *centrifugal*. However, the dominant and subdominant triads are *major*, the others *minor*. Comparing the supertonic and mediant harmonies, the latter is characteristic of more remote progressions - it is *discursive*; the former is *integral* to the harmonic and cadential system of the tonic.

Figure 2.2.

	final	non-final			
TONIC		centripetal		centrifugal	
		major	DOMINANT	SUBDOMINANT	
		minor	SUBMEDIANT	integral	SUPERTONIC
				discursive	MEDIANT

2.4. American linguistics

2.4.1. While Saussure was giving his lectures in Geneva a quite separate development was taking place in America. It was perceived that the American Indian languages were rapidly disappearing and scholars determined to capture them before it was too late. In 1911 the first volume of the *Handbook of American Indian Languages* was published. The linguistic approach engendered by this work was set forth by Edward Sapir in his book *Language* of 1921.

2.4.2. Two factors proved to be formative in American linguistics. First, the linguist had to be a practical man, an anthropologist working in the field. This respect for practical skill, experience and guesswork has survived in America and can be sensed in even the most systematic studies. Also, linguistics was seen as part of the total study of society, an insight that has only recently spread to musicology.

The other feature that proved crucial was the exotic nature of Indian languages. European linguists studied French or Danish, which were their own tongues or were very closely related to their own tongues. Familiar ideas like 'word' or 'sentence' were much harder to match with strange exotic languages; even the idea of meaning, which a European usually understands referentially, had to be reinterpreted before the functioning of Indian languages could be grasped.

2.4.3. Linguists noticed that only certain distinctions were operative in the language, the rest being totally ignored and scarcely even heard. The pertinent differences were often, according to Sapir, 'subtle and barely audible' (quoted in Hawkes 1977, 30). In one's own language it is easy to imagine that a phoneme has some sort of natural existence. In these alien languages, the abstract quality of the phoneme was obvious.

2.4.4. The masterwork of Leonard Bloomfield, also called *Language* (1933), was one of the most influential books of the century. Bloomfield elaborates the taxonomy of early linguistics and evokes a series of categories not only for sound (the phoneme and the morpheme) but also for grammar. The 'smallest and meaningless unit' of grammar, the grammatical phoneme so to speak, is the *taxeme*; while the 'smallest meaningful unit', the grammatical morpheme, is the *tagmeme*. Each of the units has its corresponding unit of meaning; the meaning of a morpheme is a *sememe*, and of a tagmeme, an *episememe*. In spite of this apparent attention to the concept of meaning, Bloomfield rejects the 'mentalistic' view of meaning. The meaning of a linguistic unit is not a thought in the mind of the hearer, the existence of which cannot be proven and the nature of which cannot be shown. It is merely a modification of the behaviour of the hearer.

All behaviour is a reaction to stimulus, and language can serve as a 'substitute stimulus' by presenting to its hearer a fact that is not really present, as when a signpost informs a traveller of the direction of a town. The behaviourism of much twentieth-century American thought is a reaction against the speculative idealism of the previous century, but it may also be seen as a response to the different functioning of the languages these scholars were examining.

2.4.5. Bloomfield studied especially the distribution of phonemes, which he considered their primary feature. However, it was not possible to isolate phonemes and establish their distribution without considering meaning, although it would have been preferable to do so because the idea of meaning is unscientific.

> Only by finding out which utterances are alike in meaning, and which ones are different, can the observer learn to recognize the phonemic distinctions. So long as the analysis of meaning remains outside the powers of

science, the analysis and recording of languages will remain an art or a practical skill (1933, 93).

Although linguistic analysis is an analysis of structure and not of meaning, it has to begin in some way with questions of meaning. The Indian informant cannot be asked, 'Is this an allophone of the same phoneme?' but rather, 'Does this mean the same?'

2.4.6. The next stage in American linguistics came with Zellig S Harris, whose *Methods in Structural Linguistics* appeared in 1951. Harris shifts the emphasis decisively in the direction of distribution. The linguist deals 'not with the whole of speech activities, but with the regularities in certain features of speech. These regularities are in the distributional relations among the features of speech in question, i.e. the occurrence of these features relatively to each other within utterances'(Harris 1951, 5). The criterion of meaning is wholeheartedly rejected in favour of *substitutability* and *repetition*.

We test the identity of phonemes by substituting one sound for another and 'seeing if the informant will accept it as a repetition'(30). There is no question of meaning: 'The test of segment substitutability is the action of the native speaker: his use of it, or his acceptance of our use of it'(31). Repetition is always readily available: 'It is empirically discoverable that in all languages which have been described we can find some part of one utterance which will be similar to a part of some other utterance'(20).

2.4.7. It has already been explained that allophones of a single phoneme occupy complementary positions in the distributional pattern of the language; clear l in English never occurs at the end of a word, dark l never before a vowel. On the other hand, two sounds that stand for different phonemes may occur in the same position; both l and r may precede a vowel. If one draws up tables of the distribution of different sounds it will be seen that some pairs or groups of sounds complement each other across the spread of the language, one sound taking over in places where another sound is absent. It may be inferred that these pairs or groups of sounds are allophones.

2.4.8. Harris also considers *suprasegmental* phonemes, which occur not sequentially with other phonemes but at the same moment. The opposition *stressed/unstressed* yields two phonemes which can only occur simultaneously with other phonemes. The words *permit* (verb) and *permit* (noun) are distinguished by the shifting of the stress-phoneme. Suprasegmentals include *pitch* and *melody* of speech; in some languages (Chinese, for example) these are essential in determining meaning. These features he calls 'secondary phonemes' or *prosodemes* (45).

2.4.9. Where earlier writers seemed to be speaking of a whole language as though they had heard everything that had ever been said in that language, Harris insisted that the focus of study was the utterance, which was 'any stretch of talk, by one person, before and after which there is silence on the part of the person'(14). The field of study may be widened from there to include other utterances, but no support is given to those normative commentators who condemn a form by saying it is 'not English'. Harris does not wish to define 'English' or for that matter Tonkawa, but only to furnish systematic descriptions of utterances. The limit of the field is not the language but the *corpus of data* which is merely 'the stock of recorded utterances'(12).

2.4.10. All actions of the analyst are actions of *segmentation* and *classification* (367), a *segment* being defined as 'a part of the linguistic representation of the time-extension of the utterance'(14-15). Even a segment, then, is not a natural element, but only part of a 'linguistic representation'; language is totally continuous and can only be divided with the aid of an analytic theory. This extends the Prague insight vis-à-vis the phoneme to every linguistic division, even the allophones that constitute a phoneme or the subdivisions of a phonemic sound if one accepts that there can be such subdivisions (some linguists divide the phoneme into *morae;* Saussure considered that it was indivisible).

2.4.11. Finally Harris offers his method as a *discovery procedure*, a systematic programme of investigation which may be adopted for any language. He admits that linguists do not, and need not, work in this manner, but feels that such a programme is the best method for the clarification and presentation of results, and that if the programme could in fact be followed it would always yield a true analysis.

2.4.12. This approach has naturally been attractive to musicians. If meaning is not at issue but only repetition, then there is some hope for music analysis, for while meaning is an exceedingly problematic affair in music, repetition assuredly is not; it is the commonest musical feature and the foundation of all analysis. Also, music is full of suprasegmentals; perhaps it is wholly suprasegmental, all its phonemes being of stress, pitch and melody.

Another musical problem is bypassed when the utterance replaces the whole language as the focus of study, for it is hard to see what constitutes a musical 'language'; musical styles and traditions seem to cross boundaries more easily than spoken languages and are less subject to standardizing forces. However, the musical 'utterance' is apparently easy to discern: it is the single symphony, the single song, the single drum solo or fiddle tune.

For some of these reasons Harris's method was seized on by Nicolas Ruwet, whose ideas will be described in the next chapter.

2.5. Hjelmslev's 'glossematics'

2.5.1. The practical business of recording and analysing real languages is never far away in the American writings. It is quite another matter with the linguists of the Copenhagen school, whose ideas are set forth in Louis Hjelmslev's *Prolegomena to a Theory of Language*, published in Danish in 1943. In this profoundly abstract work real languages are seldom mentioned. Instead, Saussure's insight that language is a logical system, independent of 'real' sounds or 'real' meanings, is developed to an extreme degree.

Hjelmslev's contempt for the traditional linguist's mingling of practical phonetics and semantics with systematic studies led him to invent a new word for his own, purified method: *glossematics*, from Greek *glossa*, language. The linchpin of his approach is the notion of *immanence*. Most language study has been more or less *transcendent* in its aims. It has aimed to solve psychological, sociological or anthropological problems and it has worked hand-in-hand with acoustics and the physiology of articulation. Any study - including musicology - can be pursued for the light it sheds on other studies; the point is to pursue it *for itself*. 'The study of language, with its multifarious, essentially transcendent aims, has many cultivators; the theory of language, with its purely immanent aim, few' (Hjelmslev 1961, 6).

Linguistics has always seemed an inductive study, i.e. an empirical one; linguistic conclusions have usually been attributed to particular field studies. Hence, the books are full of references to exotic languages. For Hjelmslev linguistics is a deductive study and consists in an elaboration of theory. He considers that 'the requirement of so-called empiricism' is fulfilled by a principle of study that is logical and epistemological rather than empirical. 'The description shall be free of contradiction (self-consistent), exhaustive, and as simple as possible.'

2.5.2. For this reason Hjelmslev has been said to proceed 'from above to below', for he aims to fix the principles of language study for all languages known and unknown. The very universality of these principles precludes their being empirical in the usual sense, for no one can know all languages, past and present, and all utterances within them. This kind of theory is not, however, merely hypothetical or provisional; its very nature determines the procedures of the operator. In its own terms it cannot be 'disproven'.

On the other hand, it arises not from mere caprice but from considerations of appropriateness.

> A theory introduces certain premisses concerning which the theoretician knows from preceding experience that they fulfil the conditions for application to certain empirical data (Hjelmslev 1961, 14).

Data, then, cannot falsify a theory; if they could it would be merely a hypothesis. But they can show it to be less appropriate than another theory, and theories depend in advance on experience of past events. No external material is allowed into this view of language.

2.5.3. Hjelmslev envisages an expression-plane and a content-plane. Both impose an arbitrary pattern on some kind of real matter; in the case of expression this matter is phonetic, to do with sounds and their articulation, in the case of content it is purport, the seamless and unanalysed universe of what can be said. Different languages never analyse and segment the universe of purport in quite the same way: 'I do not know', 'je ne sais pas' and Eskimo 'naluvara', though translations of each other, nevertheless analyse their fragment of purport in different ways. Similarly, the boundaries of content-forms are differently situated in different languages: Welsh *glas*, meaning 'blue', covers also certain shades of green and grey, while Welsh *llwyd* means 'grey' as well as 'brown'. There is thus no real meaning to an expression, but both content and expression are parts of the sign function; they exist, indeed, only by virtue of a sign function. 'The purport is... in itself inaccessible to knowledge, since the prerequisite for knowledge is an analysis of some kind'(76).

Nevertheless, it is on the level of purport that linguistics meets other sciences like physics and anthropology; as the material passes into their hands it ceases to be truly linguistic. It need not be thought that this reduces language to a ghostly commentary on an ungraspable reality. On the contrary, substance (that is, empirical reality) 'is not a necessary presupposition for linguistic form, but linguistic form is a necessary presupposition for substance'.

You can have a linguistic form without anything real (for instance, a false statement or an expression like 'unicorn'); you cannot have anything real without a linguistic form, at least on the content-plane, because unanalysed substance cannot be apprehended. It is not that forms of expression grope to express some substance or other, but that certain substances are manifestations of certain linguistic forms (that is, content-forms). At every point life is shown to be permeated and ruled by language; reality, apart from language, is ghostly indeed.

2.5.4. Hjelmslev discusses the question of *connotation*, which has been variously treated by linguistic writers. The 'literal' meaning of an expression is called *denotation*; connotation is the underlying or suggested meaning (see also above, pp.15-17). Hjelmslev isolates a number of *connotators*: style, medium, dialect, tone of voice. He concludes that the connotators are 'context for which the denotative semiotics are expression', the connotative semiotic is thus 'a semiotic whose expression plane is a semiotic' - that is, the expression plane of connotation is the whole process of denotative semiotics, expression plane and content plane together. 'A connotative semiotic is a semiotic that is not a language, and one whose expression plane is provided by the content plane and expression plane of a denotative semiotic.' The view of music as pure connotation seems blocked by this ruling, as I suggested in the previous chapter.

2.5.5. Nevertheless, the Copenhagen theories, like the views of Harris, hold out a certain promise to the musicologist.

> The decisive point for the question of whether or not a sign is present is not whether it is interpreted, i.e. whether a content-purport is ordered to it... There exist for the calculus of linguistic theory, not interpreted, but only interpretable, systems (112).

If a sign-system, to be such, need not be shown to have a particular content but only to be capable of having a content, then music would clearly be a sign-system. This seems to catch neatly the common experience of music, which is universally felt to convey something outside of itself, although one can never ascertain what is conveyed. The account of connotation illustrates, however, Hjelmslev's traditionalism when it comes to envisaging sign-systems very different from language. He is unable to contemplate connotation in the absence of denotation, for the expressive plane of a connotative system cannot be anything other than a denotative system. It has been said that music is entirely connotative; as though a man were to utter nonsense syllables in a certain tone of voice that indicated that he was angry, sympathetic and so on. And clearly the sort of connotation that Hjelmslev finds in language is at work also in gesture, facial expression, dress and manners, which are not evidently systems of denotation, as he requires. Why should there not be connotative meaning in music, even in the absence of denotation?

2.5.6. His essay on games also reveals the limitations of his view. He finds games - for instance, the game of chess - on the border of semiotic and non-semiotic. In order to ascertain whether games are properly called semiotic systems, 'we must find out whether an exhaustive description of them necessitates operating with two planes'(112). Furthermore, even if there are two planes they must not be *conformal*; that is, points of shift and distinction must not coincide throughout the two planes. In the game of chess it would seem that the terms (for example *knight*) and the content-forms (*one-forward-one-diagonal*) are wholly conformal. This is not, then, a semiotic. 'We must leave it to specialists in the various fields,' he concludes, 'to decide whether or not, for example, the so-called symbolic systems of mathematics and logic, or certain kinds of art, like music, are to be defined as semiotics from this point of view.'

In answer to him we must confess that in his terms, the semiotic character of music remains provisional, for no analysis of the content-plane can ever be undertaken to prove that it is non-conformal with the expression plane. However, we protest that the criterion is not valid, or at least not sensitive. It is only of certain kinds of language that a formal content-plane can be proposed, notably that called referential by Jakobson (above, pp. 17-19). In a phatic or poetic utterance the content is not such that it can be structured with sufficient clarity to establish Hjelmslev's non-conformality. Yet presumably he would find these utterances semiotic.

2.6. Chomsky: transformation and generation

2.6.1. It has been quipped that all the above linguistic traditions were 'B.C.' - 'before Chomsky'. Although many of Chomsky's ideas have now fallen into disfavour, the advent of generative grammar caused a revolution from which there was no turning back.

Noam Chomsky, who teaches at the Massachusetts Institute of Technology (his followers have been called 'mitniks', according to David Crystal), is known for his political activism, which he inherited, like his concern for a truly scientific linguistics, from his teacher Zellig Harris. Others may associate him with certain philosophical ideas; he has a theory of innate mental qualities which resembles a scientifically-oriented version of Platonism.

2.6.2. Amongst his many publications those that embody his most significant linguistic thoughts are *Syntactic Structures* (1957) and *Aspects of the Theory of Syntax* (1965). He sees certain anomalies in the traditional views of syntax. First, certain constructions are given quite different descriptions although they are in practice virtually equivalent. 'The man hit the ball' and 'the ball was hit by the man' must surely be versions of the same syntactic phenomenon rather than wholly distinct phenomena. Secondly, certain constructions are ambiguous. 'The shooting of the hunters' can be connected with a sentence like 'the hunters shot the game' or one like 'the soldier shot the hunters'. Thirdly, certain simple constructions, like noun phrase - transitive verb - noun phrase, work in one direction but not in the other, apparently because of something to do with the meanings of the words. Thus we may say 'Sincerity may frighten the boy' but not 'The boy may frighten sincerity'. This seems to suggest some common ground of grammar and semantics; the second sentence seems to be wrong for quite formal reasons, but not reasons of formal grammar. Semantic forms - the meanings of 'sincerity' and 'frighten' - are needed to explain the wrongness of this sentence.

2.6.3. The existing grammars of Bloomfield and Harris do not illuminate these problems. Bloomfield called his technique 'immediate constituent analysis'. It consisted in the dividing up of the elements that actually appear in the sentence. In 'The man hit the ball', 'man' is obviously a constituent. 'The man' is also a constituent, as is 'hit the ball'. But 'the man hit' is not a constituent. The levels of analysis can be shown by a 'tree diagram' (Figure 2.3).

Figure 2.3.

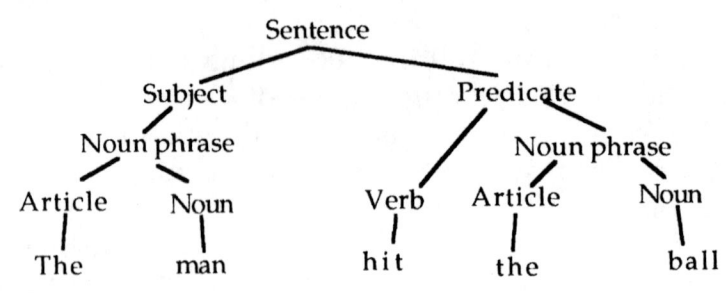

```
                           Sentence
                    /                 \
              Subject                 Predicate
               /                    /          \
          Noun phrase              /         Noun phrase
          /       \               /           /       \
     Article     Noun          Verb       Article    Noun
        |         |             |            |        |
       The       man           hit          the      ball
```

This analysis is quite adequate to explain that 'the man hit' is not a constituent, but it cannot account for the kinship of 'The ball was hit by the man'.

In the case of 'the shooting of the hunters' the same constituent analysis would have to stand for both of the possible meanings, although the sentences to which this phrase might be related have quite different constituent analyses.

2.6.4. No such immediate constituent grammar can account for the way language is really spoken and understood. The user of a language is always aware of a level of analysis deeper than that manifested in the immediate constituents. He is aware, for example, of which of the possible meanings of 'the shooting of the hunters' is intended on a particular occasion, because the underlying structure (that of 'the hunters shot the game', perhaps) is somewhere present in his consciousness.

2.6.5. This may be shown by another example. If two sentences are identical except for one expression, it is normally possible to make them into one sentence by using *and*.

    1   The scene of the movie was in Chicago.
    2   The scene of the play was in Chicago.
    3   The scene of the movie and of the play was in Chicago.

In some cases, however, this procedure is blocked. Sentence 6 is not admissible.

    4   The scene of the movie was in Chicago.
    5   The scene that I wrote was in Chicago.
    6   The scene of the movie and that I wrote was in Chicago.

If we are to formulate a rule governing the linking of items by the use of *and*, we would have to specify that they were 'constituents of the same type'. This means that we would have to refer to the analytical derivation of the expressions we intend to link; we have to delve into their analytic history.

Thus, in the history of sentence 5 there are two sentences:

7   The scene was in Chicago.
8   I wrote the scene.

There is no such duality in sentence 4. However, a sentence with a similar history in two sentences can be linked to sentence 5 by using *and*.

9   The scene that he set to music was in Chicago.
10 The scene that I wrote and that he set to music was in Chicago.

Neither 'I wrote the scene' nor 'he set the scene to music' is an immediate constituent of sentence 10. How can they be referred to in explaining its grammaticality, and the wrongness of sentence 6?

2.6.6. Perhaps it is the case that sentences are made up, not of immediate constituents combined by grammatical laws, but of transformations of underlying simple expressions according to certain laws of transformation. It would be easy to envisage a rule of transformation that would convert the simple 'the man hit the ball' into the more complex but equivalent 'the ball was hit by the man'. Similarly a transformational rule can be framed to convert sentences 7 and 8 into sentence 5. These rules are said to *generate* the sentences in question. This does not mean that generative grammar explains only the process of speaking rather than both processes, speaking and hearing. Nor does it mean that every grammatical sentence somehow begins as an archetypal construction which is subjected to certain transformations at the will of the speaker - that sentences are generated as plants are generated. The word generate is used, like much other Chomskyan terminology, in a mathematical sense, and describes not an active process but a logical relation.

2.6.7. For each language there is a small range of very simple constructions using the minimum of transformational laws; these are called *kernel sentences*. All other sentences are derived from these by means of a limited range of transformational principles. Thus syntax, like phonology, derives a wide range of possible phenomena from a small number of basic rules.

2.6.8. The pattern of immediate constituents which was previously considered to be the structure of a sentence is now called its *surface structure*. Underneath this there lies a *deep structure* that represents the sentence more truly.

2.6.9. There may, in fact, be a very deep level at which all languages are identical. Here Chomsky revives the ancient idea of Universal Grammar. He attributes such identity of basic linguistic structure not to logical necessity or historical connection but to innate structures of the mind. The mind is bound to frame utterances in a certain way because of its biological nature; 'The child's brain contains certain innate characteristics which "pre-structure" it in the direction of language learning' (Crystal 1971, 256). Many critics of Chomsky have objected to what they consider a reversion to mentalism. The idea of mind is unscientific; it is an 'impure' element in Chomsky's thought, shifting it from the level of rational theory, where Hjelmslev is safely installed, to that of metaphysical speculation.

2.6.10. Chomsky's mentalistic emphasis is perceived also in his special version of the langue/parole distinction. A language, in the sense of its abstract paradigmatic structures, is known by a speaker in the form of a capacity to frame grammatically well-formed utterances and to distinguish the well-formed from the irregular. This is called *competence*. The exercise of competence in the actual formation of utterances is called *performance*. The main difference between this terminology and that of Saussure is that the Swiss linguist speaks always in terms of language itself (in terms of *immanence*, to return again to Hjelmslev) while Chomsky is thinking of the speaking subject, who is not, moreover, merely an 'epistemic subject', the theatre in which certain linguistic procedures enact themselves, but is a human mind with certain determining characteristics.

2.6.11. It might be thought that a linguist with strong mentalistic tendencies would give a large place to semantics, for 'meaning' is largely a mentalistic idea. In fact, Chomsky's position is paradoxical. As mentioned above, he sees the interaction of grammar and semantics. The irregularity of 'the boy may frighten sincerity' seems to be midway between 'sincerity frighten may boy the', which is wholly a matter of formal grammar, and 'colourless green ideas sleep furiously', which is principally a matter of semantics. To some extent this intermediate kind of irregularity can be ordered by introducing lexical categories like 'human', 'abstract', 'count' (a 'count' noun is one that can go into the plural).

Thus it may be specified that *frighten* must have an animate object; *sincerity* is abstract and so will not do. But the lexicon, stronghold of the semantic level of language, even if adapted in this sense - by the citing of rules that govern combinations of words - cannot explain certain other irregularities, like 'the arm has a man' (as opposed to 'the man has an arm'). We do not feel that the relation of man and arm can be expressed in this way. But can our feeling be stated as a rule? Here Chomsky admits that theory breaks down.

> To conclude this highly inconclusive discussion, I shall simply point out that the syntactic and semantic structure of natural languages evidently offers many mysteries, both of fact and of principle, and that any attempt to delimit the boundaries of these domains must certainly be quite tentative. (Chomsky 1965, 163).

2.6.12. In Chomsky the emphasis shifts from phonemics, the study of the smallest elements of language, to syntax, the principles of sentence structure. In music, also, there are two main areas of analysis, the melodic/harmonic, which is concerned with the smallest units of music, and the formal, dealing with the overall structure of more or less large forms. Most modern efforts in analysis deal with form, rather than melody and harmony, even those which derive their structures from small harmonic and melodic cells, as do Schenker and Reti. Perhaps for this reason, Chomskyan theory has attracted the attention of a number of musicians, whose work is described below (Chapter 5). There are grave problems in adapting Chomsky to music theory, and these will later become apparent.

2.7. The linguistic emphasis

2.7.1. The two linchpins of twentieth-century linguistics have been:

(a) The declaration that linguistics is a *synchronic* study, concerned with language as it is understood and spoken at this moment, not with the history of language;

(b) that it is furthermore an *immanent* study, considering language as an autonomous and self-consistent system. Though language may be related to psychology, sociology, biology and acoustics, linguistics is not therefore a branch of one or any of those sciences.

2.7.2. Because of the linguist's equal concern for all languages, even those not yet discovered, linguistics sets out primarily to elaborate a theory of language. This theory is logically primary and universal. It cannot be verified or falsified because it is not a hypothesis, but on the contrary the principle on which any hypothesis must be framed and tested.

2.7.3. Linguistics tries to discover rules of segmentation and combination. Utterances must first be divided into segments according to certain criteria. The laws are then discovered whereby these segments are combined. As language is an abstract and not a physical phenomenon, the criterion of segmentation is *pertinence*. We are not concerned with all physical and acoustic differences, but only those differences that are understood as significant by a native speaker.

2.7.4. In developing such an analysis it becomes clear that language has two dimensions: the syntagmatic, whereby a segment is related to those around it, and the paradigmatic, whereby it is related to other segments not immediately present but distinct from it in some way or other. Paradigmatic distinctions may be reduced to a system of binary oppositions.

2.7.5. Laws of combination seem to apply to the segments actually found in a sentence. But in fact, the sentence may only be explicable in terms of other, simpler constructions which do not directly appear, from which the sentence is generated by a series of transformational laws. We should therefore seek laws of transformation rather than combination.

2.7.6. As for the 'real' sounds which language uses, or the 'real' meanings of its expressions, these are considered to be extraneous to linguistics proper. Neither phonetics nor semantics, therefore, is central to linguistics. However, it has proved impossible to separate language from its semantic dimension, and indeed some of the most important recent developments have been in this field (see Chapter 8, below). The independence of linguistics - its immanent status - remains an ideal rather than a reality. In musicology, this immanence seemed at first an attractive feature, for the aspect of 'meaning' in music is elusive. Nevertheless, in the eighties semiologists made good use of the writings on semantics, also.

2.8. The coming of structuralism

2.8.1. The contribution of Trubetzkoy and the Prague school to Saussurean linguistics was the distinction phonemic/phonetic based on the feature of pertinence. This brought to light an inner system of dual oppositions, demonstrated by Jakobson.

The phonetic dimension of language is acoustic and physiological; it is part of *nature*. The phonemic dimension is peculiar to one language; it is a social fact, and part of *culture*. Workers in non-linguistic fields realised that this deeper distinction, nature/culture (or 'etic/emic'), is valid throughout sociological and anthropological studies. Children sometimes resemble their mothers, sometimes their fathers; and sometimes they resemble both parents. Nevertheless, in the Trobriand Islands, while the resemblance to the mother is noticed and often discussed, the father-resemblance is ignored and discussion of it is forbidden. Mother-resemblance is emic, father-resemblance merely etic (Malinowsky 1932).

2.8.2. The linguist, like the ethnomusicologist, is a member of the anthropological team. With the advent of structural linguistics, he became a privileged member of that team, for his discipline was suddenly the only one that could claim to be an exact science. Claude Lévi-Strauss later wrote a witty description of the plight of the anthropologist at this time.

> For many years [the anthropologists] have been working very closely with the linguists, and all of a sudden it seems to them that the linguists are vanishing, that they are going on to the other side of the borderline which divides the exact and natural sciences on the one hand from the human and social sciences on the other. All of a sudden the linguists are

playing their former companions the very nasty trick of doing things as well and with the same sort of rigorous approach that was long believed to be the privilege of the exact and natural sciences. Then, on the side of the anthropologist there is some, let us say, melancholy, and a great deal of envy. We should like to learn from the linguists how they succeeded in doing it... (Lévi-Strauss 1968, 69).

2.8.3. It occurred to Lévi-Strauss that many anthropological fields - the study of kinship, for example - have much in common with language. Kinship terms like father, mother, brother, uncle have symbolic meanings in different societies; these meanings conform to a system which is not conformal with the natural relationships.

A R Radcliffe-Brown, together with many older anthropologists, assumed that the basic unit of all societies was the family, 'consisting of a man and his wife and their child or children'. Yet throughout the world, a person's most important relative, for one reason or another, is his mother's brother - his maternal uncle. This feature, called the *avunculate,* is so universal that it seems inconceivable that it can have spread simply by mutual influence.

Lévi-Strauss points out that the family, far from being the unit of social structure, is merely an etic element. It is a feature of nature; a given society may respect it or ignore it, or give it whatever significance it will.

> What confers upon kinship its socio-cultural character is not what it retains from nature, but, rather, the essential way in which it diverges from nature. A kinship system does not consist in the objective ties of descent or consanguinity between individuals. It exists only in human consciousness; it is an arbitrary system of representations, not the spontaneous development of a real situation (Lévi-Strauss 1968, 50).

The Trobrianders, mentioned above, evidently attached heavy symbolic significance to the mother-relationship, but ignored the relationship of the father.

2.8.4. Let us examine the Trobrianders more closely, with attention to the avunculate. In the Trobriand Islands descent is matrilineal; there are free and familiar relations between father and son; the special relation with the maternal uncle, however, is in this case one of antagonism. Husband and wife live in an atmosphere of tender intimacy; 'the relations between brother and sister, on the other hand, are dominated by an extremely rigid taboo... there is no greater insult than to tell a man that he resembles his sister' (Lévi-Strauss 1968, 42).

Linguistics and Structuralism

These tropical islanders may be compared with the Cherkess, who live in the Caucasus. Their descent is patrilineal, leading to hostility between father and son. 'The maternal uncle assists his nephew and gives him a horse when he marries.' Brothers and sisters, however, have an extremely tender relationship. But 'a Cherkess will not appear in public with his wife and visits her only in secret'. You insult a man by asking after his wife's health.

There are thus four types of relation which interact in a system: brother/sister, husband/wife, father/son, mother's brother/sister's son. In many societies studied by ethnologists, certain laws may be deduced governing the interconnection of these relations. The Trobrianders and Cherkess are neatly opposed, being contrary in every respect. Other social groups show, however, that the relations interact in pairs: 'The relation between maternal uncle and nephew is to the relation between brother and sister as the relation between father and son is to that between husband and wife.' We indicate free and familiar relations with +, antagonistic relations with -.

Figure 2.4.
   (a) Trobriand - matrilineal
   (b) Cherkess - patrilineal

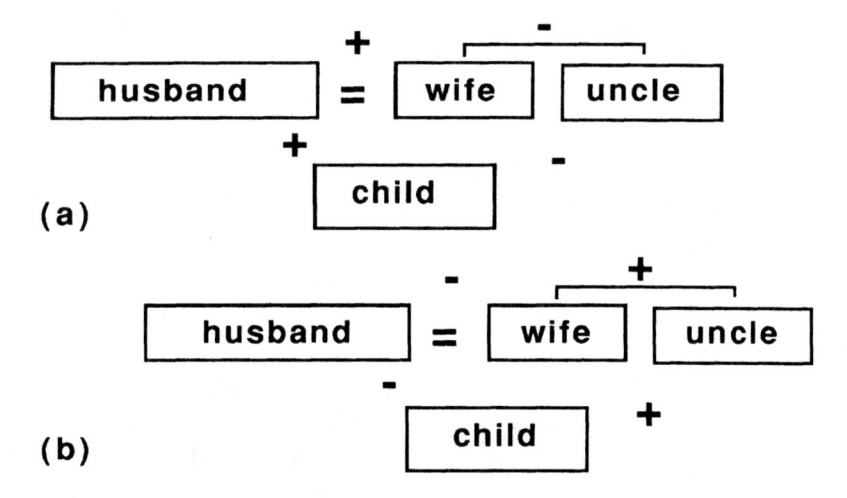

Kinship relations resemble phonemes in being selective. There are obviously many more family relations, but these are not considered important by the societies in question; they are simply etic. 'Like phonemes, kinship terms are elements of meaning.'

2.8.5. This kind of structural analysis was extended by Lévi-Strauss to many areas of anthropology; to magic, totemism, art and myth. The advent of 'structural anthropology' marked the detachment of the structural method from linguistics and its application in other fields. This method aims to reveal, not a group of phenomena analysed into a surface pattern, but an underlying model that supports a dynamic process, capable of generating new relations and adapting to new conditions. There have been structuralist studies in the fields of literary analysis, psychology, theatre, film, even cookery and fashion. The application of structural methods to semantics (see Chapter 8, below) is even something of a paradox; linguistics had dismissed the semantic level of language, but its methods, after their pilgrimage through anthropology and other studies, proved valid even in the rejected area of meaning.

2.8.6. Jean Piaget sets out to define structuralism as an independent force in modern intellectual life. He feels that its principles are already present in the great innovators of the last century like Freud and Marx. Indeed, an idea of Marx may shed light on the hiddenness of structures.

The received view of structures is usually not the right one, because it arises from an institutionalised ideology which is designed to protect a given structure. Thus, labour and production appear to be organized on principles of investment, profit and reward. The patterns of capital, surplus value, alienation and exploitation perceived by Marx were more 'truly' the structure of society and were thus hidden from view.

Music, too, is supposed to be formed of notes, intervals, chords, progressions, cadences, keys and phrases, governed by melodic and harmonic rules. These categories must be questioned; we should seek a scientifically verifiable structure for music. The structures of traditional analysis are ideologically suspect; they are not merely outmoded attempts to comprehend the object of study, but also embody an intention to preserve the state of affairs.

However, structuralism does not propose the replacement of received ideas with a new philosophy or belief-pattern of its own; it is merely a way of handling material. 'Structuralism is a method, not a doctrine, whose doctrinal consequences have been quite various' (Piaget 1971, 142). The intention is to discover hidden structures, not to impose a new conformism. It is remarkable, therefore, that the structures discovered, in areas as far apart as mathematical group theory and ethnographic kinship systems, have certain features in common.

2.8.7. A structure is a *whole* and is not dependent on any exterior agencies or conditions. Its parts are interdependent and function together; it is not merely an *aggregate* of parts. It is not a static or ideal pattern, but is dynamic. Indeed, its very nature is to generate transformations, since it is not a collection of *things* but of relationships. Its laws of transformation yield an infinity of new phenomena but never generate anything external to the system. As for the actual objects which occupy the relational nodes - the position of the maternal uncle, the phoneme *t* in English, or the kineme *forward step* in Tongan dance - these are considered to be important not for themselves but only for their positions in the web. If the dominant seventh were considered phonemic in a structural theory of harmony its psychological and acoustic features would not be relevant; only the combinational laws governing its use would be of interest.

2.8.8. Structures are *self-regulating*. This is the definitive feature which turns forms into structures, and Piaget suggests that it comes from a natural process which he calls 'equilibration'. There is a tendency in nature to move into self-sufficient equilibrium which can be found in psychology, in society, even in minerals. The system is able to handle and engross any mutants or new forms which it throws up because as well as being structured it is *structuring*. The equilibrium can only be disturbed from outside. And so, the essentially emic or cultural aspect of structures turns out itself to be based on natural laws.

2.8.9. It is important that structures are not seen as conditions of individuals. The individual speaker of a language or the individual musician is only important as a manifestation of the system; he is merely a point within the dynamic geometry. Nevertheless, he is more than just the theatre where the structure acts itself out, for he is of course active himself in the structure, though not in the individual sense. There is 'a differentiation between the *individual subject*, who does not enter at all, and the *epistemic subject*, that cognitive nucleus which is common to all subjects at the same level' (139).

There is admittedly a difficulty here; writers have differed in the scope they have given to the individual, Chomsky feeling that the form of the human intellect is innate, Lévi-Strauss finding certain permanent features in human processes of cognition whatever the culture. But not even these concessions to human agency would really alter the position of the individual within the structure; he never becomes the 'me' of phenomenology, his experience never that introspective 'lived' in which Husserl sought the conditions of being.

2.8.10. It is clear that music - or more precisely, a specific musical language, dialect or idiolect - is a self-regulating system of transformations like those described by Piaget. It is, perhaps, more apparent in music than elsewhere that significance inheres in relations, not in things. A single note is patently meaningless, but intervals, patterns, changes of volume, tempo and timbre, and above all rhythms are the prime bearers of musical significance. This is to speak of significance in the most fundamental sense, not in the lexical or referential sense which still pervades Saussure and has passed over into some writers on music. Since music is a significant system, clearly and coherently structured, musicology ought to be the leader in semiotic studies, not the intractable child it has so often been in the philosophical movements of the past. 'Wo die Sprache aufhört, fängt die Musik an'; where language can no longer offer the clue to the structure of the sign, music must step in.

3

METALANGUAGE, SEGMENTATION AND REPETITION

3.1. The problem of musical segmentation

3.1.1. The metalanguage of linguistics - the language in which theory of language is written - has developed with a high measure of universal agreement. Everybody knows what a phoneme is, even if some linguists have less need of the concept than others.

Yet musicians have never been able to agree to a common metalanguage or to base their theory on explicit definitions and methodologies. Charles Seeger comments that 'while during the last one hundred fifty years linguists have developed a superb discipline of speech about speech, musicologists have done nothing at all about a discipline of speech about music' (Seeger 1977, 38).

From the point of view of analysis, the most vital aspect of metalanguage concerns the names and properties of *segments*, those shorter or longer bits of language or music which are strung together syntagmatically, or can be grouped paradigmatically, to make up the medium as *parole* or *langue*. Since the work of the Prague school in the thirties, the segmentation of language has been based on a secure theory, that of pertinence. On the paradigmatic level, if a difference between two bits is non-pertinent, then from the theoretical point of view these two elements are the same; and on the syntagmatic level, pertinence is marked by an effect on meaning - an element too small to determine meaning not being considered a segment. Thus phonemes and morphemes are discerned; phonemic is distinguished from phonetic, emic from etic.

In music, it is true that slight changes in the sound cause apparent changes of meaning; but the changes are pretty well commensurate, and there are hardly ever any changes that cause no change of meaning. In language, the small phonetic difference between *pat* and *bat*, being pertinent, causes a major distinction of meaning. The much greater difference between the Yorkshire and Kent pronunciations of the word *pat* do not lead to any change of meaning. In music, the slight difference between two closely similar items - the opening phrases of Gluck's 'Che farò' and Mozart's 'Porgi amor', for example - indicates a change of content that is as insignificant as the phonetic difference.

There are trivial examples that can be evoked to illustrate non-pertinence in music. In ukulele music, the inversion of the chord is neither programmed by the player nor heard by the listener. This is a purely chordal style, and the shape of the chord is determined solely by the practical exigencies of technique: the chord is played in the position most convenient for the hand.

The very triviality of such examples, however, shows the difficulty of defining musical pertinence in any significant way. In most music, especially that of the West, it is scarcely possible to describe the musical phoneme as 'the smallest phonetic unit capable of affecting meaning', for musical meaning is not controlled in this way. The tiniest of phonetic changes - the shortening of a quaver to a dotted semiquaver, or the playing of a note on the clarinet instead of the oboe - always brings about a slight change of signification.

In spite of this, musicians have always had words for greater and lesser musical segments: motive, phrase, sentence, melody. No one has ever defined these terms precisely; even the painstaking definitions of Ebenezer Prout are impressionistic and normative, not based on any explicit theory. Musical metalanguage, in a nutshell, is unscientific.

3.1.2. There have, in fact, been a few attempts to define pertinence in music. In his trail-blazing article of 1958 Bruno Nettl cites the melodic minor scale; 'in the key of C, the tones "a" and "b" are used in ascent, a-flat and b-flat in descent. Thus "a" and "a-flat" are allophones of the same tone in the scale... Many folk music items exhibit this kind of tonal arrangement, using one variant of a pitch in ascent, another in descent' (Nettl 1958, 39).

The great ethnomusicologist gives another example. In a song of the Arapaho, an Indian people of the Great Plains, the following rhythmic values are found: quaver, crotchet, crotchet triplet, dotted crotchet, semibreve, '9/8 notes, 5/4 and 3/2 notes'. These can be grouped into three phonemic units, eighths, quarter-like notes and long notes. The quarter-like notes appear medially and are the most common. Eighths appear initially in phrases, long notes finally. The song final is a 3/2 note, the phrase finals the shorter variants of the long note phoneme. Quarter-like notes appear in clusters up to five, eighths in groups up to two, and long notes only singly. 'The dotted quarter allophone of the quarter-like notes appears only before a long note, but simple quarters may also appear at such points' (40).

Provisionally, there seems to be some distributional system which permits different note values to be considered equivalent - to be regarded as allophones of a rhythmic phoneme. Unfortunately, Nettl does not enlarge on this; it is not clear why a range of different values may all be subsumed in the phonemic group of the 'quarter-like note', notes approximating to a crotchet.

3.1.3. There is a kind of pertinence, not based on the idea of a musical 'language', that has been evoked for individual works. It is possible to regard certain features as variable in an insignificant way, so that their variations seem to correspond to the needs of the moment rather than some creative intention. There are countless simple examples of this; the opening interval of Schumann's piano piece 'Von fremden Ländern und Menschen' from *Kinderscenen* is a sixth, but when this phrase recurs within an ordinary rounded-binary pattern the interval is a fourth, clearly because a rising scale in the previous material has led to the higher starting note. The musical unit is not *sixth* but *rising disjunct interval*, and the difference between *sixth* and *fourth* is non-pertinent. Many examples can be given of this kind of musical pertinence. The opening motive of Beethoven's Piano Sonata in C, Op 2 No 3, ends with a rising fourth, but this later reappears as a sixth, a fifth, an octave, and greater intervals.

In his critique of François-Bernard Mâche's article on Varèse's *Intégrales*, Nattiez suggests that the note values in this piece go in groups of different lengths, the variations within the groups being non-pertinent.

Mâche had isolated a type of unit which begins with a particular rising motive, D - A flat - B flat, which he calls an 'appoggiatura'. Recurrences of this unit are remarkably similar, and Mâche decides that the differences between them are not accessible to his methods of analysis, which are based on distributional phonology. The principles of transformation 'belong to a complementary domain, and not to structural analysis' (Mâche 1971, 86).

Nattiez points out that these differences are precisely the concern of structural analysis, and that a study of them would have been much more fruitful than the listing of categories of unit which Mâche pursues. The sequel to the 'appoggiatura' is usually a series of repeated notes, mostly the note B flat. The values appear to have a certain rationale; Nattiez discovers a principle of contrast between groups of two notes, such that the second note is always longer than the first.

Figure 3.1

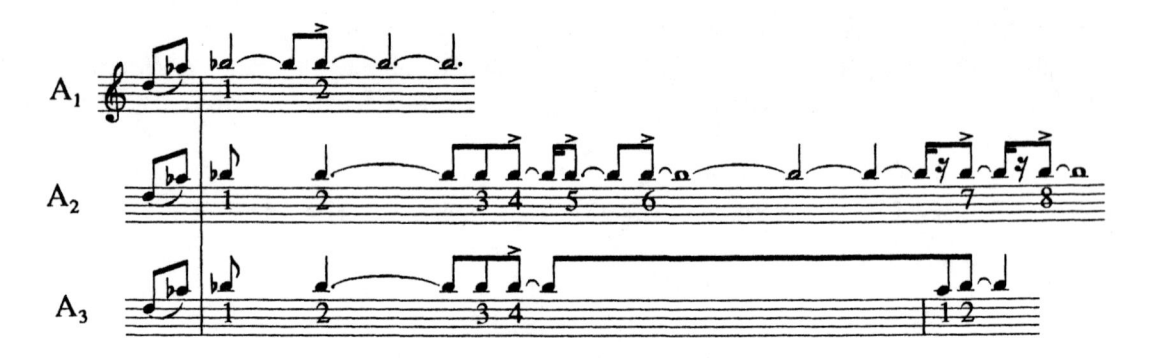

[musical notation: three staves labeled A₁, A₂, A₃ with numbered notes]

The first of these units, *A1*, makes this very clear, with minim-plus-quaver followed by quaver-plus-two-dotted-minims. In *A2* one has to imagine caesuras between the notes numbered 2 and 3, and 6 and 7. Calculating the length of notes in twelfths of a crotchet (the difference between a semiquaver and a quaver within a triplet), *A2* may be analysed as

```
            6     22
      4     7     15     93
                  15     54
```

For each pair of two notes (except across caesuras), the second is longer than the first, sometimes by considerable margins. Varèse is concerned with the abstract arrangement short-long, rather than with absolute note-values.

It is possible to calculate the margin of security that will enable a pattern to be heard as short-long. 'It is clear, if the beginnings of segments are compared, that the values 3/12 and 4/12 used either the one or the other, are opposed to values 6, 7, 8 and 9/12 which follow them... On the other hand, the difference between values as distinct as 42/12 and 93/12 is not considered pertinent since they are encountered always at the end of the unit, in opposition to a 'medial' value (between 14 and 22, or 30 and 36/12)' (Nattiez 1975, 295).

The three units quoted in Figure 3.1 are shown to contain only 5 emic values; 6, 7 and 8 are equivalent, as are 15, 16 and 22 and most surprisingly 54, 78 and 93 (all are multiples of the twelfth of a crotchet). 30/12 is isolated as a separate value because of comparisons with later units, not quoted here.

A1			30	78
A2		6	22	
	4	7	15	93
			15	54
A3		6	22	
	4	8		
	4		16	

'We do not state that [this analysis] corresponds in an absolute manner to everyone's perception: we say merely that it is aesthesically pertinent, and that it gives an image of the structure of oppositions between each value' (297).

Odd to say, Nattiez (and myself, in the comments on the Schumann piece and the Beethoven Sonata) seem to be talking about a kind of semantic pertinence, rather than the ordinary phonemic pertinence that lies behind phonological segmentation. Notably, the segments examined by Nattiez had already been isolated by Mâche according to simple principles of repetition and recurrence. Probably, the Montreal scholar has lighted on an important feature of musical semantics, but it does not help with the basic problem of segmentation.

3.1.4. The most elaborate essay in musical distributionalism based on pertinence, is that of Vida Chenoweth's *Melodic Perception and Analysis* (1972). This distinguished contribution, the work of one of ethnomusicology's most brilliant speculative minds, has unfortunately not been taken up by other students.

The basic method is derived from Kenneth Pike's standard work *Phonemics* of 1947. Chenoweth follows the same approach with musical intervals that Pike adopts with phonemes; in the illustration western intervals are used, but different intervals may be treated similarly in the case of ethnic musics.

The melody is plotted according to successive intervals, each interval being entered twice, first as preceding interval, then as following interval. Thus, in the sequence:

2ma - 3Md - 2Ma - 2ma
(2ma = minor second ascending; 3Md = major third descending)

there are three cases of distribution:

2ma - 3Md
3Md - 2Ma
2Ma - 2ma

Chenoweth uses Pike's distributional chart, adapted for musical intervals. Each interval is marked in relation to its predecessor.

	following interval						
		unison	2 m d	2 m a	2 M d	2 M a	etc
preceding interval	unison						
	2 m d						
	2 m a						
	2 M d						
	2 M a						
	etc						

Figure 3.2

Statistics may be readily compiled of the incidence of each interval, and of its environment. From these may be deduced levels of equivalence between intervals: that is, the degree to which intervals are, in Pikeian language, *contrastive* (that is, phonemic - significantly different, and thus able to occur in the same environment) or *distinctive* (distributionally complementary and thus occurring in different environments, but as part of the same phonemic group). In general terms, a contrastive distinction between intervals is the same thing as a pertinent distinction.

There are various guiding factors in deciding the equivalence of two intervals. They will be reasonably close to each other; *major third* and *minor third*, for example, are about as near to each other as dark l and clear l. They may seem distributionally complementary; if the major third appears 53 times and the minor third twice, there is reason to assume that the latter is a free variant of the former. And finally, the environment may be seen to determine a variation of interval; if a minor second always occurs after a major third, a major second after a perfect fourth, there may be reason to assume that the distinction *minor second / major second* is distinctive rather than contrastive: that is, non-pertinent.

There are five rules for discerning emic units (the Pikeian term for phonemes in a broader sense). In summary, these identify as contrastive (that is, as separate emic units) any two units which can occur in the same environment, like the *l* of leap and the *r* of reap. However, if two units occur only in different environments, like the clear l at the start of *leap* and the dark l at the end of *ball*, then these are equivalent, free variations of the same emic unit or, in linguistic terms, allophones of a single phoneme. These rules are explained at greater length by Nattiez (1975, 225-230).

Certain considerations, essential to distributional analysis in linguistics, are missing from Chenoweth's system. For example, there is no concern for *juncture*, the division between words or morphemes which alters distributional rules, although most musical styles have clear divisions between phrases (one thinks of the relaxing of harmonic rules across the phrase-divisions of harmonized chorales). Nevertheless, from the purely intervallic point of view, Chenoweth's rules for ascertaining pertinence and non-pertinence ought to make it possible to establish a distributional system for any melodic style. But they have never been successfully applied. Chenoweth's own best work lies in the field of generative analysis, and is described below in Chapter 6.

3.2. Syntagmatic repetition and segmentation

3.2.1. Before phonetic units can be grouped according to pertinence and classified as allophones, there has to be a recurrence of units throughout the discourse. It is because the voiced bilabial *b* occurs from time to time in almost any discourse in English, that this feature may be extrapolated and given phonemic status. The paradigmatic organization of language is based on *repetition*, in fact; this is especially evident in the distributional linguistics of Zellig Harris or Kenneth Pike, where a chart is compiled of recurrences of units, as has been seen in connection with Chenoweth's analysis of intervallic structure.

The kind of recurrence that structures language happens in music, too; the unification of a long passage by the constant interworking of small motives is a familiar feature. It is unusual in language, however, for items to recur *syntagmatically*, in immediate succession. Phonemes are hardly ever repeated successively in the syntagmatic chain, and successive repetition of morphemes occurs only in rhetorical or poetic utterances.

But music, unlike language, often repeats phrases syntagmatically in a very simple and regular way. A typical lyric melody begins with the symmetrical repeat of a 2- or 4-bar phrase, which usually occurs yet again a little later. The effect of this is to demarcate phrases, not on the grounds of meaning, but on the basis of repetition itself. In the 'Ode to joy' theme from Beethoven's Choral Symphony the first four bars are clearly a segment, because they recur immediately with a modified ending. The segmentation of music by simple repetition is a feature noticed by several writers.

3.2.2. The Canadian David Lidov has shown that musical repetition fulfils various functions. The kind of repetition that articulates motives and phrases, like the opening phrase of the 'Ode to Joy', he calls formative repetition. It usually takes place immediately; it is a conventional feature which 'does not attract attention' (Lidov 1979, 10). In fact, it is a *concrete* feature, rather than an abstract generalization such as the aspects of harmony, tonality and metre; Lidov seems to suggest that it is phonetic rather than phonemic, natural rather than cultural.

Quoting D Bartha's study of Beethoven (reprinted in *The Creative world of Beethoven*, edited by P H Lang) he shows that this is associated with 'quaternary stanza structure', that typical pattern of repetition, derived from traditional music, which proceeds in groups of 4-4-2-2-4 bars. Within this simple arrangement the phrases are absolutely discrete and easy to isolate - as they are in a dance tune like 'Staten Island' or the theme of the finale of Beethoven's First Symphony. So unambiguous are these phrase structures that Lidov calls them 'transparent'. Thus 'a transparent 8-measure phrase consists of two identical or very similar 4-measure halves'. If there is no such division, the phrase is called 'opaque'. It is at once clear that a lyrical imagination like that of Mozart invents plenty of transparent structures; while Brahms (as Schoenberg notices, and as is well shown in the slow movement of the First Symphony) tends to be opaque. Transparency may penetrate deep into the form; a transparent 8-bar phrase may be made up of transparent 4-bar phrases whose 2-bar halves are themselves transparent. On the other hand, the subdivisions may be respectively transparent and opaque, giving an 8-bar group that subdivides (2-2)-4, for example.

The formative role of repetition is so obvious and universal that it is seldom discussed. It even appears in contemporary music; 'innovations which lack the support of an established musical language can appeal to repetition to clarify their vocabulary and procedures'. Debussy's obsessive two-bar phrases, or Harrison Birtwistle's repetitions of whole sections, may be cited.

3.2.3. Musical repetition apparently produces the same 'double articulation' which is generated by linguistic pertinence. Just as language is articulated on the levels of the phoneme and the morpheme, so music is hierarchically divided into *motives* and *phrases*. Is it possible to distinguish the musical motive and the phrase by qualitative distinctions, as clear as those in language? Lidov attempts this, though with much less success. He first of all rejects the criterion of length; both musical units vary considerably in extent. Instead, motive and phrase may be separated by their 'minimal adequate descriptions'. The description of the phrase structure is relatively complex; that of the motive, simple and unitary. 'The principles of Riemann, Cooper and Meyer, and Ruwet are quite adequate to isolate motive: "it is of a piece, it is one thing". But phrase is "an articulated percept"' (Lidov 1975, 84-85).

In the case of a relatively transparent structure, phrases may be related to each other in a variety of different ways, giving a number of alternative descriptions. Motives, on the other hand, are related by a single feature. A medieval monody is cited as an example, 'Haut honor d'un commandement'.

Figure 3.3

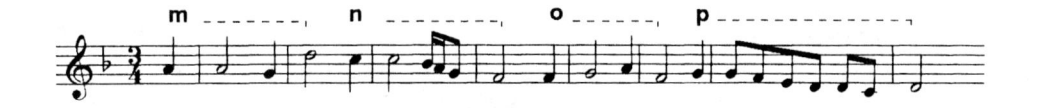

From the rhythmic point of view this melody is transparent to the level of the single bar, if one considers ligatures as single notes. Its eight bars divide 4+4, then (2+2)+(2+2), and each pair of bars divides 1+1. The tune is made up, however, of four phrases, marked *m n o p* in Figure 3.3.

The motives are rhythmically similar; each is three crotchets in length. The phrases, each made up two motives, are related in several different ways. Phrase *m* resembles phrase *p* in that both end on D. Phrase *p*, however, resembles phrase *n* since both have a contour that is mainly falling. Phrases *m* and *n* are higher in ambitus than *o* and *p*. The phrase structure of this melody takes three possible forms, defined as framing (xyyx), disjunction (xxyy) and complementation (xyxy).

Figure 3.4

	m	n	o	p	
Framing	x	y	y	x	ends on D / ends on F
Complementation	x	y	x	y	mainly rising / mainly falling
Disjunction	x	x	y	y	larger, higher ambitus/ smaller, lower ambitus

Motives, with their simple relations, tend to generate loose structures like contrapuntal episodes and development sections. Phrases are generated when motives coalesce into patterns with complex relations, like lyric themes. Thus 'syntactical strata in music, phrase and motive, might be better distinguished by their relative complexity than... by their length' (Lidov 1975, 82).

3.2.4. Viewed as a sign, formative repetition 'refers to what is repeated'; it is a marker of segmentation and thus a grammatical feature. It is usually single. When a figure is repeated more than once the attention begins to be attracted by the repetition itself; 'instead of focusing on the repeated material only, we focus on the repetition as an activity *per se* and seek a symbolic interpretation of it' (Lidov 1979, 14-15). This is called *focal* repetition. This type is a sign, not of segmentation and grammatical features, but of *connotative meaning*. It possesses extra-musical associations: 'activities that go on and on, rituals, compulsive actions, getting stuck "in a rut", emphatically accented speech, dancing, laughing etc.' Lidov gives as an example the second 8 bars of Scott Joplin's *Magnetic Rag*. Some readers will be more familiar with Chopin's Mazurka in D, Op 33 No 2, bars 65-72 and repeat. Joplin's repetitions (a figure of two bars played 4 times in a passage which is itself repeated) seem 'mischievous and compulsive, sad and consoling; the music is "stuck in a rut" but makes the best of it'.

3.2.5. It has been suggested that the most typical formative repetition occurs at once, immediately after the first statement of the phrase in question. But clearly there is no difference between the immediate repetition of the first 8 bars in a 32-bar popular song (like

Gershwin's 'Someone to watch over me') and the recurrence of these same 8 bars at the end, after the 'middle 8'. Non-serial repetition (Lidov calls it 'delayed repetition') may, therefore, be formative. But Lidov does not feel 'as sure of the conditions which should constrain delayed formative repetitions as... of those for immediate repetitions'. The chief condition governing immediate repetitions is that they shall not attract attention to the fact of repetition. Delayed repetitions are apt to sound like returns or homecomings, or, if they are multiple - one thinks of the occurrences of the refrain in rondo form - begin to take on the revolving, dog-chasing-tail quality of focal repetition.

At the other extreme, motives may present themselves ubiquitously throughout the texture of a work. This is much closer to paradigmatic repetition. The 4-note 'motto' at the start of Beethoven's Fifth Symphony is formatively repeated, one degree lower. But it functions, quite obviously, as a paradigm throughout the movement, and elsewhere in the Symphony (not to mention in other works of this composer!) If one accepts Lidov's definition of the phrase and the motive, it is probably correct to assume that motives are more often subject to paradigmatic recurrence, phrases to formative repetition. It has to be confessed that the writers on musical repetition have never thought very hard about the distinction between formative and paradigmatic recurrence. Lidov, chiefly interested in the formative effect, does not dwell on the issue of delayed repetition. Jean-Jacques Nattiez's idea of 'semiotic analysis' concentrates on paradigmatic recurrence, of course (this is discussed below in Chapter 4).

3.3. Duplication in the music of Debussy

3.3.1. The kind of music to which Lidov's ideas chiefly apply is the lyric melody in balanced phrases, based on poetic forms and derived from oral tradition. The melos of Classical music is still in this world. Debussy seldom respects this tradition much; but he has an obsessive habit of repeating short phrases. Andre Schaeffner comments on his 'systematic duplication of each melodic phrase' (quoted in Ruwet 1962, 71). This is easily illustrated: the beginning of the *Prélude à l'Après-midi d'un Faune*, the Prelude to *Pelléas*, the theme of *Danseuses de Delphes*, for instance.

This universal habit may relate, not so much to traditional music and poetic form as to the most rudimentary psychological processes. 'In a general sense, the cultural essence of repetition, and in particular of duplication, must be well grasped; duplication plays a fundamental part in the the first steps that go to make up culture and notably in the beginnings of infant language' (Ruwet 1962, 70 n.2). Ruwet quotes Jakobson on the speech of children: 'The reduplication of syllables... is a favourite procedure in nursery language... This repetitive character finds its most concise and succinct expression in, for example, *papa* '.

3.3.2. The case is not as simple as this. It is not so much a matter of 'each phrase' being duplicated, as of some phrases being repeated, others not, in a rhythm that is scrupulously worked out. And 'phrase' is a vague term; everything from the smallest motive to whole groups of phrases may be repeated, so that there are 'multiple forms of repetitions, which are situated at different stages of the structure of the work, and which are fitted one inside the other' (71).

In addition, repetitions may be subtly varied, though not in the ways of classical music - not, for example, by the replacement of a cadence to produce a harmonically complete sentence.

There is, in fact, a paradox in this music, for Debussy uses the most simple of structural devices - quasi-literal repetition - to give coherence to sequences of the most disparate material; his gift was 'to give unity to things that have no apparent links' (Schaeffner, quoted by Ruwet, 1962, 72). These two processes are connected, however. The purpose of duplication is to establish a formal equivalence between these heterogeneous elements. This is especially the case when the connections are contrastive; Schoenberg, the enemy of repetition, unifies his textures with common thematic cells, but Debussy, who wishes to juxtapose radically different figures, isolates them by means of repetition.

3.3.3. The Prelude to *Pelléas et Melisande* - indeed, each of the instrumental parts of the opera, including the interludes between the scenes - is full of near-literal repetitions.

Bar 7 of the Prelude (Figure 3.5 shows the whole piece) is one of the very few elements that are not repeated: it is a soft timpani roll. The preceding six bars contain two figures outstanding for their dissimilarity. One is modal, the other based on whole tones; one is chiefly for strings, the other for wind; one is low in pitch, the other higher; one proceeds largely in minims, the other in crotchets and quavers; finally, the second is denser in texture than its predecessor.

However, both motives are duplicated, each with slight variations. The effect of this is to isolate them contrastively, but also to bring to light certain subtle relations between them. In a certain sense motive (b) (bar 5) is a harmonic simplification of (a) (in bar 1). In (a) there are two chords, the first lacking its third; because of the modal character it is hard to say which is the tonic chord, especially as the chord on C is complete and thus stronger. But motive (b) has a single harmony, the whole tone chord on A flat.

Both (a) and (b) begin on D; in one sense (a) breaks further away, since it leaps upward a fifth. In another sense (b) is the more adventurous, since it introduces a variety of rhythmic values. The apparent intervallic simplicity of (b), however - it merely reiterates the major second D-E - conceals a common feature of the two motives. The movement across a second constitutes the bass of (a), as well as an inner part; in (b) it has moved into the melody.

Clearly this whole syntagm is repeated after the drum roll, with certain variations. Notably, the whole-tone sonority of (b) disappears, replaced with a strong sense of B flat major. So far, the structure of the Prelude could be shown as:

$$(a + a') + (b + b') + c + (a1 + a1') + (b1 + b1')$$

This analysis is reducible to (A + B) + C + (A' + B'), which is further reducible to A + B + A'. There are, indeed, repetitions within repetitions.

Turning to the last six bars of the Prelude (bars 18-23), we see a more systematic juxtaposition of repeated and unrepeated material. If a division is made after bar 20 (instead of the more obvious place after bar 19), this passage comprises two elements, each made up of one repeated motive and one unrepeated.

$$(f + f') + g \,/\, (h + h) + i$$

Of these, (f) contains two motives in counterpoint, the 'Mélisande motive' above and the 'Golaud motive' in the tenor register. If we consider only the 'Golaud motive' (since this becomes the basis of bar 20) the melodic direction in bars 18-20 is rising. It is thus contrastive with bars 21-23, where the general tendency is downward.

Figure 3.5. Debussy: Prelude to *Pelléas et Mélisande*

Furthermore, the dynamics are mirrored; in the first passage there are two crescendo marks, in the second two decrescendo marks, with one unmarked bar in each case, giving the arrangement (- < <) (> > -). In other respects the passages are contrastive: bars 18-20 are florid and rhythmically complex, bars 21-23 rhythmically plain; the 'Golaud' melody in bars 18-20 is entirely conjunct, the movement in 21-23 traces an arpeggio. Yet there is also a unifying feature. All six bars retain the elision of the third beat, which links the whole passage to motive (b) in bar 5.

If greater and smaller repetitions are traced throughout the whole 23 bars of the Prelude, an elaborate pattern emerges, with duplications on four levels. In Ruwet's chart, italics represent the serial numbers of sections, non-italics bar numbers.

1 (1-7)	*1.1* (1-6)	*1.11* (1-4)	*1.111* (1-2)	a
			1.112 (3-4)	a'
		1.12 (5-6)	*1.121* (5)	b
			1.122 (6)	b'
	1.2 (7)			c
2 (8-17)	*2.1* (8-13)	*2.11* (8-11)	*2.111* (8-9)	a1
			2.112 (10-11)	a1'
		2.12 (12-13)	*2.121* (12)	b1
			2.122 (13)	b1'
	2.2 (14-17)	*2.21* (14-15)	*2.211* (14)	d
			2.212 (15)	d
		2.22 (16-17)		e
3 (18-23)	*3.1* (18-20)	*3.11* (18-19)	*3.111* (18)	f
			3.112 (19)	f'
		3.12 (20)		g
	3.2 (21-23)	*3.21* (21-22)	*3.211* (21)	h
			3.212 (22)	h
		3.22 (23)		i

3.3.4. The question of Debussy's obsessive or mechanical repetitions dissolves if one observes his musical paragraphs in close detail. There is nothing mechanical; phrase-duplication is an integral part of contrastive and variation structures.

This sort of repetition would presumably be classed as formative by Lidov. At any rate, the habit of repeating immediately many fragments of the musical utterance is very different from paradigmatic recurrence in language; it is indeed a 'projection of the plane of association on to the plane of combination' (Jakobson's definition of the poetic mode of utterance).

3.4. Segmentation based on logic

3.4.1. Musical segmentation based on pertinence had a brave send-off, but it has proved a hard idea to work out in practice. Segmentation based on simple serial repetition is a clear and significant process, but hardly sufficient to lead to a comprehensive account.

Charles Seeger suggested that the description of music segments be based on *logical* considerations. He saw that some of the factors which pattern language were logical; the very discovery of repetitions and recurrences relies on the logical criterion of *identity*. He does not discuss pertinence; he seems to consider the linguistic phoneme a natural feature, the 'smallest and meaningless unit of signalling' (Seeger 1960, 229). He envisages similar atomic units of music; an example of a musical phoneme would be 'a single note (toneme) or beat (rhythmeme) or, better, tone-beat (museme?). In both arts, several phonemes are combined to form a morpheme... In music, a morpheme would be a motif, a pattern of design, a music-logical mood. It is at this point that resemblance ceases and difference appears. Speech-phonemes are linguistic, not logical, forms'.

The term 'mood' is here being used in a technical philosophical sense. In classical syllogistic logic the ways in which categorical syllogisms were constructed were called moods; logicians differed about the number of valid moods. In the middle ages, there were 19 moods, each with its own name. The modern theorist W S Jevons considers that only 11 moods are 'good forms of reasoning'. A mood, to put it simply, is one of the forms that can be taken by a logical proposition.

Seeger realises that linguistic discourse, on the phonological and syntactic levels, is not structured by logic but by purely linguistic forces. Logic is present on the *semantic* level.

> Although a sentence is linguistically a chain of morphemes, logically, it is a chain of sememes - a sememe being the meaning of a morpheme. Speech-logic lies entirely in the message of a signal-message complex, not at all in its signal (Seeger 1960, 229-230).

It is possible to translate linguistic utterances because language is only a medium for thought, the phonological clothing for logical structures. Music cannot be translated precisely because logical processes are at work in the utterance itself (not in its 'meaning').

> A music-logic, on the other hand, certainly lies in the signal of a signal-message complex... A music-logical cursus cannot be 'translated' into another music employing different sounds in the signal without distortion (230).

The resemblance of musical processes to semantic, rather than syntactic processes - and thus to logical operations - has been realised by another writer (see Monelle, 1991a, and below, Chapter 8).

Logic, being based on a series of abstract principles, is 'entirely free of reference to the empirical universe'. This makes logic a peculiarly suitable model for musical analysis, Seeger thinks, though its principles must be adapted. The principle of identity can be accepted; it underlies all considerations of paradigmatic and syntagmatic repetition, of course. Other logical principles like *contradiction* and the *excluded middle* have to be radically adapted or replaced.

3.4.2. Just as logic depends on oppositions - statements imply the possibility of their own negation - so music inhabits a world in which every feature has its opposite: intervals may rise or fall, notes may be short or long, tempi fast or slow, dynamics loud or soft. True, there are musical parameters, like timbre and accent, which are not structured in this way. Seeger's most telling strategy, however, is to see a similarity of principle in each of the four 'simple functions', pitch, dynamics, tempo and value. Rising in pitch is somewhat like getting louder or faster; higher pitch, greater loudness, faster tempo are more 'tense'. Music, thus, is a pattern of tense and 'detense' events on all levels. Invariance of pitch, dynamics etc. is called 'tonicity'.

If a single note (the 'museme', a note in all its parameters of pitch, value, dynamics and so on) is the atomic unit of music, then the smallest meaningful unit or 'unit of music-logical form', the musical morpheme, must consist of at least three notes because two are needed to generate logical relations, and two terms - two sets of relations - are necessary for any proposition. A figure of only two notes or events he calls 'mesomorphic', halfway to being a form; with three notes or events, a figure is 'morphic', fully-formed, and this pair of relations is called a 'binary mood'.

In terms of pitch, binary moods resemble the basic three-note neumes of medieval notation: the tense forms are (a) rising-rising (in neumatic terms the 'scandicus') and (b) rising-falling (the 'torculus'). The detense binary moods are (c) falling-falling (the 'climacus') and (d) falling-rising (the 'porrectus'). The ternary moods require four notes each; there are eight of these.

Figure 3.6.

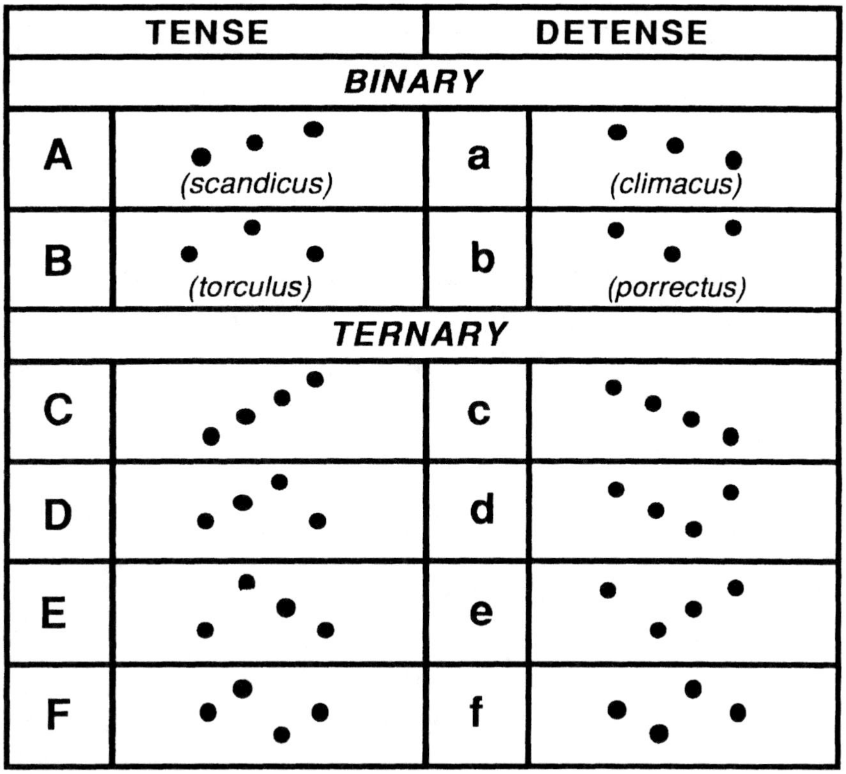

	TENSE		DETENSE	
	BINARY			
A	• • • • (scandicus)	a	• • • • (climacus)	
B	• • • (torculus)	b	• • • (porrectus)	
	TERNARY			
C	• • • •	c	• • • •	
D	• • • •	d	• • • •	
E	• • •	e	• • • •	
F	• • • •	f	• • • •	

However, the same moods may be applied to rhythmic values. It would seem that Seeger becomes confused here between rhythm and metre, for he envisages the rhythmic moods as beginning on the strong first beat of the bar and repeating themselves like medieval rhythmic modes. This makes it hard to apply his system to the developing rhythms of actual music, at least that of the western tradition.

Again, three events are necessary for a binary mood, since values are determined by points of attack; the value of the second note can only be determined by the onset of another note, which, in Seeger's rhythmic-cum-metrical system, is the first beat of the next bar. Since quicker movement generates tension, the short values are tense, long values detense. The writer connects rhythmic moods with the Greek names for metrical feet, though he is here in insecure country, since Greek feet seldom began with a stressed syllable, as rhythmic moods appear to do (see Monelle 1989).

Figure 3.7.

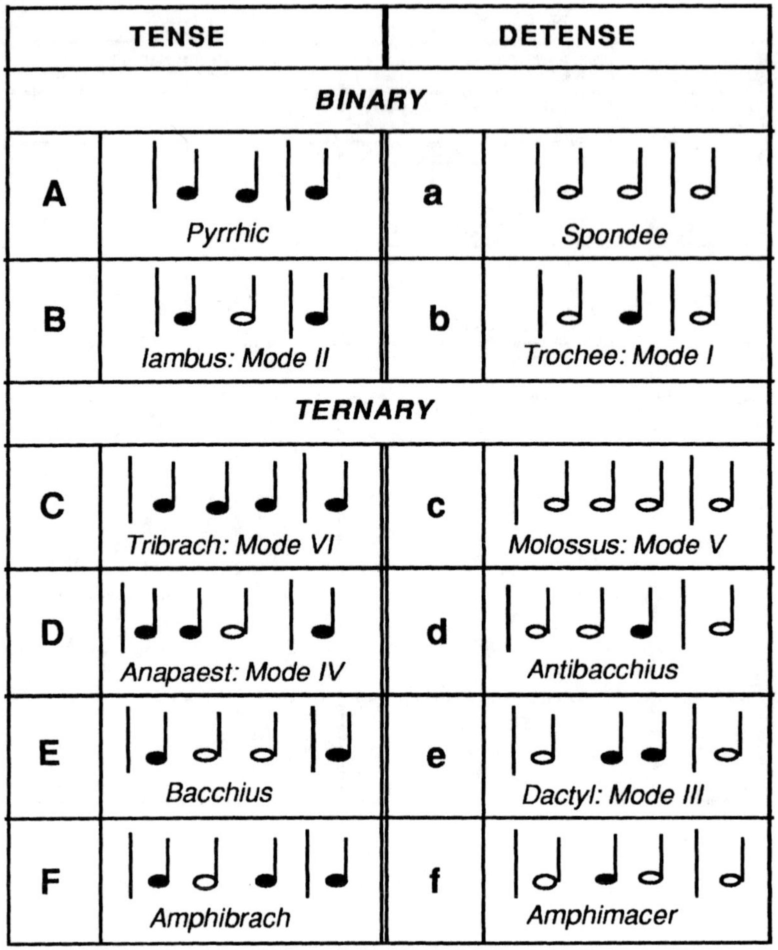

	TENSE		DETENSE
	BINARY		
A	Pyrrhic	a	Spondee
B	Iambus: Mode II	b	Trochee: Mode I
	TERNARY		
C	Tribrach: Mode VI	c	Molossus: Mode V
D	Anapaest: Mode IV	d	Antibacchius
E	Bacchius	e	Dactyl: Mode III
F	Amphibrach	f	Amphimacer

In Figure 3.7 the names of medieval modes and Greek verse feet are given.

The factor of 'centricity' makes for several variants of each mood. In terms of pitch, ternary mood D (for example) can be realised in one centric version (in which the first and last notes are the same) and four decentric versions. In the latter versions, the tension and detension (represented in Figure 3.8 by plus and minus signs) of each group of two notes - notes 1 and 2, 2 and 3, 3 and 4, 1 and 3, 2 and 4, 1 and 4 - are taken into account. Centricity (present between notes 2 and 4 in $D4$) is shown by an equals sign. Centricity is a factor in moods of rhythmic value, also.

The moods may be applied to progressions of dynamics: two crescendi succeeding each other represent mood A (rising-rising),

Figure 3.8.

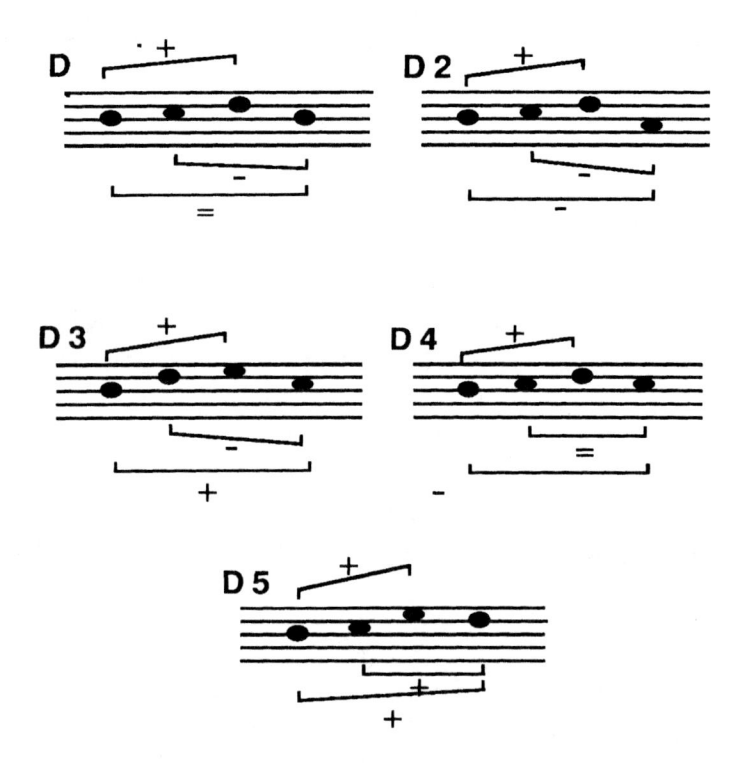

and in terms of dynamic levels, where mood A would yield [*mp - mf - f*], for example. In terms of tempo, mood A might be [*accel - accel*] or [*moderato - piu mosso - faster*].

Seeger speaks also of 'quaternary' moods, involving five notes. But longer sequences of notes are more commonly the result of 'enchainment', the joining of moods end to end by succession or elision.

3.4.3. The exhilaration of Seeger's analysis of musical movement lies in its sole reliance on abstract logic. There is no consideration of psychology or empirical method. Its limitations lie in the difficulty of application to real music. There are a few tunes that seem 'mood-bound', like the theme of Elgar's 'Enigma' Variations, which begins with decentric pitch-mood *f* in rhythmic mood *D* and continues with decentric pitch-mood *d* in rhythmic mood *d*.... and so on (Figure 3.9).

But apart from the gulf between logical analysis and real music, a much more damaging criticism of Seeger's segmentation is that it is not really a segmentation at all; the moods are analyses of

Figure 3.9.

segments *after they have been made*. No criteria are given for the isolation of segments, and any musical phrase can be divided in a dozen different ways. This analysis is best, perhaps, in the treatment of recurrent fragments, germinal motives and ostinati. And obviously, standard devices like inversion and retrogression are logical in Seeger's sense; pitch mode *a* is the inversion of *A*, while the rhythmic modes are related by retrogression: *b* and *B*, *e* and *D*, *d* and *E*, the rest being palindromes.

In Figure 3.10 are shown several germinal motives from standard works, showing how they can easily be assimilated into Seeger's logical world.

From this rigorously abstract approach we must return to a more empirical observation of musical repetition, if we are to find any realistic criteria for segmentation and taxonomy.

3.5. A 'machine' for discovering paradigms

3.5.1. The kind of paradigmatic analysis which Jean-Jacques Nattiez was to regard as defining his concept of the 'neutral level', described in the next chapter, begins with Lévi-Strauss's analyses of myths (1955; see Lévi-Strauss 1968, 206-231). This inspired Nicolas Ruwet to a more detailed examination of musical repetition.

Unlike ordinary narrative, myths have a way of returning to the same relations and functions as though time were flowing in two directions, forward and back. They resemble language in that their intelligibility rests on the recurrence of various features which can thus be listed paradigmatically like phonemes (Lévi-Strauss called them *mythemes*). For example, in the Greek myth of Oedipus the theme of fratricide/parricide occurs at intervals: the Spartoi, armed men who grew from the earth where Cadmus had sown the dragon's teeth slay each other; later Oedipus kills his father, Laios; then Eteocles kills his brother Polynices. Similarly, the names of the protagonists, as they successively appear, all imply lameness:

Figure 3.10

Beethoven, Symphony No 3

PITCH MOOD — E decentric — D centric

RHYTHMIC MOOD — f — C

Bartok, String Quartet No 4

A — a — / a — A

Brahms, Symphony No 2

F — E / f — C

Schubert, 'Great' C major Symphony

A — A — b — b — A / b — b(dim) — b(dim) — b — b(dim)

Labdacos (Laios's father) may mean 'lame'; Laios probably means 'left-sided'; Oedipus means 'swollen foot'.

    Lévi-Strauss imagines visitors from another planet who have learnt to decipher our writing, but stumble on an orchestra score. Trying initially to read it line by line, they realise that certain figures often recur in vertical alignment. They ask the question: 'What if patterns showing affinity, instead of being considered in succession, are to be treated as one complex pattern and read as a whole?' It becomes clear that an orchestral score 'must be read diachronically along one axis - that is, page after page, and from left to right - and synchronically along the other axis, all the notes written vertically making up one gross constituent unit, that is, one bundle of relations'(1968, 212).

    Applying this principle to the myth of Oedipus, the 'score' will present the narrative in the correct order, reading from left to right and top to bottom, but will arrange related features under each other.

Cadmos seeks his sister Europa, ravished by Zeus			
		Cadmos kills the dragon	
	The Spartoi kill one another		
			Labdacos (Laios's father) = lame (?)
	Oedipus kills his father, Laois		
			Laois (Oedipus' father) =left-sided(?)
		Oedipus kills the Sphinx	
			Oedipus = swollen-foot (?
Oedipus mourns his mother, Jocasta			
	Eteocles kills his brother, Polynices		
Antigone buries her brother, Polynices, despite prohibition			

3.5.2. The listing of repeated motives in myths betrays an emphasis on patterns of repetition rather than meaning. Repetition does not always occur at once, though sometimes it does. Myths, like music, appear to repeat themselves syntagmatically as well as paradigmatically; repetition can be formative. Neither Lévi-Strauss for myth, nor Lidov for music, feel any need to base their analysis on 'meaning'. Segmentation is based on patterns of recurrence, without concern for what is said.

In linguistics, as has been mentioned, the tradition least concerned with meaning is that of distributionalism, the approach of Zellig Harris and Kenneth Pike. Phonemes are discerned by examining the distribution of phonetic items throughout the language, not by questions of meaning.

This tradition of linguistic analysis is mentioned by Nicolas Ruwet in the article that gave birth to paradigmatic analysis in music (Ruwet 1966). In discussing this article, Nattiez suggests that Ruwet may also have known about certain writings in ethnomusicology. Gilbert Rouget, describing a corpus of songs from Dahomey, places letter-symbols over certain melodic figures; he does not mean to demonstrate some melodic principle or pattern but merely to record repetitions. For each of these pieces, certain fragments are repeated, others not: it is on repetition - or the absence of repetition - that our segmentation is based. When a sequence of sounds is uttered twice or several times over, with or without variants, it is considered as a unit (quoted in Nattiez 1975, 240).

Ruwet has more regard than Lidov for delayed repetition, the recurrence of musical figures after other material. This, of course, is nearer to the linguistic paradigm. At this stage, however, he is still concerned with whole phrases, as was Rouget. Soon he was to move into a discussion of short motives, laying the groundwork for a kind of paradigmatic analysis which is more distant from the idea of formative repetition. Ruwet is distinguished from Lévi-Strauss and Rouget in that his methods of segmentation are made fully explicit; his results can be checked by anyone. His system is thus a true 'discovery procedure'. This concern for scientific procedure shows the influence of Harris, and is Ruwet's principal contribution. The method becomes, in Ruwet's words, a 'machine for the discovery of elementary identities'.

3.5.3. In Ruwet's system (1966), analytical items are sought in a programmed order. One identifies:

1 The longest passages that are repeated fully, whether at once or after another passage, giving formulae like A + B + X + B + Y, where A and B are recurrent passages, X and Y non-recurrent.

2 Non-recurrent passages are considered units on the same level as recurrent passages in the respect of length. As repetitions of temporal proportion they may be written as primary units; thus A + X + A + Y becomes A + B + A + C. The resultant segmentation may now be checked by looking at pauses and at linguistic divisions in the words. This is the 'rule of equal length'.

3 If the above operations have not yielded a satisfactory analysis the following misfunctions may be suspected:

(i) non-recurrent passages are much shorter than recurrent ones and therefore cannot be considered units on the same level.

(ii) Non-recurrent passages are longer than recurrent ones. Here the non-recurrent passage may have to be subdivided, either yielding several units of level 1 - thus A + A + X becomes A + A + B + C - or shifting the analysis on to level 2 where the recurrent passages are themselves subdivided into shorter figures which may be found to recur in the non-recurrent passages. Thus, for example, A + A + X may become (a + b) + (a + b) + (x + b) + (y + b). If neither of these procedures is possible, it may be necessary to consider X as an unanalysed unit on 'level 0'.

4 Passages which seem initially not the same may be transformations of each other (rhythmic or melodic variants) according to certain principles of transformation.

(i) If pitch and rhythm are separated we may find similar contours with different rhythms or similar rhythms with different contours.

(ii) There may be permutations, additions and suppression of certain elements.

(iii) In discerning the equivalence of certain passages it may be necessary to shift from a higher to a lower level or from a lower to a higher, which Ruwet calls 'shunting'. For example, while units on level 2 - a + b + a + c - may seem to constitute the realities of analysis, it may be necessary to move up to level 1 for the purposes of subsequent work, and to determine that a + b = A and a + c = A'.

(iv) In some cases units of level 1 may seem to group themselves into even larger units. Must we therefore evoke a 'level 0'? Taking two typical formulae:

$$A + X^* + A + Y$$
$$X + A^* + Y + A$$

we find that each may become A + B or perhaps A + A' on level 0, on the fulfilment of one of the following conditions:
(a) there is some special rhythmic marking of the point shown by an asterisk, either a pause or the prolongation of a note.
(b) Y is a transformation of X.

3.5.4. As an example Ruwet takes the fourteenth-century Geisslerlied 'Maria muoter reinu mait', without its words. The score is set out in the manner of Lévi-Strauss, with repeated or transformed passages placed vertically beneath each other. It should be read in the normal way, from left to right and from top to bottom.

Figure 3.11

Because this is a simple analysis we are able to observe the stages in detail.
   1 Unrepeated passage + repeated passage (X + B + B).
   2 Negative result: X is much longer than B.
   3 X falls apart into two units each equal in length to B; and indeed they are related by transformation.
$$X = A + A'$$

4 Observing A' for a moment: this passage contains an inner repetition. On level 2, then:

$A' = x + b + y + b$

However, b, x and y are equal in duration. This may thus be rewritten:

$A' = a + b + c + b$

Turning now to the opening passage (A), the transformation which yielded A' was within the repeat of b:

$A = a + B + C + b'$

As for the later passage (B), this ends with the transformation of b.

$B = z + b'$

Figure z is equal in length to b'.

$B = d + b'$

It is now possible to pass to units of level 3, for d is in fact a shorter figure literally repeated.

$d = d^1 + d^1$
$c = c^1 + d^1$

Figures a and b do not contain such repetitions but they nevertheless may be divided into figures equal in length to d1.

$a = a^1 + a^2$
$b = b^1 + b^2$
$b' = b'^1 + b^2$

This subdivision may lead us to see that there are relations both rhythmic and melodic between these smaller units, Observe, for example, the rhythmic similarity of b^2 and d^1, and the similar contours of a^1 and b^1.

Figure 3.12

This reveals a whole web of inner motivic relations; but any evocation of a lower level, 'level 4', must be resisted. On this level the units begin to overlap. The discrete character of the units and levels is essential.

Of course, any musician could have seen this analysis at a glance. Ruwet does not offer it for itself, but as proof that his mechanical system of segmentation leads to a result which we acknowledge as realistic. Indeed, he does not even demand that the analyst actually follow his system in practice; he merely offers it as a way of verifying and clarifying an analysis reached largely by intuitive guesses. Harris had offered his procedures only as 'reminders in the course of the research and as a form for checking or presenting the results' (Harris 1951, 1) and Ruwet echoes this.

> The procedure is much more a procedure of verification, meant to keep a check that the analysis is coherent, a discovery procedure in the strict sense of the term. Doubtless it would always be possible to apply it rigorously in the given order, and the same results would be obtained, but it is much more economical and quick to use it to verify the results of an analysis obtained sometimes quite rapidly in a purely intuitive manner (Ruwet 1972, 117).

3.5.5. 'Maria muoter', a song in a popular style, clearly lends itself to Ruwet's type of analysis. His other examples are more sophisticated (they are songs by Guiot de Provins and Bernard de Ventadour, and a dance by Raimbaut de Vaqueiras) and here his methods work less well. Nattiez, in his discussions of Ruwet's ideas (1972; 1975, 244-278), makes two important contributions.

(i) The 'rule of equal length' is questioned. In some styles inequality of length may be a defining characteristic (see Schoenberg 1950, 52-101, on Mozart and Haydn). Nattiez shows that the first 7 bars of the Prelude to *Pelléas et Mélisande* cannot be analysed in segments of equal length.

(ii) Ruwet acknowledges that segmentation is based on certain criteria, especially in the case of the smallest units. Since the criteria for segmentation are many, 'it is impossible to represent the structure of a musical piece by a single schema' (Ruwet 1972, 134). Nattiez refers to the criticism of Ruwet's article by Simha Arom (1969), in which a number of different points of departure are suggested for the discovery of equivalences. Small sequences of notes may be identified and mechanically extrapolated, giving a new segmentation on the smallest level; in the example, the downward sequence C - B flat - A and the rising third A - C (Figure 3.13).

Alternatively, 'pivot-notes' can be isolated (notes which are unchanged in every phrase) and the remaining motives may be examined for equivalence (Figure 3.14).

Figure 3.13

Figure 3.14

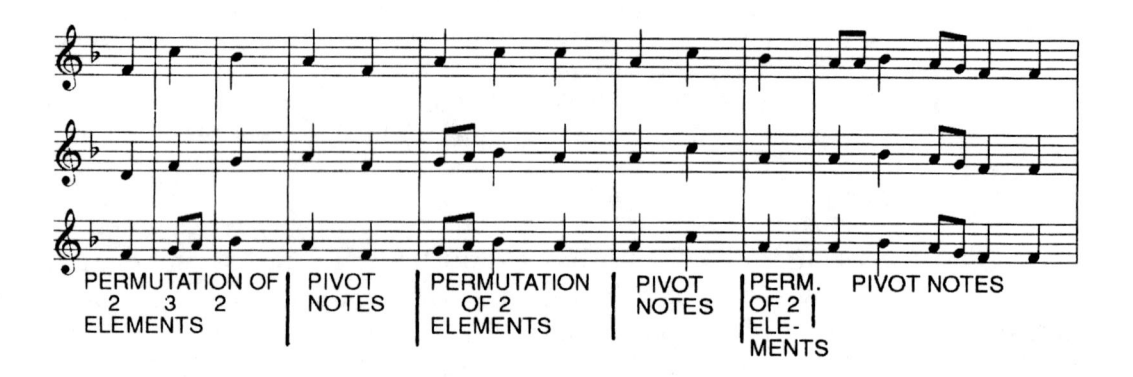

```
PERMUTATION OF | PIVOT | PERMUTATION | PIVOT | PERM.  | PIVOT NOTES
  2   3   2    | NOTES | OF 2        | NOTES | OF 2   |
ELEMENTS       |       | ELEMENTS    |       | ELE-   |
               |       |             |       | MENTS  |
```

Clearly the analyst must begin by making explicit his criteria of segmentation. 'The criteria of a paradigmatic arrangement must be known so that another researcher can criticise it in full knowledge of its basis and propose a more valid organisation... what is important in an analysis is to make explicit one's criteria" (Nattiez 1975, 264 and 340).

3.6. The problems of segmentation

3.6.1. The most effective basis of segmentation in music is undoubtedly formative repetition. Yet it is also the characteristic that is most unlike language. This would suggest that musical segmentation can never be successfully based on linguistic principles.

Yet there is no analysis without segmentation, or at least some view of salience (Schenkerian analysis takes account of the points of melodic and harmonic prominence which arise from the apprehension of musical structure). A number of conclusions result from this lengthy discussion of segmentation and metalanguage.

1   The only musical unit that seems universal and objective is the note (or single drum-stroke, gesture, or other feature). This has a number of properties, to do with pitch, value, dynamic, rhythm, timbre and attack. Unfortunately, the relations that lead to analysis only begin when two or more notes are combined; the minimal analytical unit comprises at least two notes, usually more.

2   Segmentation in music will always be ultimately based on intuition, because the relation of phonology and semantics, of expression and content, functions differently in music. The clear separation of expression and content in language, which led Saussure to regard the linguistic symbol as 'arbitrary', is not a feature of music, where every aspect seems to be linked to semantics.

3   Analytical segmentation should be based on rational and explicit principles. It is not necessary for every worker to agree on the definitions of terms like 'motive' and 'phrase', provided each analysis is backed by a clear explanation of the terms employed. If non-verbal symbols (letters or numerals) are used, it should be established to which level they refer.

4   Segmentation on rational principles is most easily applied to monophonic music. While it is true that most human music is monody, the western tradition has produced elaborate monuments of harmony and polyphony which resist rational analysis. In the next chapter there are a few examples of the rigorous analysis of harmonic music, but to speak frankly, it will again be found that monodies are the home territory of any segmentation that can be called intellectually respectable.

4

THE ANALYSIS OF THE NEUTRAL LEVEL

4.1. The neutral level

4.1.1. The approach to a musical metalanguage through segmentation based on formative repetition has led to an inconclusive result. Nevertheless, the nearest approach to metalinguistic rigour, Jean-Jacques Nattiez's 'description of the neutral level', is based on Ruwet's 'machine' for the discovery of musical units, explained above. The advantage of this over Lidov's principle of formative repetition, is that paradigmatic study - the exhaustive comparison of small units to see if they are the same or different - may be applied universally to all music and is bound to result in an analysis, however trivial. Formative repetition, on the other hand, is not a universal feature of music.

4.1.2. To understand Nattiez's adaptation of Ruwet's ideas, we need to approach the concept of the *neutral level*, for Nattiez considers that the systematic comparison of motives implies a certain theoretical stance. Things like the composer's 'intentions' and the accidents of listening - the sophistication of the listener, his attentiveness, his level of acculturation - must be eliminated for scientific music analysis to make sense. Nattiez often speaks of 'immanent' theory, a term much used by Hjelmslev. His purpose is to define music theory in its own terms; the popularity of psychological and sociological analyses has proved a nuisance to formulators of pure theory in music.

Traditional analysis - and this embraces the methods of Schenker and Reti - approached music as though it were a unified phenomenon. It is not pertinent to Schenkerian analysis to ask, where is the *Ursatz* situated? Is it in the consciousness of the composer or the listener, or in the score, or in the performance? The *Ursatz* is considered to be in the music *per se*. In a certain sense, it is to be found in all these locations; it is as though music were a transcendent fact 'discovered' by the composer and transmitted to an ideal listener. The accidents of contingency - how aware the composer was of his own devices, how experienced or sophisticated the listener, what were the composer's intentions or the listener's sympathies - have no relevance for the traditional analyst. He was indeed a pure theorist, but he was also vulnerable to criticism from the point of view of psychology or sociology, because he made no theoretical declaration of immanence. We still see music theory criticized from a psychological angle, as though theory were meant to give a psychological account of music, as well as a musical one (see especially Cook 1990).

4.1.3. Etienne Gilson stressed that art is the product of work, of making. Art is of necessity *poietic* (from ποιειν, to make; notice the distinction from 'poetic') because it cannot exist without the artist. On this level art is not seen as symbol or communication but as artifact, production. Viewed alone, the poietic level is no more than pre-semiotic.

Paul Valéry suggested that the work of the artist, and the experience of the observer, are different activities. Nothing can guarantee a direct correspondence between the artist's 'intention' and the effect his work produces on an observer. In fact, there is necessarily some divergence; no listener to a work of music can occupy the same social and cultural space as the composer, and every listener hears music differently. Valéry coined the term *aesthesic* (not 'aesthetic') for the level of reception, derived from αισθησις, the faculty of perception.[1]

4.1.4. It remained for Jean Molino (1975) to bring these notions together and to suggest a third 'level'. The symbolic phenomenon is also an object, material subjected to a form. To these three modalities of existence there correspond three dimensions of symbolic analysis, poietic, aesthesic and the 'neutral' analysis of the object (1975, 47).

---

[1] *Aesthesic/esthesic.* In her translation of Nattiez's Varèse analysis (Nattiez 1982a), Anna Barry translates *esthésique* as 'esthesic'. The normal English form of *esthétique*, however, is 'aesthetic'. It seems appropriate to write 'aesthesic' rather than 'esthesic'. The latter spelling would be normal in American English, however.

Molino, whose article is specifically about music (unlike the writings of Gilson and Valéry), clearly means to refer to the *objet sonore*, the sound-trace of music which can be recorded by an oscilloscope, and which is a purely acoustic phenomenon. He comments that musical studies were originally poietic; in the eighteenth century most books on music were manuals of composition. In the last century the viewpoint became aesthesic; Kretzschmar and Riemann essentially wrote about methods of listening. It is for us to turn to the neutral level, for only thereby can a universal metalanguage be worked out, enabling us to analyse world music without cultural bias or normative intentions - without favouring our own culture at the expense of others, or imposing a view of 'right' or 'good' music - and without embodying ideologies in our description. Semiotics is essentially neutral, in every sense; it 'threatens no one and incarnates neither the so-called unidimensional rationalism of the structuralists, nor the obscurantist pathos of pseudo-linguists tainted with psychoanalysis and/or Marxism' (Molino 1975, 61).

4.1.5. The tripartite division, poietic-aesthesic-neutral, was accepted and developed by Nattiez. In his earlier book (1975, 52) he uses the word 'work' (*oeuvre*) to describe the musical object, leaving till later the discussion of the meaning of this term. Later Nattiez uses the word 'trace' for the level of music neutrally analysed, making it legitimate to discuss the score as evidence of the neutral level. He proposes the following definition:

> It is a level of analysis on which it is not decided *a priori* whether the results obtained by an explicit procedure are pertinent from the aesthesic or poietic point of view. The means utilised for the delimitation and denomination of the phenomena are systematically exploited to their last consequences... a given procedure is taken right to the end, regardless of the results obtained (Nattiez 1987a, 35-36).

This is both more and less than the *objet sonore*, for it admits 'traces' other than mere sound, like the score, but locates the neutral level in a procedural and theoretical universe rather than in a material one.

4.1.6. In the later book Nattiez avoids the phrase 'neutral level of analysis' in this connection; this expression he now uses with quite a different meaning (see Section 4.6, below). The analysis of music without regard for poietic or aesthesic matters is called the 'analysis of the neutral level'. It is true that the theory of the neutral level has been much criticised. Sometimes Nattiez seems to be evoking the distinction phonemic/phonetic (or merely emic/etic), as though the neutral level were equivalent to the acoustic level of language. There is, however, no description of language on the phonetic level pure and simple; language can only be discussed in relation to pertinence, which is necessarily linked to the poietic and aesthesic levels. Phonetics is a study of the articulatory and acoustic character of phonemes; it does not provide any material of its own for study (Keiler 1981). When Nattiez comes to offer analyses of music on the neutral level, he uses criteria like identity and equivalence - *logical* criteria - rather than pertinence.

4.1.7. It has been objected (Blacking 1981) that neutral analysis cannot reveal the essential facts about a musical style, which are cultural and social and can only arise from a global study of the society and its practices. This objection, typical of an ethnomusicological view, is met by Nattiez, himself an ethnomusicologist. A stylistic description of a corpus of ethnic music is usually possible only with the use of abstract rational criteria, because the native musicians 'provide few clues to the process of composition' (Nattiez 1987b, 270, quoting Beverley Cavanagh), and an 'ethnotheory', a description based exclusively on informants, is impossible. At any rate Blacking, working on African ritual music, and Nattiez, on Eskimo throat-singing, were clearly in very different positions with regard to social and cultural information.

4.1.8. Sometimes one hears the complaint that the neutral level does not 'exist'. Nattiez himself devoted a little space to this question (1975, 405-408). The neutral level, he considers, is a valid concept because it is 'legitimate in relation to a given means of analysis'. It is not considered to be a metaphysical or ontological quantity but merely a theoretical notion, like a scientific law. It cannot therefore be said to 'exist' or, indeed, not to exist.

4.1.9. The tripartite division has certain salutary consequences. Ethnomusicologists sometimes suggest that ethnic music can only be truly appreciated by its own society, since outsiders can never become fully acculturated, However, various ethnic musics are visibly enjoyed nowadays in the concert-halls of the world. This is easier to explain if one sees the listener engaging with the material phenomenon of music, understood (or misunderstood) according to his own culture and experience, and when one realises that every listener, even the indigene, is in his own unique aesthesic world. 'Pertinence is relative,' says Nattiez. There can be no perfectly acculturated listener so long as the poietic and aesthesic levels remain separate.

The question of authenticity in the performance of old music is also clarified. Mozart's horn concertos were originally played on valveless instruments, which sounded quite natural to contemporary listeners. When they are so performed today they sound exotic and strange. It might be argued, therefore, that these works should be performed on valved horns, for these instruments sound more natural to modern audiences; and Mozart intended that they should sound natural, not exotic.

Mozart's intention, however, is a poietic matter. The different aesthesic position of the modern listener does not disqualify him as a perceiver of music played on valveless horns. The sound of the valveless horn is a feature of the music's materiality - a neutral feature - not a question of Mozart's intention; the modern listener may react however he will.

Nattiez himself gives the example of retrospective music analyses. Some descriptions of music employ criteria which would have been unthinkable to the composer and his contemporaries. Boulez's analysis of the *Rite of Spring* (1966) shows the influence of the second Viennese school, Messiaen and integral serialism. It could not have been envisaged by Stravinsky. But this does not make it false or intrusive; it is an aesthesic perception in confrontation with a neutral trace.

4.2. Paradigmatic analysis

4.2.1. Nattiez's special contribution was to link the idea of the neutral level to Ruwet's system of paradigmatic analysis. The latter he considers to be a 'description' of the neutral level. Because Ruwet's method is rigorously objective, independent of any preconceived notions or any considerations of composerly intention or the psychology of listening, Nattiez finds it to be a model of immanent theory. Ruwet's ideas -

> apparently rejected by their author... merit however a place of honour in this book, for the descriptions they allow provide such good examples of neutral analyses (Nattiez 1975, 239).

Figure 4.1

Naturally, Ruwet's distributional analyses of the Geisslerlied 'Maria muoter' and the Prelude to *Pelléas et Mélisande*, described above, are presented as initial examples. Nattiez also cites other analyses that conform to high standards of rationality, Mâche's account of Varèse's *Intégrales*, mentioned above, and the analysis of

Stravinsky's *Rite of Spring* in Boulez's *Penser la Musique Aujourd'hui* of 1966.

4.2.2. The most Ruwet-like of Nattiez's own efforts in this genre is his two-fold analysis of Brahms's Intermezzo, Op. 119 No. 3 (Figure 4.1 shows the first twelve bars of this piece). This fully-harmonized item is treated as though it were a monody, the melody in the lower half of the right hand being considered in isolation. A long section, the first 60 bars, is painstakingly analysed. For our purposes, only the first six bars will be described.

The first of Nattiez's two analyses is called a 'segmentation from the top down' *(segmentation de haut en bas)*. This particularly resembles Ruwet's methods in two respects: there are three 'levels' of analysis, and the units on each level are roughly equal in length.

Thus, units on level I, indicated by capital letters, are about two bars in length. On level II the units are about a bar in length, and are indicated by small letters; Greek letters are used for units on level III, which are about one beat (half a bar) in length.

Unit A, the first two-and-a-half bars, is demarcated by its paradigmatic recurrence at bar 25, where it is transposed and subject to an octave shift (making unit A1).

Figure 4.2

The octave shift in A1, together with certain other deductions from later passages, permits the separation of bar 2 as a unit on level II. This leaves bar 1 and the first half of bar 3 as units on level II also; A is composed of a, b and c (Figure 4.3).

It is now possible to envisage units on level III. Unit c is identical to the second half of unit a, and the first part of a reappears as the second half of unit b. Thus, units α, β and γ on level III can be discerned, unit γ being identical to unit c on level II.

Figure 4.3

[musical notation: LEVEL II with units a, b, c; LEVEL III with units α, γ, β, α, γ]

The next two beats are occupied with a figure that is repeated twice in sequence, followed by a repeat of its second half. This constitutes unit B, divided into d, d1 and d2.

Figure 4.4

[musical notation: d (δ, ε); d1 (δ1, ε1); d2 (δ, ε2); (ε2)]

Bars 7 and 8 are isolated by comparison with bars 49 and 50. Level III units are shown in these illustrations, their numbering partly dependent on sections of the analysis not recounted here.

Figure 4.5

[musical notation: κ, λ, ε1, γ; κ2, λ2, ε2, γ14]

4.2.3. This analysis is followed by another 'from the bottom up' (*de bas en haut*). Since, for example, unit β is by definition a subdivision of a unit on level II (in fact, of unit b in this case though the similarity of nomenclature is an accident), it cannot be made to overlap two larger units, in Ruwet's system. In fact, if the last note of unit a is taken together with the first two notes of unit b, it is found that unit α is spread across the bar line; the large unit (unit A) is made up of a short motive of four notes played three times, with an extra note. It would have been impossible to deduce this by starting with the larger units; paradigmatic considerations determined that unit b on level II began with the first beat of bar 2.

We conclude, therefore, that by working from the smallest repeated units we will arrive at a somewhat different analysis.

Figure 4.6

The left-over E at the end of the phrase is, in fact, the beginning of yet another identical unit, though this time the last note rises into a new figure. Yet it is not new; it is merely the last three notes of the original motive, transposed. Thus, the original unit is made up of two figures which overlap (Figure 4.7).

Two analyses are now offered, the segmentations being slightly different (Figure 4.8).

The first of these analyses, 'from the top down', conforms best to the harmonic arrangement of the tune and seems initially the most natural. Indeed, Julius Katchen, in his recording of the piece, seems to follow it. But another pianist, Walter Klein, stresses the melodic repetitions of analysis II; and even more striking, 'in the film *Rendez-vous à Bray* of Andre Delvaux, this piece serves as leitmotiv and becomes the object of variations in different styles. It

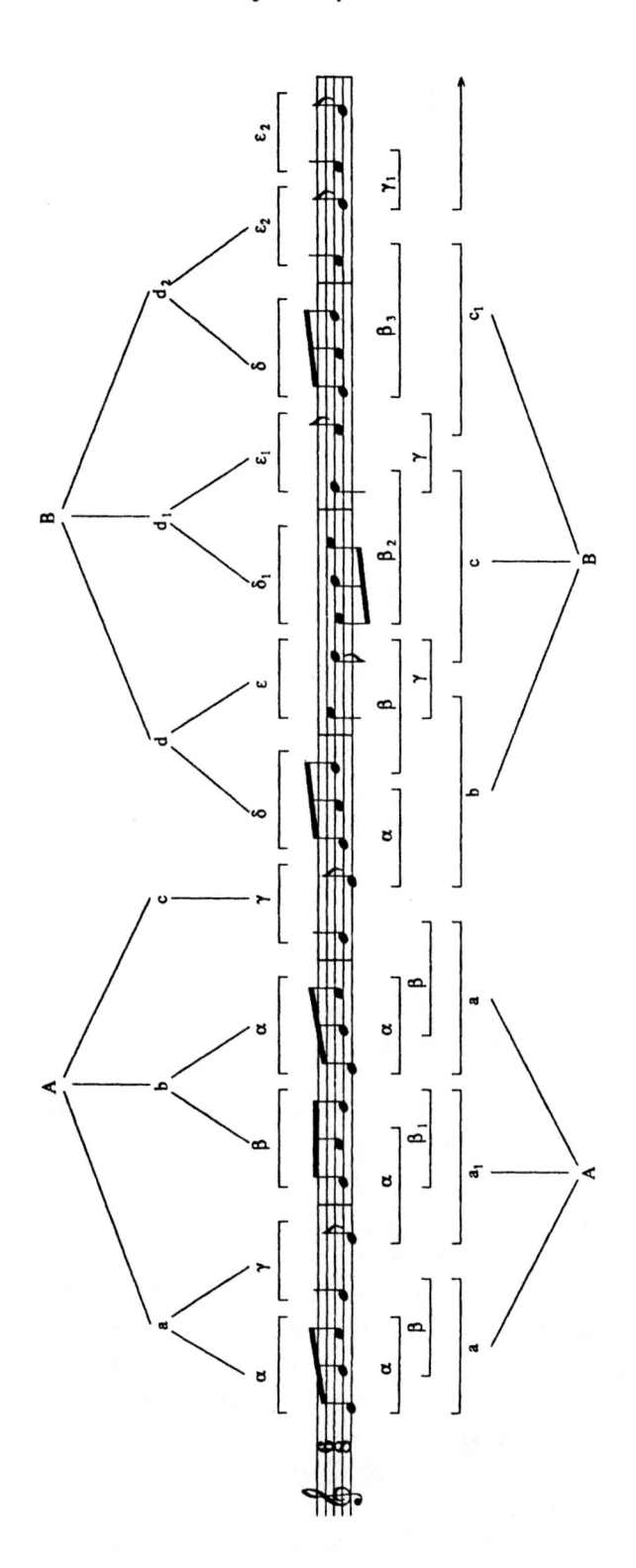

The Analysis of the Neutral Level

is the melodic unit of analysis II which serves as the theme of these variations' (Nattiez 1975, 326).

Figure 4.7

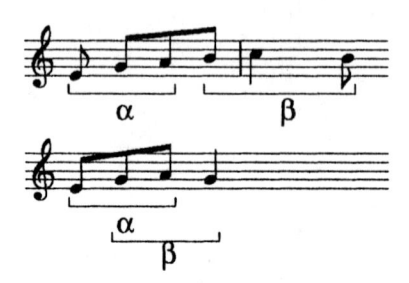

These are aesthesic phenomena, of course; the specifically neutral operations that led to the analyses show themselves capable of revealing without preference the different aesthesic possibilities. Thus, rigorous paradigmatic analysis is a revelation of the neutral level.

4.3. *A paradigmatic analysis of Debussy's* Syrinx

4.3.1. Debussy's flute piece Syrinx is particularly suited to a system of analysis derived from Ruwet, for it is an example, rare in modern music, of true monody, without any harmony. Again Nattiez produces multiple analyses, this time a three-fold description.

The first analysis is presented in the form of two paradigmatic charts representing two levels of segmentation. The accompanying chapter does not so much set out explicit criteria as offer notes and comments, in which the criteria are partly stated, partly implied.

In Chart 1 (Figure 4.9) the units are about one bar in length. However, equality of length is abandoned, partly because 'the strict distinction can no longer be maintained between units of different levels'. The unit X, merely three triplet semiquavers, is more at home on the micro-level, in spite of its kinship to unit C which is full-length. Furthermore, units may overlap; unit C begins with the last four notes of unit A2.

Chart 2 segments smaller units (on level 2, Ruwet would say) and numbers them from 1 to 66. Bars 1-8 (Figure 4.10) take us as far as unit 16. I have supplied lower-case letters in the manner of

Ruwet's level 2, though Nattiez omits these 'in order to avoid the introduction of a complex metalanguage' (Figure 4.10).

In commenting on this segmentation Nattiez both declares the implied criteria, and suggests criteria that would lead to a different arrangement. For example, unit 10 (b1 in my terms) is aligned with unit 3 (which I name b) for the following reasons:

    (i) identity of the three final notes;
    (ii) the initial note (G flat or D flat) is thus placed in the same distributional position.

However, b1 is also related to c (unit 6) because both units begin and end with the same note. Similarly d (unit 7) is related to a and a1, having the same rhythm, and this rhythm is slightly altered in d1.

4.3.2. Nattiez's third segmentation of the piece is the most complex and the most novel. It is not founded, he says, 'on anything other than Ruwet's principles of repetition and paradigmatic equivalence. But instead of being applied to musical units, these are related to the variables'.

This analysis, then, instead of placing together units which resemble each other, attempts to trace the respects in which units differ from each other. This somewhat resembles Prague-school phonology in distinguishing phonemes according to binary oppositions of pertinence (for example, Jakobson's chart of French consonants on p. 37, above), though Nattiez repudiates any suggestion of pertinence; the method 'does not fix *a priori* any limit to the number of symbols necessary to a characterisation and does not initially define which are pertinent'. As for binary opposition, some of Nattiez's variables are binary (ascending/descending; conjunct/disjunct), some merely imply this ('point of stress'; the opposite, 'unstressed', is implied), while others are simply taxonomic (the inventory of rhythms).

It could be argued that this final analysis of *Syrinx* comes closer to an explicit declaration of its criteria than any other example, by Nattiez or anyone else. First there is a 'lexicon' of variables. A few are omitted from the list that follows, which is meant to apply to the first 12 bars only (Figure 4.11).

102 *Linguistics and Semiotics in Music*

Figure 4.9

The Analysis of the Neutral Level

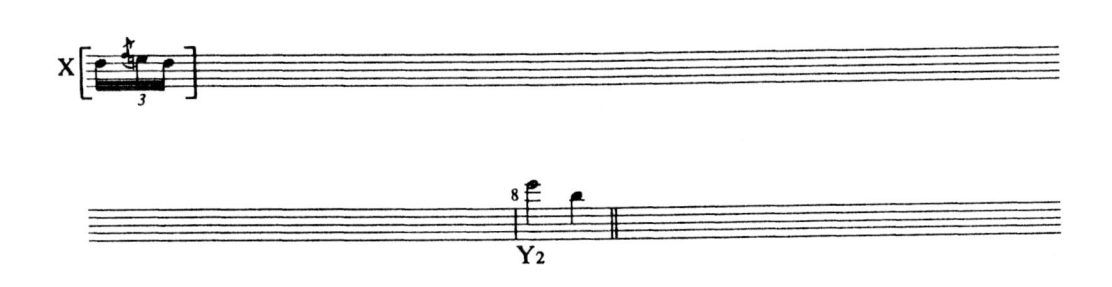

Figure 4.10

The Analysis of the Neutral Level

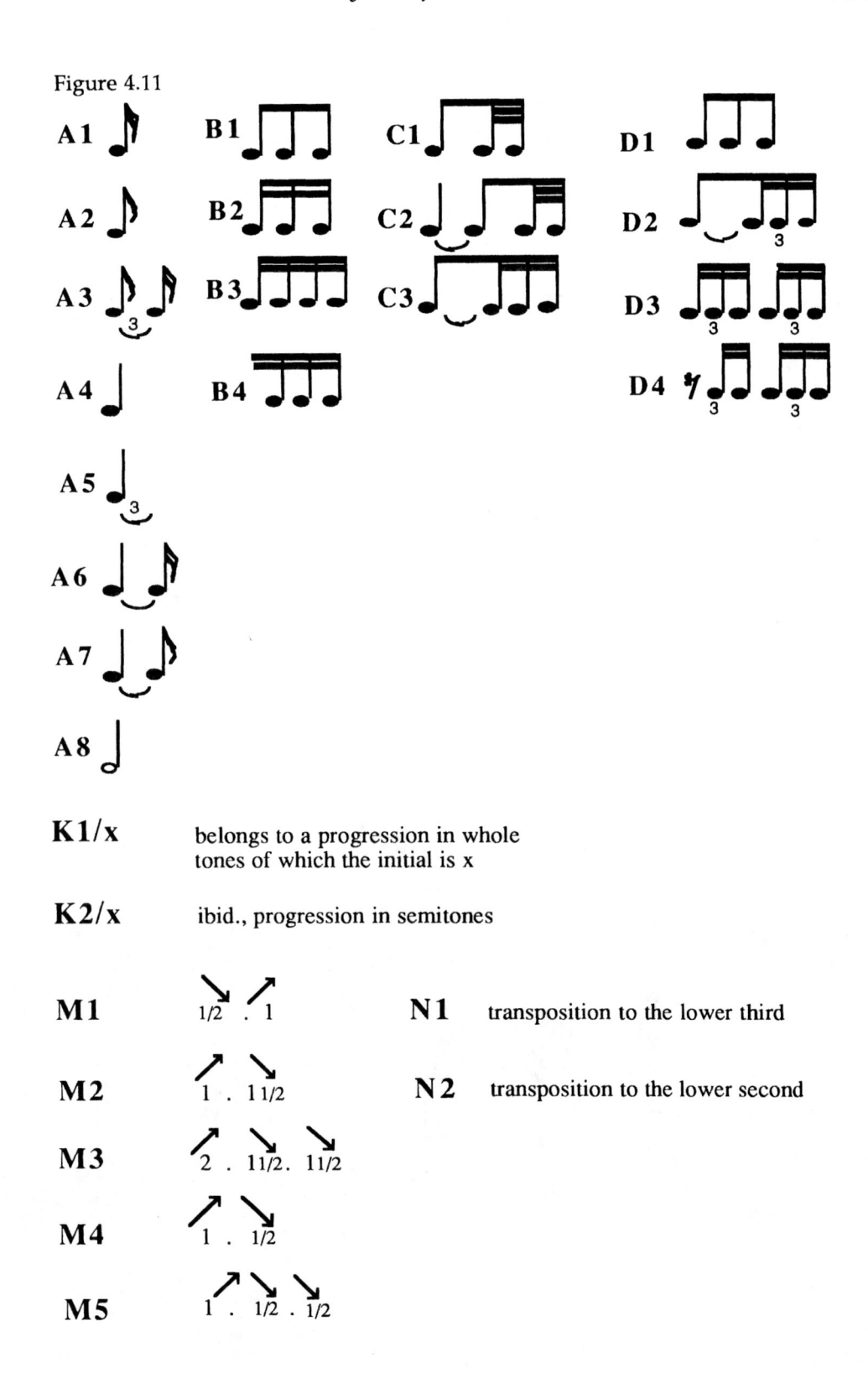

Figure 4.11

K1/x   belongs to a progression in whole tones of which the initial is x

K2/x   ibid., progression in semitones

M1   ↘ ↗   1/2 . 1   **N1**   transposition to the lower third

M2   ↗ ↘   1 . 1 1/2   **N2**   transposition to the lower second

M3   ↗ ↘ ↘   2 . 1 1/2 . 1 1/2

M4   ↗ ↘   1 . 1/2

M5   ↗ ↘ ↘   1 . 1/2 . 1/2

106 Linguistics and Semiotics in Music

Figure 4.12

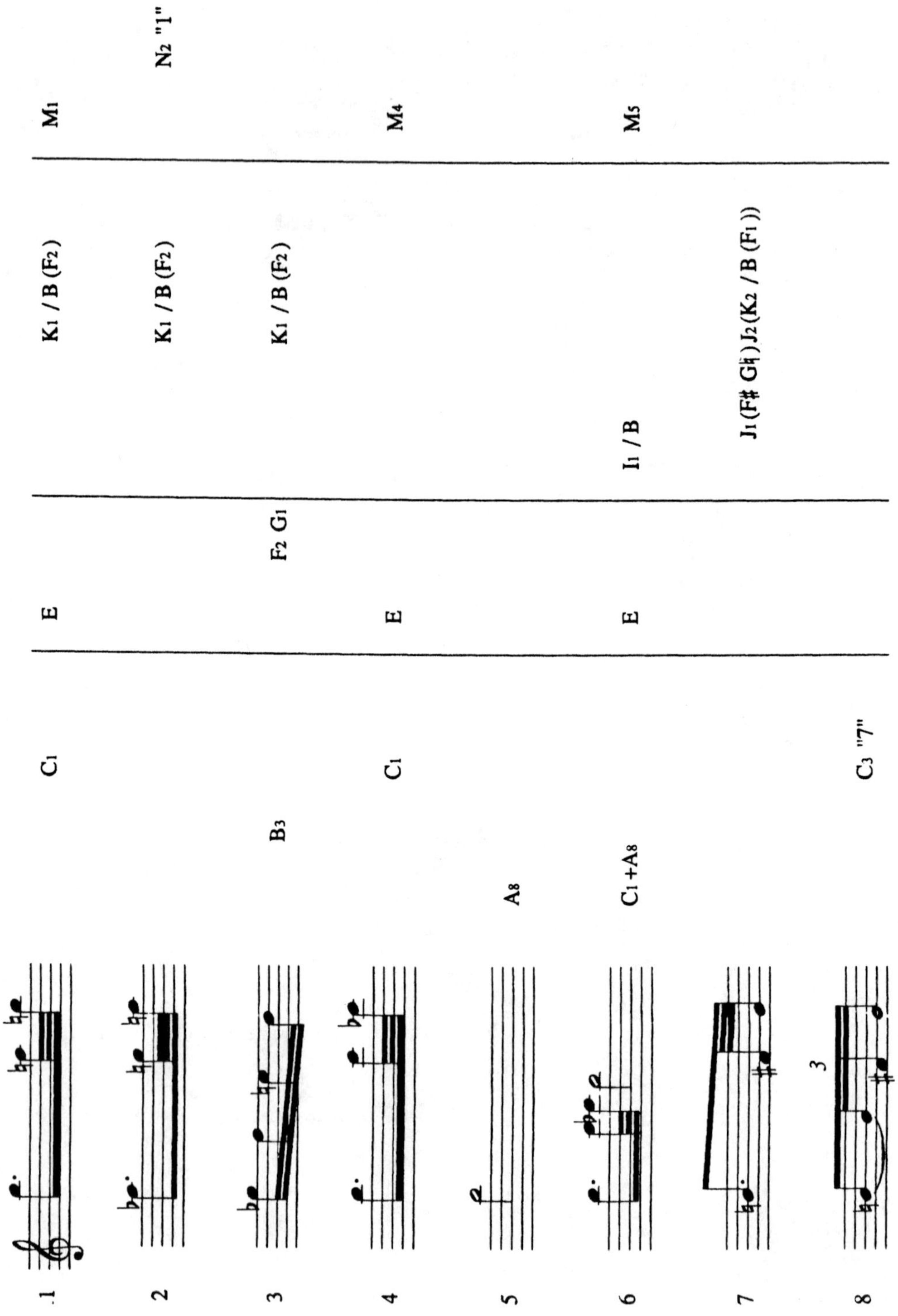

	1	2	3	4	5	6	7	8
	M_1		N_2 "1"		M_4		M_5	
	$K_1/B(F_2)$	$K_1/B(F_2)$	$K_1/B(F_2)$				I_1/B	$J_1(F\sharp\ G\natural)J_2(K_2/B(F_1))$
	E		$F_2\ G_1$	E		E		
	C_1			C_1		C_1		C_3 "7"
		B_3			A_8	C_1+A_8		

The Analysis of the Neutral Level

In the table itself (Figure 4.12), symbols are omitted if the feature is unchanged from the last segment. To clarify this, three segments are expounded at length.

Segment 1	C1	Rhythmic motif
	E	Element of chromaticism
	K1/B(F2)	Part of a progression in whole tones (descending) beginning on B
	M1	Descending semitone, rising tone
Segment 2	C1	(As before, understood)
	E	(As before)
	K1/B(F2)	(As before)
	M1	(As before)
	N2"1"	Transposition of Segment 1 to the lower second
Segment 3	B3	Rhythmic motif, in place of C1
	E	(As before, understood)
	F2	Descending
	G1	Conjunct
	K1/B(F2)	(As before)

4.4. Varèse's Density 21.5

4.4.1. In spite of the resemblance of these procedures to linguistic phonology, Nattiez, as we have seen, repudiates any criterion of pertinence. Thus his explicit criteria do not refer to anything in the culture that produced the music; neither Debussy himself nor his listeners necessarily attach significance to the opposition conjunct/disjunct, though they may do. The system is more like a chemical analysis than a linguistic one. This is an important distinction, for it is easy to confuse the neutral level with certain linguistic notions like Hjelmslev's theory of *immanence*. The 'study of language for itself' does indeed separate linguistics from psychology or sociology, but it does not exclude the criterion of pertinence. Like every other linguist Hjelmslev respects only distinctions meaningful to the language and culture under review. On the neutral level, however, the analyst studies any distinction he can rationally observe, pertinent or no. The difficult question of musical pertinence is bypassed.

4.4.2. The situation is rather different in Nattiez's lengthy analysis of Varèse's *Density 21.5*, which was written in 1975 and issued in a French edition of only 300 copies. It became more widely available when an English translation was published in *Music Analysis* (Nattiez 1982).

Here the neutral level is rather restricted in scope. Nattiez considers analyses on all three levels, poietic, neutral and aesthesic. He admits the need for intuitive decisions on the neutral level, since analysis 'is the result of human activity (and therefore has its own poietics)'. Some aspects of neutral analysis have a 'poietic presumption'; that is, they imply intentions or strategies of the composer. Ultimately the neutral level is only a theoretical device; it 'is there only to facilitate the comprehension of musical phenomena and to provide a basis for comparison'. In the English version of this article Nattiez compares his analysis with a computer analysis by James Tenney. He justifies the divergences, proving that his own method is in principle not an algorithm nor suitable as a basis for a computer programme. The 'machine' of Ruwet is decisively renounced. What really distinguishes the neutral level, then? First, 'its goal of exhaustivity or, more exactly, its refusal to look at things from an *a priori* privileged point of view'; second, 'the integration into its text of the most searching clarification possible of the method used; this has the effect of combining the results of the analysis itself with a level of methodological metalanguage that may be projected onto it' (Nattiez 1982, 329).

4.4.3. *Density 21.5*, like *Syrinx*, is a piece for flute solo. Again Nattiez proceeds 'from below to above', that is, by observing first the smallest fragments and building up from them the longer segments and sections. His account is syntagmatic, going serially from beginning to end and allowing paradigms to emerge (rather than compiling a list of paradigms and applying it to the whole score).

Rests and breathings often make segmentation clear, but when this is not the case the different musical parameters may suggest alternative segmentations. These are often presented side by side in the spirit of 'exhaustive' analysis, but the analyst always favours either one or another according to musical intuition. For example, in the first 5 bars a crotchet rest, and the virtual repetition of a short figure, make it easy to segment the passage into three (the three parts are shown by Roman numerals in Figure 4.13). In a further subdivision, the first three notes of each segment are obviously equivalent (units 1, 3 and 5). A problem arises with the remaining three fragments; from the rhythmic point of view they all contain three notes in a long-short-long arrangement (2, 4 and 6 in Figure 4.13; in 6 the last two notes are, in fact, equal; this irregularity is discussed by Nattiez).

Figure 4.13

This segmentation isolates the long G after unit 2; Varèse seems to support this by writing a long slur over the whole of units 1 and 2, stopping at the second C sharp.

The note G, however, has a special distributional position in these three units; it is always the *last* note. There is another distributional regularity; the final G is always preceded by a C sharp. The rhythmic paradigm must in this case be rejected.

Figure 4.14

However, when the passage at bars 9-11 is discussed, the rhythmic paradigm is preferred to the melodic. Initially it seems clear that this passage merely repeats the notes C - D flat, the D flat finally becoming D natural.

Figure 4.15

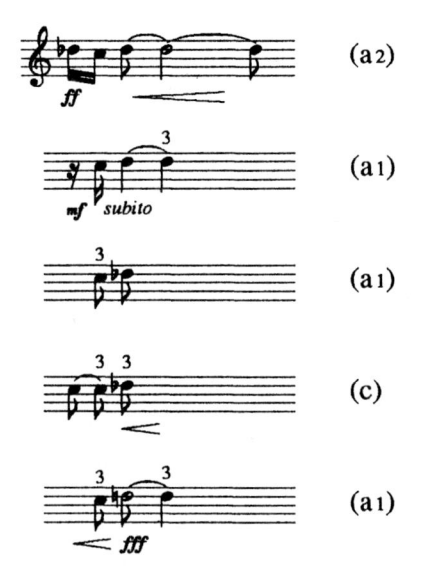

<ol style="list-style:none">
<li>(a2)</li>
<li>(a1)</li>
<li>(a1)</li>
<li>(c)</li>
<li>(a1)</li>
</ol>

This is a passage of 'permutation', however; the melodic analysis does not give a true account of our reception of the music. There is another segmentation based on rhythm. The initial apprehension of the melodic shape was a 'deception'. Nattiez has already established, in a passage not repeated here, that there are three rhythmic equivalence classes in this piece.

I	Initial short	a1	short-long
		a2	short-short-long (the two initial shorts equal)
		a3	short-short-long-short
		b	constant augmentation; each note longer than the previous
II	Initial long	c	long-short
		d	long-short-long
III	Regular rhythm	e	all notes equal

The segmentation in Figure 4.15 would place every fragment in rhythmic class I except the fourth which is sub-class c, long-short, rhythmic class II. To keep the segments within a single rhythmic class, the following segmentation must be adopted.

Figure 4.16

'The play of permutations on two notes,' remarks Nattiez, 'contributes to the principle of deception: it delays the appearance of a predictable event, the ascent to D.'

4.4.4. The alignment of segments in figure 4.16 is vertical. Under each note of the first segment there is a note in most other segments, and the last segment aligns precisely with the first.

Several of the analytical deductions, made by Nattiez on the basis of neutral analysis, are of considerable heuristic interest. Perhaps the most striking is the discovery of four modes of syntagmatic movement, *permutation, progression, flight* and *descent*. In an atonal monodic style, the systems of modality and tonality are no longer able to guide the syntagmatic chain; 'Varèse restores, on another level, what the tonal system is no longer able to offer, by alternation of distinct functional types'.

This is best illustrated by examining the distinction between *permutation* and *progression*. Permutation yields a vertical alignment of segments in a paradigmatic chart, illustrated in Figure 4.16. It is a 'brake on development' because new notes cannot be introduced. Progression, however, is based on *oblique paradigms*. This sort of movement is 'a succession of zones of privileged notes which are overshot by new added notes'. Constantly extended to the right, the chart of paradigmatic segments may eventually lead to a unit which has nothing in common with the first, though it is a natural extension of the unit preceding itself. The units are related in the manner of Wittgenstein's family relationships.

$$\begin{array}{c} A\ B\ C \\ B\ C\ D \\ C\ D\ E \\ D\ E\ F \end{array}$$

The family relations of all these units are plain, yet the last has nothing in common with the first.

An example may be found in bars 5-8 of *Density*, units 6-9 in Nattiez's segmentation. The two notes of unit 9 bear no direct relation to unit 6. The profile is oblique.

Figure 4.17

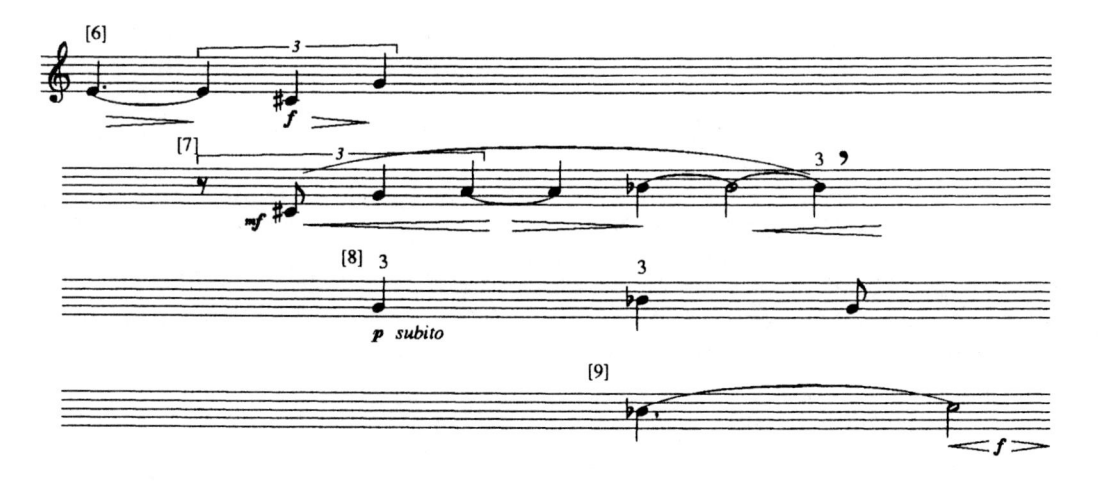

Such oblique profiles 'allow the piece to progress' because they make possible the introduction of new notes, registers and material.

4.4.5. In his closing pages Nattiez describes poietic and aesthesic approaches to *Density*. Every analysis, even on the neutral level, makes poietic presumptions. The term 'deception', applied to this piece by Nattiez, itself implies that there is somebody who wishes to deceive.

A true poietic analysis, however, would be based on information from the composer himself. As it happens, Varèse did make some comments about this piece, quoted in Hilda Jolivet's biography of the composer. But these comments prove to be unfruitful when they are applied to the music. An aesthesic analysis, like a poietic one, may be partly inferred from the score by the discernment of perceptual pertinence; that is, one may guess which features on the neutral level will seem significant to a listener. Alternatively, one may conduct controlled experiments to find out how a group of subjects hear the piece.

The most interesting information, however, can be obtained from comparing different performances of the piece. Recordings by Karlheinz Zoller, Severino Gazzelloni, Michel Debost and an unnamed flautist reveal that different players stress different aspects of the neutral analysis, as was the case with the Intermezzo of Brahms (320-324). They take surprising liberties, too, at times almost recomposing the piece.

4.4.6. Here a possible objection occurs to Nattiez. He has persistently identified the music with the score; like most analysts in the Western tradition, he analyses the score as though it were the music itself (Delalande 1987, 105).

> I have often been reproached for proposing 'score analysis', but the status we give to the score does not appear to have been clearly understood. In Western music,... the score is the composer's means of pinning his work down; it also guarantees the identity of the work from one performance to another. The score is, therefore, a *symbolic* fact which is absolutely essential to its transmission (Nattiez 1982, 320).

It can be argued, indeed, that the score is an integral part of a Western musical work. Polyphonic music could not have attained any complexity without a satisfactory notation and Western musical culture is essentially a 'score culture'. The score, admittedly, does not record everything. Nevertheless, Western history has demonstrated the 'power of writing' rather than the 'inadequacy of the score' (Deliège 1987, 243).

Unfortunately the score is not understood as a primary symbolic fact in other cultures. Usually ethnomusicologists resort to transcription in Western notation, producing not so much a score as an interpretation of one culture in terms of another.

4.4.7. Thus paradigmatic analysis, which began as a demonstration of the logical standing of the neutral level in preparation for the working out of a metalanguage and a general theory of music, ends as a tool in the analysis of scores of Western music, 'to facilitate the comprehension of musical phenomena and to provide a basis for comparison' (Nattiez 1982, 324). Different analyses of *Density* by Odile Vivier, H Halbreich, Milton Babbitt and Martin Gümbel prove that the analysts choose different aspects of the neutral level as primary (329-336). The neutral level, then, is somewhat like the sum of all possible analyses, but it is more than this: since it is an exhaustive examination according to an explicit metalanguage it may pick up features that no listener, performer or analyst finds pertinent, since all these receivers of the score are on the aesthesic level.

4.4.8. The neutral level is not a metaphysical concept; it is not a 'real object'. Of course, Nattiez never said it was. Its original association with the 'objet sonore' (which, of course, is a real object) has long been renounced. But neither does it have necessary theoretical primacy, as do scientific concepts, for its involvement with the score renders problematic its application to non-Western musics. Its claim to exhaustivity and impartiality ('its refusal to look at things from an a priori privileged point of view') gives it a certain epistemological status, however. It ought to be possible to work on the neutral level even in the absence of a score, and this Nattiez does in his various writings on Inuit (Eskimo) music. The results are inconclusive, partly because the music is no more than a rudimentary process subject to elementary generative rules (the content of the neutral level is therefore minimal), partly because neutral analysis is furnished largely as a substitute for poietic and aesthesic analyses, since the Inuit are uninformative about their own culture.

4.5. *Formative repetition in themes by Debussy*

4.5.1. There are several neutral analyses by other writers (Naud 1975; Morin 1979; Dunsby 1982; Dunsby and Whittall 1988, 218-231; Morris 1989). In various ways they show the usefulness of 'paradigmatic' or 'distributional' analysis, but they do not assist in the definition of Nattiez's master-concept. The analysis by Gilles Naud of Xenakis's *Nomos Alpha* for solo cello, and that of David Morris of Messiaen's

Abîme des Oiseaux for solo clarinet, are of interest because each of these writers compares his neutral analysis with a poietic account by the composer; by Xenakis in *Formalized Music*, and by Messiaen in *Technique de mon Langage Musical*.

Particularly successful is Marcelle Guertin's work on the first book of Debussy *Préludes* (Guertin 1981). This writer began with a wish to understand the peculiar stylistic flavour of these twelve pieces, apparently so very different one from another. She was led finally to a consideration of the initial melodic themes, examined without regard for harmony or subsequent treatment. Thus, the corpus of material for analysis is monophonic, like *Syrinx, Densité 21.5, Nomos Alpha* and *Abîme des Oiseaux*.

Like Ruwet, Guertin takes the simple fact of repetition as the basis of segmentation. She immediately notices certain similarities of arrangement. In the first prelude, 'Danseuses de Delphes', and the fourth, 'Les sons et les parfums tournent dans l'air du soir', there is an initial statement which is repeated with a slight addition. Then a fragment of the end of this figure is detached and played three times. This smaller figure is than extended somewhat. Perhaps paradoxically, this sophisticated application of the Ruwet/Nattiez technique demonstrates, in some degree, a return to David Lidov's idea of 'formative repetition'. Reviewing the themes of all twelve preludes, the standard form is reduced to three units (see Figure 4.18).

The first unit (x) is followed at once by some kind of repetition, which may be:

(a) identical;
(b) repetition with extension or addition;
(c) repetition with suppression; or
(d) repetition with substitution.

These styles of development of the theme recall Osmond-Smith's system of 'formal iconism' (Osmond-Smith 1975; see below, p. 206).

The second unit may, in fact, be divided from the first by a minimal fragment of music (as it is in 'Voiles', no. 2). It is indicated either as x' or by y:

x':   repeat of theme x, with a modification that does not alter its rhythmic length
y: complete or part repetition of x, but with extension of its length, either by addition or substitution.

Figure 4.18

1. 'Danseuses de Delphes'   4. 'les sons et les parfums tournent dans l'air du soir'

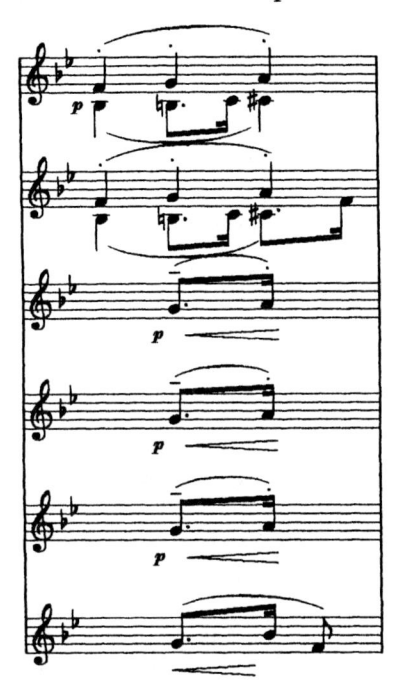

These two alternatives are shown in the example above. 'Danseuses de Delphes' begins x x'; 'Les sons et les parfums' x y. Only one prelude, no. 5 ('Les collines d'Anacapri'), departs from this system; the repetition of x is partly retrograde.

Next comes the third unit, called u or û. This is a unit of reduction, consisting of the final fragment of the unit which precedes it. When that unit was y, with its added notes, the new unit is simply a repetition of the added fragment. It is always transformed rhythmically and may be in another register. The rhythmic transformation may be seen in both examples above; 'Les sons et les parfums' also has a change of register. The symbol û indicates a transposition, rather than a mere change of register.

Sometimes the second and third units change places; u then comes between the theme and its repetition. This is illustrated from Prelude 2, 'Voiles', where the fragmentary unit is û (transposed).

Figure 4.19

Again, there is retrogradation in one case, Prelude 9 ('La sérénade interrompue'), a somewhat complex example in which only one note remains of x in y, and u is played twice although it precedes y.

Figure 4.20

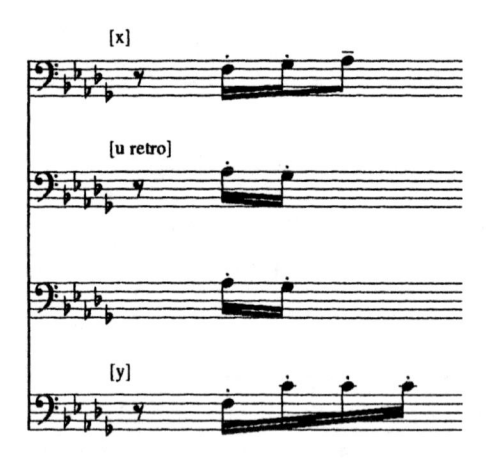

Finally, u is entirely missing from Prelude 12 ('Minstrels').

The findings of this exercise of analysis may be expressed without musical notation, in the chosen metalanguage. Paradigmatic charts are shown here for the preludes mentioned (Guertin gives all twelve).

Figure 4.21

	1. 'Danseuses'	2. 'Voiles'	3. 'Les sons'	4. 'La serenade'
①	x	x	x	x
		û		u (retro) u (retro)
②	x'	y	y	y
③	u	*	u	
	u		u	
	u		u	
	u+		û+	

This may now be reduced to a generative figure, which has two forms. First, the fundamental model, fundamental because it applies to 7 of the 12 pieces.

$$x \;+\; \begin{matrix} x' \\ y \end{matrix} \;+\; \begin{matrix} u \\ û \end{matrix}$$

This model generates, for example, 'Danseuses de Delphes' (x + x' + u), 'Les sons et les parfums' (x + y + u) and 'Les collines d'Anacapri' (x + x' + û).

Beside this there is the optional model.

$$x + û + y$$

This accounts for 'Voiles' and 'La sérénade interrompue', as well as 'Des pas sur la neige' (no. 6).

It will be noticed that u, the untransposed fragment, occurs only in the fundamental model. In the optional model - that is, when this unit comes between x and y - it is always transposed (û). This suggests that there are further distributional rules, not specifically revealed by this analysis.

Certain regularities can be observed after the section governed by the two models, as was revealed in the case of Preludes 1 and 4. Guertin does not dwell on these. Clearly her methods could be extended to much longer extracts. This research does little to clarify the definition of the neutral level, an issue with which Guertin is not concerned. But it is an exemplary specimen of paradigmatic analysis, the more remarkable for being applied to such apparently intractable music.

4.6. The semiotics of analysis

4.6.1. The previous three sections of this chapter have begun to make it seem as though music semiotics were just another analytical technique, along with Schenkerism and set theory. As I have said, this is its popular image.

To prove that semiotics is a universal theory, Nattiez writes in his more recent book about the semiotics of analysis itself. If music is a symbolic form with poietic, neutral and aesthesic levels, then surely analysis is similar. 'Since music analysis is a human product, there is no reason for it to escape a semiotic investigation' (Nattiez 1987a, 195).

There is a musicologist who writes the analysis, and a reader who interprets it; presumably the analysis has a neutral structure too, independent of the writer and the reader. As well as the 'analysis of the neutral level', there is a 'neutral level of analysis'. Just as the poietic world of a musical work is the world of the composer and the performer, so the poietics of analysis is concerned with the background, preoccupations and methodology of the musicologist; and just as the aesthesics of the work is a matter of the listener and his position in culture, so the aesthesics of analysis deals with the reader of the analytical text, who may himself be a composer, a performer or a musicologist. For there is no certainty that any reader will understand a text similarly to its writer; it is in the nature of a text to contain ambiguity. Like music itself, and like any other kind of writing, music analysis is in a dynamic relation to its writers and its readers.

4.6.2. The semiotics of analysis, however, has a rather problematic epistemological status. Analysis, as I have several times mentioned, is an aspect of *metalanguage*. If we turn it into an object of semiological scrutiny, our study is an enterprise in meta-metalanguage. This is not the whole of it; for music is not a physical object like a chemical substance, a sex chromosome or the solar system. A meta-metalanguage of physics would be different in character from the theory of physics itself, because 'the solar system was not created to be perceived' (Nattiez 1987, 193), while a metalanguage of music would be of the same nature as its subject, since music is assuredly made to be perceived (quotations are from the French edition of Nattiez's *Musicologie Générale et Sémiologie*. There is now an English translation of this work by Carolyn Abbate (Nattiez 1990)).

Paradoxically, all analysis, even 'the analysis of the neutral level', is essentially aesthesic, since the analysis, no less than the experience of the listener, is a perception of the music. Yet the aesthesic perception of the musicologist is not the same as that of the ordinary listener; the listener, to start with, experiences music in real time while the musicologist - if he is not engaged in an instant aural analysis - is already operating in the virtual time of the work. The musical time of which the analyst speaks is *imagined* time, for he is almost certainly working from a score or from memory. In any case, the analysis is theoretically distinct from ordinary aesthesics, being metalingual.

If we are to make a graphic representation of the semiotics of analysis, therefore, the analytic text must be somehow linked to the aesthesic level of the music, yet it must be on a different plane because it is metalingual. The semiotics of analysis, since it is a response to analysis, is likewise on the aesthesic level of analysis, but again, it is on an epistemologically higher plane - that of the meta-metalingual.

Figure 4.22

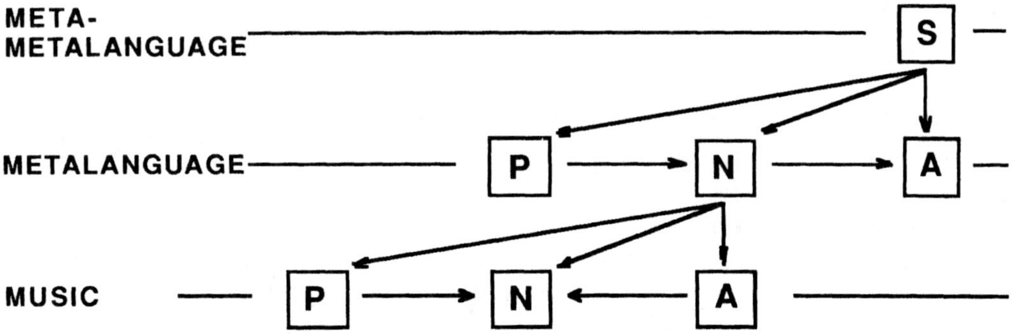

META-METALANGUAGE ─────────────────────────────── S ─

METALANGUAGE ──────── P ──▶ N ──▶ A ─

MUSIC ── P ──▶ N ◀── A ───────

This is a somewhat adapted and extended version of Nattiez's account, contained in pages 189-195 of *Musicologie Générale et Sémiologie* (Nattiez 1987). Figure 4.22, above, is a conflation and adaptation of his diagrams on p.170 and p.193. The semiotics of analysis is to be found on a kind of super-aesthesic level of metalanguage; the neutral level of analysis on a super-aesthesic level of the musical work itself.

4.6.3. On the neutral level, analyses can be classified into two main types. There are *verbal discourses*, themselves subdivided into *impressionist* accounts, *paraphrases* and *exegeses (explications de texte)*; and there are discourses in the form of *models (discours modelisés)*. The 'impressionist' type is self-explanatory; Nattiez quotes Emile Vuillermoz on Debussy's *Prélude a l'Après-Midi d'un Faune*.

The 'paraphrase' is a simple technical description of the music, without critical content: 'The figure marked (a) is immediately repeated, descending through a third, and it is employed throughout the piece. This phrase is immediately elided into its consequent, which modulates from D to A major' (Nattiez's example, taken from Annie O Warburton's essay on Bach's Third French Suite).

The exegesis (Nattiez comments that there is no real English equivalent of *'explication de texte'*; Abbate writes 'hermeneutic reading of the text') is the best kind of verbal analysis, based on 'a description, a 'nomination' of the elements of the melody', with the addition of 'a phenomenological and hermeneutic profundity which, under the pen of talented men, may engender masterworks. It is a matter of seizing the richness of the melody, bringing out salient points, without concern for system, with the explicit or implicit intention of grasping the 'essence' of the text' (203-204). Nattiez cites a magnificent example from D F Tovey's essay on Schubert's 'Unfinished' Symphony.

Analyses in the form of models, instead of speaking about music, try to simulate music in various ways. It is probably not important that Nattiez chooses the heuristic word 'model', rather than 'structure' (which writers like Miriam Glucksmann would prefer: see below, section 4.7.2); he would probably agree that models must be based on rational criteria, not ideological prejudice.

The formal simulation of music is done by selecting a single variable, then surveying the whole work, or corpus of works, in relation to that variable. Phenomena may be sorted into classes and rules of combination may be evoked. The best examples of this sort of model are those of the transformation/generation school, described above in chapter 4 and 5. Indeed, Nattiez cites Chenoweth's descriptions of New Guinea song (below, pp. 177-180).

Should we assume that one sort of analysis is better than another; that the analytical model, with its scientific precision, is to be preferred to the intuitive exegesis? 'Ten years ago,' said Nattiez in 1987 (207), 'we would have tipped the balance without hesitation in favour of formalized models.' Yet it has to be admitted that the best analyses are halfway between verbal exegeses and formalized models. The work of Schenker, Meyer, Narmour, Forte relies heavily on graphic diagrams, but makes no appeal to systems of rules; it is intellectually lucid, yet intuitively based. On the neutral level - that is to say, apart from any consideration of the actual content - it would seem that analysis works best when it is a lucid formalization of an intuitive sympathy.

4.6.4. The analyst, according to Bent, 'works with the preconceptions of his culture, age and personality.'

> The preoccupation which the 19th century had with the nature of 'genius' led to the phrasing of the initial question not as 'How does it work?' but as 'What makes this great?', and this has remained the initial question for some analytical traditions late in the 20th century. Since the 'scientific', comparative method was predominant over evaluation in such traditions, and since only works of genius possessed the quality of structural coherence, it followed that comparison of a work with an idealized model of structure or process produced a measure of its greatness (Bent 1987, 5).

This perceptive paragraph summarizes the poietic position of many analysts in our time. Nattiez gives an extensive account of the poietics of Alan Lomax's notion of 'cantometrics' (Nattiez 1987, 210-213). Clearly, any analytical insight can be viewed within its tradition: the *Affektenlehre* of Heinichen and Mattheson showed the psychological rationalism of contemporary philosophy, A B Marx's theory of thematic duality reflected Hegelian dialectics, Schoenberg's claim that the twelve-tone system was based on the nature of sound recalled the post-Kantian attempt to 'reconcile concepts with sensuous intuitions' (Norris 1989, 324). The object of poietic study of analysis must be to reveal the 'transcendent principles' that govern a particular writer's approach (Nattiez 1987, 215). The idea of 'structural coherence' as a survival of the search for 'genius' has been a common transcendent principle for analysts in the late twentieth century, as Bent points out. This tendency is deconstructed by recent writers (see below, Chapter 10).

4.6.5. It seems almost a truism to say that all analysis is made to be read, and every reading is to some degree a misreading. Yet the aesthesic level of analysis is profoundly relevant, not only to analysis itself, but also to performance and composition.

Each analyst is, of course, in a poietic position vis-a-vis his own work; on the other hand, he is in an aesthesic position with regard to the work of others, and like all scientific study, analytic theory is transmitted symbolically, aesthesics being converted into poietics with each new writer. Occasionally you can see an idea being consciously extended and distorted for a new purpose, as when Rudolf Reti develops the motivic theories of Riemann and Schering. Or it may be simply a matter of one writer's ideas being put into new words by another; the present book is full of such interpretations, in which the need to abridge and simplify has changed the language and presentation of many analyses, though this author's personal slants and background have naturally intruded.

Analysts generally show themselves, in their writings, to be readers as well as writers of analysis. But composers are readers of analysis, too; 'Brahms writes sonatas according to the form that has been explicitly theorized' (Nattiez 1987, 223). This form included the idea of a 'second subject'. It was by no means obvious that Beethoven had aimed at thematic duality; while it seemed clear enough in his string quartets, especially those of Op 18, it was much less clear in his piano sonatas. Yet Brahms consciously writes a 'second subject'; in his letters to Joachim he sometimes discusses the 'second theme'. It seems likely that the dualistic theory of certain analysts like Francesco Galeazzi and Adolf Bernhard Marx was by this time being written into the music.

Musical theorists are sometimes apt to claim finality for their ideas. Fétis said: 'Several persons, endowed with the philosophical spirit, have understood that the doctrine expounded in my work is nothing other than the revelation of the secret of art, the fundamental law without which the works of this art, produced over almost four centuries, would not have existed' (quoted by Nattiez, 1987, 224). Semiotics, by revealing that analysis is a symbolic fact subject to aesthesic perception, shows up such claims as mere fantasy.

4.7. Analysis of music or theory of music?

4.7.1. When Nattiez spoke of devising a scientific metalanguage for music, he was undoubtedly thinking of a symbolic language such as that proposed by Ruwet. Guertin's symbols and formulae constitute a metalanguage of this type. Since the principal application is in analysis, Nattiez and his followers have been thought of by musicologists at large as analysts, rather than theorists. But Nattiez considers himself a theorist, his analytical efforts a definition of the neutral level. For this reason, much of the criticism levelled at 'semiotic analysis' has been misdirected; in a certain sense, this kind of analysis is designed to *avoid* insights, for in plotting musical events exhaustively and indiscriminately it prepares the ground for interpretation, rather than being itself interpretative. It is foolish to condemn semiotic analysis because it expends much effort on a product which is, in itself, unilluminating.

4.7.2. A definition of the neutral level seems after all to be based on intuition. The principle that reveals it is not so much an objective principle as a methodological one. The neutral level is not a rule of thumb, but a principle of operation that rejects heuristic prejudices, which are socially and politically disingenuous and approach the description of new phenomena in terms of old. Neutral analysis is authentically structuralist in rejecting what Miriam Glucksmann calls 'models', which are rooted in the culture that gave the music birth, in favour of 'structures', which are revealed by rational scrutiny (see above, pp. 23-24).

Glucksmann, in her brilliant study of structuralist method, also shows that the view of science as 'proving' universal laws by empirical observation is old-fashioned and naive. Marx, Saussure, Freud, Lévi-Strauss and Althusser 'rejected the methods conventionally used in their fields of study and developed an alternative approach with a distinctive methodology and epistemology, common to all but arrived at independently. They all rejected the crude version of positivism that seeks to establish universal laws on the basis of empirical observation, and a simplistic idealism that denies the possibility of objective knowledge' (Glucksmann 1974, 139).

4.7.3. Opponents of neutral-level analysis often refer to the criteria of *verification* and *falsification*, considered to be the hallmarks of scientific theory. But even in the physical sciences, no theory is based on verification; only laws and theorems can be so based. In science 'conscious conceptualization on the part of the investigator must intervene between observation and explanation... Observed phenomena are only the raw material from which concepts may be elaborated to describe the real structures of the world' (Glucksmann 1974, 140-141).

The mark of good theory is not verifiability but *intelligibility*. The leading explicator of modern scientific method, Karl R Popper, shows that science advances toward 'theories of an ever higher level of universality', but cannot go to the highest level straight away because such a step would at present not be testable; it would be a return to metaphysics. Only the uninformed imagine that scientific method 'starts from observation and experiment and then proceeds to theories... This legendary method... still inspires some of the newer sciences which try to practise it because of the prevalent belief that it is the method of experimental physics' (Popper 1959, 279).

The belief of the scientific amateur, that scientific laws arise from observation and are proved by it, is ridiculed by Einstein.

> There is no logical path leading to those... highly universal laws from which a picture of the world can be obtained... They can only be reached by intuition, based upon something like an intellectual love (*Einfühlung*) of the objects of experience (quoted in Popper, 1959, 32).

Nattiez's methods err, perhaps, more on the positivist side than on the heuristic. His mixture of intuition with observation cannot disqualify him as a scientific semiologist; yet Nattiez himself sometimes suggests that conclusions must be objectively verifiable. His own conclusions are clearly falsifiable *in his own terms*; they are 'capable of being tested', to use Popper's formula. Yet his observations are conducted on a basis of appropriateness (Hjelmslev's word) rather than on purely objective grounds.

Musical theory based on explicit criteria and a declared methodology is clearly in the spirit of human science. There seems no reason to exclude Nattiez's work from this category; the neutral level is not a 'thing', but a declaration of objectivity and impartiality. This theorist renounces ideology and established ideas and calls for patient and painstaking observation. The call is imperative, even if his own results are of limited scope.

5

TRANSFORMATION AND GENERATION

5.1. Chomsky's generative grammar

5.1.1. The work of Ruwet and Nattiez derives largely from the distributionalism of Zellig Harris. Another linguistic tradition, the transformational-generative grammar of Chomsky, has proved to be relevant to music in several ways. The idea of 'transformation', the invocation of a 'deep structure', the division of linguistic activity into competence and performance, the envisaging of a universal grammar based on innate structures of the mind, all these notions have seemed sympathetic to musicians. It has even been possible to develop computer programmes from generative analyses and thus to analyse music. The intelligibility and expression of musical performance also seems to be hierarchically generated (Clarke 1988).

5.2. The contribution of Bernstein

5.2.1. The musical connection with Chomskyan theory was made by Leonard Bernstein in his Norton Lectures at Harvard in 1973 (Bernstein 1976). In his personal and idiosyncratic way he saw a relation between the transformations which generate sentences and can turn one sentence into another, and the transformations which a musician imposes on thematic material. He was impressed, also, by the way in which linguistic deletion can produce ambiguity, a process he discovered also in music; and he suggested that poetic language, and especially the device of metaphor, was a kind of super-surface structure in which transformational laws are used to lend ambiguity and transparency to ordinary language, just as musical devices are employed to generate a highly ambiguous surface structure in music.

5.2.2. He is able to associate the Chomskyan idea of transformation with musical transformations, that is, the development and fragmentation of motives and themes. He takes a series of very simple transformations of the sentence 'Jack loves Jill' and compares them with variants of a short musical phrase, seeing a certain semantic parallel between the inconclusive 'Does Jack love Jill?' and a phrase ending with an augmented chord.

Figure 5.1

(Reprinted by permission)

5.2.3. There are transformational rules which make possible the contraction of several expressions into one, like the forms using *and* mentioned in Chapter 2. A simple rule would lead from (1) to (2) here:

(1) Jack does not love Jill + Jack does not love Mary + Jack does not love Gertrude.
(2) Jack does not love Jill or Mary or Gertrude.

This is called *deletion* and it forms the basis of much sentence generation in Chomskyan theory. Now, one may assume that the 'Royal Theme' in Bach's Musical Offering (Figure 5.2d) is derived by a process of deletion from three other figures (Figure 5.2 a-c).

Figure 5.2

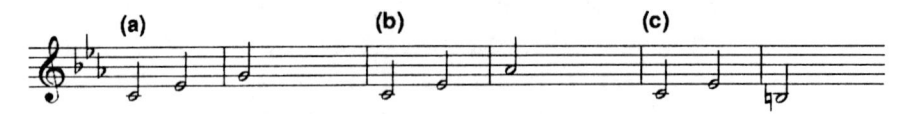

(Reprinted by permission)

5.2.4. Operations of this kind often produce ambiguous expressions in language, as explained in Chapter 2. A process including deletion reduces the sentence 'The hunters shot the game' to the phrase 'the shooting of the hunters'. But this phrase can also be got by deletion from another sentence, different in meaning: 'The soldier shot the hunters'. Our interpretation of 'the shooting of the hunters' depends, therefore, on the context.

In like manner the opening figure of Mozart's G minor Symphony may be metrically strong-weak or weak-strong, because a hypothetical accompaniment lead-in has been deleted. In Figure 5.3a, a two-bar introduction throws the first strong accent on to the first bar of the theme; in 5.3b the introduction, now three bars in length, suggests that the theme begins in a weak position. Mozart writes the ambiguous 5.3c, deleting the necessary introduction.

Figure 5.3

(Reprinted by permission)

Our instinct to place the first structural accent on the first perceptible strong beat leads us initially to hear the figure as a strong-weak pattern. But context will later prove it to be weak-strong; the first bar of the theme is an upbeat to the second.

5.2.5. In justifying his idea that poetic language is a kind of super-surface structure derivable by transformational rules from ordinary prose, Bernstein concentrates on the device of metaphor. When Romeo rapturously proclaims that 'Juliet is the sun' he is really comparing Juliet to the sun and finding that they have a common quality, namely radiance. Hence 'Juliet is the sun' is derivable by deletion and transformation from something like 'The human being called Juliet is like a star called the Sun in respect to radiance'. The difference from ordinary transformation is that the resultant string is not merely ambiguous but actually nonsense if taken at its face value.

Most transformational processes in music, argues Bernstein, are of this order; two things are equated with each other, because although they are obviously dissimilar, they have some feature in common which does not have to be stated; it is intuitively perceived. The first two bars of Brahms's Fourth Symphony are followed by another phrase that is at once apprehended as 'the same' because its rhythm and intervallic shape - a falling third and a rising sixth - are shared with the first phrase.

Figure 5.4

This procedure, then, is 'transformational' for Bernstein in two senses: because it resembles metaphor, the second phrase being equated with the first although in many respects it is different, metaphor being itself the product of transformation; and because the second phrase is a transformation of the first, just as 'Does Jack love Jill?' is a transformation of 'Jack loves Jill'.

5.2.6. Bernstein constantly refers to both interpretations of transformational theory in his lengthy exposition of Beethoven's 'Pastoral' Symphony (156-189). Of the first four bars he says:

> What Beethoven does with that, in true Beethovenian style, is immediately to develop it, to vary it, to *transform* it. Right away we can spot one obvious transformation: what was this has now become this. And so we already have a metaphor... (159).

The sort of transformation embodied in the varying and development of a musical phrase - this is the traditional musical sense of 'transformation' - can, it is true, be viewed in Chomskyist terms. The second phrase of Brahms's Fourth Symphony can be derived from the first by stating an alphabet - the scale of E minor - and invoking some rule governing the inflexion of the leading note, then 'rewriting' the first phrase on the principle of a downward transposition by one scale degree.

However, it is unusual in language to structure an utterance by stating a simple sentence, then repeating it in various transformations. The underlying forms that explain the syntax of a sentence of language are *in absentia*; they are part of the sentence's deep structure. Bernstein mentions the idea of deep structure from time to time but does not develop it.

5.3. Embedding and left-branching

5.3.1. Other writers have considered this idea at greater length. Allan R Keiler finds in the harmonic structure of tonal music the processes of embedding and left-branching which Chomsky finds in his analyses of English, and is able to express these in the form of tree-diagrams (Keiler 1977, 1978, 1981).

The simplest examples are patterns of a few chords within a key. Keiler's method of analysis shows that there is a hierarchy of relations between the chords based on the primacy of cadential movement. At the most immediate level chords relate as V-I (written D-T, dominant-tonic). Other chords are analysed as dominants and tonics on other degrees.

Figure 5.5.

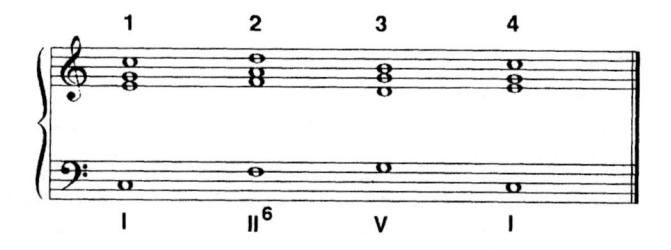

In Figure 5.5 the version in Roman numerals is an 'immediate constituent' analysis. But clearly, chord 3 is a function of chord 4; chord

2 is a function of chord 3. Chord 1 is not related to chord 2, except insofar as it is related to the whole process of chords 2-3-4. Using Keiler's metalanguage a tree-diagram can be constructed.

Figure 5.6

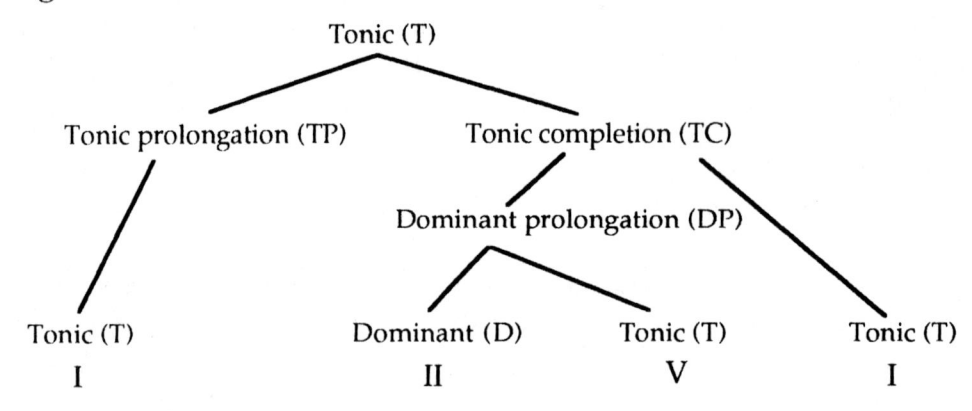

```
                        Tonic (T)
                       /         \
            Tonic prolongation (TP)   Tonic completion (TC)
              /                    /                      \
                         Dominant prolongation (DP)
                          /              \
          Tonic (T)   Dominant (D)    Tonic (T)         Tonic (T)
             I            II              V                I
```

The resemblance is obvious to Chomsky's diagrams of sentence-construction. Following Chomsky, Keiler uses the term *embedding* for the process whereby the D-T of chords 2 and 3 becomes the subsidiary element in the 'tonic completion' of chords 2-3-4. And as in the analyses of transformational grammar, real terms (actual harmonies) enter only at a late stage; most of the analysis is logical and formal.

5.3.2. Apparently the interpretation of D-T in Keiler's system is somewhat different from conventional theory, for the chords may or may not be inflected within a key and may or may not be unmixed triads. In the above analysis chord 2 (an uninflected supertonic chord) is taken to be a dominant function of chord 3 (a dominant chord). This becomes even more apparent when we approach real music. The tree-diagram of the first section of the Courante from Handel's Suite no 14 shows a pattern of harmonic sequences in bars 5-11 which is analysed as a series of D-T resolutions, each dependent on the one that follows (Figure 5.7).

   This is a process of embedding on deeper and deeper levels which resembles the process of 'left-branching'. In the phrase shown in Figure 5.8 each word is dependent on the one that follows and the hierarchical primacy of words rises progressively from first to last word.

Figure 5.7

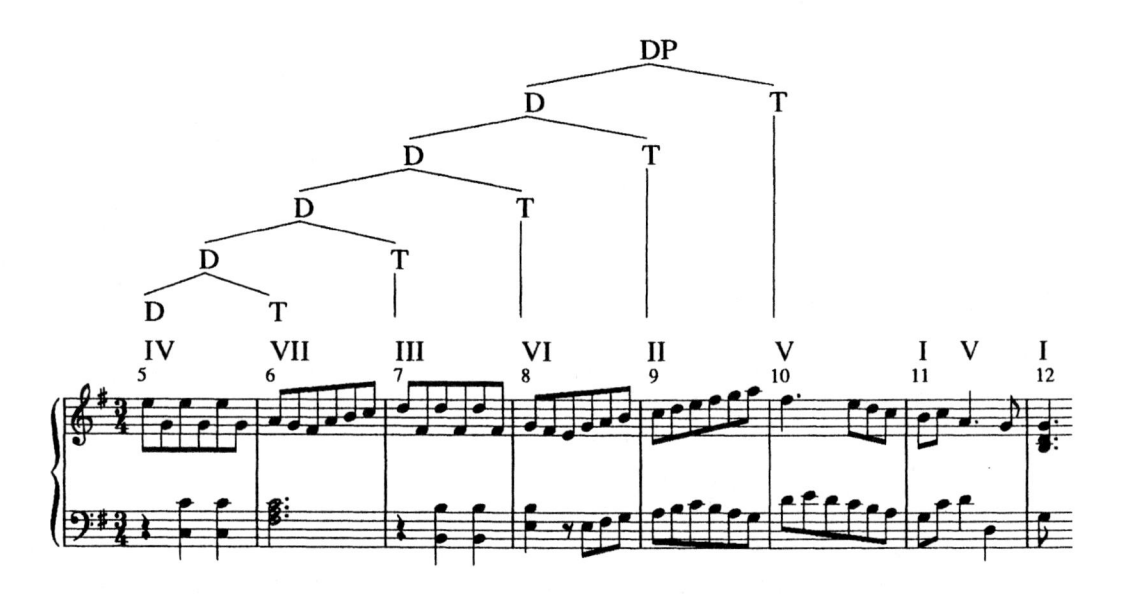

[Musical score with tree diagram above showing hierarchical D-T (Dominant-Tonic) relationships culminating in DP. The chord labels below the tree read: IV, VII, III, VI, II, V, I, V, I at measures 5, 6, 7, 8, 9, 10, 11, 12.]

Figure 5.8

[Tree diagram over the phrase:] very clearly constructed bridges

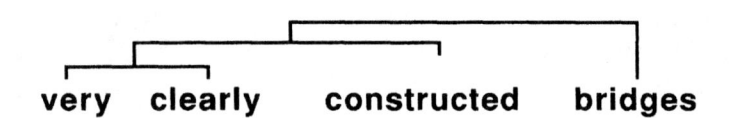

5.3.3. This type of analysis handles well the question of modulation. When a section ends with an inflected modulation to the dominant, traditional theory seems to suggest an analysis in two keys at once. The final chord is the dominant with respect to the whole piece, but a tonic chord with respect to its immediate environment. Keiler's system merely finds it to be a T within an embedded D-T progression, itself hierarchically subordinate to a larger tonic prolongation that will lead - in the second section of binary form - to a similarly extended tonic completion.

5.3.4. The idea of 'deep structure' and the use of terms like 'prolongation' bring to mind the theories of Schenker. Keiler is aware of this but claims that Schenker tends to suppress local details in favour of an overall picture. The hierarchic view of harmonic structure shows how a chord can be heard in a foreign key, yet take its place in a larger structure in the home key.

> It would thus be a pity, in the interests of describing only general properties of tonal grammar, to claim, for example, as Schenker would, that there is no question here at all of any local sequence of keys, but rather only voice-leading details within the frame of reference of a single key. While this is true for the harmonic structure, local key reference is still an important part of the grouping design... i.e. part of another interrelating hierarchy (1981, 163).

Nevertheless, the relation of deep structure to Schenker's Ursatz has occurred to several writers as well as apparently underpinning Keiler's theory.

5.4. Deep structure and transformation in jazz

5.4.1. The relations of deep structure and transformation to jazz improvization have been noticed by Alan J Perlman and Daniel Greenblatt (1981). The improvizer is like a native speaker of a language; possessed of competence in the language of jazz, he is able to make an infinite variety of sentences by the operation of a limited range of devices on an underlying structure. Here the deep structure is represented by the chord changes of the song on which he is improvizing, with the slight reservation that these chords may themselves be embellished or varied by the player, according to certain rules of substitution which seem to group chords phonemically. In some cases, these optional alterations of chords have led to the creation of a new song; Charlie Parker's *Ornithology* is based on the changes of *How High the Moon*, suitably 'improved'.

On the basis of the underlying structure of chord changes, the improvizer creates a surface structure by fitting a series of learnt or invented melodic tags - 'licks' in jazz terminology - on to a 'shallow structure' of available notes. For example, if the basic chord is B flat 7, one set of available notes would, of course, be the diatonic scale of E flat major. Another would be the 'diminished' scale, in which the sixth and seventh degrees are chromatically lowered, giving minor and augmented ninths on the root. Fragments of improvization show John Coltrane in *Giant Steps* using the first of these alternatives, Charlie Parker in *Donna Lee* the second (Figure 5.9).

Finally, licks are selected to comply with the note-sets that have been chosen. At this point Perlman and Greenblatt see a semantic element in jazz playing, for these licks are usually echoes of other players or of various styles, in such a way that an experienced listener can actually trace the sources and influences of a jazz solo as it is played.

Figure 5.9

The greatest player not only weaves the richest and subtlest texture of different suggestions; he actually creates new figures which, initially incomprehensible, are eventually accepted as features of this player's style and are copied by others. This consitutes the 'meaning' of jazz improvization.

5.5. *Lerdahl and Jackendoff: generative analysis*

5.5.1. The most extended application of generative theory to music is embodied in the analytical method of Lerdahl and Jackendoff (1983). Musician Fred Lerdahl and linguist Ray Jackendoff propose a comprehensive analytical view which is musically sensitive as well as theoretically rigorous.

Their object is to write a transformational/generative grammar of 'classical Western tonal music'; such a grammar would be a contribution to psychology and cognitive theory. Like Chomsky, they take the basic procedures of musical and linguistic comprehension to be features of mind, and thus to be dependent both on learned and genetic constraints; though they confine themselves to tonal music, they feel that their most fundamental insights concern universal human musicality, just as Chomsky reached a concept of universal grammar through a study of English.

5.5.2. They declare that a generative grammar need not be an automaton for the manufacture of new music or language - a 'sentence-spewing device'. Indeed, their system is an analytic grammar rather than a generative one, and it would need extra processing before it could generate music in the practical sense. This system is based on the intuitions of a listener and thus describes the process of musical perception rather than composition.

5.5.3. The authors do not make a show of their dependence on Schenker; the first frank admission of influence has to wait until page 106. Nevertheless, the whole book is an elaboration and clarification of Schenker's theories, though the authors make an important addition to Schenker in considering also rhythm and metre. They assume that the listener, confronted with a complex musical surface, grasps it by simplification into a hierarchic structure ultimately composed of a few simple events or of one event only. The analysis of musical hearing thus proceeds by reduction, which is 'a step-by-step simplification... of the piece, where at each step less important events are omitted, leaving the structurally more important events as a sort of skeleton of the piece'. The kinship with Schenkerian 'foreground', 'middleground' and 'background' is obvious.

5.5.4. However, where Schenker is content with intuitions these writers try to proceed from intuition to systematic rigour. In Chomskyan theory the criterion is *grammaticality*. In music, grammaticality is harder to define, and ambiguity is omnipresent. Although the authors offer a series of *well-formedness rules*, rules of grammaticality, they find an additional need to propose *preference rules*, which 'designate out of the possible structural descriptions those that correspond to experienced listeners' hearings of any particular piece'(9). There are no such rules in linguistics, though they are reflected in certain aspects of language study. Such rules, in leading to a preferred reading rather than merely a grammatical one, reveal the essential ambiguity of music and prove the undertaking to be partly critical, rather than merely a matter of logical classification.

5.5.5. The method proceeds by four operations. First *grouping*, which is the same as segmentation - the dividing of the musical surface into sentences, phrases and subphrases. Second, the perception of *metrical structure* - the tactus, strong and weak beats, subdivisions of the beat, and *hypermeasure* elements, time units larger than a single bar. Third, *time-span reduction*, structuring each group around a *head* or most important event. Finally, *prolongational reduction* reflects the intuition of tension and relaxation in structuring small and large time-spans according to their most tense events and the resolution of tension.

5.5.6. Some aspects of grouping and metrical structure are revealed by the actual notation of the music. For example, the position of the strong beat is made clear by the bar-lines. Lerdahl and Jackendoff are faithful, however, to their intention to record the experience of a listener, and they show how metrical structure can be deduced from the aural shape of music. As for grouping, they are able to show how simple intuitions of a hierarchy of smaller and larger groups are founded on systematic rules.

5.5.7. It is in the area of reduction that these writers expound the most novel and controversial part of their system. As already explained, they propose two kinds, called *time-span reduction* and *prolongational reduction*.

Music is not heard as a series of chunks of material, but in relation to salient events to which other events are related in various ways. Within any time-span (group or metrical subdivision) there is a most important event or *head* which gives sense to the other events. In the following cadence from Bach's arrangement of the chorale *O Haupt voll Blut und Wunden* the second chord dominates the first in that it is a resolution of the dissonant and ambiguous character of the first. Within the time-span of this half-bar, a purely metrical division, the second chord is head.

Figure 5.10

In this case the afterbeat dominates the downbeat. Later in the same arrangement (here somewhat simplified) the downbeat chord, instead of resolving on to a more stable and less ambiguous chord, moves to a first inversion of itself, a less stable chord. In this case the downbeat dominates the afterbeat. Notice, however, that the succeeding two chords return to the afterbeat-dominated arrangement of Figure 5.10. Like Keiler the authors see this as a kind of 'branching' and indicate it with a tree-diagram.

Figure 5.11

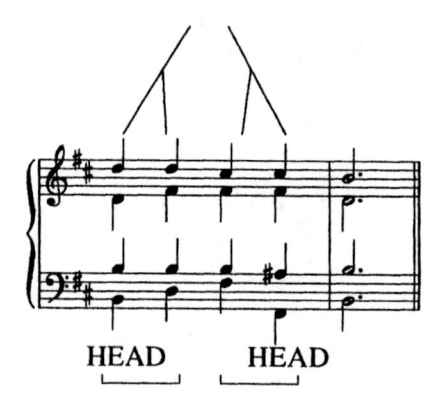

These examples are concerned only with metrical subdivisions. As the analysis becomes more extensive, it is necessary to engage with analytic groups - musical, rather than merely metrical sections. The chorale divides naturally into phrases; each phrase has a head, and is subdivided into subphrases, each with its own subordinate head. This pattern can be shown be a tree-diagram showing left- and right-branching. In the case of the first phrase of the chorale, the overall head is the first chord. This dominates its right branch, the identical chord (chord 8) which comes last in the phrase (Figure 5.12). In the subphrases, chord 1 also dominates its right-branch on chord 5, but chord 5 dominates its left-branch (chord 4) on the lowest level.

5.5.8. This type of tree-diagram, with its left-branching and right-branching, is familiar to the linguist. These writers have several modifications to add, however, of which the most important is *cadential retention*. It is argued that every time-span has two salient structural accents, the beginning and the cadence, which form the 'pillars of tonal organization' or 'points of gravity'. In some cases the beginning will dominate the cadence (such is the case in Figure 5.12).

Figure 5.12

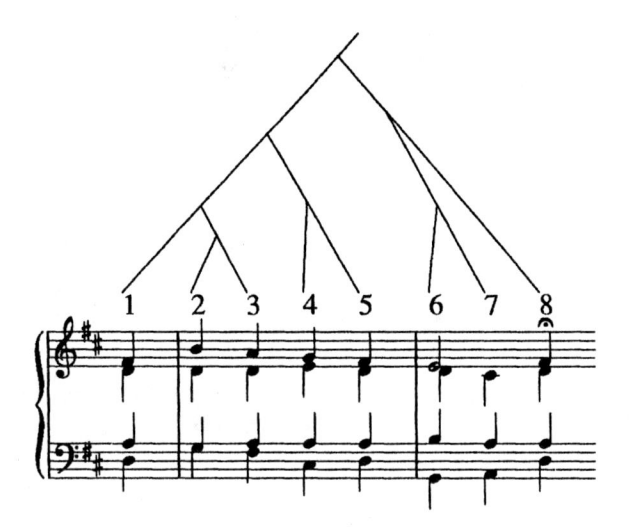

In other cases, the cadence dominates, and this may be confused if either of the chords in the cadence is selected as head. The two chords in the cadence are thus taken together as a single event, the two stems in the tree-diagram being joined by an ellipse. This may be observed at the end of the first phrase of Mozart's Piano Sonata, K 331.

Figure 5.13

5.5.9. A time-span is a subdivision by metre or grouping, on which further operations are to be conducted, beginning with the discernment of a head. Once heads are defined at all levels of time-span reduction, the analysis follows. All rules of time-span reduction are therefore concerned with the isolation of the head.

The first two rules of time-span reduction require that the head should be in a metrically strong position, consonant, and harmonically close to the local tonic. In the first metrical group of the second phrase of *O Haupt* (Figure 5.11) all these considerations apply. In the second metrical group the harmonic considerations outweigh the metrical ones; the metrically strong chord (on the third beat) is too dissonant to be allowed, and the head is placed on the fourth beat, left-branching on to the third.

The choice of head may also be influenced by factors from other levels of the analysis; on one side by metrical structure, on the other by prolongational reduction, which will be dealt with in a moment.

5.5.10. The remaining preference rules are concerned with cadenced groups - musical 'phrases'. If a phrase ends with a cadence it is always best that the cadence be head, and that the first subordinate time-span have a head near the beginning. In the first phrase of Beethoven's Sonata in E, Op 109 (Figure 5.14, not the example given by Lerdahl and Jackendoff) the composer's metrical arrangement leads us to question the placing of head in the first subordinate time-span (x). The first chord is clearly favoured harmonically, but so soon in the piece its choice as head would disturb metrical stability, leading to metrical solecisms later in the movement. The last subordinate time-span (z) ends with the cadence, which is retained as its head and is indeed head of the whole phrase (a).

If we choose the second chord as head of (x) as indicated in Figure 5.14a, the resultant reduction (5.14b) is unsatisfactory (in the second subordinate time-span (y) the second chord has again to be favoured for reasons of parallelism). The reduction at 5.14c is much better. A rule is needed directing us to favour an early head in time-span (x) because it is the first time-span in a cadenced group, that is, in time-span (a).

The metrical instability which is unavoidably generated is part of the composer's plan, and this is confirmed by comparison with the simpler Sonata in G, Op 79, last movement, of which the Op 109 phrase is a variant. Here we find no instability; metrical factors confirm the analysis. In Figure 5.15 this passage is transposed into E for the sake of comparison.

Figure 5.14

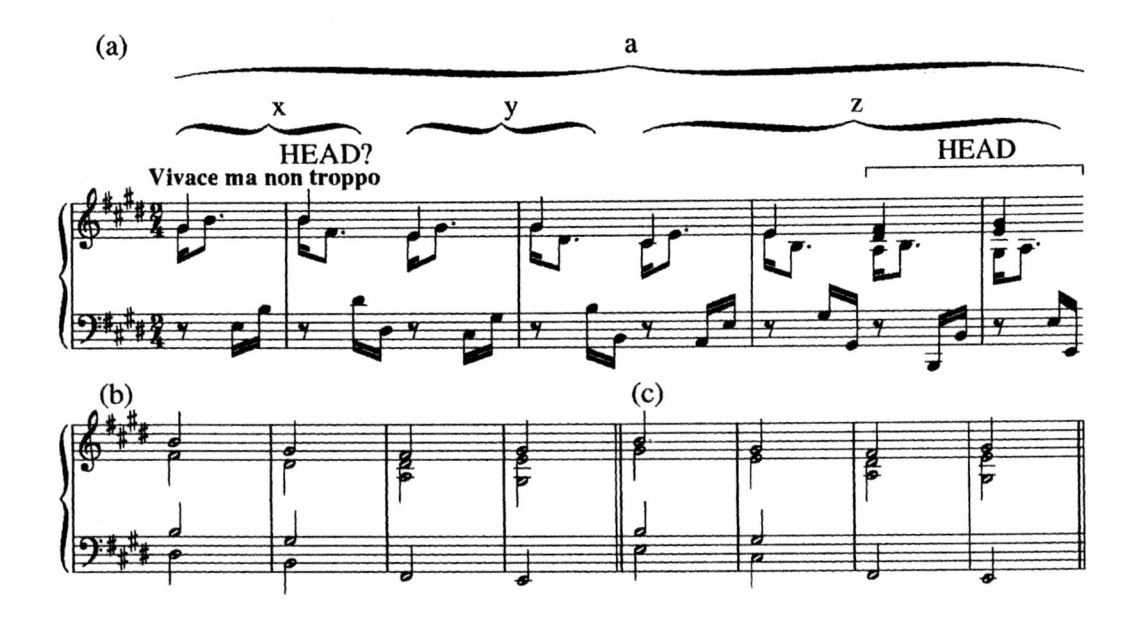

Figure 5.15

5.5.11. The analyses produced by rules of time-span reduction fail to account for an important intuition in the hearing of tonal music. The whole mechanism of progression and resolution, of reprise, development, drama and climax, is dependent on the experience of tension and relaxation that is most familiar in a tonal cadence. A well-wrought tonal piece seems to mount to a climax of tension and then relax progressively into its final cadence, perhaps with certain inner patterns of tension and relaxation along the way.

5.5.12. An analysis of the patterns of tension and relaxation is by no means the same as a time-span reduction. Lerdahl and Jackendoff use a similar tree structure to indicate these patterns, highlighting the differences between the two kinds of analysis. The analysis of tension is *prolongational reduction*. Here the salient event - which gets the main branch of the tree - is more relaxed, so that a process of tensing is represented by a right branch, a process of relaxing by a left branch. The meanings of these diagrams are given both for time-span reduction and prolongational reduction to stress the difference. The most obvious initial effect of this new kind of reduction is to alter the interpretation of a cadence, which is always a relaxation and therefore a left branch.

Figure 5.16

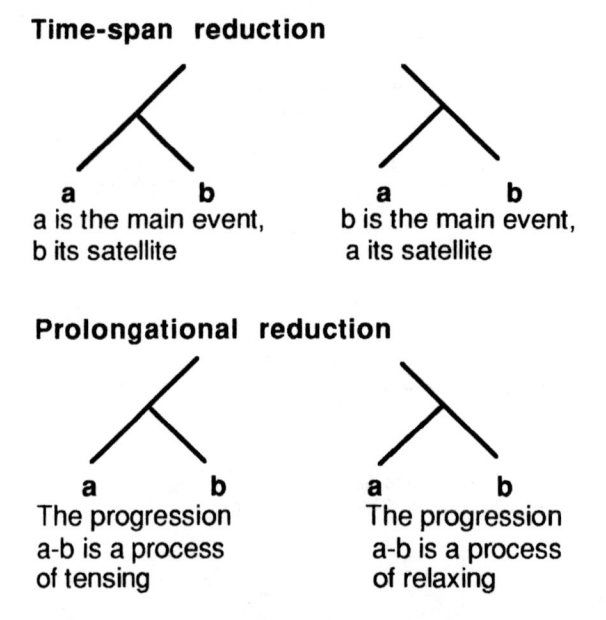

Time-span reduction

a   b   a   b
a is the main event,   b is the main event,
b its satellite   a its satellite

Prolongational reduction

a   b   a   b
The progression   The progression
a-b is a process   a-b is a process
of tensing   of relaxing

In prolongational reduction there are three kinds of branching. An ordinary progression from one note or one chord to another is indicated by the simple diagrams in Figure 5.16. When prolongation is accomplished by merely repeating a note or chord, or by inverting the chord, or placing the melody on a different degree, there is *strong prolongation* (exact repetition) in which the branches are joined by a small circle; or *weak prolongation* in which the circle is filled in. This kind of reduction is particularly relevant to the *Ursatz* of a whole movement, in which the tonic key of the beginning progresses to the dominant at the double bar, then returns to the tonic for the recapitulation, and ends with a V-I cadence.

Figure 5.17

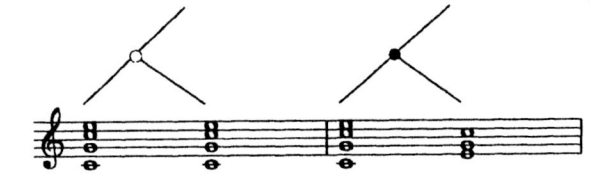

In Figure 5.18 the movement from exposition to recapitulation (chord 1 - chord 3) is a strong prolongation; the whole movement (chord 1 - chord 5) is a weak prolongation. A time-span reduction is given also for this *Ursatz*; this reveals that the beginning of a reprise is syntactically part of the final section of the piece, parallel to the first section; but in terms of tonal drama the reprise heightens the tension which is to be released in the cadence.

Figure 5.18

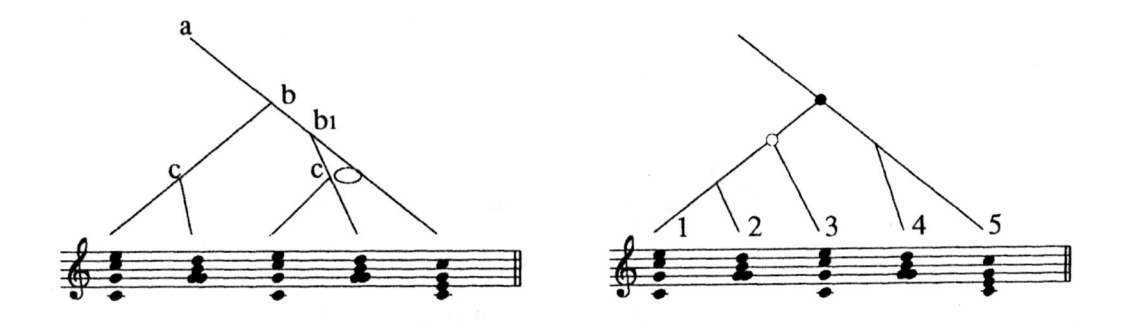

5.5.13. An example may be given of the working of the rules. The authors give a simplified time-span reduction of the first four bars of Mozart's Piano Sonata in A, K 331 (Figure 5.19).
If we assume that the most general outline of the prolongational reduction is the same as that of the time-span reduction - that is, the last chord is attached as a right branch to the first - then we must ask, what is the next most important feature in the prolongational reduction? We are told first to favour events important in the time-span reduction. The most important events are those on level c: the first chords of bars 2 and 3.

Next, however, we are required to favour an event stably related to either of the two ends. The most stable event is the tonic chord at the start of bar 4, a strong prolongation of the first chord. In this case the rule of stable relation overrides that of time-span congruity; it is enough that the most important event comes on one of the next two levels below the outlining level (here the outlining level is level b; the two available levels are therefore c and d and the tonic chord at the start of bar 4 is, indeed, on level d).

Figure 5.19

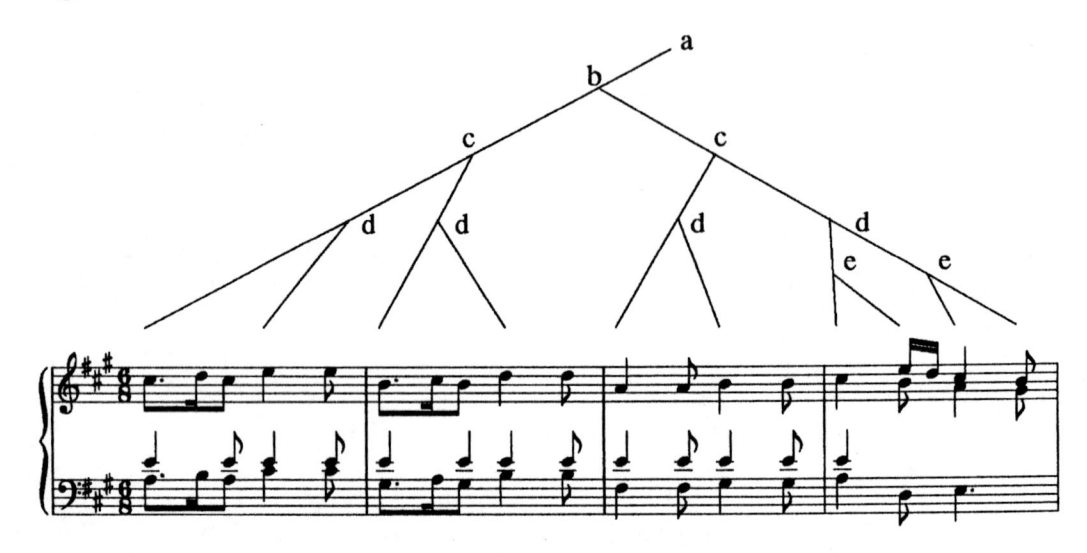

Since the whole region between the beginning and the start of bar 4 has been bracketed by the initial operation, the chords at the start of bars 2 and 3, on level c of the time-span reduction, are still the most important in time-span terms and would tend to be adopted. But again the rule of stable relation conflicts; the most stable event is the tonic inversion halfway through bar 1, a weak prolongation of the opening.

But this would lead to our classifying everything in bar 2 as a function of the second chord in bar 1. Clearly this is wrong; bar 2, a melodic sequence, is parallel to bar 1. There has to be a rule of parallelism to establish that the events of bar 2 are similarly classified to those of bar 1, save only that the head of bar 1 dominates that of bar 2 (Figure 5.20). The remaining chords in bar 1 and bar 2 are both weak prolongations of their predecessors.

The rest of the phrase may be reduced in similar fashion. Compared to the time-span reduction, the prolongational reduction is closely similar on the local level, different on the global.

Figure 5.20

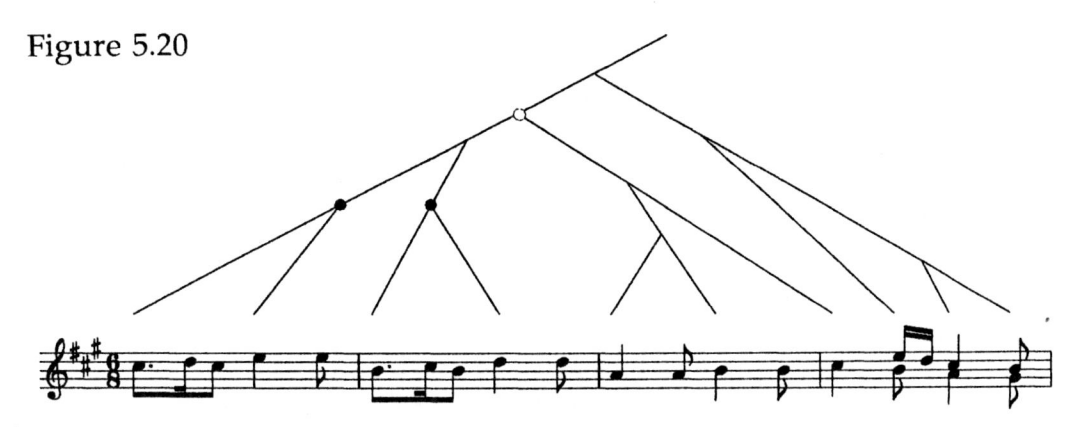

5.5.14. In analysing larger and larger syntagmata the authors find normative prolongational structures in Western music. Familiar formal routines like binary form and sonata form are expressions of these. There is even a rule for the normative structure of a syntagm, whatever its length.

Lerdahl and Jackendoff have been criticized in several ways. It is objected that Chomsky's transformational rules permit the rewriting of a single deep structure as various surface structures, all retaining the same paradigmatic material. They are thus dynamic rules which offer infinite possibilities in the creation of new utterances on the level of performance or *parole*. The rules of Lerdahl and Jackendoff are analytical rather than dynamic. They do not really describe the working of a language, but merely dissect the hearing of an experienced listener. The theory is not really 'generative'.

However, Chomsky's rules may themselves be used analytically as well as generatively - they may explain how a hearer makes sense of a sentence spoken by another. Indeed, in discovering his rules Chomsky had to follow exactly this path, beginning from well-formed surface structures and deducing the rules that generated them. The rules of Lerdahl and Jackendoff generate analyses, while Chomsky's rules generate English; but this does not *prima facie* disqualify Lerdahl and Jackendoff as generative theorists.

5.5.15. A more practical complaint is that these authors essentially indicate two analyses - the time-span reduction and the prolongational reduction - for every piece of music. It is tiresome in practice, and may be intellectually unsatisfactory, that a single integral analysis cannot be formulated. It may be, however, that this duality reflects the linguistic duality of grammar and semantics. Chomsky sees a mingling of these two sides of language, seeing that the ill-formedness of a sentence like 'The boy may frighten sincerity' is partly a semantic matter. He tries to solve the problem by extending grammatical rules to include semantic considerations; he never envisages separate grammatical and semantic structures.

Hjelmslev, on the other hand, positively states that a system for which the grammatical and semantic segmentations are identical is *not a semiotic*, and he throws out a challenge to musicians to prove such a discrepancy (Hjelmslev 1961, 113; see above, p. 46). If time-span reduction sets out the pattern of syntax which 'means' the tonal drama of tension and relaxation revealed by prolongational reduction, then music may have the duality of 'expression-plane' and 'content-plane' that Hjelmslev demands.

5.6. *The computer analysis of chorales*

5.6.1. Grammars as explicit as this suggest the possibility of computer analysis. Another researcher has, in fact, attempted to use a computer for harmonic analysis (Winograd 1968). The ambiguity of tonal music is again acknowledged. To cope with it, the computer has to be provided with a finite set of routes in its search for the correct parsing of a chord, and since several different routes may lead to an acceptable parsing (while some, of course, may not) there has to be a numerical scale of levels of meaningfulness. There is thus a preferred parsing, recalling the preference rules of Lerdahl and Jackendoff.

In computer analyses of language, as opposed to music, hierarchies of ranks have been decreed, such as sentence/clause/group/word. The computer is commanded to 'rankshift' in its search for a classification. For the sake of harmonic analysis, Winograd distinguishes five ranks: composition/tonality/chord group/note. Here 'composition' means the whole piece and 'tonality' means 'a group of successive chords functioning in the same tonality'. Clearly the identity of a chord is dependent on tonality and this may change without warning. A simple rankshift to tonality level may be enough to identify the new chord, or it may be necessary to return to composition level to make sense of it. There may, however, be 'rankshifted tonalities as constituents of other tonalities' giving a 'recursive structure or hierarchy of tonalities'. For example, in a piece in C major, a minor triad on D may be II, or VI of IV, or IV of III of IV, and so on.

A chord group may be complete (containing a cadence) or implied (containing a pattern 'dominant preparation - dominant');

hence tonalities may be simple (ending with a cadence) or modulating. Each chord is defined with regard to root, type, and inversion, and is then classified according to context; for of course its identity depends on key.

5.6.2. Because musical parsing is so heavily dependent on context, ordinary generative grammar is replaced by *systemic grammar*. This specifies three possible types of relation between A and B. First, A may be *conditional* on B. Thus, if a chord is classified as 'major' then it must be a harmonic, rather than a passing chord. Secondly, A may *exclude* B. If a chord is classified as a triad, then it cannot also be a seventh. Thirdly, A may be one of an exhaustive list of features, A-B-C-n. For example, a seventh chord may be figured 7, 6/5, 4/3, 4/2, and nothing else. Part of the systemic grammar is here given (rather simplified) for the classification of a chord that has already emerged as 'harmonic' (not a passing chord).

Figure 5.21

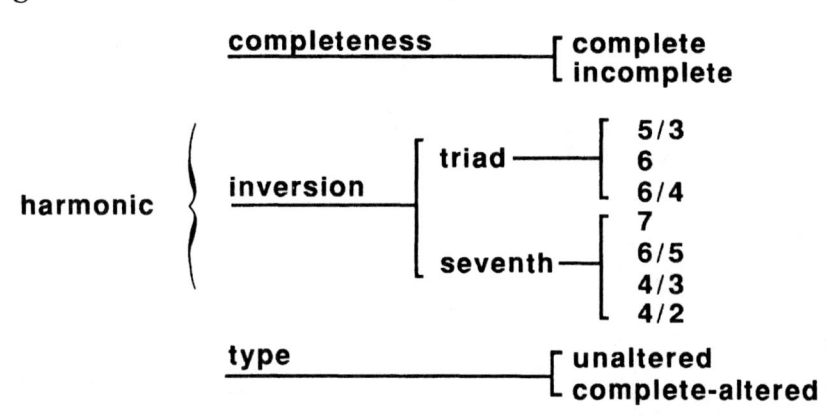

```
                  completeness ─────── ┌ complete
                                       └ incomplete

                                       ┌ 5/3
                               ┌ triad ─┤ 6
               ┌ inversion ────┤        └ 6/4
harmonic ──────┤               │        ┌ 7
               │               │        │ 6/5
               │               └ seventh┤ 4/3
               │                        └ 4/2
               │
               └ type ───────── ┌ unaltered
                                └ complete-altered
```

The actual analysis proceeds backwards, that is, in reverse direction to the music. As each new event is encountered, a possible parsing of the string is constructed, taking into account all possible continuations. Naturally a number of different possible parsings develops as the analysis continues and each of these is retained. Occasionally a new event will show one particular parsing to be impossible; it is then dropped. Even so, a very large number of possible paths soon develops. There has to be some way of eliminating many of these before the procedure gets unwieldy. Hence a 'plausibility value' is assigned to each of the parsings up to a given point. 'Instead of carrying all these forward, we can select only the most promising - those which are most likely to lead to good parsings' (30). This may lead to the rejection of the only correct parsing, so that the analysis later breaks down. To avoid this the whole operation is preceded by a scan of the piece to establish certain limiting rules, in particular the overall tonality. Some allowance is made for notes outside of tonalities (passing notes) and for one type of chord that is tonally irregular, the Neapolitan.

5.6.3. The final output is 'a single best "reading" for the composition'. In most cases this reading matches that of a human analyst with striking fidelity. When it does not agree, the reasons are to do with counterpoint; if a chord arises through chiefly linear causes the computer is driven to seek out an unnecessarily complex solution. Other errors arise when the fifth of a chord is missing and the computer is obliged to supply a fifth in order to classify the chord.

In Figure 5.22, the first three phrases of the chorale *O Traurigkeit*, the recognition of passing notes in bar 1 is quite subtle and the machine sees correctly that the music modulates to the relative major with a glance at the dominant thereof. The only mistake comes with the starred chord in bar 3 which was 'analyzed as serving a linear function rather than a dominant function. This happened because it did not resolve in any normal way, and thus did not seem to function within the semantic rules.' This chord would be heard as the dominant of A minor.

Figure 5.22

5.6.4. This researcher envisages an extension of computer analysis to other aspects of music. The sort of systems he finds in harmonic structure 'abound in music, with systems of pitches, durations, chord types, inversions, key, time-signature and numerous others'.

Presumably grouping, time-spans and prolongation could be included in the list. He also sees a reciprocal influence on computer analysis of language, for having treated the classification of chords within a key as a semantic procedure, he sees that language also may perhaps be reduced to a semantic model instead of the usual syntactic one, 'thus introducing a first step towards the processing of language in terms of meaning and understanding'. The view of harmony as a semantic matter - as an aspect of the meaning, rather than the syntax, of music - has influenced one reading of musical semantics (below, pp. 236-242).

5.7. *Generating music by rule*

5.7.1. There has, in addition, been an attempt to compile a real generative grammar for music; that is, a grammar that generates new material which can itself be used to test the efficacy of the grammar. Sundberg and Lindblom (1976) propose such a grammar for the Swedish nursery tunes of Alice Tegnér. The extremely conventional nature of this corpus made it suitable for this work. The writers adopt the tree diagrams of prominence contour from Chomsky and Halle's theory of phonology (1968). In the linguistic version this diagram is meant to indicate positions of stress.

5.7.2. The lowest layer is composed of separate beats. On the level above, the beats are paired into 'feet'; the next binary division is into 'bars', then 'sub-phrases', 'phrases' and the whole 'period' of eight bars (Figure 5.23).

The levels of prominence, from 1 to 5, are shown at the base of the diagram. These are allotted by making feet left-prominent, all other levels right-prominent, excluding bar level. Beats 1 and 2 comprise Foot 1 which is left prominent. Beat 1 is therefore more prominent than beat 2. All other feet are similar.

Subphrase 1: 1 2 1 2 1 2 1 2

Foot 4, however, is prominent because the subphrase is right-prominent. The prominent beat of foot 4 must therefore be heightened.

2 3 2 3 2 3 1 3

The phrase, comprising two subphrases, is also right-prominent; so the prominent beat of foot 8 must be heightened.

3 4 3 4 3 4 2 4 3 4 3 4 3 4 1 4

150   *Linguistics and Semiotics in Music*

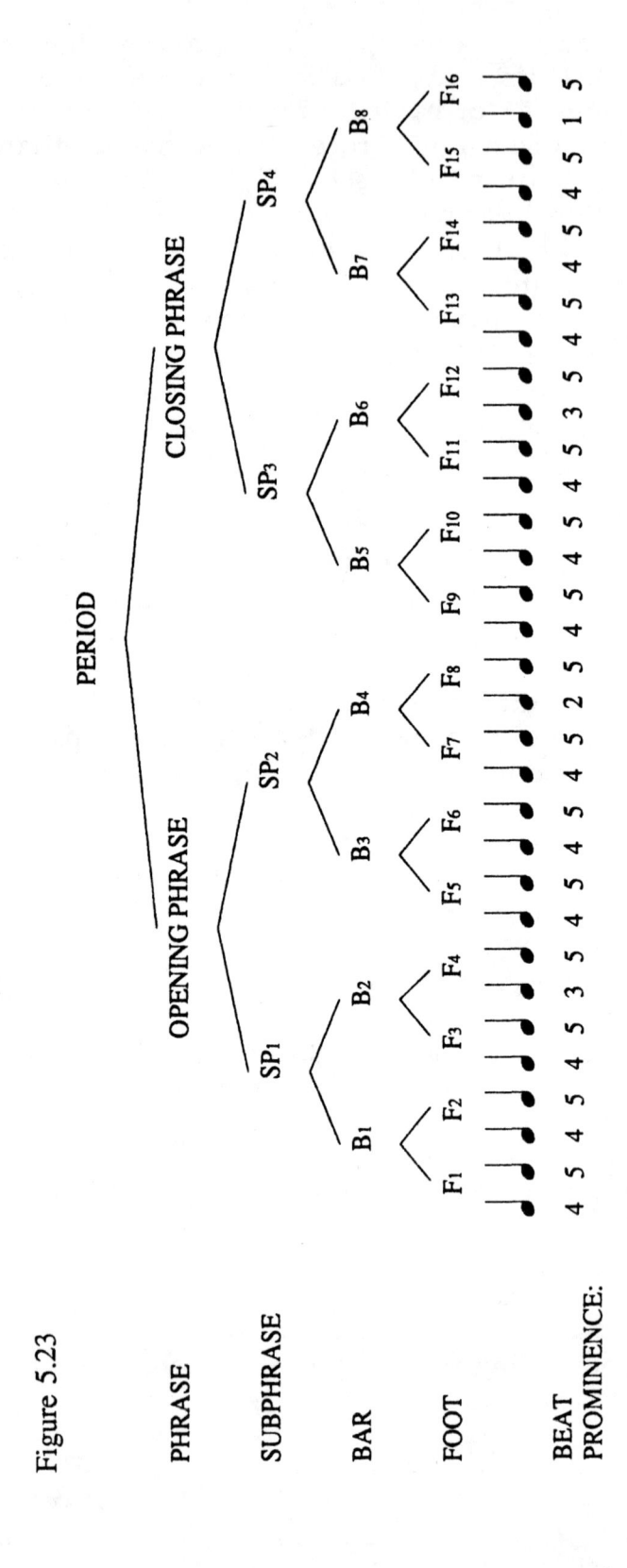

Figure 5.23

PHRASE   PERIOD
                    ╱   ╲
          OPENING PHRASE   CLOSING PHRASE
           ╱   ╲   ╱   ╲
SUBPHRASE SP1   SP2   SP3   SP4
         ╱ ╲   ╱ ╲   ╱ ╲   ╱ ╲
BAR   B1 B2 B3 B4   B5 B6 B7 B8
        ╱╲ ╱╲ ╱╲ ╱╲   ╱╲ ╱╲ ╱╲ ╱╲
FOOT   F1 F2 F3 F4 F5 F6 F7 F8 F9 F10 F11 F12 F13 F14 F15 F16
       ♩ ♩ ♩ ♩ ♩ ♩ ♩ ♩ ♩ ♩ ♩ ♩ ♩ ♩ ♩ ♩
BEAT
PROMINENCE: 4 5 4 5 4 5 3 5 4 5 4 5 2 5 4 5 4 5 4 5 3 5 4 5 4 5 4 5 1 5

Transformation and Generation

Since the whole period is similarly right-prominent, the prominent beat of foot 16 must be heightened, completing the prominence pattern as in Figure 5.23.

5.7.3. Next the actual rhythm of the tune is generated (Figure 5.24, which also shows harmonies and pitches).

Figure 5.24

4 564 5	46563 5	4 564 5	4 562 5	4 564 5	46563 5	4 564 5	4 561 5
A	B	A	C	A	B	A	C
♩♫♩♩	♫♫♩♩	♩♫♩♩	♩♫♩♩	♩♫♩♩	♫♫♩♩	♩♫♩♩	♩♫♩𝄽
D	Em7	A7	D	D7	Em7	A7	D

(i) Determine the sequence pattern. There may be two basic bar-shapes, A and B; bars 5-8 must repeat bars 1-4.

(ii) *Catalexis*. Delete prominence rank 5 when it follows prominence ranks 1-2-3, or 1-2, or 1 alone (in Figure 5.24 this leads to a crotchet rest on the last beat of all).

(iii) Insertion. 'We may insert additional prominences of rank 6 after prominence ranks 4 and 5 in the first bars marked A and B.' This leads to the addition of quavers; also dotted notes may be added, though these do not appear in the example. In Figure 5.24 this makes possible quavers in bars 1 and 2, which are the first 'A and B' bars.

(iv) The insertions and dottings are transferred to the bars that are similar in the sequence pattern. Thus in Figure 5.24 bars 3 and 4 are similar to bar 1; the metrical pattern of bars 1-

4 is obligatorily repeated in the last 4 bars, apart from the deletion in bar 8.

This gives the complete rhythmic pattern in Figure 5.24.

5.7.4. Now the harmonic structure must be generated. First, all notes of prominence rank 5, and some of prominence rank 4, are deleted. In the given example it is possible to retain only one chord per bar. The locations of these chords are indicated by the retained prominence ranks.

| 4 | 3 | 4 | 2 | | 4 | 3 | 4 | 1 |

Next, 'introductory' and 'target' chords are distributed. These are stable chords, recalling the 'structural beginning' and 'structural cadence' of Lerdahl and Jackendoff. The introductory chord in bar 5 is optional; in fact, it is not adopted in this tune.

| I | | | T | | (I) | | | T |

'Anticipatory' chords (those that prepare cadences) and 'rest' chords (less stable than target chords, but not preparing cadences) are now allotted. I or A chords alternate with R or T chords.

| I | R | A | T | | A | R | A | T |

Harmonic distance from the tonic is now indicated by numbers, and these are translated into actual chords - in this case in D major.

Figure 5.25

```
‖    | 2   | 1  | 0 ‖ 3  | 2   | 1  | 0  ‖
‖ D  | Em7 | A7 | D ‖ D7 | Em7 | A7 | D  ‖
```

With these two inputs, the rhythmic structure and the harmonic structure, the actual music is now generated. Only chord notes are permitted for prominence ranks 1, 2 and 3. For prominence rank 4, chord notes may be used, or adjacent notes (passing notes between two already-assigned pitches). The same rule applies to prominence ranks 5 and 6, the frequency of adjacent notes increasing. The sequence pattern must be maintained. The final result has already been shown in Figure 5.24.

5.7.5. Finally a set of tunes is given, generated by neutral and random operations within the system; these tunes, the writers believe, are acceptable to Swedish listeners as similar in style to the Tegnér melodies. In Figure 5.26 tune *a* is by Tegnér, the other two generated by rule. Apparently *b* is a fair imitation of the style but *c* suggests that refinements are needed to prevent unmusical traits.

Figure 5.26

Nevertheless, the tunes generated by these rules evince more than mere bland conventionality; even the more inept examples seem to reflect Tegnér's folk-oriented Nordic style. As Sloboda (1985) agrees, Sundberg and Lindblom succeed in showing that rules alone can generate music of a specific style.

5.8. Generation of tunes by computer

5.8.1. If generative rules can be formulated with such precision, clearly tune generation, like analysis, can be entrusted to a computer. It must be stressed that the established practice of computer composition is not at issue here. In computer composition the style is largely a product of the medium: computer music is a respected segment of the contemporary musical world. But the question of generative grammar, as discussed in this chapter, has to do with traditional musical styles. Clearly a computer composition is a product of generative grammar, but is the music of Bach and Mozart based on generation and transformation? The computer can help us to decide this by putting into effect our grammar after it has been deduced.

5.8.2. Mario Baroni and Carlo Jacoboni formulate a computer programme for the composition of chorale melodies in the style of those harmonized by J S Bach (Baroni and Jacoboni 1978). They proclaim:

> Our task is that of generating a sort of grammar with which we can describe the musical texts we have chosen for study. Such a grammar, if it were complete, would be able to generate examples of the studied language different from the original ones we began with, as happens with the grammars of natural languages. One can thus speak of a sort of generative grammar of the studied texts, giving the term a more general meaning without precise parallels with the formal Chomskyan approach (11-12).

After careful consideration of this corpus they proceed to the 'formulation of a hypothesis consisting of determined laws intended as synthesized statements which are capable of describing relationships that feature in many different circumstances (the heuristic-inductive stage of the analysis)' (24-25).

5.8.3. Using these laws, new phenomena are generated and the laws are corrected wherever the generated material is inappropriate. They treat the note as minimal unit, though all the features attributed to it depend on its relation to other notes: duration, metrical position, degree of the scale and pitch. The last of these, pitch, is not 'an absolute value of the frequency of the sound wave' but is considered only in relation to other pitches before and after. Here, above all, is a system of 'differences in which there are no positive terms'! Nevertheless, larger musical units are respected in roundabout ways; the 'phrase', an obvious feature in a chorale with textual lines and pauses, is taken as given, and the beginning and end of the phrase are distinguished from the central body, these areas being separated as 'fields' to which different rules apply. In spite of the necessary precision of their technique, these researchers do not distinguish a tone from a semitone or a major third from a minor third.

Their grammatical rules apply to notes no shorter than a crotchet. Shorter notes are considered to be decorations and are controlled by their own set of transformational rules.

5.8.4. They conclude with the complete grammar, from which the following rules are samples:

> Rule 11: In the central body, transitions of a third without decoration involving degrees which are not strong, are used only if they are descending and only if the second of the two basic notes is not a mobile degree (73).

> Rule 23: Ascending cadences are never decorated (85).

This grammar becomes the basis of a computer programme. Its effectiveness is demonstrated by a collection of new chorale tunes (first two phrases only). Again, I offer two samples.

Figure 5.27

The impression is that Baroni and Jacoboni are more successful than Sundberg and Lindblom. All their melodies feel 'Bachian' and none have grossly unmusical features .

5.9. John Blacking on musical competence

5.9.1. The ideas and methods of transformational-generative grammar are taken up by various ethnomusicologists. Their work is discussed in the next chapter. The writings of John Blacking, however, are of special relevance here, for he concerns himself with two concepts that are at the heart of Chomsky's thought: the idea of *competence* and the theory of *Universal Grammar*. As explained in

Chapter 2, competence - the mental counterpart of the Saussurean *langue*, linguistic structure as understood by the individual mind - is not necessarily conditioned by the genetic structures of the mind; such a connection would make all linguistic competences fundamentally the same. Chomsky, however, seems to assume that there is a connection; at the base of all languages there lie features that are human and universal, recalling the 'universal or philosophical grammar' of James Beattie (1788).

5.9.2. Whenever Blacking talks about musical grammar, he invariably assumes that it implies some elements universal to the species.

> What is therefore of much interest in the search for the characteristics of a musical language comparable to human speech, is not only the varieties of musical grammars, but also the common principles by which musical grammars are constituted (Blacking 1984, 369-370).

For this writer, competence is grounded in a universal human faculty. This may seem to conflict with the perception that some people are 'musical', some not. Blacking points out that the competence necessary for making music is also needed for hearing it. Almost everyone can enjoy and make sense of music; 'Musical genius cannot exist without listeners' (Blacking 1971, 20).

Musical competence is different from linguistic competence in that the latter is most commonly exercised in speaking; the musical kind is more often exercised in listening. Thus, if we consider composing, conducting, singing or playing an instrument to be 'musical performance' then the relation performance/competence is different in music; most humans do not show their competence in performance. Furthermore, musical performance is not necessarily the only measure of musical ability and 'may not necessarily be an expression of essentially musical competence'. Indeed, an experienced listener will often make more of a performance than the performer himself or even the composer.

Chomsky's shift from *langue* to competence reflected a mentalistic view, a psychological reinterpretation of language. Blacking's persistence in seeing competence in universal terms reflects a sociological and ideological view; for him competence, a quality common to mankind, replaces 'musical ability', an élitist quality possessed by the few who are trained in conservatoires. The idea of competence attracted him because this was a quality acquired by almost all children in the first few years of life, not a freak ability genetically programmed into a few exceptional individuals. Thus, he divides competence into two faculties:

> Particular musical competence is the innate or learned capacity to hear and create the patterns of sound which are recognized as music in the context of a particular musical tradition; and universal musical competence is the innate or learned capacity to hear and create patterns of sound which may be recognized as music in all cultural traditions (1971, 21).

5.9.3. Examining the Venda, a tribe of the Transvaal, he admits that some persons are superior performers, but this is usually because they have had more opportunities to learn about music, perhaps as sons or daughters of musicians. The Venda consider that, in recognizing the ability of exceptional performers, listeners prove that their own competence is equal to that of the performers. 'The Venda may not consider the possibility of unmusical human beings, but they do recognize that some people perform better than others' (1971, 26).

Certain aspects of Venda musical activity suggest that their competence is not wholly confined to their own culture, but reflects a universal mental quality. They are able to apply themselves creatively to the European songs which reach them. Their own tradition is constantly developing in a creative way, as though there were forces within it that are not part of it. Venda children invent their own free variants of tribal music, incorporating new features like the speech-tones of newly-invented words or rhythms connected with functions other than those native to the songs. These variations form a unique category of Venda music and suggest musical energies in the childish mind that have not been taught by culture, 'a creative use of features of the musical system which extends beyond techniques that might have been learnt in society'.

Blacking sees a comparison between some of these techniques and those discussed by Reti (1962 and 1967) for Western music. It may be possible, then, to progress to a theory of universal musical competence, the dynamic structural force that necessarily lies at the basis of all deep structure in music.

5.9.4. Quite apart from the élitist issue, the theory of musical competence sheds a rather different light on music studies from most of the other ideas discussed here. 'Neutral' theory aims to elucidate qualities that are inherent to music regardless of whether they are perceived or appreciated by listeners. Schenker (and thus, probably, Lerdahl and Jackendoff) evoke structural details which, to be sure, must necessarily underlie any hearing of the music, but which may go largely unnoticed by all but the most experienced listeners. Yet linguists hardly ever consider the 'most experienced speakers' - they are not concerned with specially expert speaking or listening; linguistic performance and competence are part of the ordinary experience of any human being. It seems, therefore, that Blacking is right in finding musical competence - whether cultural or universal - in every human listener. Indeed, the analysts referred to in this book, not only Lerdahl and Jackendoff but also Sundberg and Lindblom, Ruwet, and Nattiez, spend much of their time discussing simple musical phenomena accessible to any listener. It may be at this level, the level of the Geisslerlied and Tegnér's nursery songs, that musical structure most closely approaches that of language. A criticism often levelled at distributional analyses of music, that they employ a complicated paraphernalia to uncover simple and trivial features, may reflect the prejudice of the older linguists castigated by Chomsky for concerning themselves only with 'exceptions and irregularities'. A theory of music must primarily be a theory of the simplest workings of the most regular music.

5.10. A glance back at Chomsky

5.10.1. Of the various approaches described above, two come nearest to real Chomskyan theory: those of Keiler, and of Sundberg and Lindblom. In true transformational-generative grammar most of the stages are abstract and logical, real terms only entering at the end. Rules are used to 'rewrite' each term in a previous string, the initial category being an abstract conception like 'sentence'.

Initially, the sentence may be *rewritten* as noun phrase, auxiliary, verb phrase (Chomsky 1965, 68).

$$1 \quad S \longrightarrow NP \frown Aux \frown VP$$

The verb phrase is now rewritten as verb and noun phrase.

$$2 \quad VP \longrightarrow V \frown NP$$

Noun phrases may be rewritten either as determiner plus noun, or simply noun alone.

$$3 \quad NP \longrightarrow Det \frown N$$
$$4 \quad NP \longrightarrow N$$

The word the is a determiner.

    5   Det ⟶ *the*

A verbal auxiliary may be a modal.

    6   Aux ⟶ M

May is a modal; sincerity and boy are nouns; frighten is a verb.

    7   M ⟶ *may*
    8   N ⟶ *sincerity*
    9   N ⟶ *boy*
    10   V ⟶ *frighten*

At the end of this process the left term in stage 1 ('sentence') has been progressively rewritten as *Sincerity may frighten the boy*.

5.10.2. Although Keiler's system may seem to be analytical rather than generative, it does in fact function in a similar way to Chomsky's. In the simple chord sequence of Figure 4.5, by changing the terms for some of Keiler's categories we may write a system of rules which function exactly as do Chomsky's, real terms entering only at the end.

    1   P ⟶ TP⌒CadP (Cadence prolongation)

    2   CadP ⟶ Cad⌒T

    3   TP ⟶ T

    4   Cad ⟶ HD (Hyperdominant)⌒D

Introducing real terms:

Figure 5.28

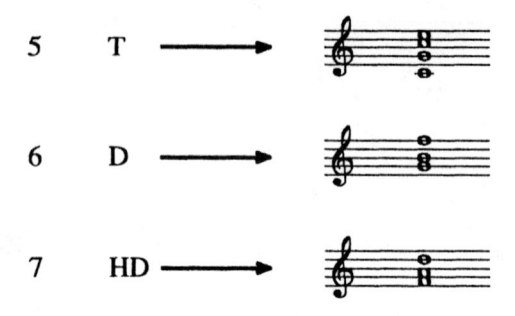

This interprets a tree diagram similar to Keiler's (the original diagram is Figure 5.6).

Figure 5.29

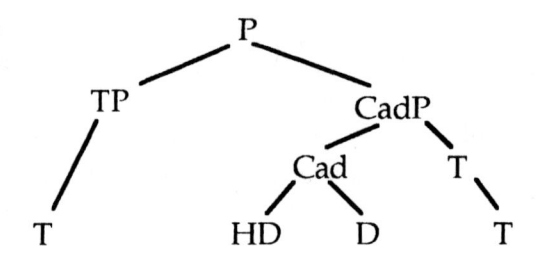

At every stage there are alternatives which are rejected, just as Chomsky rejects the myriad linguistic alternatives to arrive at a particular sentence.

The similarity to Chomsky is striking. To achieve it, an important feature of Keiler's theory has had to be obscured: the relation hyperdominant-dominant is the same as that of dominant-tonic. This is the sense in which Keiler speaks of 'embedding'; clearly there can be a second hyperdominant (V of V of V) and so on. No such feature exists in language because grammatical categories are in some degree qualitative, while all musical features are relational. It is unthinkable that some grammatical component could be a noun phrase in relation to one part of the sentence, a verb phrase in relation to another. It is precisely this kind of double identity which gives music its impetus.

5.10.3. The system of Sundberg and Lindblom is similarly based on abstract categories expanded by rules, real terms coming only at the end. But because it is based on a theory of phonological stress, it is wholly context-oriented. Its dependence on Chomsky and Halle's *The Sound Pattern of English* makes it no easier to relate to the grammatical theories of the Cambridge master. In these theories, context is incorporated by rather cumbersome rules. For example, the simple fact that transitive verbs take a noun phrase as object, intransitive verbs do not, is indicated in the following manner:

$$V \rightarrow [+V, \begin{cases} + \text{ transitive } / - NP \\ - \text{ transitive } / - \# \end{cases}$$

The distinctions abstract/non-abstract, animate/inanimate in subject and object give rise to impressive collections of context-sensitive rules. If Sundberg and Lindblom were to express their tune-generator as a transformational grammar, almost every parameter governing every note of the tune would be context-sensitive. Only the initial operation (Period --- Opening phrase --- Closing phrase) is transformational.

5.10.4. Transformational rules and categories are aspects of *metalanguage*. Schenkerian reductions, instead of converting musical expressions into metalinguistic abstractions, convert them into other, simpler musical expressions. Someone may protest that the graphic analyses of Schenker are, in fact, written in a musical metalanguage, music-about-music. Lest we run away with this tempting sophistry, it must be pointed out that music simply does not contain the two levels of grammar and phonology which are essential to language. Music, indeed, is a system of relations, and so is grammar; but you do not hear grammar when you hear language - you hear phonology. There is no phonological relation between *sincerity* and *frighten*; the relation is grammatical. In music, abstract grammar is realised and syntax dances before us. In order to apprehend linguistic grammar we have to devise a technical metalanguage which is itself not grammar, of course, but discourse about grammar. To discuss musical grammar we similarly need a metalanguage which is not grammar. But all music is grammar, even Schenker's brief *Ursätze*. Hence we need a symbolic, logical metalanguage to discuss music.

6

LINGUISTICS AND WORLD MUSIC

6.1. *Studies based on phonemics, phonology and pure structuralism*

6.1.1. Ethnomusicologists were the midwives of music semiotics. Heralded by Nettl and Bright, its first definitive master was Jean-Jacques Nattiez. The study of world music makes especially urgent the need for radical theory, since the whole edifice of Western musicology, its terminology, methods and notation, prove to be ethnocentric when applied to the musics of other cultures, or even to the folk and popular styles of the home culture. Working alongside linguists and anthropologists, the ethnomusicologist found that he was floundering in vague amateurism.

Chomskyan generative theory has been much favoured in the area of world music; and exponents of transformational-generative grammar, in this as in other fields, do not always call themselves 'semiologists'. Nevertheless, it seems appropriate to describe their work in the context of a semiotic study.

6.1.2. It was natural, however, that the first efforts should aim at a musical phonemics, based on the criterion of pertinence. Nettl, describing an Arapaho Peyote song in which he found nine pitch phonemes and two rhythmic phonemes, the two kinds of phoneme combining only in certain patterns, remarked: 'This is similar to a type of linguistic statement in which certain vowels in a given language are said to occur in short and long forms, others only short' (Nettl 1958, 41). This seems to foreshadow a kind of distributional analysis, but the criterion for distinguishing phonemes is not made clear.

Mâche, too (1971), having discerned six levels in music analysis of which level 2 is the 'definition of phonemes' and level 4 the 'definition of monemes' (which are like morphemes), proceeds to an analysis of Varèse's *Intégrales* in which he discovers five monemes. Each moneme has from one to three 'components'. But are these components phonemes, in fact? It is hard to say, because of the impossibility of commutation; in music, it makes no sense to replace one component with something different and see if the music is 'the same'. If we do commute, there is always a musical change, yet it is not a radical change as when we change *pat* to *bat* by commutation of one phoneme.

6.1.3. Considering the many admissions of failure or near-failure in the field of musical phonemics, it is surprising that there is one study that seems almost wholly successful, even if it is strictly speaking a study of dance rather than music. This is Adrienne Kaeppler's analysis of Tongan dance (1972). Her methods are derived largely from Goodenough's theory of componential analysis (described in an article in *Language*, 32/2, 1956).

She finds dance analogues of phonemes and morphemes which she calls *kinemes* and *morphokines*, using the terminology of Ray L Birdwhistell's 'kinesics' (his *Introduction to Kinesics* was published in 1952). 'Kinemes are those actions and positions which, although having no meaning in themselves, are the basic units from which all dance of a given tradition is built' (Kaeppler 1972, 174). Not all differences and distinctions are considered kinemic: 'If [my teachers] said it "didn't matter" or if they didn't perceive differences in what I did, I concluded that the movements were only allokines of a kineme...'

> Occasionally in Tongan dance the torso bends or twists but this is not considered significant or emic to the Tongans... Indeed many Tongans do not even consciously perceive [torso movement], just as Americans are seldom conscious of the sound of glottal stops.

Thus, while there are eleven leg kinemes, including 'forward step', 'bend the knees low in place', there is only one head kineme, 'a tilt where the head moves quickly to the right side'. In spite of this there is much head movement in Tongan dance; it is not kinemic but merely 'adds style to a dance, makes a dance more aesthetic, and differentiates good dancers from poor dancers'.

Although the definition of the morpheme usually makes some reference to semantics, and although there is a strong semantic component in Tongan dance which Kaeppler later discusses, she avoids semantics in defining the morphokine. This element is the smallest unit that is recognized as a movement; morphokines do not necessarily 'have narrative or pictorial meaning (although they sometimes do)'. Only certain combinations of kinemes are permitted, and morphokines are analysed both with regard to the kinemes that make them up, and with regard to their external distribution - what morphokines can occur together. In spirit this analysis is distributional though it differs from orthodox distributional linguistics in a number of ways. First, linguistic phonemes and morphemes always appear consecutively, rather than simultaneously (except for stress-phonemes or *prosodemes* which must occur with other phonemes). Kaeppler's morphokines tend to occur in simultaneous groups. For example, a complex arm movement may be made up of arm kinemes, wrist kinemes and finger kinemes. As such, it is an intelligible and separable morphokine. It may be performed, however, at the same time as an equally intelligible leg morphokine.

Secondly, some of the morphokines are called 'environment morphokines'; these are positions, in the midst of which other morphokines may be danced, for example 'arm extended forward in middle level'. The writer compares these to 'the tone of voice in speech'. The tone of voice is not usually considered phonemic, however, except in tone languages.

Thirdly, there are morphokines which are 'not significant at the kinemic level but are important at the morphokinemic level'. That is, they are inseparable from certain other morphokines and are not recognized in any other combination. They are, as it were, morphemes that are not made up of phonemes.

Most interesting, certain morphokines have Tongan names with extrachoric meanings, like 'from here to there' or 'rainbow'. Morphokines can be combined into 'motifs' (Kaeppler does not venture into grammar and call them 'sentences'), with names like 'crown', 'give', 'sweep', 'unwind', 'scatter'. Dance can thus be used to illustrate poetry. Most movements, however, are sufficiently ambiguous to represent many different poetic ideas. The phrase 'flower of the tropic bird created' is illustrated by three movements of which one clearly resembles that of a bird. The other two are more generalized, the slower signified by a universally 'beautiful' movement and 'created' by a movement meaning 'above', which is later used for 'breeze' and 'fragrance'. Since Tongan poetry is itself arcane and symbolic, it is as though poetry and dance meet on a level of literal meaning from which each radiates into different vistas of ambiguity. In any case, many movements have no extrachoric meaning at all.

> Movements either interpret poetry or create beauty. They present an abstraction to which dancer and spectator alike may attach meaning of his own choosing or which can be enjoyed aesthetically as movement (213).

This study is distributional (rules are shown governing the occurrence of items within the structure of the language) but not generative (no rules are given showing how danced patterns are developed by the transformation of simpler units). There is, in fact, a very convincing generative study, Alice Singer's work on Macedonian dance (Singer 1974), which also contains a useful critique of Kaeppler's article. With all its intellectual acumen, it will not be discussed here.

6.1.4. Kaeppler's theory is a kind of phonemics of dance. Any phonological theory is bound to be based on phonetics, and phonetics can itself be based either on acoustical or on articulatory principles. That is, the sound of language may be studied, as heard by a listener or a measuring instrument; or we may study the physiological manner of sound production. Acoustical phonetics has generally been thought more relevant to music. There is one exception to this. In analysing the traditional drumming of the Garhwali-speaking area in northern Uttar Pradesh, Anoop Chandola (1977) uses articulatory methods of description. In this style of music, the type of drum-stroke is more important than the sound it makes, and distributional rules can be formulated for the articulatory aspect of drum performance.

The six types of Garhwali drum are played in pairs. For example, the *dhol*, a large two-headed copper or brass drum with deerskin and goatskin heads, is generally accompanied by the *damau*, a higher-pitched single-headed drum resembling a small kettledrum. Drums are struck sometimes with the fingers or palm, sometimes with sticks, sometimes with the knee, though the damau is played only with sticks. There are two types of stroke, one producing a hum and called an 'open' stroke, the other pressing against the drumhead to give a dull sound, called a 'closed' stroke. The drumhead may be struck on the corner or in the centre, and there are certain sliding strokes.

Strokes may be classified according to the articulatory agent (palm; fingers 1-5; stick; knee; in each case, left or right), the place on the drumhead (corner or centre of the left or right head), and the manner of striking (closed, open, slide). The letters J to V are used for the various strokes, though their meanings change for each drum. A few examples of dhol strokes are given here.

N: The dhol sound (stroke) represented by this symbol is produced by a left hand slap which uses fingers 2-4. The slap strikes the corner of the left face of the dhol. The stroke is open.

O: This is produced by a left hand slap which consists of fingers 3-5 plus the palm at the base of these fingers... The place of articulation for this stroke is the corner of the left face. The stroke makes an open sound.

L: This open stroke is articulated on the center of the right face with a stick held in the right hand (Chandola 1977, 40).

The Garhwali performance consists of a traditional story sung in improvized verse, the stanzas usually accompanied by soft drumming and separated by loud drumming. Two performances of the same story may be closely similar, for vocal melodies and drum rhythms are associated with particular stories. There are two performers, both of them drummers and singers, though one is the lead singer and the other the principal drummer. There may be dancers also. In certain circumstances the drum rhythms and verse texts are fixed; in others, less so.

> In the example of the marriage... the drummers' distribution of rhythms and texts is fixed for each occasion. However, in other contexts, drummers have more options as to the quality and quantity of rhythms, intonations, and texts. In other situations, besides the song texts, the drummers may use spoken language intermittently... (12).

There is thus a high level of improvization, but it is constrained in various ways. The drum-strokes are combined into certain set patterns; there are eleven such patterns for the dhol-damau pair, of which the first is given here as an example (the damau has only two available strokes, M with the left stick and N with the right).

Dhol:	N L N	L N L	N L L	O
Damau:	N M N	N M N	N M N	N M N

Certain constraints operate in the formation of these patterns. No pattern may begin with a closed stroke. The slide stroke, V, can be preceded only by an open stroke. The stroke M on the dhol must be followed by L. Two strokes can occur together: N and O, N and L, but not S and M, S and V and so on. Certain patterns are thought appropriate to the different sections of song texts.

Clearly, a whole system of distributional and generative rules could be framed for Garhwali drumming, amounting to a complete grammar of the genre. In addition, the underlying systems of drum performance could perhaps be related to textual aspects, both syntactic and semantic. Chandola does not attempt this, as he admits. It is a pity, for this seems a uniquely interesting example of the operation of a transformational grammar, with its possible link-up with the linguistic analysis of a song text.

6.1.5. Before turning at last to the applications of generative grammar to ethnic music, we ought to consider a couple of exercises in pure structuralism, unrelated to phonetics or phonemics.

Rouget and Schwarz (1970) offer a structuralist solution to the problem of describing and transcribing ethnic musics. The Western listener will tend to transcribe what his own tradition leads him to hear. For this reason, according to Hornbostel, only a recording suffices to represent an ethnic performance. To transcribe is to introduce phonemic distinctions without proper foundations. However, phonemic distinctions may perhaps be discerned by comparing one musical language with another, for according to Martinet, to describe a language is to show how it differs from others.

Rouget and Schwarz take two brief extracts of female song: a dithyramb/lullaby sung by a Griot from the Sudan, and a shamanic song on nonsense syllables, sung by a Fuegian Indian. To ensure the strictly phonetic basis of the study, they utilise acoustic instruments which measure exact pitch, duration, intensity and the frequency spectrum - the relative levels of overtones of the fundamental. The latter instrument enables them to judge the level of consonance of the intervals without reference to Western triadic and tonal principles. If the harmonics of different notes tend to coincide (as, of course, the harmonics of notes in a triad would do) then these notes are in a consonant relation. If, for example, the third harmonic of note 7 is the same as the fourth harmonic of note 10, then these notes are harmonically related: consonance is a 'relation between spectra'. Since the Griot singer uses an equiheptatonic scale, and since like Western singers she is seldom exactly in tune, such an abstract criterion of consonance becomes vital. Rouget and Schwarz define song, in fact, by reference to 'an incontestable pre-eminence of harmonics on the sound'; without this, the performance is speech-song. The Griot singer enunciates each syllable separately and sings each note at a level pitch. It is thus easy to subject her performance to tests of pitch and consonance. The Fuegian, on the other hand, never defines notes but sings in a constant *portamento*. Nevertheless, some relations of pitch can be discerned: 'Disons qu'il y a entretien de la consonance' add the authors, punning on the word 'entretien' - this could mean, 'consonance is maintained', or 'there is a dialogue with consonance'. In other respects the two singers are very different. While the Griot uses a wide range of note values, related irrationally to each other, the Fuegian's note values are uniform. The Griot sings at a constant dynamic level with a slight increase at ends of notes; the Fuegian's intensity changes constantly.

Viewed acoustically, the two musical 'languages' may be analysed according to a series of binary oppositions.

Griot	*Fuegian*
Variety of note values	Uniformity of note values
Absence of accent	Presence of accent
Maintenance of intensity	Variation of intensity
Vocalic timbre unimportant	Vocalic timbre important
Legato without portamento	Marcato with portamento
Punctual sound (i.e. conforming to discrete pitches)	Diffuse sound

Since pitch is controlled by the larynx, intensity by the breathing apparatus (the *soufflerie*, more than just the lungs), these two vocal styles may be opposed by the primacy given respectively to each of these functions. This engenders a second scheme of oppositions, based on R Husson's classification of the singing voice (in *Le Chant*, 1962). This scheme corresponds to the articulatory aspect of phonetics.

Linguistics and World Music

Griot	*Fuegian*
Reduced glottic tonus	Raised glottic tonus
Raised sub-glottic pressure	Weak sub-glottic pressure
Larynx very low	Larynx raised
Soft palate low	Soft palate raised

Vocal body *schema*:

Strong abdominal component	Strong thoracic component
Growth of diffuse pallesthesic sensitivity of the rhino-pharyngeal and nasofacial regions	Growth of sensitivity of the larynx and the pharyngeo-buccal cavity

The writers find these distinctions appropriate to the African and American singers, considering their general cultural contour. The Griot's intonation is based on the immutable pitches of a xylophone; while throughout the Americas, wind instruments predominate. The Fuegians have an accented style of dancing which leaves its mark on their singing.

6.1.6. Indian classical music has seemed especially suitable for analysis on linguistic principles, for like language it bases an improvized surface on the complex raga system, as speech depends on phonology and syntax.

However, the only truly syntactic study of Indian music is not, in fact, based on linguistic syntactics, but on a purely rational system derived from Piaget's standard study *Structuralism*, which was mentioned in Chapter 2 (Piaget 1971). The *raga* (the word may mean 'colour') is a set of melodic traits called 'limbs' *(avayava)* which give the performance, to Indian listeners, a certain mood. Writers usually characterize ragas by quoting their characteristic melodic shapes; this can be observed in the study by Harold Powers, summarized below.

It occurred to Heikki Nylund, however, that a purely syntactic system could be derived from the melodies that define a raga, on a higher level of abstraction than the lists of melodic shapes. Piaget speaks of 'lattice' or 'network' structures which 'unite their elements by the predecessor/successor relation' (Piaget, 1971, 24, quoted by Nylund, 1983, 47). Indian musicians, too, classify notes by their positions in melodic shapes; notes are ascending *(arohi)*, descending (*avarohi*), oblique (*vakra*) or direct (*sarala*). An ascending note is one that is followed by a higher note; a descending note is followed by a lower note; an oblique note is part of a movement in one direction (for instance, preceded by higher, followed by lower); a direct note is a point of change of direction (preceded by lower, followed by lower, for example). The melodic complexion of a note, therefore, is determined by its position in a sequence of three notes: predecessor, note, successor. It ought to be possible to describe the character of a raga by listing the possible sequences of three.

Each raga makes a selection from the available notes of the Indian system. This system has seven degrees which are very roughly equivalent to the degrees of the Western scale, though strictly speaking they are an ordering of 22 tiny intervals each equal to slightly more than half a semitone. The 'natural' form of the scale, expressed with C as keynote, has flattened E and B, thus:

C D E flat F G A B flat

Some of these notes can be raised or lowered, however (this account is based on Cooper, 1977).

As well as using a particular selection of notes from this overall system (including 'chromatic' notes), each raga is limited to certain starting and finishing notes. Other rules apply: 'When two variants of an element [for instance, 4 and 4#, the very out-of-tune F and F#] are available, the upper is used in ascent and the lower in descent' (Nylund, 1983, 48).

Nylund now writes syntaxes for three ragas, *Bihag*, *Hambir* and *Kedar*, which share the same scale selection: 1 2 3 4 4# 5 6 7. He can then show that certain melodic progressions are common to several ragas, others unique. Let us observe the melodic potential of the note 7 in *Bihag* and *Kedar*; initial notes are preceded by a bracket, finals followed by a bracket.

```
         Bihag                    Kedar

              2              1         2
         (1   1)
              7                   7
          5   6              6         6
          4                   5
```

Linguistics and World Music 171

This means (for *Bihag*) that note 7 may be preceded by an initial upper 1, or by lower 5, or by 4; it may be followed by upper 2, or by a final upper 1, or by lower 6. It is clear that certain sequences involving the note 7 are common to both ragas, others unique.

$$\begin{array}{c} 2 \\ 7 \\ 5 \end{array}$$

could occur in either raga, while

$$\begin{array}{c} 1) \\ 7 \\ 4 \end{array}$$

would imply *Bihag*. Longer sequences can be read from the syntax in groups of three notes. As an example, we may consider a sequence given by Nylund which encompasses 11 notes before distinguishing between Bihag and Kedar: (1 4 3 5 4# 5 7 6 5 7 6... In order to relate this to the syntax, the notes should be arranged in threes (it does not matter how the division is made):

$$\begin{array}{l} (1\ 4 \quad 5\ 4\#\ 5 \quad 6\ 5\ 7 \\ 4\ 3\ 5 \quad 5\ 7\ 6 \quad 7\ 6... \end{array}$$

The complete syntax for *Bihag* demonstrates the grammaticality of each of these progressions.

```
         2         7        6  7              6
(1  1)            6        5          5       5
    7             4+  5    4+ 4+      4+
5   6                      4  4              3 → 4
4                          3  3

         7        5        3              4
5   5             4+  5         2      2   3
    4             4   4    7   1)      1
(3  3)            3                    (7  7
(1                1   2
```

An exceptional feature of *Bihag* - the fact that 4# may be approached from above, although it is the upper variant of 4 - causes the slight oddity in this diagram, for whenever 5 is followed by a descent to 4# the next notes are always 3 - 4. This is indicated with an arrow.

The 11-note sequence given by Nylund illustrates a feature common to improvized performances. 'The presentation of the common features of two or more ragas is sometimes utilized in the beginning of a performance to keep the audience in suspense as to the raga being presented' (Nylund, 1983, 50). The selection of formulae common to more than one raga must not continue for too long; this would 'distort the raga ultimately chosen'.

The melodic 'ring' of a raga is not truly captured by Nylund's syntax. Indian musicians admitted to him that they never thought of ragas in this way, though the analysis was correct so far as it went. This is consistent, however, with the views of Lévi-Strauss (in *Structural Anthropology*) and Piaget that cognitive systems are fundamentally unconscious: 'Cognitive structures do not belong to the subject's consciousness but to his operational behaviour' (Piaget 1971, 68). It would be a more serious matter if the syntaxes were insufficient to describe each raga exhaustively; if it were found that two ragas, though audibly different, possessed the same syntax. Nylund has not found this to be the case, but he admits that further study of ragas might yield an example.

6.2. Studies based on generative theory and semantics

6.2.1. Nylund's analysis of Indian ragas approaches transformational-generative theory; his raga syntax is a dynamic system which generates an infinite number of strings. If we turn to a real generative account, however, the difference is at once apparent in the tree-diagrams, sets of transformational rules and flow-charts.

Cooper (1977) shows that an abstract generative pattern can account for the scalic modes of ragas. It will be recalled that each raga makes a selection from the available notes of the Indian system; this 'scale' of the raga is called a *that*. The 'chromatic' notes may be included in a given *that*; as we have seen, degree 4 may be raised, while degrees 2, 3, 6 and 7 can be lowered (in the approximate Western equivalent, lowered 3 would be a very flat E flat). Degrees 1 and 5 are fixed.

There are 10 *thatas*, but over 200 ragas. If the options were to operate without constraints there would be far more thatas, clearly. What, then, are the constraints? The following selection of thatas, with their Indian names, may suggest a clue. An incorrect form is also given.

1	2	3	4	5	6	7	
					(*Bilaval*, the natural scale)		
1	2	3b	4	5	6b	7b	(*Yavanapuri*)
1	2b	3b	4#	5	6b	7	(*Todi*)
1	2	3b	4	5	6	7	(incorrect)

Cooper follows Indian theory in dividing the scale into two tetrachords, called *purvanga* (the lower) and *uttaranga* (the upper). The highest note of *purvanga*, which can be sharpened, is separately classified, giving in both tetrachords a fixed note and two variable notes, the lower variable (LV) and the higher variable (HV). The deep structure is thus:

Figure 6.1

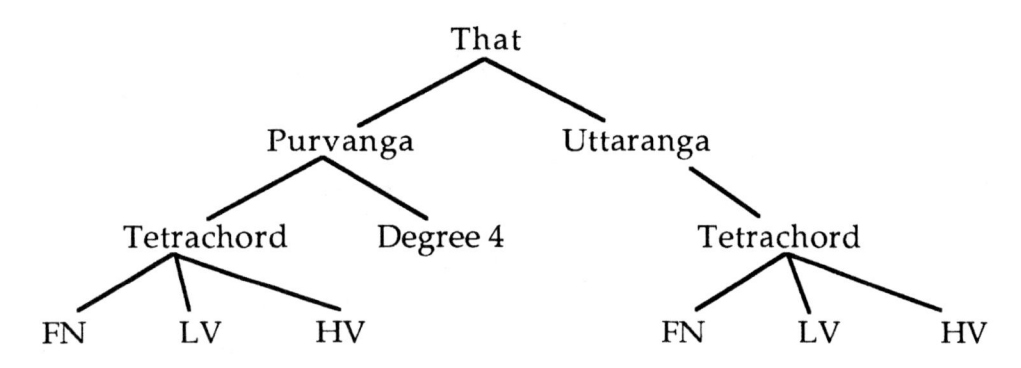

```
                        That
                       /    \
                 Purvanga    Uttaranga
                 /    \           \
          Tetrachord  Degree 4    Tetrachord
          / | \                   / | \
         FN LV HV                FN LV HV
```

It can be seen (by observing *Yavanapuri*) that all variables may be flattened except degree 2, the lower variable of purvanga. Thus the initial sequence 1-2-3b is possible. Why, then, is the last sequence incorrect in the above list? Cooper discovers that this incipit is possible only in the context of 6b-7b, the flattening of both variables in uttaranga. In addition, when the lower variable in purvanga (degree 2) is flat, the corresponding note in uttaranga (degree 6) must also be flat. The rules governing formation of thatas can be stated in a chart which somewhat resembles a flow-chart (Figure 6.2). A possible route would be: 'Start by sharpening degree 4; optionally flatten degree 2; optionally flatten degree 6; optionally flatten degree 3.' This is programme A, and if all options are taken up the result is 1-2b-3b-4#-5-6b-7, which is the that todi (see above). The chart generates all grammatical forms, and no ungrammatical ones (Figure 6.2).

Cooper then offers rules for the deletion of notes to generate hexatonic and pentatonic scales, which are also found, and to find vadi and samvadi, the two melodically primary notes comparable to final and confinal in Western modes.

It does not escape his notice that all these features are paradigmatic and on the level of abstract grammar. The whole point of turning to Indian music was to compare its level of performance with that of language, since it is wholly improvized. The rules which permit actual performance within the limits set by the raga system, which he calls 'melodic functions', are not sketched.

Figure 6.2

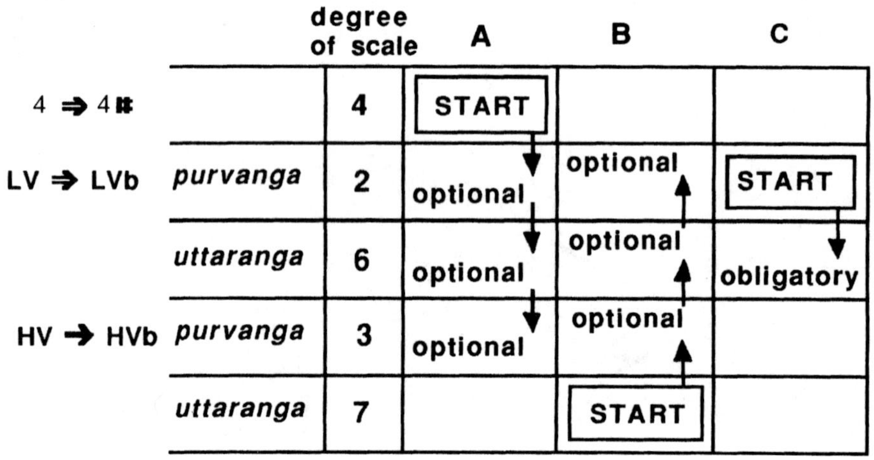

	degree of scale	A	B	C
4 ⇒ 4♯		4	START		
LV ⇒ LVb *purvanga*	2	optional	optional	START
uttaranga	6	optional	optional	obligatory
HV ⇒ HVb *purvanga*	3	optional	optional	
uttaranga	7		START	

The nature of the melodic function which generates well-formed possible extemporizations from the final output trees of the grammar is not clear, although it looks as if it might provide an interesting, albeit difficult, area for future research (27).

Nylund's study, being concerned with note-order rather than merely *that*-construction, is closer to performance. Even this, however, is not powerful enough to generate actual improvization, but only to determine what is syntactically correct.

6.2.2. Another piece of research, in progress when Cooper was writing, came nearer to the actual note-sequences of improvizations. Harold Powers (1976) decided to approach the problem in terms of *structural semantics* rather than generative grammar, using the taxonomy of John Lyons (1963). As a structuralist Lyons stresses that *sense* is prior to meaning; 'having meaning' comes before 'what meaning'. The absence of cognitive, referential or ostensive meanings in music is no obstacle to a study of musical semantics in structuralist terms. Linguistic items are related semantically in a series of 'lexical fields', later called 'lexical systems', governed by certain types of paradigmatic relation: terms may be incompatible (tulip/rose), loosely synonymous (adequate/sufficient), hyponymous (tulip/flower) or opposite-complementary in various ways (male/female; high/low; husband/wife). In terms of general discourse (here I expand on Powers's account) one can proceed hyponymously, confirming and making more specific the existing expression.

> Things are improving; John has returned the book he borrowed.

One can proceed on a level of loose synonymy, adding little to the first statement while not contradicting it.

> John's work is better; he has higher marks.

Two statements may be complementary by stating the converse of each other.

> John bought Mary's house; Mary sold the house to John.

And of course, utterances may contradict.

> Mary is brighter than John. John is brighter than Mary.

In practice hyponymy and incompatibility are the commonest paradigmatic relations within the vocabulary, and probably hyponymy is fundamental also in structuring discourse. That is to say, successive utterances confirm, expand and make more specific the semantic proposition declared at the outset.

It is opportune, remarks Powers, that the structural theories of Lyons destress the aspect of referential or cognitive meaning, for this is precisely what music lacks. Nonetheless music has a sense; within a musical discourse it is possible for a particular syntagm to be confirmatory, neutral, or nonsense on many levels - in relation to its immediate surroundings, or in relation to the whole piece, mode, or tradition. This is particularly clear in the Indian raga system. A raga is, of course, a melodic style or 'melody-type' as well as a scale, and there are characteristic motives which typify a particular raga; these are called *anga*. An anga may announce the lower part of the register within a raga; this pitch area, as well as the motives that characterise it, is called *purvanga* (as we know from Cooper), *purva* meaning 'lower'. Since *uttara* means 'higher', the upper pitches, and their characteristic motives, are called *uttaranga*. Indeed anga may betoken the whole span of a raga; they are then *raganga*. Two examples of anga may be given.

Figure 6.3

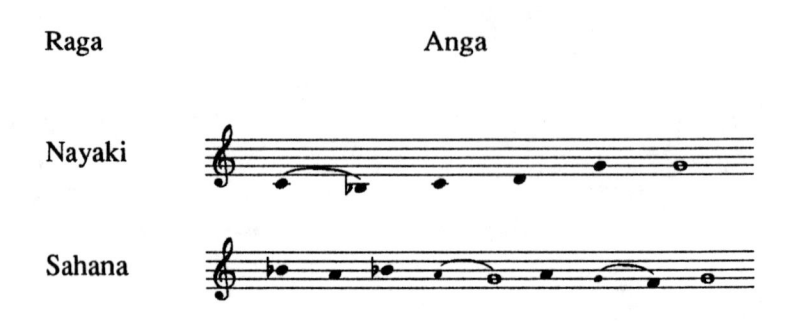

                Raga   Anga

Nayaki

Sahana

When a musical figure is improvized it may strongly announce or confirm a particular raga by conforming closely to the anga. It may, on the other hand, be merely grammatically acceptable, not contradicting the raga but not establishing it unequivocally,. In North Indian technical language these two kinds of figure are called avir-bhav and tiro-bhav. Another figure may be 'wrong' in that it suggests a different raga, or is merely ungrammatical, not suggesting any raga, 'nonsense'. There are thus four kinds of acceptability.

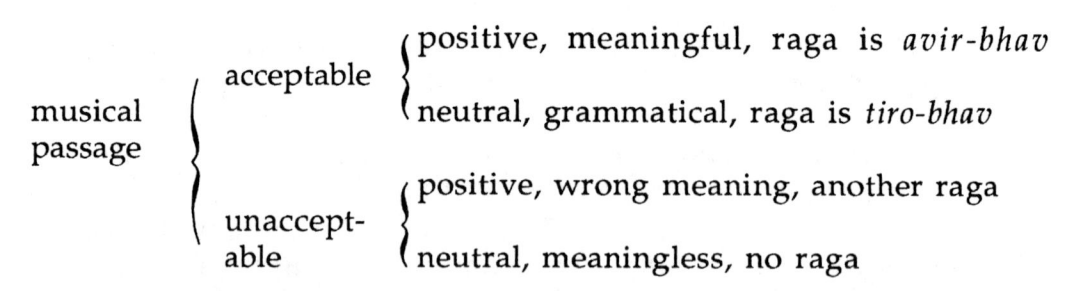

musical passage
- acceptable
  - positive, meaningful, raga is *avir-bhav*
  - neutral, grammatical, raga is *tiro-bhav*
- unacceptable
  - positive, wrong meaning, another raga
  - neutral, meaningless, no raga

Certain anga may be common to several ragas, and many figures played by Indian musicians may suggest several ragas at once, because ragas tend to go in families. These families are understood semantically by Indian theorists and even given associative meanings. Thus the Indian writer Omkarnath Thakur gives a semantic account of one anga which is common to several ragas.

> *Purvi* is an evening raga... the anga (lower 7 - 2b - 3) of *puriya, puriya-dhanasri,* and other sunset-ragas is prominently used in it.

There are, however, anga which distinguish between closely similar ragas within a family, and ways of continuing the more ambiguous anga so that a single raga is determined. In *puriya-dhanasri*, for example, the motive (lower 7 - 2b - 3) must lead immediately to (4# - 2b - 3) 'otherwise there would be some semblance of *puriya*', a different raga.

The hierarchy of motive - anga - raga - raga family - Indian classical system is hyponymous in the way that paradigmatic relations are hyponymous in linguistic semantics, and the syntagmatic relations of motives, confirming or contradicting previous statements, are hyponymous/incompatible like those of successive utterances in discourse. Purvanga and uttaranga are complementary; together they confirm the whole range of a raga in both its registers. Like Cooper, Powers concludes that 'Indian classical music seems much closer to language than its Western counterpart'.

6.2.3. Vida Chenoweth applies the technique of transformational-generative analysis to a corpus of traditional songs of New Guinea. Her study is closer to generative linguistics than that of Cooper, because her grammar generates actual songs, not merely their grammatical basis. Of her various studies, the most elaborate is the work she undertook, in collaboration with Darlene Bee, on the singing of the Awa tribe, who live in the south-east section of the eastern highlands (1971).

Figure 6.4

Though there are ten categories of Awa song, they all evince a musical grammar which the writers analyse, not by proposing a scale of pitches but by listing 13 intervals in relation to the 'tonal centre'. These intervals are given relative status in the system according to their 'functional relationship to the tonal center of a given melody, their relative strength rhythmically, and the kinds of variations in which they occurred'. Of primary status is the minor third which is the 'Awa scale nucleus'. This interval may have prefixes, infixes or suffixes according to certain rules of musical syntax, giving a list of 'rhythmically weak adjacent tones'. The emic scale resulting from this grammar is shown in Figure 6.4.

In this notation B flat is the tonal centre and G - B flat the scale nucleus. The actual order of intervals in a given song is controlled, however, by the following grammar, to which I supply a key.

$$(4d -) + <m3 + (\{ - M2a - / - m2d - ; - M2a> + (- 4a)\})$$

Key
Hyphen following = a prefix
Hyphen preceding = a suffix
Hyphen boundaries = an infix
< > encloses kernel
; = either/or
a = ascending
d = descending
M = major
m = minor

To clarify the functioning of this grammar certain consequences may be drawn from it. The note a perfect fourth below the scale nucleus (D in Figure 6.4) may occur as a prefix at the beginning of a melody; the note which fills in the minor third of the scale nucleus (A in Figure 6.4) may occur as an infix - a neighbour-note formula - between repetitions of the G or the B flat; above the B flat there may be a major second (C) occurring as a suffix, and even a perfect fourth above this (F). In the example below these possibilities are shown ((i) to (v)) together with two impermissible formulae ((vi) and (vii)).

Figure 6.5

Awa singers do not always actually sing the notes emically constituting their melodic system. The perfect fourth can be replaced by a tritone, and major thirds, apparently not part of the system at all, can result from non-pertinent variations, as in Figure 6.6, in which

(a) was actually sung in place of the regular (b), giving the suggestion of a major third between A and F (I have transposed this example into the same register as Figure 6.5).

Figure 6.6

(a) etic   (b) emic

These rules are considered to work within the phrase. Awa songs contain from two to twelve phrases of similar length. 'No interval other than the unison is repeated, and no more than two adjacent intervals proceed in a common direction.' As a further restriction, songs are of three types: those in which development is restricted to the scale nucleus (in this case G - B flat); those which develop also below the tonal centre (taking in D); those which develop above the tonal centre (to F). These types do not occur together in the same song. For the first of these types (development restricted to the scale nucleus) Chenoweth and Bee rewrite the grammar as a flow chart. The notes are digitalized; I translate them into music notation in Figure 6.7.

Figure 6.7

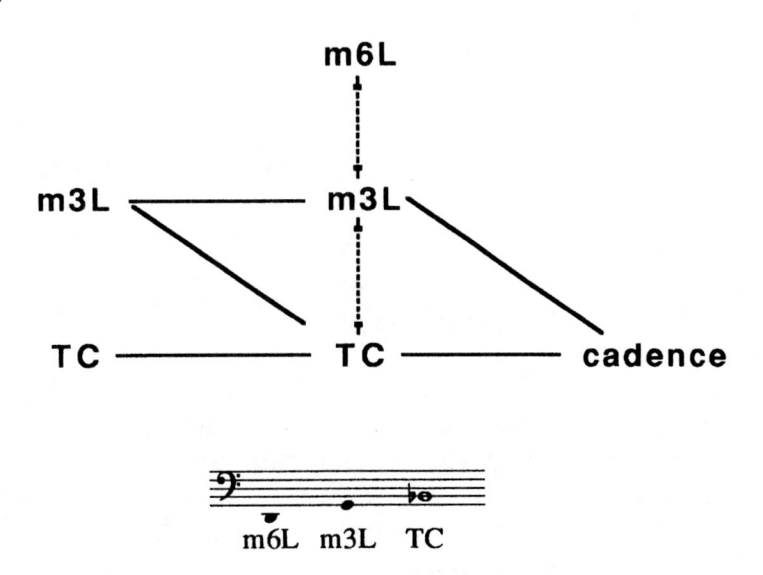

m6L

m3L — m3L

TC — TC — cadence

m6L m3L TC

The formal grammar expressed by this flow chart is as follows.

{m3L; TC + TC} + {(TC) + m3L + (m6L + m3L); + TC}n + cadence

Elements in round brackets are optional. 'n' means 'repeat the section between curly brackets an indefinite number of times'. The grammar is interpreted thus by the authors:

> [The melody] may begin on either a minor third lower than the tonal center or on the tonal center. If it begins on the tonal center there must be at least one repeat of the first note. The melody may end with either the tonal center or the minor third. The core of the melody consists of alternations between these two with an optional progression of a minor third plus a minor sixth and back to a minor third (779).

Finally, Chenoweth and Bee summarize the melodic grammar of the Awas in a graphic display based on concentric circles (781), a very ingenious device in which melodic phrases may be generated by proceeding from the outer circumference to the centre.

Earlier, Chenoweth had written similar studies of the music of other New Guinea tribes, the Gadsups (1966) and the Dunas (1969). In the latter case, the grammar was used to generate new songs, as Sundberg and Lindblom did with the Tegnér melodies. The Duna informants 'readily accepted the new songs'. On the other hand, the Awa grammar described above was used in an attempt to generate some melodies in the style of another tribe, the Usarufa. This enterprise 'made it immediately obvious that... their music systems are significantly different'.

6.2.4. Equally elaborate, though somewhat different in methodology, is the transformational grammar written by Judith and Alton Becker for the Javanese gamelan genre called *Srepegan* (Becker 1979). This is a simple kind of monody, sung and played on ideophones, which accompanies the puppet theatre. The Beckers are respectively musician and linguist.

They point out first that actual intervals, which govern Western music at the top of the hierarchy, are dependent in Javanese music on the particular gamelan (instrument) being played, for each type of gamelan is tuned differently. The intervals are only relevant, therefore, at the lowest level, the level of performance. In their article, these writers transcribe melodies as they would sound on a pentatonically-tuned *saron*, a small xylophone.

Srepegan is made up of four-note figures called *gatra*. These are all end-stressed, and go in threes, the last note of every third gatra being marked by a large gong. The group of three gatra is called a *gongan*. After three gongan the pattern repeats itself; this is considered to be a point of juncture. Examples of gatra are given, with their realization on a pentatonic saron and the serial numbers assigned by the Beckers.

Figure 6.8

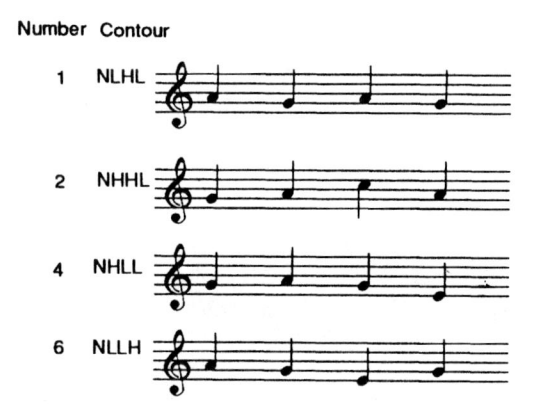

Number	Contour
1	NLHL
2	NHHL
4	NHLL
6	NLLH

Certain factors are controlled by mode *(pathet)* notably the overall pitch of the sequence, which is governed by the last note of the second gongan (the 24th of the sequence). This is chosen because this gongan always ends with the same gatra, namely gatra 2.

The general stylistic constraints of gamelan music are also operative. The Beckers' grammar, however, controls the formation of nine-gatra sequences within all modes, except that they show how pathet controls overall pitch.

Srepegan, then, consists of three gongan, each of three gatra. The # symbol indicates juncture, the point of separation across which rules of distribution are inoperative, like the division between two words in spoken language.

Srepegan = # G_i + G_j + G_i #

It will be noted that gongan 3 broadly recapitulates gongan 1. To arrive at the actual gatra within this pattern, the following formula is taken initially. As will be seen, 'a' and 'b' do not necessarily indicate the same music each time. 'a' is optional and may be omitted.

$$\text{Srepegan} = \# [(a) + 1 + b] \ [1 + 1 + 2] \ [(a) + 1 + b] \#$$

Sometimes Gi is double; there are two Gi's together. For this reason we introduce a further rule.

$$a = (Gi >< 1)$$

This means, 'a is gatra 1; or a whole Gi unit; or both together.'

The first gongan may therefore be simply $[1 + 1 + b]$ where $a = 1$. On the other hand it can be $[Gi + 1 + b]$ where $a = Gi$, which could be realised as:

$$[1 + b] \ [1 + b]$$

where a in the conjoined gongan is suppressed, or

$$[1 + b] + 1 + [1 + b]$$

where a in the principle Gi is realised as G + 1, and a in the conjoined gongan is suppressed. There are several other possibilities.

The grammatical constraints on b are subject to context. b may be gatras 1, 2, 3, 4, or 6. In the first gongan the final b (not the one in any conjoined gongan) is always gatra 1. The slash means 'in the context of' and the short underline indicates where the b in question is placed.

$$b = 1 \ / \ \# \ Gi \ [a + 1 + \_ \ ]$$

In the final gongan, before juncture, b is gatra 3 provided a is realised as gatra 1.

$$b = 3 \ / \ Gi \ [1 + 1 + \_ \ ] \#$$

In the case of conjoined gongans, where a is realised as an additional gongan, b is gatra 4 if the conjoined gongan comes at the beginning of the sequence, after juncture.

$$b = 4 \ / \ \# \ a[1 + \_ \ ]a$$

Linguistics and World Music

The small a's indicate that the whole passage between square brackets is a realisation of a. If the conjoined Gi comes at the beginning of the last gongan, thus after Gj and not after juncture, then b is gatra 6.

$$b = 6 \;/\; Gj + a[1 + \_\;]a + Gi \;\#$$

In all other contexts, b is gatra 2.

It is now possible to generate actual sequences, at least as far as the internal melodic contours within each gatra. An example is given within the mode *slendro pathet sanga*.

Figure 6.9

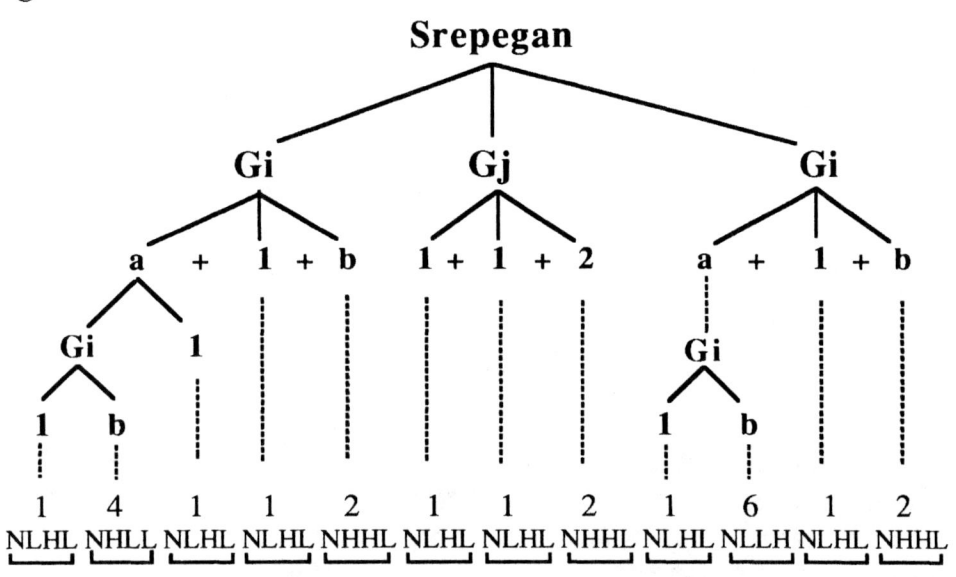

Srepegan

```
              Gi              Gj              Gi
           /      \         / | \          /      \
          a   +  1 + b    1 + 1 + 2       a   +  1 + b
        /  \                                / \
       Gi   1                              Gi   1
      / \                                 / \
     1   b                               1   b

     1   4   1   1   2   1   1   2   1   6   1   2
    NLHL NHLL NLHL NLHL NHHL NLHL NLHL NHHL NLHL NLLH NLHL NHHL
```

Examples are now given of modes and their appropriate pitches.

II	*slendro pathet nem*
V	*slendro pathet sanga*
VI	*slendro pathet manyura*

We may now fix the very last pitch in the whole sequence, the last note of b in the final Gi. Where the note already fixed is V, then the last note is also V. If the note already fixed is another note, II or VI, then the final note is three pitches below in the pentatonic system (V or II). We have now fixed the pitch of two gatra within the whole sequence.

The pitches of the remaining gatra may now be assigned. Their last notes are normally in the pattern [x+1 + x+2 + x] within the single gongan - that is, note + one note higher + two notes lower, for example, V + VI + III.

It should now be possible to give the actual pitches of the middle and last gongan in the example above, disregarding the conjoined gongan. In *slendro pathet sanga* the last pitch of G is V so the following pitch contour may be deduced.

Figure 6.10

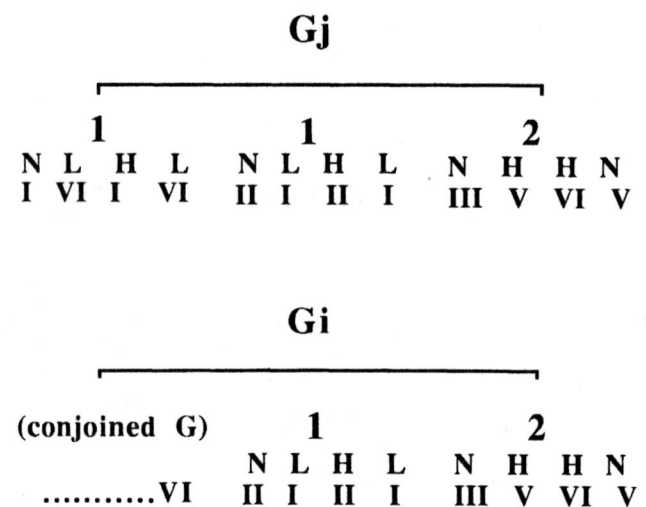

```
                         Gj
         ┌─────────────────────────────────┐
           1           1              2
         N L H L     N L H L        N H H N
         I VI I VI   II I II I      III V VI V


                         Gi
         ┌─────────────────────────────────┐
                          1              2
     (conjoined G)      N L H L        N H H N
     ..........VI       II I II I      III V VI V
```

In order to fix the pitches of the first gongan a more general rule must be introduced. This is a rule of the gamelan system, not specifically of *srepegan*. It is thus hierarchically superior to the rules so far stated. This is important, for it sometimes conflicts with the rules of *srepegan*. Indeed there is a conflict in the example given above.

This rule states that the last note of each gongan is automatically the last note of the first gatra within the next gongan. Initially, it enables us to fix the last note in the first gongan of the given sequence, which has to be VI, and the last note of its first gatra, which has to be V (as it follows the last gongan when the sequence is repeated).

According to the rules of *srepegan,* however, the first gatra would end with 1, in order to preserve the pattern

   (x+1 + x+2 + x)

within the gongan. The conflict is thus:

Figure 6.11

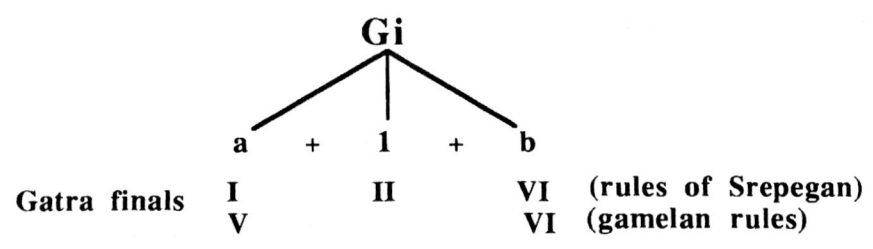

```
                    Gi
                   /|\
                  a + 1 + b
Gatra finals      I    II    VI   (rules of Srepegan)
                  V          VI   (gamelan rules)
```

In this case a conjoined gongan is introduced in order to preserve the sequence of finals prescribed by *srepegan* rules. In the conjoined gongan, which is merely (1 + b) in form, the first gatra final has to be V, of course. The other gatra has to end with 1 because it precedes the first gatra of the main gongan, also ending with 1. This gives a thoroughly ungrammatical conjoined gongan with pitches V + I.

Figure 6.12

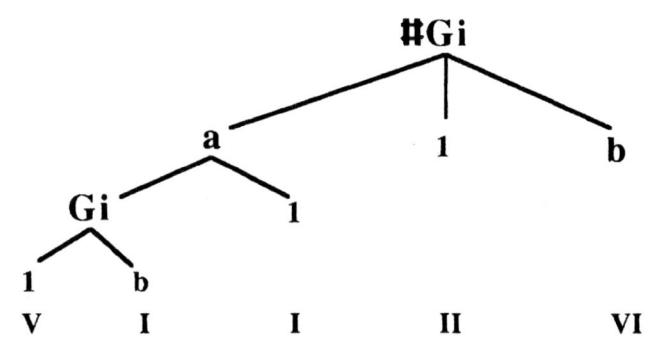

```
                          #Gi
                         /  |  \
                    a    1    b
                   / \
                 Gi   1
                /  \
               1    b
               V    I    I    II    VI
```

In the conjoining of the extra Gi notice that the realisation of a retains gatra 1 and is thus (Gi + 1).

In this particular melody a conjoined gongan is introduced also into the last gongan in order to preserve symmetry.

Figure 6.13

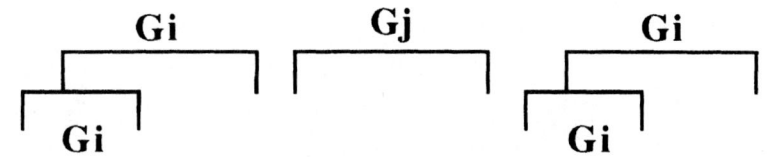

```
        Gi         Gj         Gi
   ┌─────┐    ┌─────┐    ┌─────┐
 ┌──┐                    ┌──┐
  Gi                       Gi
```

Conflict occurs here also, this time involving *pathet* rules. In the final Gi (disregarding the conjoined gongan) the first gatra final would be V, as this was the last note of Gj. By the normal *srepegan* rules the gatra finals would be:

Figure 6.14

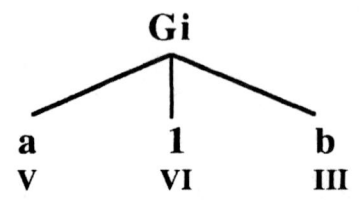

```
           Gi
         / |  \
        a  1   b
        V  VI  III
```

The rules of *pathet*, however, decree a final pitch of V for the whole sequence, not III. In this case, b ends with V; the conjoined gongan has V as its first gatra final, and having only the two components (1 + b) is grammatically completed as V + II. The note II can now be taken as first gatra final in the main gongan, which of course becomes ungrammatical in *srepegan* terms.

Figure 6.15

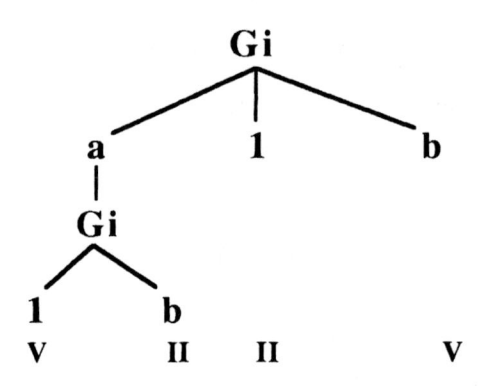

```
              Gi
            / |  \
           a  1   b
           |
           Gi
          /  \
         1    b
         V    II    II    V
```

The whole melody is now given including its sounding pitches on a pentatonically-tuned saron (Figure 6.16).

The complexity and precision of this grammar do not blind the writers to the flexibility and change which are always at work within a living system. Actually, levels of constraint are always shifting. 'A higher level constraint may be working its way down the hierarchy, as tonality seems to be doing in the West... musical systems have a living, changing quality' (32).

Figure 6.16

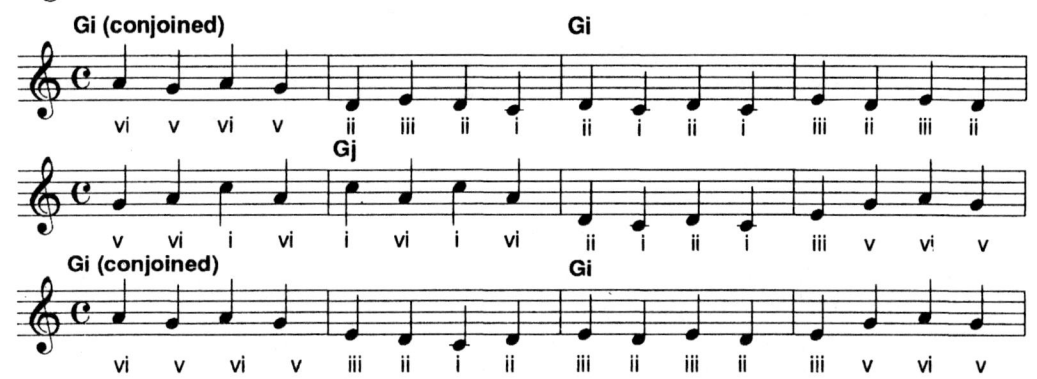

[musical notation figure with labels: Gi (conjoined), Gi, Gj, Gi (conjoined), Gi and scale-degree annotations (vi, v, iii, ii, i, etc.) beneath the notes]

6.3. Meaning in ethnic musics

6.3.1. The Beckers are resolutely syntactic and generative. Yet some ethnomusicologists admit to a semantic level in the music they study. It seems that most societies envisage extra-musical meanings in their music. Boilès (1973), after clearly distinguishing musical syntax, semantics and pragmatics, considers that 'semiotics sheds doubt on the validity of every analysis that is content with formal analysis for its own sake'. For example, a scale or a melodic formula may be simply 'the result of syntactic rules' but it may also have 'a designatum of considerable interest for the culture in which it originates'.

Western analysts have tended to avoid semantic explications of music, concentrating particularly on harmony. But harmony is itself an 'indexic sign', marking phrase and accent and thus delimiting units of meaning; Western harmony has the same function, in fact, as voice intonation in Western languages (an intuition shared with Janácek, who tried to suggest voice intonation with musical harmonies; see Karbusicky 1983).

Actually, if the universe of reference is clearly enough defined, it is usually easy to discuss the semantics of music. Balinese scales are considered appropriate to particular characters in Balinese theatre; and in the case of one repertory (the gamelan *Gambuh*) 'each scale is a signifier of which the designatum is a type of actor or action'. Similarly, if the music of the *geza* of Japanese *kabuki* theatre is considered, both timbre and melody are seen to have designata. Each instrument has its own special evocations, and for each there is a range of melodies with particular meanings. Thus the *shamisen* represents natural sounds, psychological moods or moments of time. Its range of melodies includes *yuki*, evoking snow (a natural sound); *shinobi sanju* establishes a mysterious atmosphere (a psychological mood); and *kangen* suggests a court scene of times gone by (a moment of time). A lexicon can be drawn up, linking the instruments and melodies with their respective evocations. Boilès's own fieldwork was with the Otomis in the state of Veracruz, Mexico. He found the different musical levels related to different semantic fields: 'Sequences of ordered musical pitches designate entities, while rhythmic models designate actions, and the formal structure designates a disposition of the Otomi world'. This writer reminds the semiologist that he is not concerned merely with formal analysis, but with systems of signs, and describes the kind of meaning music can have.

6.3.2. The most impressive demonstration of this is contained in Boilès's study of the 'thought-song' of the Tepehua people of Veracruz (1967). This is a type of ritual song used in a ceremony called *Halakiltunti*, 'the moving of the things', in which a spirit is summoned and enters into the body of the priest. The 'things', ritual objects, are converted to gold, marijuana is chewed and dancing ensues. Each stage of this process is accompanied by music which is considered to be song though it is chiefly played on violin and guitar. The songs are textless, but informants can always give the texts when asked. These texts cannot be sung, however; they do not fit the music. The songs are indispensable to the ritual and have a remarkable power in themselves: 'Songs associated with the marijuana spirit can induce euphoria even without actual use of the drug.'

Here, then, is a corpus of wordless music with specific meanings that can be expressed in words. Every song contains a group of 'continua' (two or more), each of which is repeated a number of times. A single continuum contains four short figures, each four semiquavers (or one crotchet) in length. Thus a continuum lasts for one bar of 4/4 time. The manner in which the four motives signify is tersely summarised.

> The first two motives of a continuum form a noun phrase, and the last two function as a verb phrase. The noun phrase consists of a noun (motive A) and a prepositional phrase or a relative clause (motive B), the latter being an imbedded sentence. The verb phrase is composed of an optional gerund, a participle (motive C), and a verb (motive D). Prepositions, adjectives, verbal adjectives, adverbs, and gerunds are denoted by the intervals which join one motive to another (272).

Linguistics and World Music

I present a graphic interpretation of this analysis.

Figure 6.17

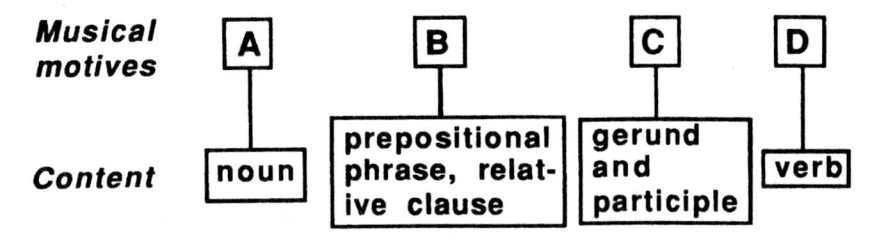

	A	B	C	D
Musical motives				
Content	noun	prepositional phrase, relative clause	gerund and participle	verb

Intervals are given in cents, rising and falling. Thus 175r, a rising interval of almost two semitones, means 'presence, act of being present'. Interpretations are also subject to context; in the position of first motive, 350f + 175r means 'divine thought'. If the interval of 175r is reduplicated, this is associated with 'giving'. 'Thus the combination of 350f + 175r + 175r forms a noun phrase which is translated "the given divine thought".' Different interpretations would apply to terminal strings.

An example is now given of the operation of this code. The analysis in cents is shown with an approximate transcription on stave. This is the first continuum of a song with three continua.

Figure 6.18

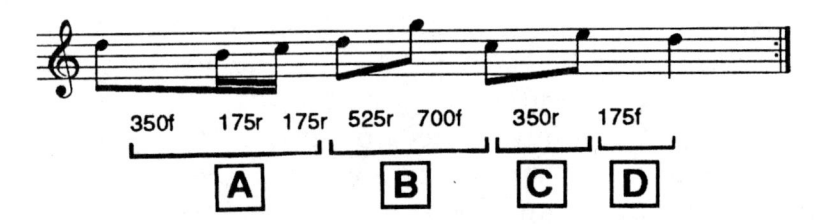

350f 175r 175r 525r 700r 350r 175f
  A   B   C   D

The whole rhythmic context has the meaning 'asking pardon'. In the noun phrase A, the noun (350f + 175r) means 'divine thought'. The reduplication of 175r signifies an adjective: 'given'. B is in this case a relative clause or embedded sentence, with the noun 525r meaning 'salutation' and the verbal adjective 700f ('being happy'). C is a participle: 350r, meaning 'arriving'. Finally the verb is represented by a tense marker only: 175f, meaning past tense. This continuum is interpreted, 'The given divine thought, whose salutation was happy, has arrived'.

It is clear from this example that the same interval can have a number of meanings according to context. In this respect Tepehua thought-song resembles the Tepehua language in which the same morpheme, in different contexts, can have several unrelated meanings. There are, moreover, similar processes of morphemic positioning and reduplication in the semantic operation of Tepehua speech.

6.3.3. A similar shamanic ritual provides the setting for a group of American Indian songs studied by Norma McLeod (1971). These Kutenai songs, like the Tepehua songs described by Boilès, are wordless, and are sung to nonsense syllables. Each song has its place in the Kutenai 'blanket rite', calling on the spirits individually and following the degree of trance of the shaman. Though they have no words they are felt to be essentially related to the spirits and the stages of the ritual; if the right song is not sung at the right time, the ritual is ineffective. McLeod has not found a grammatical structure that might lead to specific interpretations in the forms of sentences, however. The songs mean 'the power of spirits, the identification of a particular spirit, and the relationship between spirits'. The spirits come, it is said, because 'they like to hear their songs... the song is a link between the human and spiritual worlds'.

Like the spirits themselves, the songs are related in groups, each group having distinct structural features in common. There are even hints of symbolic meanings: the song for Black-tail Deer 'has a little tail on the end' (it has a coda). There is little or no structural similarity of songs in different groups. The various songs for woodpecker-spirits are all in minor thirds and isorhythmic. These structural features are sometimes realised by the Kutenai themselves; they say that the into-trance songs are 'slow and little', the out-of-trance songs 'jumpy and big'. Indeed, the latter group are faster and more rhythmic and have wider intervals.

6.4. The boundaries of semiotic studies

6.4.1. With such graphic interpretations of music we approach the far boundaries of semiotics and structuralism, and begin to pass over into other studies. Several writers have understood musical significance in social terms. Whatever the wisdom and virtue of this strategy, it shifts musical theory into the fields of sociology, psychology and anthropology and banishes the much-sought universal theory of music to an even further horizon. Certainly, a music analysis that makes reference to the kinship, social status and sex of the performer or listener cannot be considered 'neutral' or 'immanent'.

Antonin Sychra (1973) observed two kinds of rhythm in Moravian and Slovak folksongs. Some are dance-like in a fixed tempo, some declamatory and rhapsodic. Yet some songs exist in both rhythmic formats. It seems that social changes, especially the urbanisation of the peasantry, have caused dance-songs to be adapted in this way in order to provide for an individual, subjective expression instead of a collective experience. Change of social function, linked with a change in the social circumstances of the singers, can thus cause a musical change in the songs themselves.

> The semantic intention, that is, the principle producing the choice and hierarchisation of creative means, is often fatally linked to social function, as is aptly seen in the antinomy of the languorous song and the dance song of Moravia and Slovakia (33).

6.4.2. The chief advocate of a sociological view of music was John Blacking. His various publications on the Venda, which have been mentioned in Chapter 4, show that social function is a vital factor in forming music, that many purely musical features are best explained in social terms, and that just as society can change music, so musical changes can reciprocally change society. He proposes 'Cultural Analysis', the analysis of music as total cultural entity. He envisages structural oppositions which pass beyond the bounds of the purely musical and embrace the whole social event: 'tone/companion tone, tonic/counter-tonic, call/response, individual/community, theme/variation, chief/subjects etc' (1971, 104). Two pieces of music may sound alike but are classified quite differently for social reasons. Alternatively, two closely-related pieces may sound quite different.

The undoubted wisdom of Blacking's view must not blind us to its anti-theoretical tendency. This writer does not wish to see a universal theory or 'linguistics of music' because he feels that systematic theories can only falsify ethnographic data. Unfortunately, there has been something of a British fashion for the decrying of pure theory, as I have suggested above in Chapter 1.

> Methods of analysis which are used by other disciplines such as linguistics or systematic musicology, should not be applied to the Cultural Analysis of a musical tradition, since they may impose on the data a structural bias which distorts its intrinsic pattern (1971, 104).

In spite of his opposition to systematic theories, this writer sometimes uses linguistic terminology. His version of the Chomskyan ideas of competence and performance has been discussed already. In addition, he describes the musical phenomenon itself as 'surface structure' which must be elucidated with reference to a 'deep structure' of historical, political and social facts. This witty metaphor is misleading, however, for Chomsky's deep structures are purely linguistic, revealed by the kind of systematic analysis which Blacking rejects. To tell the truth, this writer is a critic of linguistic and structuralist views 'from outside'. He does not re-focus these views on a wider or a different experimental field, but on the contrary he considers them intrinsically linked to comparatively narrow fields - especially to linguistics, which is inseparable from language - and therefore deceptive in the study of music, for music is a human and cultural process.

6.4.3. The voices of reaction proved powerful, and ethnomusicologists have shown less interest in semiotics in the eighties. The problems lamented by Norma McLeod, however, problems of ethnocentricity and lack of a systematic metalanguage, continue to plague the subject. The refusal to apply rationality is not a praiseworthy denial of racism but, on the contrary, a surrender to obscurantism. Rationality is not merely a Western mythology; it is the necessary ground of all academic study, and it is still needed in the anthropological field. Without it, there can only be ethnocentrism of a much more unpleasant kind.

7

ICON, INDEX AND SYMBOL

7.1. *The semiotic theory of C S Peirce*

7.1.1. The roots of semiotics lie partly in scientific method and practical fieldwork. When Nattiez speaks of making music semiotics into a science, he recalls the scientific methodology of linguists like Harris and Bloomfield; and when ethnomusicologists like Chenoweth and Kaeppler adapt linguistic methods to practical analysis of ethnic music they recall the American tradition of linguistic study, typified by Sapir. However, semiotics has another root.

In traditional philosophy *semiotic* is a branch of epistemology, with a history going back to Aristotle and beyond. Music semiotics may be something more than an adaptation of linguistic and scientific method to music studies; it may be a theory of music with an epistemological basis of its own, not necessarily dependent on induction.

7.1.2. The writings of Charles Sanders Peirce (rhymes with verse) have been particularly influential. Because this American philosopher wrote in English there has been a tendency to use the term *semiotics* for this branch of the study, reserving *semiology* for the linguistics-based scientific branch chiefly developed by French writers (French *sémiologie*). This is a practice which I have not followed, preferring 'semiotics' for the whole field.

7.1.3. Peirce considered that semiosis, the functioning of something as a sign, was present when three things came into play: a *sign*, an *object* and an *interpretant*. A road-sign indicates the proximity of a crossroads. This sign-function requires an approaching driver to interpret the sign. There may be persons unable to interpret it thus, or who would interpret it otherwise. The driver interprets the sign - he is its interpreter, but cannot be its *interpretant* for this is defined as another sign; in this case, perhaps, a sentence in the Highway

Code. The sign-function may be summarised as, 'A means B by virtue of C'.

This suggests an infinite regression; if the interpretant is itself a sign, then in its turn it will need an interpretant. The road sign is interpreted by an official sentence; this verbal explanation is significant by virtue of a greater sign, the whole system of the Highway Code. This interpretant will need an interpretant, and so on ad infinitum. This is shown in a diagram of G-G Granger (1968, 114).

Figure 7.1

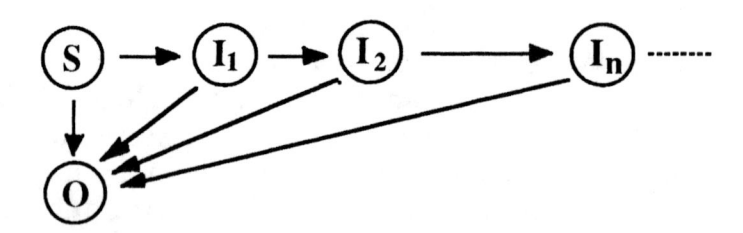

$$S \rightarrow I_1 \rightarrow I_2 \longrightarrow I_n \text{--------}$$
$$\downarrow$$
$$O$$

The interpretant, then, is not a person who interprets, but 'any sign which interprets another sign, whether that interpreting sign be a thought in somebody's mind, a written translation, a sentence spoken, or anything else that is interpretative' (Greenlee 1973, 26).

7.1.4. In his classification of signs, Peirce makes a number of threefold divisions or *trichotomies*. These are all governed by his basic ideas of *Firstness, Secondness* and *Thirdness*. It is important to get the flavour of these essential notions before embarking on Peircean taxonomy, for they are the foundations of his epistemological theory.

Firstness is the area of pure possibility. Before we can perceive a man, it is necessary that such things as men may exist, and that it is possible to perceive them.

Secondness, the most obviously 'real' plane, is the area of 'happening-to-be'; not only is it possible that a man may exist, but there happens to be a man before me now and I perceive him. 'The real is that which insists upon forcing its way to recognition as something other than the mind's creation'. This is the level of 'experience'.

Thirdness is the area of purpose, intention, relation, will, understanding, cognition. When I see that the man is the porter, that he intends to give me a message, that his arrival may interrupt my work or raise my spirits, I enter the domain of Thirdness.

In the case of a sign function, it initially appears that all three elements are on the level of Thirdness. Thus the road sign, the crossroads and the Highway Code are all real experiences which I fully understand in relation to myself.

Peirce applies this consideration, however, to a *thought* which is a sign: a dream or a scientific theory (though in a certain sense all thoughts are signs). Within the mind, 'the first, the second and the third are all three of the nature of thirds... while in respect to one another they are first, second and third. The first is thought in its capacity as mere possibility; that is, mere mind capable of thinking, or a mere vague idea. The second is thought playing the role of a Secondness, or event. That is, it is of the general nature of experience or information. The third is thought in its role as governing secondness. It brings the information into the mind, or determines the idea and gives it body. It is informing thought, or cognition' (Peirce 1931-1958, 1, >537).

Mental firstness is merely the possibility of thinking; when a thought occurs to us, this possibility is realised and we move into Secondness. But this thought is of no use to us until we have understood it and related it to other thoughts; a thought that is grasped and used has entered into Thirdness. 'But take away the psychological or accidental human element, and in this genuine Thirdness we see the operation of a sign.' This acute insight touches the heart of Peircean semiotics.

If we imagine that the sign is a thought, not in a human mind but in the mind of semiosis itself, then this sign, as an unmeaning, pre-semiotic object, inhabits Firstness (it is the possibility of signifying), the object Secondness (something-to-signify, the realisation of the sign's potentiality), and the interpretant Thirdness, since it adds understanding, relationship, purpose to the signification of the sign. Notice that all three levels, in this reading, are logical rather than mental or psychological; the interpretant is no more a human thought or mind than the sign or the object, but all are part of the structure of signification.

7.1.5. Peirce now embarks on his first trichotomy of signs. 'A sign is either of the nature of an appearance, when I call it a *qualisign;* or secondly, it is an individual object or event, when I call it a *sinsign...;* or thirdly, it is of the nature of a general type, when I call it a *legisign* (1931-1958, 2, ¶243-246). A qualisign is 'a quality which is a sign'. For example, the colour red is a sign of danger. This is true independently of any particular red object like a traffic light or fire warning, and although actual signs of danger may incorporate other signs. Thus we need to interpret an object as a traffic light before its redness signifies danger, and such interpretation may involve sign-processes other than the qualisign. Nevertheless, the redness itself, in this context and apart from the other pointers, is a qualisign.

The sinsign ('single' or 'simple' sign) is a real object or event which functions as a sign. In real life we encounter only sinsigns, for every sign must be incorporated in a sinsign to become an object of perception. The redness of the traffic light may be a qualisign, but the particular traffic light which I see at this moment is an 'individual object' and thus a sinsign.

A legisign ('a law which is a sign') is 'not a single object, but a general type which, it has been agreed, shall be significant. Every legisign signifies through an instance of its application, which may be termed a *Replica* of it... The Replica is a sinsign. Thus, every Legisign requires Sinsigns' (2, ¶246). To this Greenlee adds that sinsigns, in their turn, require qualisigns, for it is through some quality that sinsigns are understood as signs.

The legisign is best understood as a type or class of which a sinsign is token. A word or sentence of language is a legisign, for it may occur in many different places yet is always the same. When I write or speak the word 'man' it is significant not through itself, but by its paradigmatic relation to an item in the English lexicon. 'Man', the lexicon item, is a legisign, yet we never encounter it in this form; it must be written or spoken on a particular occasion, thus represented by a sinsign.

The features of Firstness, Secondness and Thirdness appear in this classification. A quality is a mere potentiality; though it can be conceived in isolation, it needs to be incorporated into some object to become real. A sinsign, being an actual object, is clearly in the realm of Secondness. Finally, classes or types are formed by the conceptualising intellect; the legisign is a creature of Thirdness.

A particular performance of Beethoven's Seventh Symphony is a sinsign; the score, or rather any score (the defining features of a score of the work, apart from any individual copy), is a legisign; the key of A major, or the instrumentation for Classical orchestra, are qualisigns. This is somewhat illuminating, in that it makes of the symphony a *logical* item not a real phenomenon. If the symphony is a legisign it can never be encountered directly, but only in the form of sinsigns, tokens of the type. A performance is indeed a sinsign, but so is an individual copy of the score; it is extremely questionable that a score is a copy of only part of the work, as is often claimed, or that the piece is 'really' present only in a performance. Every performance is a sinsign, it is true; but this is only a sign by virtue of a legisign, the symphony itself.

7.1.6. This trichotomy concerns the nature of the sign rather than the object or interpretant (because 'sign' is sometimes used to mean the whole process of signification as well as merely the thing which signifies, Peirce sometimes uses *representamen* for the latter sense). If the classification is made with regard to the object, we have 'the *rheme*, a sign which represents a possible object' (2, ¶250), 'the *dicent*, (or *dicisign*), a sign which represents an actual object' (2, ¶251), 'and the *argument*, a sign which represents a legal object' (2, ¶252). It is noteworthy that Greenlee (1973) and Karbusicky (1986) regard this as the 'interpretant classification', because the changing status of the object controls the sign's relation to the interpretant.

If my child gives a sudden cry, this may arise from physical pain. It may, however, signify other things, or nothing at all. By virtue of having a possible object, this sign (or possible sign) is a rheme. Its identification as a rheme does not depend on its signifying pain; merely on the possibility that it may signify *something*.

The dicisign is more familiar. Because it is meant to stand for a real object or event, it can be true or false. 'It *conveys* information, rather than being a sign [like a rheme] from which information may be *derived*' (2, ¶251). An ordinary proposition ('There is a man in the room') is a dicisign.

The *argument* is best represented by a logical syllogism, a condition on which such-and-such is the case. Its interpretant is then the conclusion which is intended to be drawn from the premisses which form its conditions. It must be a legisign.

7.1.7. The final classification of signs - the one most discussed in the fields of aesthetics and music - has regard to the *manner of relation to the object*. If the relation of a sign to its object is one of *resemblance*, this sign is an *icon*. A figurative painting is an icon, or the imitation of a nightingale or cuckoo by an orchestral instrument. A diagram, too, is an icon, even if it represents only logical relations; the diagram by G-G Granger of the sign function (Figure 7.1, above) is an iconic sign, though the relationships represented are intellectual rather than visual. Even an algebraic equation is partly iconic, since it represents the logical relations of the stages in deduction by groups of terms placed under each other.

Iconism is potentially present in anything, for 'anything is fit to be a Substitute for anything that it is like'. It is a feature, therefore, of the Firstness of something. Icons are divided 'according to the mode of Firstness of which they partake. Those which partake of simple qualities, or First Firstnesses, are *images;* those which represent the relations, mainly dyadic, or so regarded, of the parts of one thing by analogous relations in their own parts, are *diagrams;* those which represent the representative character of a representamen by representing a parallelism in something else, are *metaphors*' (Peirce 1940, 105).

It is noteworthy that musical signs have been thought of as images (the representations of nightingales and cuckoos) and as metaphors (see Ferguson 1973) but never, apparently, as diagrams, unless one considers a few cases of resemblance between musical forms and physical objects; the suggestion, for example, that the five parts of Stravinsky's *Canticum Sacrum* represent the five domes of St Mark's.

The second type, the *index,* 'is a sign which refers to the Object that it denotes by virtue of being really affected by that Object' (1940, 102). It is 'in dynamical (including spatial) connection both with the individual object, on the one hand, and with the senses or memory of the person for whom it serves as a sign, on the other hand' (1940, 107). The index depends on 'association by contiguity, not association by resemblance or intellectual operations'.

A bullet-hole in a glass pane is an index, signifying a past shot. The rolling gait of a man Peirce sees in the street indicates that he is probably a sailor. A rap on the door, a low barometer, a weathercock, a spirit-level, all these things are indices. A spontaneous cry is also an index, provided it arises from some cause. The direct connection of indices to objects or events gives this style of signification the character of Secondness.

The naive interpretation of music aesthetics - that music is the expression of some real emotion or other - represents music as an *indexical* sign, like a spontaneous cry. In this form, such a view is untenable. But there are other good reasons for finding indexical functions in music, as we shall see in due course.

Though onomatopoea is a kind of icon, and though Peirce finds certain iconic features in the syntax of language, and indices in formulae like demonstrative pronouns and prepositional phrases, it is clear that the linguistic sign is not typically iconic or indexical. 'Icons and indices assert nothing' (1940, 111). Consequently, these types of sign cannot be true or false, though icons may represent imaginary objects.

The third type of sign, according to this classification, is the *symbol*. This is the closest thing to Saussure's definition of a linguistic sign.

> A Symbol is a Representamen whose Representative character consists precisely in its being a rule that will determine its Interpretant. All words, sentences, books, and other conventional Signs are Symbols... [A symbol] must *denote* an individual, and must *signify* a character. A *genuine* symbol is a symbol that has a general meaning (Peirce 1940, 112).

When I say, 'Socrates is a man,' the word *man* denotes an individual, namely Socrates; but it *signifies* a general category or 'character'. The symbol, dependent on an agreed or cultural nexus apprehended by the mind, is wholly plunged into Thirdness. It signifies a category; 'not only that, but it is itself a kind and not a single thing'. Symbols are not usually invented by an individual mind, but are generated by culture. 'They come into being by development out of other signs, particularly from icons, or from mixed signs partaking of the nature of icons and symbols' (115). Their meanings change in response to social and historical pressures.

Although an interpreting mind is needed to recognize an icon or an index, the connection of sign to object is in these cases not actually established by the mind.

> The icon has no dynamical connection with the object it represents; it simply happens that its qualities resemble those of that object, and excite analogous sensations in the mind for which it is a likeness. But it really stands unconnected with them. The index is physically connected with its object; they make an organic pair, but the interpreting mind has nothing to do with this connection, except remarking it, after it is established. The symbol is connected with its object by virtue of the idea of the symbol-using mind, without which no such connection would exist (114).

Musical symbols sometimes betray their origins in indices or icons. The *reveille*, an army bugle-call, has meaning because of a 'rule that determines its interpretant'; but in the first place it was, perhaps, merely a loud clamour designed to awaken the soldiers - an indexical sign. The doleful appoggiatura had acquired a conventional expression of grief by the eighteenth century; the texts of Italian madrigals of the sixteenth century show that it was originally an imitation of a sigh - an icon.

7.1.8. Some combinations of the three trichotomies are clearly impossible. It has already been commented that an argument must be a legisign; actually, it must also be a symbol. A rheme, on the other hand (a sign of a possible object) has many possibilities: a logical term is a *rhematic indexical legisign*; a real, individual diagram is a *rhematic iconic sinsign*; a feeling of red, not realised in an object, is a *rhematic iconic qualisign*. However, there can be no such thing as a symbolic qualisign; only legisigns can be symbols. A chart can be constructed to show the possibilities of combination, based on the rule that no sign may be combined with any sign to the right and below it.

Figure 7.2

	Sign	Ground	Object
FIRST	qualisign (1)	icon (4)	rheme (7)
SECOND	sinsign (2)	index (5)	dicisign (8)
THIRD	legisign (3)	symbol (6)	argument (9)

There are ten classes of sign, represented by the combinations: 369, 368, 367, 358, 357, 347, 258, 257, 247, 147 (Feibleman 1960, 93).

7.2. The limitations of iconism

7.2.1. The idea of the iconic sign is naturally attractive to musicians. Perhaps a sad aria is meaningful because it resembles a cry of sadness. Perhaps a rapid musical passage derives its meaning from a resemblance to quick physical movement, as Hanslick thought when he found the 'dynamic properties' of reality in music. The classical theory of imitation was related to music in the eighteenth century (see, especially, Batteux 1746, summarized in Chapter 1, above), when a resemblance was suggested between certain musical styles and certain human emotions.

It is important, therefore, to consider for a moment Eco's critique of iconism (Eco 1979, 191-217). The idea that an iconic sign is 'similar' to its object, or has the 'same properties', raises a number of questions which cannot be answered without a radical modification of the idea of iconism.

If an icon has certain properties in common with its object, then its functioning as a sign has scarcely been explained: the question is, which properties? Sign and object cannot have all properties in common; this would imply a relation of *identity* rather than a sign function. Consider a drawing of a horse which is no more than a continuous black line. Visually, the drawing has nothing in common with the horse, for the horse contains no black lines. There is, however, a graphic convention which leads us to perceive a horse in a mere tracing of its outline. In any case, the 'outline' of the horse is itself a culturally encoded concept; the drawing uses a conventional method to represent a perceptive model. At every stage, culture and convention govern the act of drawing; this would make the drawing a symbol, not an icon, in Peirce's sense.

Certain relations of resemblance are even more obviously cultural. It is said that saccharine is 'like' sugar, because it shares a property of sugar: it tastes sweet. But a refined cook will assure us that saccharine is also very unlike sugar. The similarity depends on a cultural opposition (*sweet/bitter* according to Eco).

Peirce's classification of a logical diagram as an iconic symbol is obviously absurd, thinks Eco. The representation of abstract relations with spatial layouts is based wholly on convention, and every diagram must establish its own rules for the conversion of one kind of relation into the other.

Such phenomena, apparently iconic signs, are not signs at all. Kandinsky pointed out that a line can suggest force, weakness, stability, imbalance and so on. This painterly feature has been studied by the psychology of empathy *(Einfühlung)*. Actually these 'expressive' effects are merely stimulations of the nervous system, acting directly and not through any sign-function. Occasionally, a sign-function is present as well, when a certain stimulus has been culturally recorded so that part of its effect is due to a learned convention. This sign is not iconic, however.

The resemblance of a figurative painting to its subject is, somewhat surprisingly, a matter of convention, as Ernest Gombrich shows in *Art and Illusion* (1956). Constable developed a new technique for portraying light in a landscape.

> Constable's painting *Wivenhoe Park* was inspired by a poetics of the scientific rendering of reality and to us seems decidedly 'photographic', with its detailed portrayal of trees, animals, water and the luminosity of a patch of field caught by the sun. And yet we know that when his works appeared for the first time no one felt that his technique of contrasting tones was some sort of imitation of the 'actual' effects of light, but rather that he was taking a strange liberty. Constable therefore had invented a new way of coding our perception of light, and of transcribing it onto canvas (Eco 1979, 204).

Similarly, Dürer portrayed a rhinoceros covered with scales and overlapping plates. This established a convention which lasted for two hundred years. Even explorers, who had seen real rhinoceroses, had to portray them with overlapping plates because this was the only way to signify 'rhinoceros'. We accept a certain representation as true to experience because it conforms to a codified system of expectations. 'Maybe an "iconic" solution is not conventional when it is proposed, but it becomes so step by step, the more its addressee becomes acquainted with it' (Eco 1979, 204-205).

Some of the codified features of an icon represent things that are known rather than seen. A child will draw a car with all four wheels in sight. The conventional sign for the sun - a circle with radial lines emanating from it - does not resemble the 'real' sun, but it matches our awareness that rays of light emanate from the sun. At least, we *imagine* that light behaves in this way; this constitutes our 'perceptual model'.

An apparent icon may even turn out to be the object itself, rather than a representation of it. When a child pretends to shoot a pistol, gripping an imaginary butt and pulling an imaginary trigger, the action is the same as that of really firing, except that the pistol is missing. 'The red that appears in the drawing of a red flag is not "similar" to the red of the real flag: it is the same red.' These phenomena are called 'intrinsically coded acts'.

It is even tempting to reduce aspects of 'resemblance' to isolated oppositions, iconic phonemes. For example, the addition of stripes to a drawing of a horse would be sufficient, for European observers, to turn it into a zebra. If there were a society that knew only zebras and hyenas, but had never seen horses or mules, stripes would not be pertinent; some detail of body-shape would have to be selected to distinguish between a zebra and a hyena.

Such codified oppositions are called *iconic figurae*. Unfortunately, they cannot be systematically discerned for any work of art or visual representation. 'Free variants outweigh pertinent features.' Typically, an iconic sign is a complex text, hard to analyse further into *figurae*, establishing its own iconic idiolect.

Eco dismisses the iconic sign. 'Iconism is not a single phenomenon, nor indeed a uniquely semiotic one.' Indeed, Peirce's whole enterprise - the multiple classification of signs - seems ill-advised to Eco.

7.3. Expression as icon

7.3.1. Eighteenth-century writers accounted for music by the classical theory of mimesis. The significance of music was due to a resemblance to verbal intonation and to the human affections, revealing an 'affinity with the soul' (Neubauer 1986, 43). The Romantics turned to an aesthetic of expression, considering that art represented the artist's nature, rather than human nature in general. Expression is no more than a species of imitation, however; it is not an alternative to mimesis. Neubauer thinks that the belief in a mysterious affinity between emotion and musical sound was founded on the Pythagorean tradition. Because inanimate nature, the human soul and music are all rooted in numerical proportions, relations of similarity can be produced which seem hard to comprehend or analyse.

It is to be expected, therefore, that the earliest semiotic writers on music would assume it to be an iconic sign. Peirce himself seems to have taken this view (Karbusicky 1987a, 24). Charles Morris's influential *Signs, Language and Behaviour* (1946) was based on a behaviouristic view which is now unfashionable and might be thought peculiarly unfruitful for music studies.

Morris disposes of the naive form of expressionism, in which music is thought to be the expression of real emotion. 'A sign... is expressive if the fact of its production is itself a sign to its interpreter of something about the producer of the sign... [But] such "expressiveness" has nothing to do with the mode of signifying of signs, since any sign whatsoever may be expressive' (1946, 68). If I exclaim, 'I am in despair!' I make a statement about myself which, as a sign, is no different from 'I am tall'. But the listener, hearing it - especially if it is spoken breathlessly and with passion - will learn something about me with which he will empathise; my despair will have been 'expressed'. 'The expressiveness is not part of the signification of the sign in question but rather the signification of another sign, namely of a sign which consists in the fact that a certain sign is produced.' There is, then, no such thing as an 'expressive sign'. In Peircean language my exclamation may be simply a *symbolic legisign*.

The expressiveness of music clearly does not depend on the fact of its being produced; that is to say, we do not form some conclusion about the condition of the musician, merely from hearing him perform. Like a speaker, he is making a significant statement which embodies a meaning; the 'emotion' or 'expression' is somehow in the music, not in the performer. Music, then, is not 'expressive'.

7.3.2. Music can be considered a sign-language 'if the iconic sign is made central (though not all-sufficient) in the analysis' (193). Morris follows the eighteenth century in attributing this iconism to a hidden affinity between experiences of various kinds. Iconicity is 'a property of auditory and visual signs alike... A sound may be iconic of things other than sounds... There is a large agreement between persons who are asked to pair musical improvizations with persons or with paintings' (191).

However, music is not simply a tissue of symbolised emotions. 'An icon can designate, but it can also appraise or prescribe' (194). A musical work may indeed present a certain emotion or emotional process, but it may also offer a critique; the emotion may be ironical or parodistic. Even 'a command can be... signified musically by the use of sounds similar to the speech melodies of spoken imperatives'. The language of music may be 'less adequate than spoken language for some purposes of communication but more adequate for others'.

7.4. Wilson Coker on icon and index

7.4.1. Morris's ideas on music are worked out at greater length by Wilson Coker (1972). Agreeing with Morris, he declares that 'the type of sign that appears to be centrally important in art works... is the iconic sign' (1972, 30). His exposition of the theory of iconism follows Peirce; the resemblance between sign and object 'need not be extensive... being an iconic sign is a matter of degree'. He follows Morris in attributing the iconism of music to synaesthesia. Although each of the senses has its own unique field, there are certain qualities that can be perceived by several senses; the sharpness of a needle can be seen as well as felt. 'Our responses to many different stimuli, perceived by different sense organs, feel or seem to be similar... [there is] a noticeable cross-sensory participation in a common response to variegated stimuli' (56). Coker calls this 'sensory isomorphism'.

The significations of artistic icons are *values*. 'Value arises within an act, within which a property of an object or situation in relation to someone, consummates or frustrates his interest; hence, value elicits positive or negative preferential behaviour' (32). Music sets up situations in which certain outcomes are expected; these outcomes are then permitted or obstructed, causing feelings of frustration or gratification, pleasure or pain. This bears an evident similarity to life-experience; in real truth, the value of an object is in our assessment of the object, not in the object itself. Nevertheless, we are apt to say that something we value 'has value'; therefore, we may locate the signification of an artistic icon in the value which the musical gesture seems to possess.

7.4.2. In spite of this twofold approach to iconic signification - in terms of sensory isomorphism, and of values - Coker considers music to be *autonomous,* its meaning chiefly *congeneric.* 'In a work of art... there are internal relations only', he comments, quoting DeWitt Parker's *The Nature of Art* (1939). Congeneric meaning is the same thing as 'intrinsic' or 'endosemantic' meaning; one gesture 'means' another in a different part of the work, or even in another work. David Osmond-Smith calls this 'formal iconism' (see below).

Non-musical meanings, be they onomatopoeic, emotional or synaesthesic. are called 'extrageneric'. Congeneric iconism may extend to timbre; even where the musical content changes , an iconic relation may be established by selecting the same timbre.

7.4.3. The *index* is also an important musical feature for Coker.

He understands the term in Morris's rather modified sense, rather than Peirce's. An index 'focuses one's attention, attracting then directing attention; and it specifies more or less the location of an object or an event in space or time' (89). Indices are exemplified by pointing gestures (indicating the object pointed at), bookmarks (indicating a page), buoys, beacons or lighthouses (indicating sandbanks).

In music, some notes or properties are more prominent than others. '*Musical indices* are the salient points within musical gestures... [they] outline the boundaries of musical space-time... [and provide] signposts along the pathway of a gesture's sonorous motion'. In terms of pitch the first, last, top and bottom pitches, and the most dissonant and consonant intervals, may serve as indices. A simple example is given from Ernst Toch's Third Symphony, where the highest notes of each section of the phrase serve as indices of the tonal motion, outlining a descent in fourths. There are also indices of harmony, duration, tempo and intensity.

Figure 7.3

(Used by permission)

To a semiologist, certain of Coker's ideas seem confused. Undoubtedly sensory isomorphism and signs of 'value' would have to be classed as extrageneric, though Coker presents them as though they were integral to his theory of congeneric meaning. It is doubtful that musical repetitions can be regarded as signs of each other, whether iconic or no, though *variants* may be considered signs; for as Eco makes clear, a relation of *identity* is not a sign relation. This is especially true of the iconism of timbre; when Debussy presents the theme of *Nuages* again and again at the same pitch on the cor anglais, the timbre of the instrument is the same each time, like the red colour of the flag in Eco's example; it is an 'intrinsically coded act'.

Nevertheless, this early attempt marked the path for efforts in the field of musical sign-classification. Later writers have been more wary.

7.5. *'Formal iconism'*

7.5.1. David Osmond-Smith's essay on iconism in music (1972) is contemporary with Coker's, but it is considerably more sophisticated and shows a knowledge of Eco's theories.

Musical iconism in the most obvious sense 'tends to be of peripheral importance' in music. However, synaesthesia forms the basis for many musical effects, which are sometimes so vivid that the score itself seems to resemble the object; when water is represented by arpeggio figures, these *look* like waves on the page. Still, words are almost always necessary to elucidate the meaning. Only in very few cases (like Delius's *First Cuckoo*) could the signification be guessed without a verbal commentary.

Some iconic habits in music are based on synaesthesia. 'High' and 'low' notes can be used to suggest physical position or movement, but also for other oppositions like light/dark; in Handel's 'The people that walked in darkness' low pitch is used iconically.

Dynamics may be iconic, and so may timbre (some tone colours are considered 'dark').

Musical iconism is much constrained by the limitations of musical structure. 'Iconic elements... are even more subject to the formal considerations that are music's primary concern than would be the case, say, in a representative painting.' Musical icons, therefore, tend to be confined to those phenomena which are *suitable* for musical representation, especially those with repetitive rhythms like galloping horses. A single event, like the descent of the guillotine in Berlioz's *Symphonie Fantastique*, is harder to picture.

In practice most programme music tends to subordinate graphic iconism to the creation of mood. 'The tendency... is not so much to represent the aural landscape as to suggest certain emotional atmospheres or moods, whose precise dramatic significance is revealed by some metalinguistic commentary.' Consequently an evocation of a scene will omit features that are not conducive to mood; pictures of the sea 'will tend to ignore... the squawk of seagulls' (Osmond-Smith did not know Hubert Bath's *Cornish Rhapsody* which contains that very effect).

7.5.2. Music is a sign of its own style, but this signification is indexical rather than iconic. However, when another style is suggested, alien to the piece in question, by means of quotation, parody or pastiche (as in Stravinsky's *Pulcinella*), a kind of iconism comes into play which clearly illustrates Eco's dictum that the object of an iconic sign is not a referent but a 'perceptual model'. There is need for caution; some elements of this sort of iconism may not be signs at all. In the trumpet-calls of Beethoven's *Missa Solemnis* 'the melodic and rhythmic formation constitutes an iconic sign (referring to the cultural unit 'trumpet call'), the timbre of the trumpet is an intrinsically coded act'.

7.5.3. The evocation of mood is connected with the communication of emotion in music. While one should not aim at some sort of absolutism in which certain figures and styles must convey the same emotions for all human listeners, it is certainly possible to relate musical formations and affective states 'amongst a specific cultural group during a specific historical period'. This may have something to do with the connection of related processes in the physiology of the brain. Whatever the case, there seems no reason to restrict iconicity to those musical sign-processes whose interpretants can be clearly traced. 'All forms of musical communication in which the formal structure conveys to the listener something above and beyond itself would seem to be based upon iconic processes: explicitly in the case of the iconic sign, instrumentally when seeking to manipulate the social or historical connotations of a certain style or piece, and unconsciously in the case of emotive communication.'

The affective character of music is due to a socially and historically established iconism, using the fact of related processes in the brain, of which the interpreter is not consciously aware. This 'subconscious iconicity' is partly dependent on the onomatopoeic and synaesthesic images of conscious iconicity, and partly the direct product of the music as abstract form.

Osmond-Smith has moved away from the naive standpoint that icons resemble objects. With Eco, he sees that cultural conventions enter into iconism, both at the stage of the 'perceptual model' and in the formation of the sign. The world contains no objects, but only cultural units; an emotion, a mood, a parodied style, all are perceptual models which provide material for iconic representation.

This writer has, however, been no more successful than the eighteenth-century theorists in establishing a connection between the musical icon and its expression; 'subconscious iconicity' seems close to that 'affinity of the soul' which was cited by Batteux.

7.5.4. It is possible to be much more precise in speaking of internal iconism, the resemblance of a phrase to its variants within the fabric of a musical work, what Osmond-Smith calls 'formal iconism' (Osmond-Smith 1975). This can be traced according to two codes, the *stylistic*, understood and agreed by a whole social group within an extended period of time, and the *idiosyncratic,* unique to the idiolect of the piece in question. It has both paradigmatic and syntagmatic modes. Paradigmatic rules determine the extent to which sub-units can be varied within a musical unit, before iconism ceases and *dissemblance* sets in. Syntagmatic rules determine sequences of units and sub-units; some sequences are *uni-probable* (unit A *must* be followed by unit B) while others are *multi-probable* (unit A may be followed by unit B or unit C, or by any unit).

In the combination of minimal units (rhythms of a single beat, or pitch-combinations of a single interval) certain stylistic constraints come into play in progressing to the next level; for example, a conventional cadence formula is made up of certain predetermined units. Idiosyncratic constraints will prove to be of greater force, however, at the level where combinations of units begin to turn into 'themes' and thus take on an *iconic relation*.

Both rhythms and pitch-combinations can be subjected to various types of modification. In *addition* extra notes or sub-units are attached to the end of the unit. In *suppression* one or more sub-units are removed. A combination of the two devices produces *substitution;* a sub-unit is removed and replaced with a different sub-unit. Rhythmic units may be subjected to *syncopation,* or if they are syncopated, to *metric normalisation.* Both rhythms and pitch-combinations may be *re-arranged* or *retrograded. Augmentation* and *diminution* are available both for rhythms and pitches; in the case of rhythms, by the lengthening or shortening of values, and in the case of pitches, by the widening or narrowing of intervals. Combinations of pitches may be *transposed,* or *displaced* melodically (that is, shifted in pitch without change of key).

When rhythm and pitch are considered together, addition and suppression normally affect both parameters at once; if a sub-unit of pitch is removed, its rhythmic configuration usually disappears as well. The retention of a previous rhythm with a new pitch contour, or of previous pitches with a new rhythm, are exceptional cases and examples of *inter-parametric displacement.* Substitution and permutation, however, normally affect only one parameter; typically, a substituted sub-unit of pitch will conform rhythmically to the sub-unit it replaces.

Having classified the ways in which musical units may be varied, Osmond-Smith proposes the 'hypothesis' that his classification may form the basis of a methodology to measure the degree of iconic relation between musical units, and to set the boundary to iconism, where resemblance begins to fail and a new unit comes into being. He does not describe exactly how this iconic calculus could be set up.

7.6. *Music as indexical sign*

7.6.1. Unfortunately the whole business of 'congeneric' or 'formal' iconism is open to question. It is, of course, logically faulty to describe something as a sign of its own qualities. Osmond-Smith, however, having discussed the imitation of other styles, continues: 'Granted that the pastiche of an alien style is iconic, then presumably reference to the stylistic norm of one's own period is equally so.' This is to make a tree the sign of greenness, for a style can only be described as a quality of the works of a given period. But the central tenet of formal iconism - that a repetition or variation is an icon of its antecedent - is itself illogical. A literal repetition, such as the immediate reprise of the exposition in classical sonatas, bears a relation of *identity*, which according to Eco destroys the notion of iconism (Eco 1979, 192). A thing cannot signify itself. If it is objected that, since the passage and its repetition are perceived separately and successively, their relation is not exactly a relation of identity, then presumably they must be *replicas* or *specular reflections* of each other. But a specular reflection 'cannot properly be called an image... it does not stand *for* something else; on the contrary it stands *in front* of something else, it exists not instead of but because of the presence of that something'.

Perhaps it should be ruled that only *variants* of a given musical figure (not replicas) can be considered icons. But again, a difficulty arises. It may not be thought a serious matter that sign and object cannot be distinguished one from the other; but such is the case. It would be naive to assume that the *first* statement of a figure is always its standard form, the object of all subsequent 'iconic' variants. Some composers make a point of presenting their material in enigmatic form at the start, so that the standard form or 'theme' of a work seems to come near the end. Such is Bartòk's technique in his string quartets (Monelle 1968 and 1970). Often there is no one statement that can be isolated as the theme; the theme seems to emerge as a composite product of the various statements. In the first movement of Beethoven's *Eroica* Symphony, both first and last statements of the theme (Figure 7.5, a and b) contain elements which prove inessential. The theme may be a more abstract feature (c).

Figure 7.4

It seems clear that themes and their variants are 'replicas ruled by *ratio facilis*' (Eco 1979, 202). They 'reproduce certain pertinent features established by their type' and are like phonemes, for example, related to an emic model. 'Why should we not assume,' asks Eco, 'that the actual recognition of token signs is governed by a principle of similarity and is therefore an example of iconism?' Answering his own question, he shows that iconic signs are produced by rules of transformation, not by the trivial accidents of common qualities: that is to say, by *ratio difficilis*.

But musical repetitions and variants are *tokens of a type*, it seems clear. 'The presumed "iconism" that should govern the correspondence of a token to its type is not a *theorem* that semiotics could demonstrate; it is one of its *postulates*. The very notion of a sign and of its replicability... depends on postulating that such a recognition is possible... Thus a token is not a sign of its type' (Eco 1979, 203). The whole structure of epistemology is based on the relation of token to type; the very term 'sign' denotes a type of which individual signs are tokens. It would be worrying if we were obliged to see an iconic relation between every logical class and its members.

7.6.2 If one reads the eighteenth- and nineteenth-century writers on expression theory they do not, in fact, seem to speak of iconism at all. The sounds of music are 'signs of our emotions' in the sense that they *stimulate* directly the emotions they embody; there is no question of *resemblance*.

> Sounds, in melody, do not work on us simply as sounds, but as signs of our affections, of our sentiments; it is thus that they excite in us the movements that they express (Rousseau, *Essai sur l'Origine des Langues*, 1753, quoted by Karbusicky, 1986, 1).

According to Imberty, the Enlightenment writers, especially Du Bos, described the impression of music as based on 'the isomorphism of the syntactic order and the natural order of the passions, an isomorphism which is the basis of all systems of signs, at a more general level, an isomorphism which supports the very possibility of signs to signify' (Imberty 1973, 188). This was to see the indexical function as the basic mode of signification and thus to see affective expression in music as an archetypal form of sign.

The indexicality of music was considered to have its origin in the intonation of the voice. 'The intonation and colouring of the human voice are the most conspicuous forms of indexicality; they are directly connected to situation and psychic movement' (Karbusicky 1986, 61). The human voice is 'of all things most conformal to our spirits', according to Descartes. Mattheson spoke of the 'sympathetic properties of sound', both of the voice and of instruments (in the *Vollkommene Kapellmeister*, 1739), and Christian Wolff (in the *Psychologia Empirica* of 1738) located the earliest vestiges of music in interjections, which resemble animal cries as direct expressions of emotions. Rousseau agreed with this; 'exclamations, cries, groans' are traces of musicality in the basic speech of man' (Karbusicky 1986, 62).

This *Ursprache*, the original primitive speech which gave direct voice to inner feelings, was the root of music's power to convey emotion. In his *Kalligone* of 1800, Herder said that 'the power of sound, the call of the passions belong sympathetically to the whole species, to its body and spiritual life. It is the call of nature, the energy of inner movement (*Energie des Innigbewegten*)... it is harmonious movement' (quoted in Karbusicky 1987a, 28). This idea turns up again and again and gave Edmund Gurney the title for his work on music aesthetics (Gurney 1880). Schumann writes: 'That would be a poor art, that had only sounds, and no language or signs for spiritual states!' and Pozdnysev, the narrator in Tolstoy's *The Kreutzer Sonata*, proclaims: 'The music places one suddenly, instantly, in the same spiritual state in which the creator of the music found himself!' (both quoted in Karbusicky 1987a).

Even Hanslick, otherwise an opponent of the idea of emotional expression in music, admits that there is a natural connection between sounds and feelings, echoing closely the words of Herder.

> Every shaped tone carries - if only indeterminate - a semantic load... Tones possess fundamentally and individually, like colours, symbolic meaning which produces an effect outside of and primary to any artistic intention... [they have] a force, placed by nature in sympathetic association with certain moods (*Vom musikalisch-Schönen*, quoted by Karbusicky, 1987a, 28).

There is no question of resemblance; music is in dynamic connection with feeling. Karbusicky relates this to the Aristotelean ενεργεια. The sign-function of this sort of 'dynamic index' is *synergistic*, based not merely on contiguity but on contiguity-in-motion, like a chain of rafts floating on the sea which are bound to conform to the moving shapes of the waves. The directness of music, which has impressed many philosophers, its ability to accelerate the pulse or move to tears, recalls Peirce's comment on indices: 'they direct the attention to their objects by blind compulsion' (Peirce 1940, 108). This seems to answer to the experience of music in a more satisfactory way than Susanne

Langer's 'presentational symbol', which sounds like a combination of Peirce's symbol and icon; music, according to Langer, is a 'logical picture' of emotional life (Langer 1953, 222).

Music and the passions are both the 'work of nature'. Music is a sign of a natural order of which it is essentially a part; emotional life also partakes of that order. The relation of music and feeling is metonymic rather than metaphoric, indexical rather than iconic.

7.6.3. Nineteenth-century authorities tend to list the functions of music, placing the index alongside other functions. Hermann Kretzschmar finds in music (a) feelings, moods and states (that is, *indexic* functions), (b) images (*iconic* features) and (c) motives, themes, shapes, structures. These last elements are not signs at all, but are activities of abstract construction and free play which generate musical extension (Kretzschmar 1887). Hans Engel echoes this, but is more precise; he detects (a) the empty play of forms, (b) constructivist shaping, (c) affect, (d) symbol, (e) energy and (f) magic (Engel 1950). He makes no mention of iconic qualities, but he includes symbols and, as Karbusicky comments, the indexical quality is differentiated in (c), (e) and (f).

Some of the most obviously physiological and psychological effects in music, like the crescendo and the sforzando, suggest that music's indexical function may be connected with *Gestalt* theory. This was first applied to music by Ehrenfels (1978/1890). Gestalt psychologists speak of 'melodies' of thought, an idea reached by another route by Asafiev (Asafiev 1976/1942, 931; see below, Chapter 9).

7.6.4. Symbols - in Peirce's sense - also appear in music, but here one has to confess, with Karbusicky, that logically-defined qualities 'never appear pure'. Even a straightforward musical icon, like the call of a cuckoo, may be connected to an indexical function (it may proclaim, 'Spring is here!') The cuckoos and quails in Beethoven's Pastoral Symphony have also a symbolic function'; they symbolize the whole of nature and the emotions associated therewith. In any case, symbols (as already explained) often have their origin in icons. The 'sighing' appoggiatura, it has been commented, was originally an icon of a real sigh. As early as the lament of Dido in Purcell's *Dido and Aeneas* (1689) it had become a conventional symbol of grief, and it was freely used for centuries with this meaning, even in instrumental music. It survives in the 'servitude' motive in the

Ring. Its iconic associations have been forgotten; it has become part of the 'language' - a symbol.

The trumpet-calls in the *Missa Solemnis*, discussed by Osmond-Smith, are examples of symbols that have been culturally transferred. A striking example of this is given by Philip Tagg (below, pp 287-290).

All these examples contain much that is indexical, however. The 'servitude' motive has the chromatic harmony and dark instrumental timbre which are 'naturally' associated with solemn and ominous feelings. Musical sign-functions are always mixed (Monelle 1991c, on which the remainder of this chapter is based).

7.7. *Rheme, legisign and sinsign in music*

7.7.1. Is music qualisign, sinsign or legisign? There has been much agonizing about the nature of music, and especially the status of the *score*. Western analysts always work with scores; but it has been objected that 'the graphic element of the musical sign is not music, not even its reflection, but only an *aide-mémoire*. Music only exists in the state of sonorous manifestation' (R Siohan, quoted by Nattiez, 1975, 110). If the 'state of sonorous manifestation' means performance then analysts have a difficult problem, for all performances are different. Yet the score does not record the whole of music; some knowledge of performance practice is needed in order to decode it.

Célestin Deliège takes a different view. The Western tradition, with its complex polyphony based on rhythmic synchronization, needed the score for its development; our musical culture is essentially notational and proves, not 'l'insuffisance de la partition' but 'la puissance de l'écriture' (Deliège 1987, 243).

The question is further complicated by considering oral traditions in which it is possible to speak of music items which may be performed on many occasions without losing their identity, but not of scores; and of contemporary aleatory works, in which the score provides only part of the information necessary for a performance of the piece, and every performance differs radically from all the others. The problem of identifying the 'physical mode of existence of the musical work' (Nattiez 1975, 109, quoting Etienne Gilson) has all the marks of a logical problem treated, mistakenly, as though it were a theoretical or empirical problem.

7.7.2. If music is a sign, then each individual performance is unquestionably a *sinsign*. In Peircean theory some sinsigns are unique, others tokens of legisigns. The latter variety can easily be recognized, for they are grouped into classes; all traffic-lights, all pronunciations of the word 'man', resemble each other. All performances of a given musical work, then, since they resemble each other closely, are sinsigns of the same legisign. Legisigns are logical entities, never encountered empirically. The score, therefore (each individual score) is also a sinsign, defining the pertinent features necessary for an identification of the piece. *Pace* Gilson, the piece has no 'physical mode of existence'; its mode of being is logical, not physical.

7.7.3. The individual work is not the only example of a musical legisign. All works contain features in common with other works, with all the works of the one composer, with all works of a period and place, with all Western music, (or Indian, or Luganda). There are, then, *stylistic* legisigns. Each of these signs has an interpretant-relation to the next; the 'language' of a whole culture interprets the style of an epoch and the style interprets the work. Each stage of the process of identification involves qualisigns; but while some qualisigns are peculiar to this one work and no other, others are qualities of both the work and its style, and a few of work, style and language.

Figure 7.5

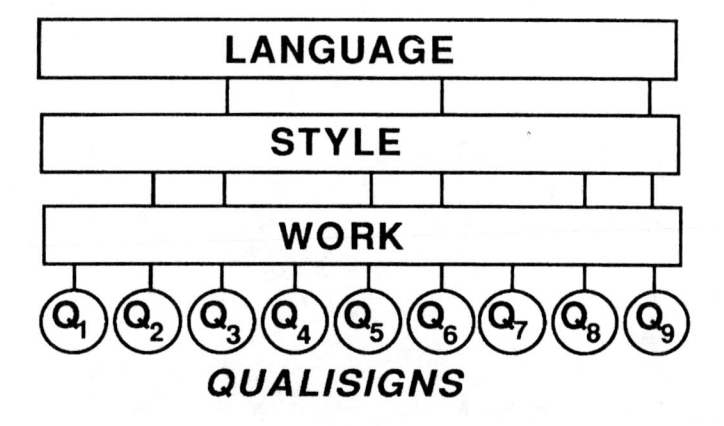

```
        ┌─────────────────────────┐
        │       LANGUAGE          │
        └─────────────────────────┘
           ┌────────────────────┐
           │       STYLE        │
           └────────────────────┘
             ┌──────────────┐
             │     WORK     │
             └──────────────┘
              Q₁ Q₂ Q₃ Q₄ Q₅ Q₆ Q₇ Q₈ Q₉
                    QUALISIGNS
```

At each level, the level above acts as interpretant. This is a modified form of the interpretant chain of Granger (Figure 7.1).

To locate a work of art in the area of the legisign is to attribute to it Thirdness. This is logically satisfactory but intuitively a little troubling. There is something pristine and naive about the artwork that seems out of place in the fully-digested world of Thirdness; there is something *first* about art. 'Notice the naivete of firstness,' Peirce wrote to Lady Welby. This may be due to the classification according to *object,* which is dealt with below. It may also be connected with the multi-level interpretant structure of the artistic sign. It is easy to imagine that the *work* (rather than the individual performance) is a sinsign, interpreted by the legisign of style, as though the work were a unique and actual event or thing (whereas, of course, it is a class of events or things). In this case the sonorous object - the material reality of a performance - would become a qualisign. This seems to be Tarasti's view: 'In the lowest musical dimension (that of a musical work)... any musical "unit" or "member" in the syntagm has its own legisigns, which have served as models or types for its creation, for its particular shape as a sinsign, and for its qualisigns - i.e. its concrete, aural qualities' (Tarasti 1987, 446). Treating the *work* as a sinsign brings it one level nearer to the vernal infinities of Firstness, and gratifies those people, like Gilson and Nattiez, who would like to attribute a 'physical mode of existence' to the artwork. But it is illogical, and will not do.

7.7.4. Peirce's classification according to the object (*rheme/dicent/argument*) is discussed in my article in *The International Review of the Aesthetics and Sociology of Music* (1991c). Karbusicky finds this distinction particularly intractable; it is 'above all logically conceived. In order for this to accommodate music, an art form which lacks concepts, one would have to consider very distant parallels' (Karbusicky 1987a, 25). The parallels may not be so distant.

It will be recalled that a rheme is a sign of a possible object; a dicent of a real object; and an argument of a legal object. It is easy to find common ground between Peirce's 'possibility' and the idea of *virtuality* which Susanne Langer uses to characterize aesthetic expression. If the two could be equated, then the parallel sought in vain by Karbusicky may be at hand. Unfortunately Langer takes an 'autonomous' view of music and does not acknowledge its indexic character. She accepts its affinity with poetry but denies its representative or narrative function.

If, however, the object of the musical sign is an indexed sequence of emotions and moods, there are two considerations to be taken into account: (a) this sequence is imaginary, and (b) it inhabits a dynamic world which moves, changes and reaches a conclusion. Viewed in this light, music has much in common with fictional narrative. Perhaps it is to be expected that a work lasting forty minutes, if we admit that it has an affinity with poetry, begins to resemble Byron's *Don Juan* rather than Herrick's *To Daffodils*. Music generates 'virtual time', as Langer says; but like a novel, it also tells of 'virtual events'. 'The events in a novel are purely virtual events, "known" only to virtual people' (Langer 1953, 295).

Virtuality, in the aesthetic sense, is not possibility *tout simple*. Though the events of fiction are not real events, they have the quality of *verisimilitude*. This means, not merely that they are 'like' life, but that the artist has used skill to persuade us that life is like this; he sets out, not only to picture life but to modify our conception of it. In a certain sense, the novelist portrays life as it 'might be'; he portrays its possibilities rather than its actualities.

> The 'livingness' of a story is really much surer, and often greater, than that of actual experience. Life itself may, at times, be quite mechanical and unperceived by those who live it; but the perception of a reader must never fall into abeyance... Virtual events, however subdued, have character and savor, distinct appearance and feeling-tone, or they simply cease to exist. We sometimes praise a novel for approaching the vividness of actual events; usually, however, it exceeds them in vividness' (Langer 1953, 292).

The curious and correct implication of this is that much bad art is 'truer to life' in a trivial sense, because it cannot heighten our perception of life. The emotional trajectory of many student compositions is lukewarm and incoherent; but life is often like that, too.

Charles Batteux called art 'a lie, with every semblance of truth'; and Schiller spoke of *Schein*, semblance, Konrad von Lange of *Scheingefühl*, seeming emotion. The novelist sets out, not merely to communicate a possible world, but to bring to life a world that is apparently real. It would be easy to communicate all the information of *Anna Karenina*, including descriptions of emotions, without eliciting any sympathy or moving the reader in any way. Synopses of operas are like this - this is why they are so tedious to read. The world of the artwork is much more: it is a *seeming real* world. If the artistic sign has for object a chain of heightened possibilities, in that it portrays emotions in their most possibly-intense form, then it is also a very particular kind of rheme, for it is a sign of a virtual object, that is, a seeming-real object.

On the manifestation of a phenomenon that serves as an object for a rheme (a 'happening-to-be'), the rheme becomes a dicent, a sign of a real object. But the artistic rheme has within it a seeming-phenomenon which gives it already the character of a dicent; as we perceive the level of virtuality, we observe the rheme's conversion into a *seeming-dicent*. Art then, is the condition of a rheme which governs its transformation into a seeming-dicent.

7.7.5. One can go further than this, for the seeming reality portrayed by a literary narrative has its own inner logic which is, in fact, different from that of real life. Real events have causes and consequences which can be described by logical discourse; this kind of discourse is classed as *argument*. These causes and consequences are apparently present in the seeming reality presented by fiction, but in fact the course of events is shaped by another kind of logic, that of narrative. For this reason we can often predict the outcome of a story, or at least perceive a hierarchy of probabilities which have nothing to to with the probabilities of life. A certain outcome is 'inevitable' or 'telling', another is 'sentimental'. When Dickens wrote the alternative ending to *Great Expectations* (in which Pip and Stella were finally united), people saw that it was less satisfactory and that the original unhappy outcome was truer to the tale, more in keeping with the stylistic and emotional tone of the novel. Beethoven detached the *Grosse Fuge* from the Quartet in B flat, Op 130, because he realised it was the wrong conclusion to the other movements. Bartòk began an exuberant quick finale to his Sixth Quartet, but abandoned it and wrote a desolate slow movement when he understood the emotional direction of the rest of the work.

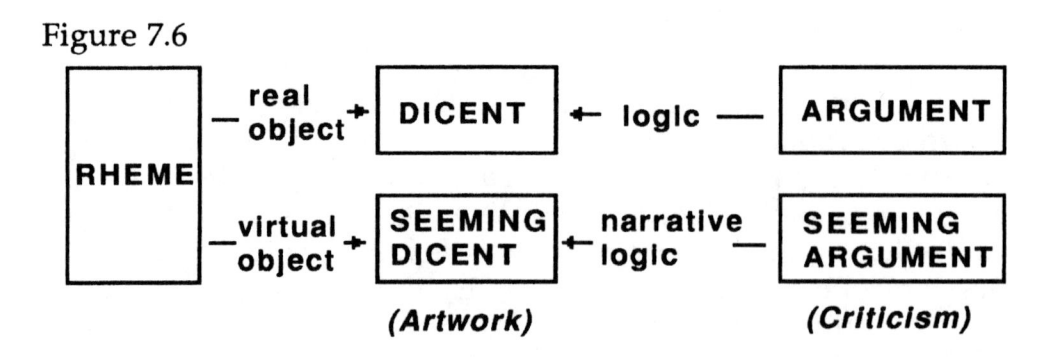

Figure 7.6

```
                  real                                
          ─ object ─► DICENT  ◄─ logic ── ARGUMENT
RHEME                                                 
          ─ virtual ─► SEEMING ◄─ narrative  SEEMING
            object     DICENT     logic   ── ARGUMENT
                      (Artwork)           (Criticism)
```

The sort of discourse which discusses this inner aesthetic logic, as opposed to phenomenal logic, is called *criticism*. If fictional narrative is seeming-dicent, then criticism is surely *seeming-argument* (Figure 7.6). If music is understood as fictional emotional narrative, then its participation in the working of *Schein* gives it resonances in each part of the object-trichotomy. For this reason, music criticism is not just analysis, but purports to trace emotional trajectories and patterns of probability and inevitability.

7.7.6. For Peirce, a rheme may afford information - it may signify a real object - but it is not so interpreted. The meaning of this is clear for literary and visual art; David's *Oath of the Tennis-court*, and his portrayal of Napoleon, may be treated as having real objects. But this is to reduce them to the level of mere illustration; as paintings, they are interpreted as rhemes rather than dicents. A book of history or biography may be praised as an accurate account, but this is not to praise its artistic qualities. Paradoxically, portrayals of real objects must be treated as seeming-dicents and discussed with seeming-arguments if they are to be considered as art, though in another sense they are real dicents.

Music, however, can never function as a real dicent. It manifests to the full the Firstness of the rheme. Nor is music only a matter of virtual *time*; as emotional fiction, it expresses virtual objects and virtual events; it even performs the 'virtual gestures' which Langer finds in dance (1953, 178).

7.7.7. The musical work, in its most typical form, is a *rhematic indexical legisign*; the actual peformance, or a copy of the score, is a *rhematic indexical sinsign*. Within its texture are to be found qualisigns of theme, rhythm, harmony, style, evocation, some of which may function iconically or symbolically. The tendency to regard the work as a sinsign, which is seen in Tarasti, is partly due to its functioning as a manifestation of style, as though it were a single event related to a category of events; and partly to its pervasive odour of Firstness, caused not by its mode of signification but the profound virtuality of its object and its incapacity to function as dicent or argument.

Peirce was certainly the most adventurous logician of our age. His ideas are still discussed, even by the anthropologically-minded writers who find his work too limited, too confined to pure theory. A systematic application of his semiotic theory to music produces, at least, a definition of the musical work and a justification of the activity of music criticism, which cut through the knots and tangles of much confused polemic. Cultural, political and moral viewpoints change, but logic is indispensable and Peirce is a better guide than most.

8

SEMANTICS AND NARRATIVE GRAMMAR

8.1. Music and semantics

8.1.1. If music is a sign with an identifiable object, as Peircean theory seems to suggest and Karbusicky intends us to think, then it ought to be possible to discuss musical semantics, the machinery and patterning of musical meaning. Indeed, intuitive and heuristic musical commentary has always done so. Music is regularly described as 'searching', 'affirmative', 'grand', 'heroic', 'lamentation', or given metaphoric interpretations: 'Night winds sweeping over churchyard graves' was Anton Rubinstein's description of the Finale of Chopin's Sonata in B flat minor.

Since music moves forward in time, a systematic semantic analysis is bound to resemble a *narrative* description. The treating of music as narrative is a very old habit; it was an established attitude in the nineteenth century.

8.2. The historicity of semantic accounts

8.2.1. According to Anthony Newcomb, any analysis of Romantic music which ignores the semantic and narrative aspects is simply unhistorical (Newcomb 1984).

Schumann's Second Symphony is often considered deficient by modern analysts, who are preoccupied with purely formal matters. Newcomb points out, however, that contemporary critics praised the work for its working out of an inner programme; they felt that its musical unity could only be understood by considering the signification and metamorphosis of its themes.

Speaking in general of the symphony genre in Schilling's *Enzyklopädie der gesammten musikalischen Wissenschaften* of 1838, Gottfried Wilhelm Fink compared it to a 'dramatically constructed *Gefühlsnovelle*'; and Schumann himself said, 'When I play through Schubert, it is as though I were reading a novel of Jean Paul composed into music' (Newcomb 1984, 234). In Schumann's Second Symphony contemporaries would have found a 'plot archetype' that was familiar from many other works, identified as 'suffering followed by healing or redemption'. For this reason - and not because of any matters of abstract form - the work was usually compared to Beethoven's Fifth. Ernst Gottschald in a review of 1850 finds that the *Grundidee* of the whole composition is 'struggle leading to victory', and he accounts for the unconventional form of the finale by tracing a gradual emergence and crystallization of the main themes. Newcomb himself explains the apparent incoherence of this finale by showing within it a dramatic development that even includes references to other music, notably Beethoven's song cycle *An die ferne Geliebte* (Newcomb 1984, 243-247). Not only does the movement make sense as a piece of emotional fiction, but it also parallels a development in Schumann's life at the time - his illness and depression of 1845, and his eventual recovery.

8.2.2. In fact, Ludwig Finscher condemns 'the habit, even in current musicological practice, of avoiding the interpretation of content by falling back on mere description of form, with a concomitant relegation of questions of content to the realm of the ineffable' (in an article in *Über Symphonien: Festschrift Walter Wiora*, 1979, quoted by Newcomb, 1984, 248). Semantic analysis of Romantic works is not fanciful; on the contrary, neglect of the semantic dimension is historically unsound.

8.3. Grammar and design in Beethoven

8.3.1. Newcomb avoids the technical language of semiotics. There is another semantic/narrative analysis, however, by a leading semiologist, David Lidov.

The popularity of the *Allegretto* from Beethoven's Seventh Symphony is due, perhaps, to the extreme formal simplicity of this movement, joined to its evident profundity. It was the subject of one of Berlioz's perceptive descriptions; again, the contemporary sensibility turned to drama and narrative in explaining musical structure.

> The rhythm consists exclusively of a dactyl followed by a spondee...
> It first occurs in the lower strings of the violas, cellos and double basses, marked *piano*; with the intention of being repeated shortly there-

after in a *pianissimo* full of menlancholy and mystery. From there it passes to the second violins while the cellos chant a kind of lamentation in the minor mode; the rhythmical phrases rising continually from octave to octave, and thereby arriving at the pitch of the first violins. These, by means of a crescendo, transmit it to the woodwinds in the upper region of the orchestra where it then explodes in all its force. Thereupon the melodious plaint, being stated with greater energy, takes on the character of a convulsive lamentation; irreconcilable rhythms agitate painfully one against another - these are the tears, the sobs, the supplications, in short, the expression of unlimited grief and of a devouring form of suffering.

But a gleam of hope has just appeared; these agonizing accents are followed by an airy melody: pure, simple, soft and resigned - patience smiling at grief...

The orchestra, after a few alternations reminiscent of anguish and resignation, as if fatigued by such a painful struggle, presents only fragments of the original theme and dies away exhausted. The flutes and oboes take up the theme with a murmuring voice, but they lack the strength to finish it: and the ending falls to the violins in a few barely perceptible pizzicato notes. After this with a flicker of fresh animation, reminding one of the flame of a lamp about to die out, the woodwinds exhale a profound sigh upon an indecisive harmony and all is silence.

8.3.2. It is extraordinary that the unusually schematic structure of the movement does not emerge from Berlioz's analysis at all. It is basically a set of variations, interrupted twice by an episode chiefly in the tonic major. Yet Berlioz tells the story of a grief that rises to almost unbearable expression, gives way to a serene hope, and finally sinks exhausted. Apparently there are two processes at work to give shape to this music, one connected with musical syntax and traditional formal procedures, the other arising from the emotional trajectory which Beethoven chose to compose into the work.

These two processes Lidov calls *grammar* and *design*. A purely grammatical analysis would concentrate on the union of two forms, variation form and ABA song-and-trio form, allowing for a few unaccountable aberrations like the appearance of a fughetta. None of the music's unique and personal features would be explained by such an analysis; 'grammar is primarily social' (Lidov 1981, 154).

Some aspects of the 'meaning' of the piece might be suggested, like the contrast of minor and major and the steady crescendo. But the most significant underlying processes have nothing to do with grammar; they are closer to semantic processes. If the movement is considered, not as a grammatical syntagm but as a discourse, then the ability of music to relate to outside reality - its ability to be 'about' something - is accounted for in a way that is intellectually acceptable. In verbal language, grammar permits predicative statements which have referential 'meaning'. But musical grammar sets up no such possibilities. The patterns of linguistic discourse, on the other hand, appear to be more of a stylistic matter; while musical discourse-patterns are the basis of music's eloquence.

8.3.3. The processes in question - here Lidov draws on the ideas of Lévi-Strauss, especially those expounded in his analysis of Ravel's *Boléro* (in *L'Homme Nu*) - are those of opposition and mediation. In an initial presentation, two opposed principles are set up; in an intervening sub-structure, their reconciliation is prefigured; finally they are mediated, though deeper levels of abstraction and intellectualization are suggested, the whole discourse being framed in such a way that its sign-function is clarified, as though it were placed within inverted commas.

8.3.4. The opening of the movement - the theme of the variations, and Berlioz's dactylic/spondaic rhythm, 'full of melancholy and mystery' - is dark and deliberate, homogeneous, with the slightly macabre voicing of violas, cellos and basses (Figure 8.1). Its marchlike step seems funereal (or pavane-like, Lidov omits to say). The melodic austerity and the absence of ornament indicate a kind of nobility; 'from the courts of Austria to the salons of Paris, we find ubiquitous the paradox of social manners that the conduct of conversation even about the warmest, loftiest, and most radical ideas was expected to be cool, elegant and restrained... the suppression of spontaneous emotion in voice or gesture was a point of honor and duty' (Lidov 1981, 150).

Figure 8.1

The second version of this theme introduces a contrasting feature, a melody for cellos and violas in unison, Berlioz's 'lamentation'. It is a 'richly ornamented line... [with] a complicated and almost improvisatory rhythm' (Figure 8.2). Ornament is 'a sign of eloquence of expression. It represents the freedom of the musical line to give voice to the passions which motivate it'. The basic opposition of the movement presents itself as two ways of responding to sadness: 'its ornamented melody - elaborate, eloquent, confessional - laments. Its plain march, stoic and taciturn, intends to hold its tongue, to keep quiet'.

Figure 8.2

The series of repetitions of 'march' and 'lamentation' then proceeds according to a pattern. Each time an instrument or combination of instruments plays the march, it passes into the lamentation in the next variation; initially violas and cellos, then second violins, first violins and winds.

The A major interlude (at bar 101) partly mediates the opposition of the first section, since the melody is played simultaneously in plain and ornamented form: plain on the clarinet, while the violins add a figured version, elaborating the theme in broken chords (Figure 8.3). But this is no more than 'an insubstantial space of ephemeral feeling'; the non-structural key (C major, the relative, would have been more 'grammatical'), the harmonically perverse ending with a transition to F major, show that this passage is ultimately irrelevant. Its almost whimsical design yields finally to 'the harsh reality (grammar) of the A minor theme'. The resolution of conflict is no more than a fantasy; 'another resolution must be won on home territory'.

Figure 8.3

The true mediation begins with the return of the march at bar 150. The sedate A minor theme is in the bass, stationary on E; the 'lamentation' is played by a flute, two clarinets and an oboe, depersonalized and sphinx-like. In between, the violins and violas exchange semiquaver figures which defuse the tension of this tragic statement (Figure 8.4). This neutralizing of individual characters 'mollifies the contrasts which had seemed so striking... While the sixteenth notes release tension in higher speed, the dynamic energies of the Allegretto are waning'. The mediation of oppositions by means of the work's design constitutes a meaningful manoeuvre comparable to the bringing together of subject and predicate in a linguistic expression. Finally, the extrinsic meanings attributed to the opposed terms (aristocratic restraint; tragic expression) become redundant; by the shifting of its oppositions into unity and agreement, the music takes on the character of a sign.

Figure 8.4

There is a more radical shift in store. Having allowed the music to 'speak' by moving its oppositions into unity, Beethoven steps outside the persona of the author or speaker in this discourse to thematize the semiotic process itself. The fughetta, which Berlioz does not mention, is obviously a variation on the march and its lamenting adversary, but it lacks the character of both. It 'neither suffers nor expresses: it plays; it abstracts. Its tone is neutral... Now the music, in the most exacting sense, becomes a sign. It stands for something which is absent'. In the climax there is a noisy reminder of the original theme, now bereft of its mystery.

Even the major-key interlude, which now reappears in part, loses its power to modulate and wander tonally; it is a mere reference. Finally, the theme is broken up into two-bar fragments, descending step by step through the orchestra. 'The theme here is simply the original, stolid march, but in its progressive descent in register it has the effect of a lament.' This is mediation, but mediation of a new kind, because the tone is now abstract; the fughetta has transported the whole discourse away into a world of abstract reference and memory.

There have been two significant shifts in this piece. The first is a normal aspect of narrative structure: oppositions are presented, then mediated. The second is a shift within the semiotic process itself. The author speaks of a tragic drama; but then the author disappears, leaving signs that must speak for themselves. And lastly, the musical sign is framed or isolated with six-four chords, one at the start, one at the end. Nothing could be more ungrammatical, more clearly a facet of design; in a movement that is mostly so deeply embedded in simple grammar, design is given the first and last words.

8.3.5. When Lidov speaks of 'march' and 'noble' style, he seems to demonstrate the validity of Newcomb's premisses for the Classical style, as well as for Schumann; that is to say, you cannot fully understand Classical music without knowing the semantic world of contemporary culture.

However, he also begins to approach the 'intonation theory' of Boris Asafiev, explained in the next chapter. Indeed, Marta Grabócz uses similar terms in her analysis of Liszt (Grabocz 1986), which is expressly based on intonation theory. Like several other analysts of this type, Lidov makes no mention of Asafiev; the Russian writer is still little known in the West.

8.4. Topic, rhetoric and structure in Classical music

8.4.1. The most systematic delineator of the Classical style is even more closely allied to intonation theory than is Lidov, but like the Canadian, he makes no reference to Asafiev. Kofi Agawu makes use of two semantically-oriented methodologies in showing the interworking of design and structure in a group of chamber works by Haydn, Mozart and Beethoven.

8.4.2. Classical music is peculiarly suitable to demonstrate the action of expressive topics; baroque pieces tended to stick to a single topic, but variety was in the essence of Classical style. Furthermore the topics themselves had not begun to dissolve into private and personal expressions.

Agawu takes his list of topics from Leonard Ratner's *Classic Music: expression, form and style* (1980). He omits a few of Ratner's topics, but nevertheless manages to isolate twenty-seven topics.

1 alla breve	15 Mannheim rocket
2 alla zoppa (syncopated)	16 march
3 amoroso	17 minuet
4 aria	18 musette
5 bourrée	19 ombra
6 brilliant style	20 opera buffa
7 cadenza	21 pastoral
8 sensibility (*Empfindsamkeit*)	22 recitative
9 fanfare	23 sarabande
10 fantasy	24 sigh motif
11 French overture	25 singing style
12 gavotte	26 *Sturm und Drang*
13 hunt style	27 Turkish music
14 learned style	

Thus, the opening of Mozart's 'Prague' Symphony leads from French overture into sensibility, followed by singing style and hints of learned style and fanfare.

8.4.3. This begins to read like a musical lexicon. The trouble with such an approach is that musical syntax remains unaccounted for; topical references are not arranged into coherent syntagms, as are the words of a language. Yet the musical sign is pre-eminently a syntactic form. This was the chief criticism of Deryck Cooke's system in *The Language of Music*.

8.4.4. Agawu's strategy to overcome this difficulty is to consult a different tradition, the application of rhetorical categories to music. Johann Mattheson (in *Der vollkommene Capellmeister*, 1739) proposed a structural model for a vocal composition, using terms derived from rhetoric.

Exordium-Narratio-Propositio-Confirmatio-Confutatio-Peroratio

Some of these categories are specific to vocal music, and others are dispensable. Clearly the 'exordium' is an invariant element, however, as well as the 'peroratio' - the beginning and the end. This analysis is discussed at greater length in Bent 1987, 6-8.

Writers were clear that the statement of an idea was distinct from its elaboration, and that the ending of a piece was a matter of more than grammatical closure, but needed rhetorical expansion. Agawu compares this view with the three elements of the Schenkerian *Ursatz*, the two-voice structure common to much tonal music, characterized by the harmonic movement I-V-I and the melodic progression 3-2-1. This model, usually considered an abstract grammatical feature, is 'necessarily an instance of a rhetorical strategy'.

Figure 8.5

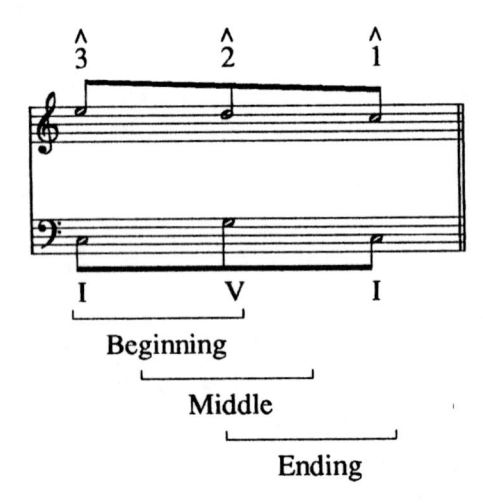

$\hat{3}$ $\hat{2}$ $\hat{1}$

I V I

Beginning

Middle

Ending

8.4.5. In his definition of *beginning* Agawu quotes Edward Said's *Beginning: Intention and Method* (New York, 1975). The beginning is 'the point at which, in a given work, the writer departs from all other works... Beginning is the first step towards the intentional production of meaning.' Thus, a mere introductory flourish or *Eingang* is not the beginning. The beginning proclaims the material and intent of the piece, and foreshadows its overall structure. 'The features of the smaller piece are then mapped onto that of the larger one.' Consequently, the beginning will itself have a beginning, middle and end, though it has to be open-ended, able to lead into its own continuation.

A *middle* is a sign 'whose dependent status is uppermost... all middles are, on the deepest level, dominant prolongations'. Rather than presenting their own ideas, they are commentaries on previous ideas. They are characterized by process, and are often built on a circle of fifths. Middles are open at both ends.

The end uses rhetorical devices to emphasize the close, 'notably repetition in various dimensions and on various temporal levels'. It is open at its beginning. It is important to see that each of these elements is a *rhetorical* sign; while beginnings normally come at the beginning, it is possible for the beginning to be a rhetorical end (Haydn's String Quartet in D, Op 64 No 5, is cited), or for the middle to contain a rhetorical beginning, as when sonata movements contain a new theme in the development section. Furthermore, the beginning-middle-end paradigm is valid for the shortest syntagms, as well as whole movements. It may equate to exposition-development-recapitulation, but the exposition alone must have a middle and an end, and even the initial statement of theme must have the same tripartite structure, perhaps in just a few bars. As was shown in the Schenker *Ursatz*, the three elements usually overlap.

8.4.6. If the extroversive content of Classical music be revealed by topical reference on the level of surface design, and the introversive structure be investigated in Schenkerian terms and expressed according to the beginning-middle-end paradigm, then we might expect that design would reflect structure; that is, that important structural points would be marked by notable changes of topic. But in fact, Classical form is at its most expressive when the two levels are in *disagreement;* 'the basis of any expressive structure must be premised on the noncoincidence of domains'.

Beethoven's String Quartet in A minor, Op 132, is a remarkable example. The harmonic structure of the first movement shows a 'high level of continuity', but the topical design continually fails to articulate the main structural points. The relation between domains is 'one of disjunction, a disjunction whose rhetorical force transcends the normative disjunction between domains that lies at the heart of every expressive structure'.

This may be shown with a short passage, bars 19-22 of the movement (Figure 8.6). The three topics in play are 'fanfare', 'sensibility' and 'cadenza'. However, the harmonic event of these bars is a shift from the Neapolitan chord on B flat to a dominant chord (on E), via the 6/4 chord. The *fanfare* topic is clearly presented by the instruments in unison, but is in the most unlikely harmonic position, on the Neapolitan chord. This is followed by a chromatic insertion to reach the 6/4 chord; the topic of *sensibility*, characterized by sighing appoggiaturas, enters just after the bass move from B flat to A, and *cadenza* sets in as the chromatic shift reaches F, just before the arrival on the second inversion. This exemplifies in miniature the dialogue of structure and design that permeates the movement, as well as much late Beethoven.

Figure 8.6.

[musical notation: Allegro, bars 19-22, transitioning to Adagio]

8.4.7. As an example of the functioning of all levels, both introversive and extroversive (and incidentally, one in which the levels are in better agreement), let us take the opening of Mozart's String Quintet in D, K 593. This is an extract in which the harmony quite clearly states the tonic chord, then moves away towards supertonic and subdominant, then returns to a rhetorical extension of the tonic. That is to say, it has a discernible beginning, middle and end (Figure 8.7).

The rhetoric of closure brings out a topic different from the rest of the passage: a lyrical melody over static accompanying chords, the topic of 'singing style'. At the centre of the passage is evidently another topic; Agawu follows Ratner in calling this a 'fanciful roulade', not a topic from our list. Perhaps it could be classified as 'cadenza'.

The little flourish of a trill and a dotted figure at the beginning suggest the 'march' topic, though the motion together of the first violin and first viola also suggest a horn-call, the viola part shaped liked a fanfare. At this rapid tempo the short upbeat, staccato, on dominant harmony, also hints at a bourrée.

A Schenkerian graph of this passage would show a melodic descent from 3 to 1 over a simple I-V-I cadential progression. This already suggests the beginning-middle-end paradigm. But it does not emphasize the lengthy prolongation of the final chord; 5 bars out of the total 12 are based on the last element in the *Ursatz*. From the end of bar 2 there are many chromatic notes; clearly there is harmonic mobility in the central part of this passage. The first two bars are typical of a beginning; they outline the tonic triad, starting (after the upbeat) in root position and ending in first inversion - for the end of the beginning, as explained above, has to be open. Also, the opening bars present the 3-2-1 progression that dominates the

Semantics and Narrative Grammar 231

whole passage; the beginning shows the 'global progression in miniature'.

Figure 8.7

The three paradigmatic elements should be seen to overlap. *Middle* begins, then, with the tonic chord which ends beginning (Figure 8.8). It is sequentially based, taking the ascending bass fourth from the opening of the piece (A-D) and moving it up: B-E, D-G, E-A. The process involves an ellipsis; C sharp - F sharp is implied, as shown in Figure 8.8.

The ending amplifies the resolution of the harmonic and tonal progression, first with a cadence in 'hammer strokes', then two more cadences that echo the first.

It would be simple to affiliate a topic to each of the sections; march for beginning, cadenza for middle, singing style for ending. But there is more to it than this. As beginning gives way to middle there are 'heavy-footed cadential figures', with accented upbeats, that suggest a clumsy peasant dance. And in the midst of the 'singing' extension of the final cadence there is a shred of fanfare (in the second violin at bar 10), linking this to the viola part at bar 2. In typically Mozartian manner, there is a change of texture and mood for every phrase of this extract; a military opening, with hunting connections, gives way to a rustic scene, then a dash of virtuosity, decisive hammered chords, and a touch of opera with military echoes. The topical 'plot', like 'an episode from *commedia dell'arte'*, is partly deployed within the architecture of the rhetorical structure, partly self-justifying.

Figure 8.8

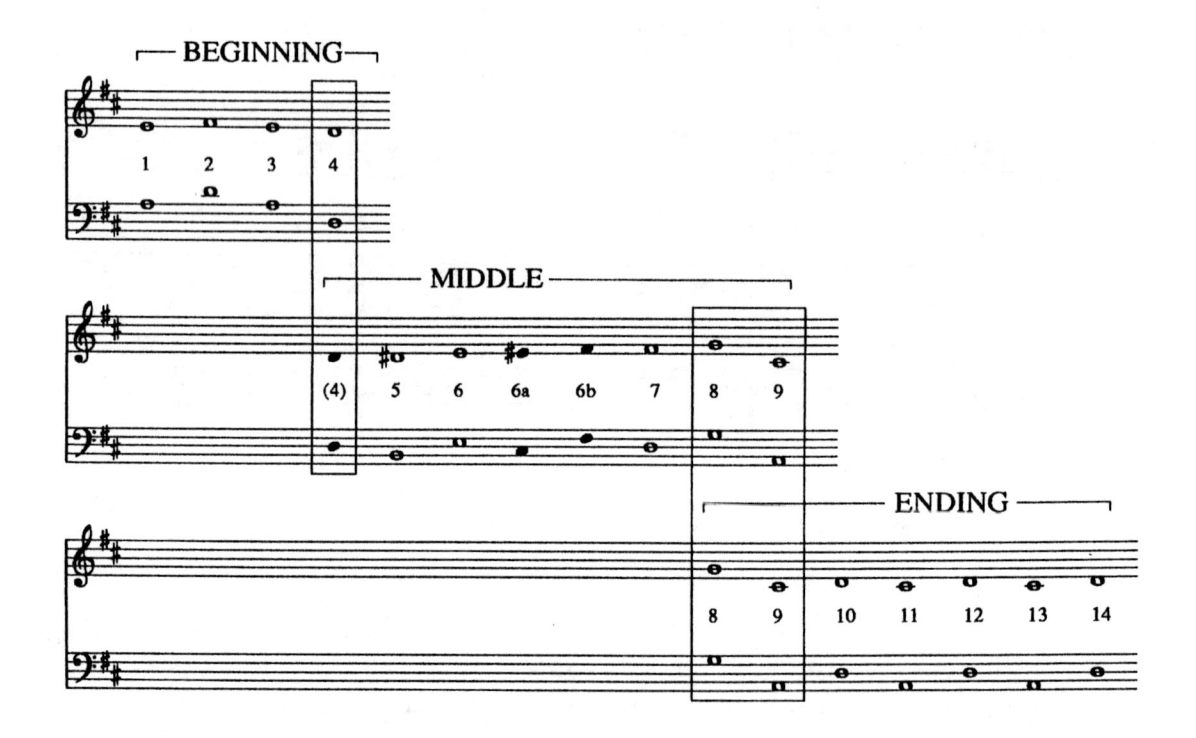

8.5. Structural semantics

8.5.1. A semantic study of music, then, can take the form of a search for simple reference: for the military or peasant style, or for specific topics like 'fanfare' and *'Sturm und Drang'*. It can also imply a narrative view; the conception of music as emotional or moral plot.

Semantics itself is now a study of some sophistication, with its own structuralist side. Referentialist studies would seem naive to proponents of the traditions of structural semantics, like John Lyons, whose theory was the basis of Harold Powers's article on Indian Classical Music, mentioned above in Chapter 6.

Just as a word is a token of a lexical field, so a musical phrase *(anga)* may be a token of the raga. Ragas are themselves related in fields, so each raga is also a token of a greater field. As was commented above, neither Lyons nor Powers shows much interest in what a verbal or musical symbol represents, but only in the structure of the signified. Like structural linguistics, the structuralist version of semantics sees significations as positions in the web of the signified, 'without positive terms'.

We now have an account of structural semantics which is more exhaustive that that of Lyons. This is the *Sémantique Structurale* of Algirdas Julien Greimas (1966). This magisterial survey, the last monument of mainstream French structuralism, has been richly suggestive for musicians.

There are two sides to Greimas's theory, which may be called *deductive* and *inductive*. The first of these, the theory of *semeanalysis*, is a systematic study of the structure of meaning itself. The second, *narrative grammar*, is an application of basic theory to literary narrative. Both have been adapted by musicians. It is as though the two aspects of naive semantics, referentialism and narrativism, had been given companions in the more rigorous world of structuralism.

Figure 8.9

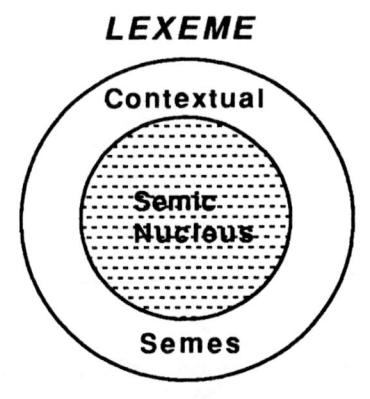

LEXEME

Contextual

Semic Nucleus

Semes

8.5.2. The basic linguistic expression - the word or phrase - is called a *lexeme*. Every lexeme is a 'stylistic constellation'; in a way characteristic of the language and of the style of the writer and the work, it groups together atoms of meaning in a characteristic pattern. These atoms are called *semes*. Some of the semes in a given lexeme are permanent and invariant, and form the *semic nucleus*. Around this are grouped semic variables. The selection of appropriate members of this group is made according to context. These variables are called *contextual semes* (Figure 8.9). The addition of the appropriate contextual semes to the semic nucleus gives the signification of the lexeme on this occasion. It is now called a *sememe*. For example, when two lexemes are placed together, they must have certain contextual semes in common, or the syntagm will not make sense. These linking semes ensure intelligibility; they are not *grammatical* links, such as ensure sense and continuity on the syntactic plane.

Figure 8.10

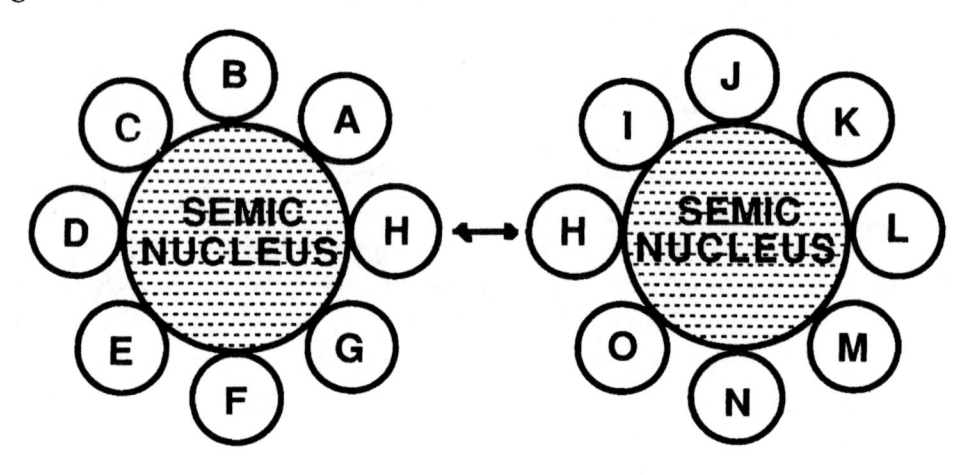

As discourse progresses, certain contextual semes are found to affect a certain area, greater than a phrase or sentence; these are called *classemes*. A classeme which persists throughout a whole utterance - a poem or novel - is called an *isotopy*.

8.5.3. It follows that in most sememes within an actual utterance, certain semes are rejected because they are not confirmed by context. For example, in the expression 'the dog is barking' both terms are ambiguous if taken separately. *Dog* can be located on the axis animal/thing (a fire-dog is not an animal). Such an axis is called a *semic category*. In any context, only one of these semic alternatives may be chosen. The selection is made by examining the context: here, the other lexeme. *Bark* is similarly located on an axis of signification, animal/human (because humans bark also, but the word takes on a different meaning when used thus). Bark does not embrace the seme *thing;* this must therefore be rejected from the first lexeme, making it clear that the dog is in this case an animal. Similarly, dog does not embrace human, so a similar choice is possible for the second lexeme. The semes *thing* and *human* have been rejected as they were not confirmed by context.[1] Their appearance is irrelevant and accidental.

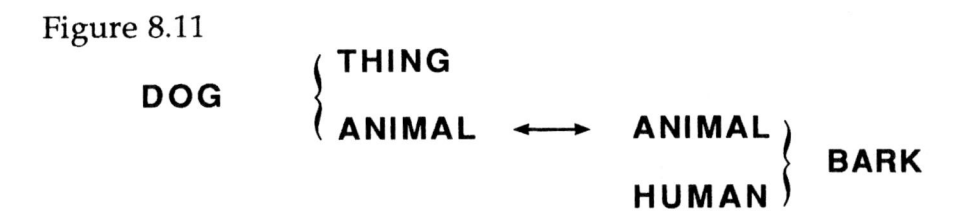

Figure 8.11

DOG { THING / ANIMAL } ⟷ { ANIMAL / HUMAN } BARK

However, the seme *animal* is present in both lexemes; it has been expressed twice. No doubt it will appear many more times as the discourse proceeds, if we continue to hear the story of this particular dog. Each time it appears it becomes more *redundant*. Redundancy sets in at the moment when a discourse begins to become intelligible; without redundancy language is meaningless nonsense, while too much redundancy creates meaningless repetition. Both kinds of meaninglessness have parallels in music, for music also achieves intelligibility by reiteration. In this respect, it resembles the *semantic* level of language, rather than the grammatical or syntactic level.

Figure 8.12

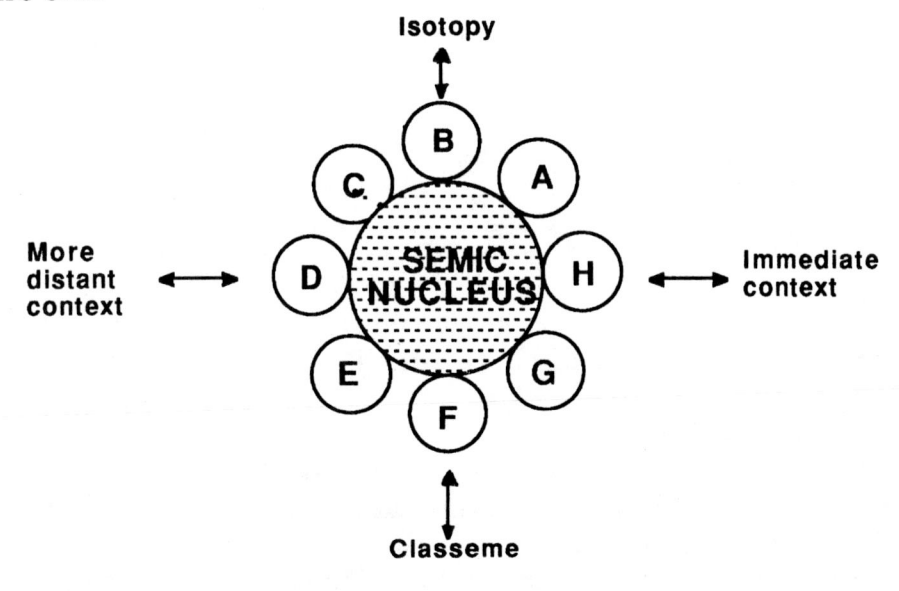

[Diagram: A central "SEMIC NUCLEUS" surrounded by circles labeled A, B, C, D, E, F, G, H. "Isotopy" points up from B, "Classeme" points down from F, "More distant context" points left from D, "Immediate context" points right from H.]

---

[1] Greimas's terms have been translated by the author. There is an American translation of the *Sémantique structurale* (Greimas 1983) which was not consulted at the time of writing this chapter.

8.5.4. In a longer discourse, the wider context affects the configuration of a particular sememe. Certain semes may by operative, not merely because they form an intelligible link with the adjacent sememe, but because they are confirmed for this section of the discourse by a local classeme, or because they relate to an isotopy which governs the whole discourse.

8.6. *Lexeme and context in the* Tristan *Prelude*

8.6.1. The establishment of meaning by context may be observed in music also. Let us consider Wagner's *Tristan* Prelude, a piece which seems peculiarly eloquent in spite of the absence of conventional form. It is a *locus classicus* for analysts, 'A form that has come into being simply as the outcome of the ideas' according to Ernest Newman (1949, 211). The opening gesture, as Newman himself points out, contains two lexemes. Each apparently has its own 'nucleus' of meaning, though in music it is hard to say what this is - and each contains several contextual semes.

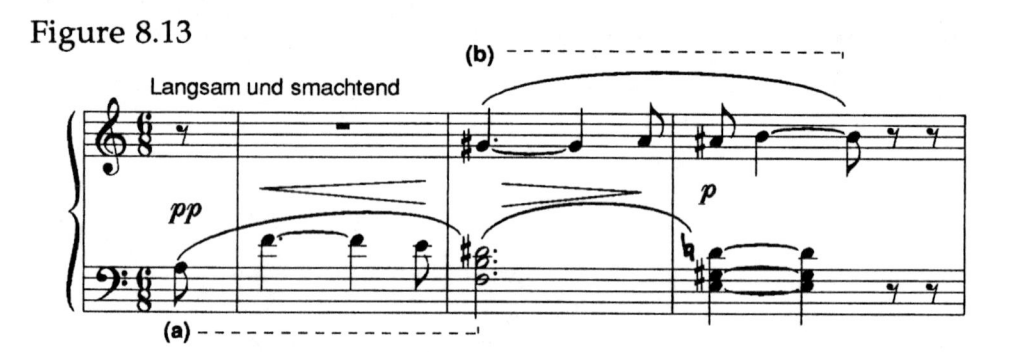

Figure 8.13

The first lexeme is for cellos alone, without harmony. It spans the interval of a minor sixth, then falls in a brief chromatic scale. Beginning softly with an anacrusis, it ends on the strong beat, growing a little dynamically as it falls. Lexeme *b* contrasts in almost every way. It is for wind, harmonized, narrow in compass, beginning on the strong beat and ending with a feminine rhythm in quavers. The only seme in common with *a* is the chromatic scale. This does not mean, of course, that the chromatic scale is the only semantically important feature of *a*. Other features may be part of the nucleus, or may assume importance in a broader context.

At this stage harmony and tonality are uncertain. The closing chord of lexeme *b* is, in fact, a dominant seventh in A, but since it is never resolved this key remains no more than a possibility. The sequence of this passage at bar 4 adds nothing apart from the interval that separates it, a minor third. In some pieces this might be significant; for example, it might suggest a key. In this piece it merely confirms the tonal uncertainty, and this is reinforced by the constant chromatic movement of the parts. In fact, everything up to bar 16 confirms the semantic material of bars 1-2; the chromatic scale, the common feature of lexemes *a* and *b,* is thus the classeme that governs this whole passage.

8.6.2. To describe a chromatic scale as a 'classeme' is to imply that musical items normally thought to be grammatical or syntactic are, in fact, semantic. 'Chromatic scale' somehow describes the meaning rather than merely the classification of this feature. This apparently perverse approach is neither questioned nor justified in the article in which I propose this method (Monelle 1991a).

The idea of treating 'syntactic' features as though they were semantic originates in Winograd's computer analysis of harmony (Winograd 1968). This view conflicts, in fact, with Greimas's own view of music. You cannot classify the signified on the basis of the signifier, he says; it is nonsense, therefore, to say that 'music has a musical significance' (Greimas 1966, 11). Music is described on the basis of the signifier, not the signified - its signification, like that of any signifying system, is 'simply human'.

However, it is impossible to know whether terms like 'chromatic' or 'contrapuntal' are descriptions of syntax or of meaning. Many musical terms ('chromatic', for example) are metaphors, suggesting that literal descriptions of musical phenomena are almost nonexistent.

The principal reason for taking ordinary musical language as semantic rather than syntactic, is that music behaves like the semantic side of language. The constant repetition, varied or otherwise, which forms the basis of musical structure has no counterpart in linguistic syntax or style; only in verse prosody does language approach the structure of music, and this is arguably already music to some degree. In its most typical forms, written prose or ordinary speech, language specifically avoids patterns of repetition.

Yet underlying this non-repetitive pattern of morphemes, there is a pattern of semes and isotopies which tends toward redundancy and relies on repetition to achieve intelligibility. At this level, the structure of language resembles that of music.

Perhaps surprisingly, Greimas and Courtès, in the article on isotopy in their dictionary of semiotics, confess that it is often hard to find a dividing-line between the content-plane and the expression-plane: this distinction, vital to Hjelmslev and traditional linguistics, begins to dissolve. Quoting F Rastier, they define isotopy as 'The iterativity of linguistic units (manifested or not) belonging either to the expression-plane or to the content-plane, or, more broadly, as the recurrence of linguistic units'. Maybe music demonstrates the coalescence of expression-plane and content-plane to an even greater degree.

8.6.3. At bars 16-17 of the Prelude to *Tristan*, there occurs a semantic event which demonstrates how musical argument proceeds.

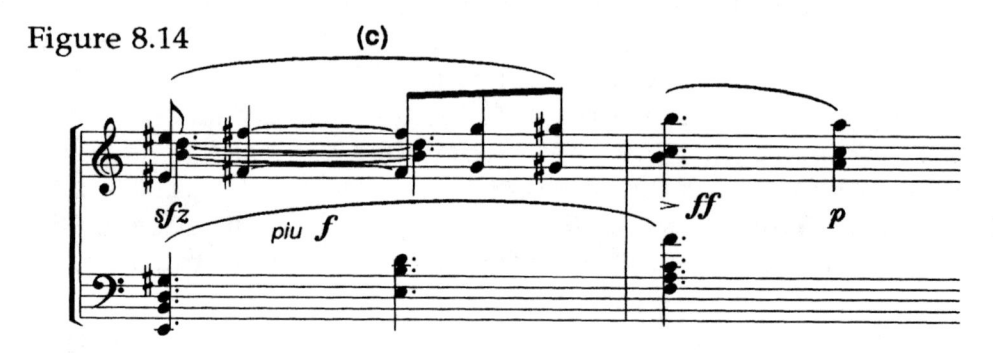

Figure 8.14

The classeme *chromatic scale* links this semantically to the previous, but there is an intuitive feeling of arrival and further departure, as though the sense of the music had crystallized in these two bars. Other semes are present; the feminine quaver rhythm now comes at the start, together with the same chord over which it was first heard, a dominant seventh (here a ninth) in A. The passage has a more strongly diatonic feel; although its two keys, A and C, are related by a third rather than a fifth, the arrangement in two root-position simple chords (the second with an appoggiatura on the eleventh) makes it easy to hear the first chord as V of VI in C. In any case, the final descending interval is a tone, thus necessarily diatonic. Since the closing notes are long in value, the rhythm of *b* is effectively reversed. The semantically important character of these bars is underlined by their expanded orchestration and by the high dynamic level (*più f* rising to *ff*). Yet their semantic content does not seem to go far beyond the previous, except for the suggestion of diatonicism and the rhythmic reversal. The element of diatonicism is new - if it were not rapidly confirmed it would be 'meaningless' and would go unnoticed. In fact, the following passage confirms not only the diatonicism of these bars, but returns to another seme from bar 1 which had been abandoned for a while: the wide interval. At the same time a new seme, the dotted rhythm, is introduced and immediately confirmed in the sequel.

Figure 8.15

The whole melody is now diatonic and the tonality obviously C major. The accretion of semantic material may be examined in the tables.

Figure 8.16

W	Wide interval	
C	Chromatic scale	
F	Feminine quaver figure	
D	Diatonicism	
T	Dotted rhythm	

Bars 1-2	W + C	
	C + F	
Bars 16-17	C + F + D	
Bars 17-19	W + F + D + T	

The two bars between bar 17 and bar 19 are more profoundly diatonic than anything in the Prelude, except their own reprises when these occur; any chromatic movement within them can easily be explained in terms of passing notes and applied leading notes, and the melody is entirely without chromaticism.

However, the following bars are full of chromaticism (as well as semes F, W and T) and the real converging point of the argument is at bars 25-26, where diatonic harmony (the key clearly E major) accompanies a chromatic line that contains every other seme: wide interval, feminine quavers and dotted rhythm.

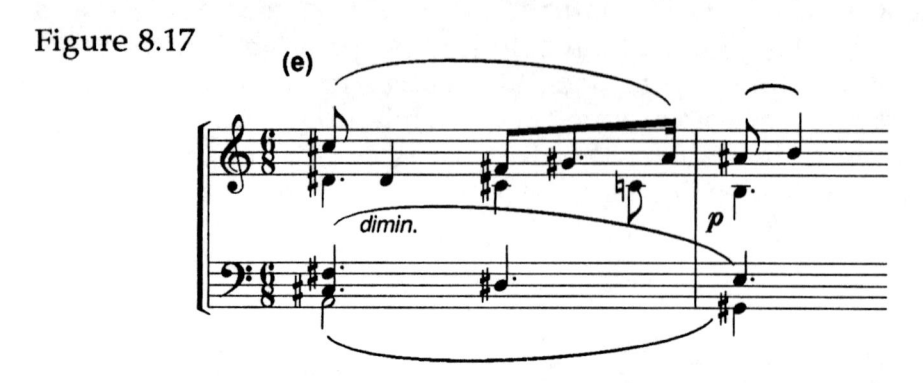

Figure 8.17

It is noteworthy that the last four notes of this melody are identical in contour and pitch to motive *b* at the beginning, though the harmony was different at that point.

The melody of the next 4 bars is resolutely diatonic in E (the C natural is a free allophone in this style) and continues to present semes T and F, seme W lapsing for a while.

Figure 8.18

The reiteration of this figure, with its conclusion on G sharp and A, marks a passage of low semantic content and high redundancy. This is in order to present an important figure in the bass, which combines the wide-interval seme W with a new seme, that of one-note-to-a-beat equal dotted crotchets (Figure 8.19).

Figure 8.19

(g) [musical notation in bass clef]

The pattern of semic accretion may again be tabulated.

Figure 8.20

		W	C	F	D	T	E
1-2	a	⊛	⊛				
	b		*	⊛			
16-17			*	*	⊛		
17-19		*		*	*	⊛	
25-26		*	*	*	*	*	
26-30				*	*	*	
Bass, 28-29		*					⊛

⊛ = first occurrence
* = redundant occurrence

8.6.4. Breaking off this semantic analysis of the Prelude, it is interesting to turn to the traditional *Leitmotiv* names as they are accepted and adapted by Ernest Newman and Albert Lavignac.

Figure 8.21

MOTIVES AND MEANINGS

Sememes	*Semes*	*Leitmotiv*
a	W + C	Confession of love; grief, sorrow
b	C + F	Desire
d	D + T + W + F	The glance
e	D + C + T + W + F	The love-philtre
f	D + T + F	The magic casket
g	W (+ E)	Death

It is easy to imagine connections between the musical figures and their 'meanings'. Desire is an irrational and disruptive force, and is thus matched by semes C and F, which are harmonically and rhythmically destabilising. The tremor of modesty and shame that followed the meeting of the lovers' eyes - 'Dort den Helden, der meinem Blick den seinen birgt, in Scham und Scheue abwärts schaut' - is suggested by the slightly restless rhythm of seme T. The relentless slow tread of seme E, which was just coming in as the analysis broke off, is like the inevitability of death.

It is interesting to note also that the whole semantic material of this passage, apart from seme E, which in a sense marks a new departure, is concentrated on lexeme *e*, the 'love-philtre'. If this identification is correct, then all the sorrow and passion are focussed not on love or on death but on an extraneous force for which the lovers are not responsible. This was certainly what was intended by Gottfried of Strassburg.

8.7. Semic systems

8.7.1. A number of semic axes have come into play in this short passage of instrumental music. Consider, for example, the axis *discrete/glissando*. The operation of this axis depends on the presence of pitched sounds; in fact, on the element *pitched*. This axis has no relevance to, for example, a drum solo in a North Indian *gat*. On the other hand, many singers - for example, the Fuegian *selk'nam* described by Rouget and Schwarz (1970), not to mention many Western opera singers - would define the two pitches, but join them by a marked portamento, so that both glissando and discrete pitch were present. If the discreteness of pitch is taken as marker, then there are four possibilities, depending on the presence or absence of *d* (the element of discrete pitch) and of *D* (the condition in which pitch may be discrete or not; that is, the presence of pitched sounds). A chart may be drawn, opposing the positive, negative, neutral and complex forms of the term *D*, comparable to the chart of semic terms on page 25 of *Sémantique Structurale*.

Positive	d	(presence of d)	(Tristan)
Negative	not-d	(presence of not-d)	(Xenakis, *Shaar*)
Neutral	-d	(absence of d and not-d)	
		(*Gat* drum solo)	
Complex	d + not-d	(presence of D)	
		(Fuegian *selk'nam*)	

(Monelle 1991b).

Xenakis's *Shaar* is a piece for strings, written in glissandi; the *Gat* drum solo contains no discernible pitches, either discrete or glissando; the Fuegian song has discrete pitches, joined by portamenti.

8.7.2. In another article (Monelle 1991b) this system of contextual analysis is applied to an instrumental work, the Fugue in B flat minor from Book 1 of Bach's *Das wohltemperirte Clavier*. In that piece the opposition conjunct/disjunct is operative within the world of discrete pitches, as well as diatonic/chromatic, operative in the *Tristan* example. Another opposition, between primary intervals (the fifth, fourth and octave) and other intervals is noticed. There are, in addition, semic axes of rhythm. All of these are significant within the isotopies of key and texture which apply to the whole fugue.

These oppositions make it possible to expand the semic system of *discrete pitch*. Even the unfamiliar side of this system - with the marker *glissando* - is characterised by a binary opposition. Non-discrete pitch events may be *rhetorical*, using portamento, vibrato and *Sprechgesang* as declamatory devices in the expression of a sung text, or in the imitation of such declamatory devices on an instrument, in which case they are usually combined with discrete events; or they may be freely non-discrete in the manner of birdsong and the sounds of wind and machinery. Thus the semic system of *pitched sound-event* can be sketched (Figure 8.22). This would have to be rewritten for non-Western musical styles; the opposition diatonic/chromatic might become *gapped/inclusive*, for example.

Figure 8.22

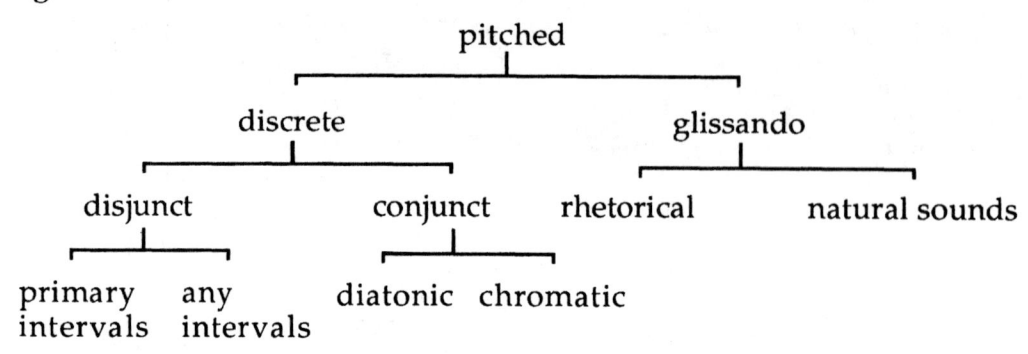

```
                        pitched
           ┌───────────────┴───────────────┐
        discrete                        glissando
      ┌─────┴─────┐                ┌────────┴────────┐
   disjunct    conjunct        rhetorical      natural sounds
   ┌───┴───┐   ┌───┴───┐
primary  any  diatonic chromatic
intervals intervals
```

8.7.3. The application of semeanalysis to music has important consequences. It is impossible to regard some feature or other -the key, the underlying harmonic structure, the theme, the rhythm - as paramount, for all are semantic features collaborating on equal terms. The approaches of Schenker, Réti, and Lerdahl and Jackendoff would each be incomplete in the eyes of semantics. The distinction of *sense* (established by redundancy) and *signification* (by variancy) illuminates musical features like variation, development and reprise. To reprise a passage is to make one's discourse intelligible; to vary a figure is to be eloquent. The more repetitious the discourse becomes, however, the more it approaches 'total cliché' (Greimas 1966, 36); the less it is redundant, the more it approaches a 'schizophrenia' leading to non-communication. This seems to be a lesson for certain manifestations of contemporary Western music.

Finally, extra-musical interpretation is not excluded. The meaningfulness of a musical feature may, indeed, include extra-musical meaning, especially when linguistic syntagmata are attached to the music in the form of sung words, programme or title. The distinction extrinsic/intrinsic has no particular importance; beyond meaning and sense lies meaningfulness, whether it can be interpreted or not.

8.8. Narrative grammar

8.8.1. Greimas's thought also has an inductive side, related to the narratives of novels and folk-tales. Indeed, the last section of the *Sémantique Structurale* is devoted to an analysis of Georges Bernanos's *Journal d'un Curé de Campagne*. In his later writings, notably the two volumes of *Du Sens* (Greimas 1970, 1983; see also Greimas 1987), he elaborated a theory of *narrative grammar* in which the deductive and inductive levels are brought together. This grammar is pre-linguistic; since it deals with the levels of meaning which constitute a common structural level, far below the level of manifestation (that is, of actual story-telling), it can generate various kinds of manifested meaning in 'cinematographic and oniric languages, figurative painting, and so forth' (Greimas 1987, 64) as well as discourse about meaning, that is, semiotics. It is reasonable to assume that music may be one of the languages in which narrative structures may be manifested.

8.8.2. On the deepest level, signification is structured by the logical principles of contradiction, contrariety and implication. Thus *black* and *not-black* are *contradictory*. *Black* and *white* are *contraries*. *White* implies *not-black*. These terms can be arranged in a square.

Figure 8.23

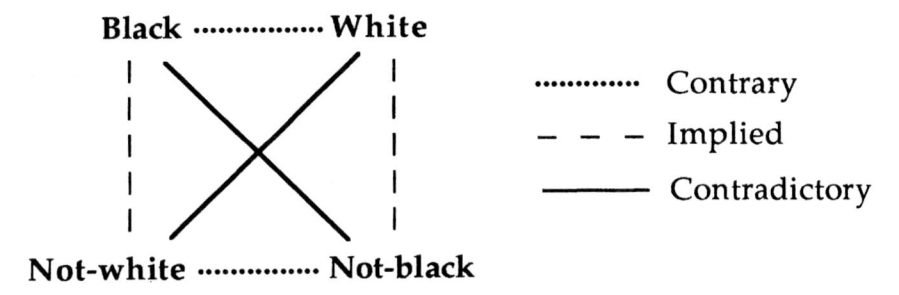

$$
\begin{array}{ccc}
\text{Black} & \cdots\cdots\cdots & \text{White} \\
& \times & \\
\text{Not-white} & \cdots\cdots\cdots & \text{Not-black}
\end{array}
$$

$\cdots\cdots$ Contrary
$---$ Implied
$\underline{\hspace{2em}}$ Contradictory

Removing the real terms, we are left with the classic 'semiotic square'. Clearly 'black' and 'white' constitute a category or semantic axis, i.e. a complex seme (S) incorporating two other semes (s1 and s2).

Figure 8.24

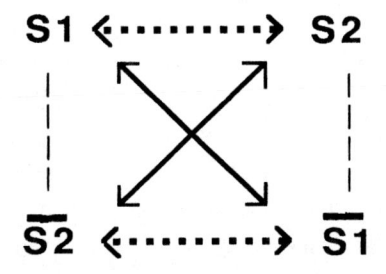

$$
\begin{array}{ccc}
S_1 & \longleftrightarrow & S_2 \\
& \times & \\
\overline{S_2} & \longleftrightarrow & \overline{S_1}
\end{array}
$$

It is apparent that 'black' and 'not-white' are not synonymous. But in fact, their non-synonymity (for example, 'not-white' includes red and green) is less important than the kind of assertion they make, one affirmative, one negative, as will be seen when we move on to the level of narrative.

The three directions of relation are called axes (relations of contradiction: S and $\bar{S}$), schemata (relations of contrariety: s1 and s2) and deixes (relations of implication: s1 and $\bar{s2}$). This arrangement may be illustrated with non-trivial terms, closer to the features of an actual narrative. In the following case it could be said that one of the principal terms is *marked*, the other *unmarked*; that is, on the semantic axis of *truth*, *being* is marked by the presence of truth, *seeming* not so marked.

Figure 8.25

TRUTH

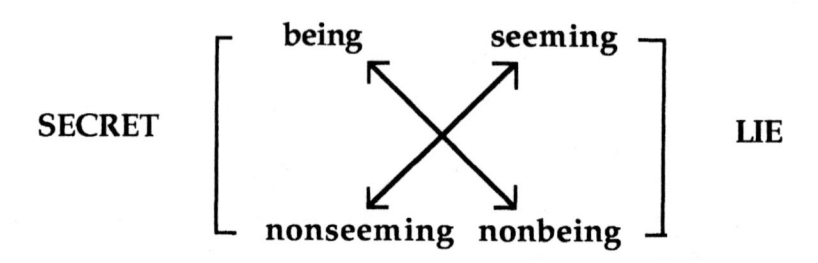

SECRET $\begin{bmatrix} \text{being} & \text{seeming} \\ & \times & \\ \text{nonseeming} & \text{nonbeing} \end{bmatrix}$ **LIE**

FALSEHOOD

In this case (Greimas 1987, 110) the combination of *being* and *nonseeming* produces something which is true, but is not seen to be so; the opposite combination, of *seeming* and *nonbeing*, goves something which is untrue but appears true. In this narrative, therefore, the opposition *secret/lie* will have structural importance. This is evidently a non-trivial observation.

8.8.3. This is the level of deep structure. Before showing how this may generate the next level we may summarise the levels of signification. The semiotic square is non-syntactic; it is a pattern of terms and qualities, related logically. The next level, that of narrative grammar, replaces the static terms with narrative utterances, descriptions of actions, turning what was a logical analysis into the basis of a story (although the 'characters' and the exact nature of the actions are not yet specified). The abstract level of narrative grammar is now elaborated by importing certain themes and motifs (stock characters, stock situations) from the culture in which the story is being framed: these are called *discoursive structures*.

Next, the actual materials of the story are added; the characters with their names and descriptions, the actual events, and finally, through linguistic realization, the actual words in which the story is told. This is the level of manifestation.

DEEP STRUCTURE
NARRATIVE GRAMMAR
DISCOURSIVE STRUCTURES
MANIFESTATION

Greimas's theory of narrative grammar derives from Vladimir Propp's analysis of Russian folk tales (Propp 1958). Taking 100 stories, Propp argued that all the tales were made up from limited elements, defined as *roles* and *functions*. The roles had general titles like villain, helper, hero, false hero; a function was 'an act... defined from the point of view of its significance for the course of action of the tale as a whole' (Propp 1958, 20). 31 functions were identified. It may be observed that functions were not defined by their actual nature, but by their place in the action; in Wagner's *Ring*, although Alberich obtains power by stealing the gold from the Rhinemaidens, Siegfried by killing the dragon, the function of obtaining power is the same.

In Greimas the roles are called *actants* and are defined systematically by abstract qualities, like the basic terms of deep structure; Propp's roles are somewhat *ad hoc* and indeed are stigmatized by Claude Brémond for being features of *parole* rather than *langue* (in *Le Message Narratif*, quoted by Culler, 1975, 209).

8.8.4. The basic unit of narrative is the narrative utterance, NU, defined as the function of an actant.

$$NU = F(A)$$

In this form the narrative utterance resembles a simple sentence, subject-predicate, as in 'Siegfried killed the dragon'. But there is another kind of utterance in which three actants are involved in the function: sender, object and receiver. This kind of utterance is called *translative* because something is lost on one side, gained on the other. In its positive form, a translative utterance might proclaim: 'Wotan gave the Ring to the giants.' The negative equivalent might be, 'Alberich stole the gold from the Rhinemaidens.' Sometimes, an apparently simple utterance may turn out to be translative; thus, 'Siegfried took authority away from Wotan.' It is then classifiable with the theft of the Ring under the function heading, 'loss of power'.

Not all functions are operative, or in Greimas's term, 'doings'. Some may be 'virtual', connected with potentiality rather than actuality; the virtual or 'modal' functions are *wanting, knowing, having to* and *being able,* called *modalities.* Clearly a modal function tends to lead to an operative function (John wants to become king; John fights a battle). In addition, a modal function may itself become the object of an operative function. In the complex function following, John (S_1) knows something; Peter (S_2) is ignorant; John tells Peter - John gives knowledge (the object, O) to Peter. This, then, is a translative utterance of which the object is a modal utterance.

$$TU = S_1 \longrightarrow O:knowledge \longrightarrow S_2$$

This slightly complex utterance is a typical expression of narrative grammar. It will be noticed that none of the terms - actants or functions - have any semantic contents; we are still on the level of abstract structure. Propp's 'roles' (hero, helper etc.) are far too near the surface of manifestation to be acknowledged by Greimas at this level.

8.8.5. At this point semantic material is introduced. On the next level, actants are replaced by *actors;* the former are 'of syntactic nature', the latter 'of semantic nature'. Because an actor may be complex - he may embrace several actants, or several actors may be needed for a single actant - he is more like a *lexeme* in language, a natural manifestation of a complex of meanings. An actor exists in culture as a *theme* or *motif* taken from a 'discoursive dictionary'. We may assume, then, that the dictionary of Russian folk tales contains actors like hero, villain, helper - Propp's 'roles'. Narrative structures, acquiring this minimal cultural accretion, become discoursive structures. It would seem that Propp's analyses are on this level. However, actors exist simultaneously on the levels of discoursive structures and narrative grammar; an actor is a cultural item functioning as an actant. A simple illustration of the four levels of signification may be given from Wagner's *Das Rheingold.*

Wotan *(the hero-god)* obtains power from the giants *(the dupe)* by *contract*. Alberich *(the anti-hero)* obtains power from the Rhinemaidens *(the dream-woman)* by *theft*. Wotan steals Alberich's power *(theft + trickery)* and recovers his power from the giants by a *spurious contract*.

The discoursive themes and motifs are italicised in this summary. To move on to the level of narrative grammar, actors shall become actants.

Figure 8.26

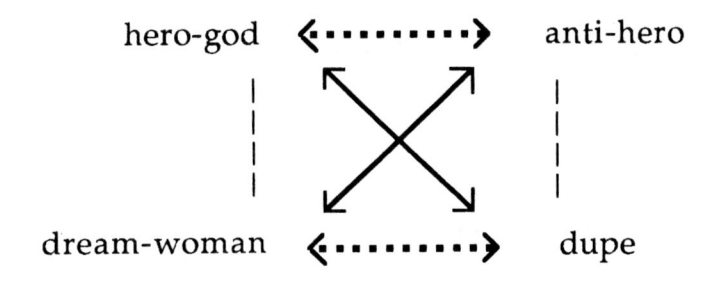

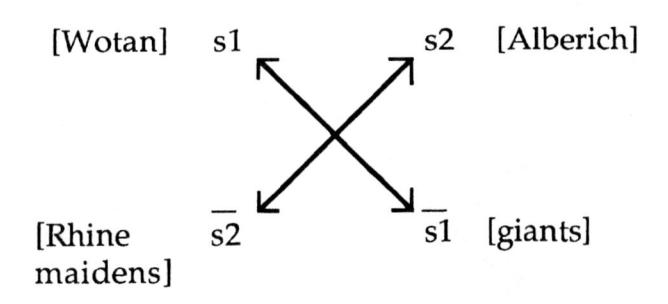

$$
\begin{array}{ccc}
\text{hero-god} & \longleftrightarrow & \text{anti-hero} \\
\updownarrow & \times & \updownarrow \\
\text{dream-woman} & \longleftrightarrow & \text{dupe}
\end{array}
$$

$$
\begin{array}{cccc}
[\text{Wotan}] & s_1 & s_2 & [\text{Alberich}] \\
 & \times & & \\
[\text{Rhine maidens}] & \overline{s_2} & \overline{s_1} & [\text{giants}]
\end{array}
$$

The functions, similarly, are logically related.

Figure 8.27

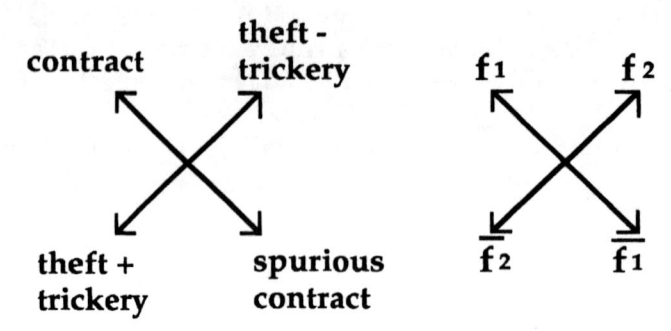

```
         theft-
contract  trickery       f₁        f₂
    ↖   ↗               ↖   ↗
     ╳                    ╳
    ↙   ↘               ↙   ↘
theft +   spurious       f̄₂       f̄₁
trickery  contract
```

The narrative grammar of *Das Rheingold* may now be written.

$$f_1 = \bar{s}_1 \longrightarrow O \longrightarrow s_1$$
$$f_2 = \bar{s}_2 \longrightarrow O \longrightarrow s_2$$
$$\bar{f}_2 = s_2 \longrightarrow O \longrightarrow s_1$$
$$\bar{f}_1 = \bar{s}_1 \longrightarrow O \longrightarrow s_1$$

Since in every case the object (O) is power, this narrative sequence may be said to describe the *microuniverse of power*. The deep structure may now be established.

Figure 8.28

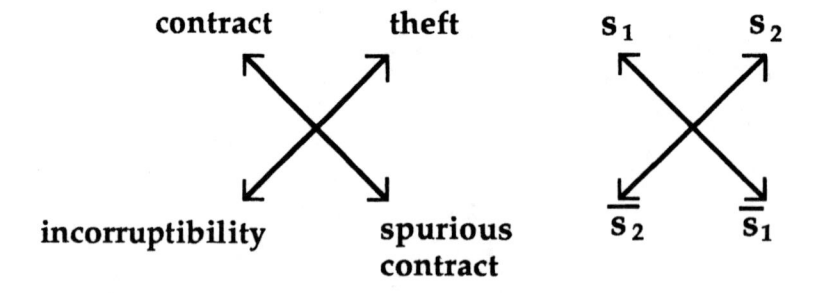

```
contract      theft          s₁        s₂
    ↖   ↗                   ↖   ↗
     ╳                        ╳
    ↙   ↘                   ↙   ↘
incorruptibility  spurious    s̄₂       s̄₁
                  contract
```

It will be observed that *contract* and *theft* represent a semantic *axis*; they are *contrary* modes of economic relation. *Contract* and *spurious contract* are a *schema* and are *contradictory*. *Contract* and *incorruptibility* are a *deixis*, related by implication: the incorruptible can pursue economic relations only in the form of contracts. *Das Rheingold*, then, is a narrative exposition of a logical configuration.

8.9. Myth and music

8.9.1. Greimas's narrative grammar is applied to music by Eero Tarasti, a Finnish musicologist who worked in Paris with Greimas before ethnomusicological work in Brazil. Initially, Tarasti turned his attention to the working of myth in music; the derivation of Greimasian theory from the folk-tale analysis of Propp made this seem an obvious departure. An insight of Lévi-Strauss, however, was the real starting-point. Real myths, the strangely drab but demoniac tales collected by anthropologists (rather than the prettified versions contained in *Tanglewood Tales*), impress the Western listener, as has already been remarked, by their repetitiousness. So repetitive are some myths that mythical time seems to lose its linear character and become circular, or flow in several directions at once.

Lévi-Strauss realised the similarity of this to musical patterns like fugue and rondo. In his famous analysis of the story of the 'Lewd Grandmother', a myth of the Klikitat Indians (Lévi-Strauss 1981, 163-182), successive recurrences of the same 'theme' suggest a fugal exposition, stretto and conclusion. Elsewhere, he finds a mythical theme presented not only fugally but also in inversion (Lévi-Strauss 1970, 147-163). He is also able to analyse Ravel's *Bolero*, an especially repetitive piece, as though it were one of these myths with recurrent themes; because the passages enter successively, never together as in a fugue, he calls it a 'fugue laid out flat' (1981, 660).

Both myth and music possess a relation to time which is 'of a rather special nature: it is as if music and mythology needed time only in order to deny it... Music transmutes the segment [of time] devoted to listening to it into a synchronic totality, enclosed within itself. Because of the internal organization of the musical work, the act of listening to it immobilizes passing time' (Lévi-Strauss 1970, 16). Music is like 'a myth coded in sounds instead of words' (1981, 659). It is noticeable that, at the point in Western history when myth lost its sway over people's minds, music began to develop - particularly the form of the fugue with its resemblance to mythic structures. Music, then, is the mythology of the modern world.

For Lévi-Strauss the first great analyst of myth was Wagner. 'If Wagner is accepted as the undeniable originator of the structural analysis of myths..., it is a profoundly significant fact that the analysis was made, in the first instance, *in music*' (1970, 15). However, it is also clear that Wagner is in a different position vis-à-vis myth from the primitive musician. For him, mythical structure has entered into music and become musical structure; yet, in composing mythical music-dramas he uses music to demonstrate mythic structure itself - to present a 'structural analysis of myth'. This suggests that the principles of myth are present at two levels in Wagner's music.

8.9.2. Tarasti confirms Lévi-Strauss's supposition by showing that primitive music, coming from societies in which myth is still alive, is extremely simple. Indeed, its complexities, such as they are, can be shown to derive from mythical content, not from musical motivations. For example, the simple but lengthy songs of the Suya Indians of Brazil have a two-section structure which, according to Anthony Seeger, 'coincides with the dualism of the cosmos and social groups' (Tarasti 1979, 49).

8.9.3. The repetitive structures of myth are compared with instrumental music. The meaning of a syntagma in both languages is conditioned by its position, earlier or later in the story or composition. Thus, the 'initial situation' is characterized by Propp as a privileged position; a mythic theme appearing at this point will possess additional meaning derived from its initialness. In music, too, the introductory gesture has special importance: Tarasti quotes the passage for two harps at the beginning of Smetana's *Vysehrad*. Similarly, a theme that recurs and thus 'alludes to something earlier, in the distant past, to which the... message must be related', takes on new meaning, both in myth and music.

> Consider a composition where, for example, after a long development and many incidental passages a theme which is introduced at the beginning of the work, reappears at the end. Now, however, its meaning is completely different from what it was when it first occurred in the composition (1979, 68).

This feature, common to myth and music, is not found, for example, in drama or the novel, where exact repetition is uncommon.

8.9.4. The main part of Tarasti's book is concerned with music that has specifically mythical content: Wagner's *Ring*, Sibelius's *Kullervo* Symphony and Stravinsky's *Oedipus Rex*. Since Greimas's theories are partly dependent on Propp, it is possible for Tarasti to make 'functional' analyses of these works, as well as isolating semes, lexemes and isotopies after the manner of Greimas. His analyses bring together both aspects of Greimas's thought, semeanalysis and narrative grammar.

In pure musical analysis (as opposed to the analysis of mythic elements in music) it is conceivable that 'size, length, speed, intensity, density, continuity, tension' might be considered as semes, organized on axes like 'long/short, slow/fast, soft/loud, thick/thin, continuous/discontinuous, tense/relaxed' (Tarasti 1979, 73). This is apparently to recommend an analytical technique similar to my own (above), but Tarasti considers these semes to be aspects of the signifier - the music itself - rather than the signified, which for him is the mythical meaning. He would not, therefore, agree that musical classifications are already classifications of the semantic plane.

8.9.5. Since the mythical element is itself a seme, it is interesting to seek out characteristics 'on the level of the signifier' which indicate the mythical seme. The imitation of ritual songs and dances, the use of archaic scales, the timbre of certain instruments - harp, horn and cor anglais - may convey the mythic atmosphere. In many works the mythical seme becomes an isotopy, of course. Indeed, it is this kind of work with which Tarasti is chiefly concerned.

In subdividing the mythical isotopy, this writer never truly reduces his semic material to the atomic level. Each seme is a relatively complex affair, and their musical character is demonstrated 'ostensively' - that is, by music examples. Seventeen semes are discovered: the nature-mythical, the hero-mythical, the magical, the fabulous, the balladic, the legendary, the sacred and so on (86-129). The examples are drawn from a broad sphere, from Liszt, Glinka, Strauss, Tchaikovsky and others as well as the three composers who form the main subject of the book.

In examining the Ring, Tarasti divides the mythical isotopy into three sub-isotopies, those of 'nature or myth', 'society or saga' which is 'comprehended as events related to a familial structure', and 'fairy tale, or beings and events occurring outside nature and society' (178). The musical motives clarify this division by separating into the three isotopies. Sometimes a single character has three *Leitmotive*, one in each isotopy; Siegfried, for example, has his *Heldenthema* (no 39 in William Mann's motivic chart: see Mann 1964) which confirms his place in the world of nature; secondly, the heroic motive based on his horn call (no 57), placing him in the isotopy of saga; thirdly, the horn call itself (no 44) which comes from the world of fairy tale. Similarly, for Brünnhilde the 'awakening' motive (no 53) signifies nature-isotopy, the love motive (no 58) saga-isotopy, and the sleep motive (no 42) fairy tale.

8.9.6. The mythical semes can be traced in the Ring. For example, the balladic seme 'is associated with two factors: a soft 6/8 or 3/8 metre and flattened tonality'. It appears at the beginning of *Siegfried* in Mime's narration and Siegfried's reply, in F minor and G minor. 'Siegfried's narrative, his ballad of his own life also begin in G minor and triple metre', but the area of flat keys is quitted when he speaks of the prophecies of the bird; the balladic seme is no longer dominant and this lengthy lexeme is complete (218).

8.9.7. Even more significant, the musical organization is often dependent on details of narrative grammar rather than purely musical development. The basic structure of a translative utterance:

$$S \longrightarrow O \longrightarrow R$$

is reflected when the receiver's music echoes that of the sender, even when the sender is absent and merely implied. Thus Erda receives from nature the knowledge to become an oracle for Wotan.

$$\text{Nature} \longrightarrow \text{Knowledge} \longrightarrow \text{Erda}$$

The 'nature motive' is consequently varied to form the motive of Erda. In the relation between Wotan and the giants, the forming of the contract to build Valhalla makes Wotan sender, the giants receiver.

$$\text{Wotan} \longrightarrow \text{commission to build Valhalla} \longrightarrow \text{Giants}$$

Consequently the giants have a motive which recalls Wotan's 'spear' motive.

Figure 8.29

Returning to *Siegfried*, the mythical functioning of music can be shown by dividing the hero's life into a set of Proppian functions, basing the sequence on Jan de Vries's *Heldenlied und Heldensage* (Bern 1961).

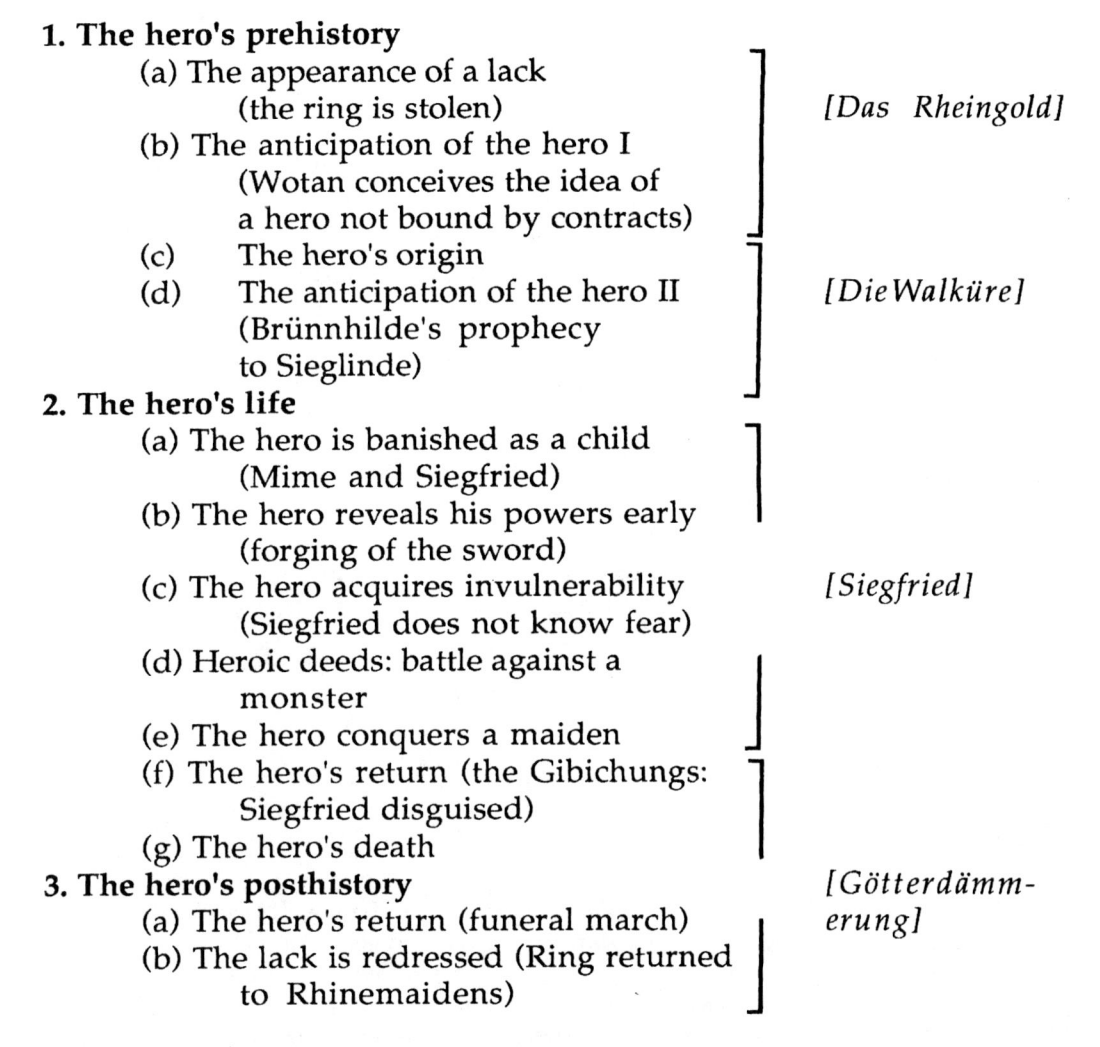

1. The hero's prehistory
    (a) The appearance of a lack
        (the ring is stolen)   *[Das Rheingold]*
    (b) The anticipation of the hero I
        (Wotan conceives the idea of
        a hero not bound by contracts)
    (c) The hero's origin
    (d) The anticipation of the hero II   *[Die Walküre]*
        (Brünnhilde's prophecy
        to Sieglinde)

2. The hero's life
    (a) The hero is banished as a child
        (Mime and Siegfried)
    (b) The hero reveals his powers early
        (forging of the sword)
    (c) The hero acquires invulnerability   *[Siegfried]*
        (Siegfried does not know fear)
    (d) Heroic deeds: battle against a
        monster
    (e) The hero conquers a maiden
    (f) The hero's return (the Gibichungs:
        Siegfried disguised)
    (g) The hero's death

3. The hero's posthistory   *[Götterdämm-*
    (a) The hero's return (funeral march)   *erung]*
    (b) The lack is redressed (Ring returned
        to Rhinemaidens)

It has been commented that Act I of *Siegfried* is largely dominated by the balladic seme. This section also reveals with unusual clarity the question-and-answer quality of myth; scholars have described myth as a question posed by primitive man to nature. In the view of André Jolle:

> Man is confronted by the world and poses a question to it. In reply he receives his own words back and thus creates a mythical being... Where this kind of creation of the world occurs as questions and answers, there ap-

pears the form called myth (Tarasti 1979, 19, based on André Jolles, *Einfache Formen,* Halle 1930).

In Scene 1 of this act Siegfried questions Mime about his own origins; in scene 2 the Wanderer sets riddles for Mime. In every case the questions acquire a mythical quality by having their answers already incorporated in the music, even the Wanderer's last riddle, which Mime, of course, cannot answer: 'Who will forge Notung anew?'

When Siegfried quizzes Mime about his parents, his 'dreamy, chromatically-rising motif' expresses the function of questioning; it is, in any case, a quasi-inversion of the motive which accompanies Sieglinde's questioning of Siegmund after his first entrance in *Die Walküre,* Act I. Siegfried's questioning motive is immediately followed by the *Schwesterliebe* motive from *Die Walküre;* the question is doubly answered before Mime has a chance to speak. The motives are as follows.

Figure 8.30

Similarly, the motifs anticipating Siegfried's forthcoming deeds are in many places hidden on an unconscious level in the orchestral texture as, for example, when Siegfried looks at his reflection in the water and the Siegfried motif is heard played by horn in *piano, aber bestimmt,* or when the Wälsunga motifs are incorporated in the forest murmurs in the second act as though in reply to Siegfried's question about his parents (208).

In the first scene of this act the questions are never answered in the text; only the music shows that they contain their own answers. The analysis is made, on the mythical level, in music, as Lévi-Strauss guessed. In scene 2, the scene of Mime and the Wanderer, the riddles are answered in the text also. Nevertheless, the answers are already in the music. As the Wanderer asks, 'Welches ist das Geschlecht, dem Wotan schlimm sich zeigte, und das doch das liebste ihm lebt?' ('Which is the tribe that Wotan treated harshly though its life is dearest to him?') the orchestra quotes the motive of the Wälsungs (no 33 in Mann's table). Similarly the questions, 'What sword must Siegfried wield?' and 'Who will forge the sword anew?' contain their own answers in musical form.

8.9.8. The answering of a question at the moment it is asked is a feature of the power of myth to conflate time, to put effect before cause and conclusion before inception. In the third scene of this act, this potentiality is classically shown. Mime, learning that he is to meet his death from 'him who knows no fear', tries to teach Siegfried fear.

> Haven't you ever felt, in the dark forest, at twilight in some dark spot... a dizzy flickering that flares around you... Didn't burning fear make your body shake, trembling in your breast with anxiety, didn't your heart burst with pounding? (William Mann's translation: Mann 1964, vol 3, 35-36).

Siegfried will, in fact, learn fear when he encounters Brünnhilde on the mountain top, encircled by fire. Accordingly, the orchestra plays the motives of fire (no 14) and of magic sleep (no 43).

Because Tarasti regards the ability of music to leap across time as main evidence of the survival therein of mythical structures, the funeral march in *Götterdämmerung* is for him a 'core-lexeme'. The whole life of the hero is recapitulated musically.

> In fact, from this core lexeme we may decode the intrinsic substance of the Siegfried saga as presented by Wagner. The three themes in the middle of the march represent those three levels, or isotopies, the conflicts among which are 'mediated' by this hero's life and actions. First we hear the sword motif, which also is the very first musical motif in the whole *Ring* anticipating the forthcoming hero and which belongs to the isotopy of saga, society. This is followed by two appearances of the Siegfried motif which refers to the hero's mythical task of mediation and expresses the relation between the hero and the mythical isotopy. Finally in this section we hear Siegfried's hero motif whose origin, Siegfried's horn call, alludes to the fairy tale isotopy (220).

Finally, then, the three isotopies which form the basis of the work's semantic structure are brought together into a single lexeme, and this is accomplished in the *music*, not in the text or on the stage. The 'secret of form' in Wagner, sought by Alfred Lorenz in the purely musical fields of *Barform* and arch form, is to be found, after all, in the structures of myth.

8.10. Narrative patterns in instrumental music

8.10.1. Wagner's *Ring* (not to mention *Kullervo* and *Oedipus Rex*) might be thought to lend itself to an analysis founded on narrative grammar, because of the relations of the mythical story to the kind of material studied by Propp. But Tarasti applies structural semantics and narrative grammar to instrumental music, too. He is able to adapt the concepts of isotopy and modality, as well as to derive semiotic squares from the semantic structures of instrumental pieces.

He is, in fact, not alone in pursuing this methodology in the analysis of instrumental music; Màrta Gràbocz also uses the terminology of Greimas in her book on Liszt's piano works. Although her work is primarily based on intonation theory (and is therefore described below, in Chapter 9), she adapts this to the patterns of narrative grammar, suggesting that the music is best understood as a heroic drama; not only in works inspired by literature and landscape, but even in the pieces with abstract titles like the *Grand Solo de Concert* and the Sonata in B minor. She presents elaborate tabulated analyses of several works; but her use of the Greimas terminology is idiosyncratic (her 'isotopies' seem to function as classemes, for example) and it will be better to approach this method through the writings of Tarasti.

8.10.2. In Greimasian methodology, isotopy is viewed in terms of the three categories of *spatiality*, *temporality* and *actoriality*. Each of these categories can be a field for *débrayage* and *embrayage*, words which are hard to translate but mean something like 'disengagement' and 'engagement'.

The spatial category has two dimensions, external and internal. In Tarasti's musical interpretation of the theory, external spatiality is concerned with register. Music may be narrow in register, extremely low or extremely high, or widely spaced. Characteristically a piece may begin with notes in the middle register, then steadily add notes of wider compass: this is *débrayage*. The range may then be gradually contracted until the original narrow compass is restored: *embrayage*. This process is particularly obvious in piano music, where the player's hands are visibly débrayées.

Internal spatiality, in tonal music, concerns relation to the tonal centre. Classical form clearly prescribed a system of *débrayage/embrayage* in its regular trajectory from tonic to dominant, and back to the tonic through related keys.

8.10.3. Temporality is a matter of pace and rhythm. In narrative the central point of temporality is now, the time in which the story unfolds. The musical 'now' is a centrality of tempo - merely moderate, or centrally placed with regard to the standard pulse of a particular piece - and a regularity of rhythm, without strong rhythmic contrasts. Again referring to classical music, the first movement of a sonata or symphony might be considered to set the 'now' of temporality, from which the slow movement and rapid finale represent a débrayage.

Actoriality is related to thematics. Tarasti makes no attempt to distinguish between actor and actant, but suggests that the listener identifies with the main theme of a piece as though it were the protagonist in a drama. This theme can depart and be replaced with other themes, or it can be partly present in the form of a development or variant. The theme is thus the *ego* of the narrative, which has three points of centrality: *hic, nunc et ego* (Tarasti 1989, 3).

8.10.4. The modalities of *devoir, vouloir, pouvoir* and *savoir* are essential for Greimas's narrative grammar. Tarasti is able to interpret these in a convincing manner.

Savoir - knowing - has its counterpart in *musical content*. A theme rich in material for development, an episode full of new musical ideas, a passage that introduces new procedures or departures, all of these are examples of *savoir*. Redundancy limits *savoir*, however; a passage of repetition or development is not considered to be 'knowing'. 'The reverse of *savoir* is redundancy, poverty of information; *savoir* is thus the cognitive moment of music' (1989, 5). In this respect Tarasti accords with my own approach (above, p. 240).

Classical composers often concentrated *savoir* into a small space. The two hammerstrokes which begin Beethoven's *Eroica* Symphony are not rich in information; they constitute a conventional dramatic gesture. The six bars that follow are, of course, the informational fountainhead of the movement and a concentration of *savoir*. They are followed by sections poor in *savoir*; first because of ordinary cadential and scalic procedures, afterwards because the development of the theme implies comparative redundancy.

Pouvoir has to do with technical resources. Clearly the compass, technique and characteristics of the instrument present limitations of *pouvoir*. Limits are also imposed by style; the opening gestures of Bartòk's Fourth Quartet would not be part of the pouvoir of classical music.

Style also imposes obligations. A classical movement must end in its original key; a serial work must conform with various versions of the tone row; a classical Indian improvisation must reflect the raga. These obligations represent musical *devoir*.

Musical *vouloir* is likened to the 'implication' which Leonard Meyer traces in musical figures. It is 'the internal trend *(tendance)* of music, its movement towards something'. Most Western music has substantial passages that are preparatory, developmental, valedictory; they seem to be *en route,* passages from one fixed point to another.

8.10.5. The Greimasian notions of being and doing (*être* and *faire*) are also matched in music. Being is 'the state of repose, statism, consonance'; doing is 'action, happening, dynamism and dissonance'.

Between these extremes are found *devenir*, 'becoming', and *paraître*, 'seeming', the latter significant in combining with 'nonbeing' to form the element of *lie*, which Tarasti translates into musical terms.

8.10.6. Most of the music analysed by Tarasti is for piano, though there is a song analysis (1991), which deals with the question of interpretation also. His analysis of the Seventh Prelude in Debussy's Second Book ('...La terrasse des audiences du clair de lune') is representative (Tarasti 1989).

This mysterious and evocative piece contains no traditional 'development' and matches no established form, except that its presentation of fragmentary references to the original theme may suggest a rondo. Nevertheless, its haunting effect suggests an empty theatre in which something unnamed is acted out; perhaps *Pelléas et Mélisande,* or a recitation of *L'Après-midi d'un Faune,* for both of these, Tarasti thinks, are echoed in the music. In any case, one can speak of a thread of narrativity, 'un récit sans aucun récit concret'. The substance of the narration concerns the desire for an object of value, which is continually frustrated; finally it is satisfied, but in a rather equivocal way. The work is empty of indexic meaning in the sense of intelligible Romantic gestures.

8.10.7. Like some of the literary works analysed by Greimas, this piece is pluri-isotopic. The stillness of the opening is due to a long C sharp pedal in the lowest register; this is an isotopy of *être*, being. But within this very pedal there is the germ of an isotopy of *faire*; it becomes apparent that it is a dominant (the piece is in F sharp major) and must lead to some resolution.

In other respects, the first bar is full of *savoir*; it is spatially *embrayé* at the very beginning (compressed into the central register) but the tempo is *débrayé*, being very slow.

Figure 8.31

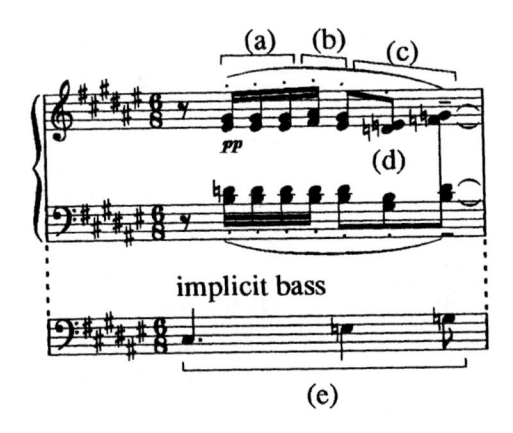

The thematic material is various in its content:

(a) repeated notes suggest movement towards some goal: *vouloir*.
(b) The appoggiatura figure (A sharp-G sharp) classically means 'lamentation, nostalgia, quest';
(c) a V-shaped motive, called a 'neume', which, together with
(d) parallel chordings, contains an element of *non-devoir*, because of the irrational shift to G natural and the traditional ban on parallels.
(e) An implied bass ascent C sharp-E-G, more clearly seen in the altered reprise at bar 20; this stresses the forward-directed *vouloir* of the theme.

8.10.8. This theme is the principal 'actor' of the narrative. It appears five times during the piece, always much varied (at bars 1, 7, 20, 25 and 39). When it comes, its inner *vouloir* leads to a transitional passage that culminates each time in frustration, *inachèvement*, and the reappearance of the theme; except for the last time, which leads to success and the attainment, in part, of the 'object of value'.

The initial statement, entirely built on the C sharp seventh, is frustrated by the simple device of an interrupted cadence; the return of the theme at bar 7 begins on a chord of D sharp minor (the submediant chord). The feeling of *inachèvement* is heightened by the *subito pp*, as it will be on several later occasions. There is a spatial *débrayage*; the figure is spread over three octaves, and moved high on the keyboard.

Figure 8.32

This leads at once to a *débrayage* of inner space; the key changes to B flat, and between bars 9 and 13 there is a passage of impatient joy, 'un peu animé et léger', a sort of fool's paradise which leads, after all, to nihilism. At bar 13, over an inversion of the ninth on C sharp (the dominant effect of the opening), there appears, not the theme or some resolution of its potencies, but a flaccid near-quotation from the *Prélude à l'Après-midi d'un Faune*, debilitating, projecting *non-vouloir*.

Figure 8.33

The section from bar 16 to bar 20 is, in Greimas's term, a process of 'premodalisation'. There is an air of 'becoming' (*devenir*) and the 'cradling' motive, together with the C sharp pedal, which now comes in all registers, hints at the return of the theme. The feature of pluri-isotopy is well shown; the pedal, as before, reflects *être*, 'a kind of stagnation', while the rising chromatic tenor suggests the modality of *vouloir*. And all the time, the appoggiaturas of the theme harp on the idea of passionate nostalgia.

Figure 8.34

The appearances of the theme at bars 20 and 25 suggest a 'passage à l'acte', a movement of the actor towards the dénouement. At bar 20 the theme is waltz-like though not much bound by the routines of a real waltz (by the waltz *devoir*), and at bar 25 there is the maximum *débrayage* of both internal and external space; the theme is presented in E flat, spread over more than 5 octaves.

This promises to lead to a musical climax. The crescendo at bar 28 heralds the loudest passage in the piece, which takes its material largely from bars 1-3 and extends a dominant seventh in C, with tiny fanfares in the tenor register that recall *Pelléas*. This is a pre-modalisation of even greater power; there is a strong *vouloir-faire*. However, the tonal *débrayage* and the non-functional chordings prefigure an unsatisfactory outcome.

There is, in fact, a return to F sharp major at bar 32, though the harmony is still an inversion of the ninth. Worse than this, the thematic material is not that of the actor, but the flaccid motive from bar 13 which recalls *L'Après-midi*.

Everything led us to expect a solution; and the restoration of the tonic, with widely-spaced chords, suggested at first that one had been found *(paraître)*. But it was not so; the promised 'object of value' was an empty sham *(non-être)*. In Greimas the combination *seeming* + *non-being* indicates *lie*. The *subito pp* section at bar 32, then, is a musical 'lie'.

Even the final variant of the actor, at bar 39, is unsatisfactory. There is internal and external *embrayage*, and the range is again narrow, in the central register of the piano. The tonic of F sharp is attained, but the note itself does not yet appear in either melody or bass, and the theme, instead of having the air of glorious success, is fragmentary. The actor has not vanquished, but has acquired 'un beaucoup plus grande expérience'.

The ghostly coda (bar 42) is texturally unique in the piece; its chiming, mechanical open fifths evoke an empty moonlit scene. Finally the appoggiatura - which vacillated throughout between a major and a minor second - is crushed into acciaccature, scarcely audible ('Timbrez légèrement la petite note', instructs Debussy), decisively minor seconds.

8.10.9. Using Greimas's categories of *euphorie* and *dysphorie*, this piece contains four actions or narrative utterances, leading respectively to conclusions that are neutral; dysphoric; seemingly euphoric (a lie); and euphoric. In each case the actor is transformed by an unsuccessful quest that leaves him fragmented, scattered. Even the final appearance is tragically vitiated; the end is cold, lonely.

Using symbols of narrative grammar, the narrative programme of the Prelude may be plotted (this is written in one continuous line by Tarasti; I have separated it into three lines for clarity, and appended a key).

$E = \text{être}$ $A = \text{acteur}$
$m = \text{modalité}$ $v = \text{is deprived of}$
$F = \text{faire}$ $\wedge = \text{possesses}$
$O = \text{object of value}$

$Em_1 (A \vee O); Fm_2 [A' \longrightarrow (A'' \vee O)];$
$\qquad\qquad Fm_3 [A'' \longrightarrow (A''' \vee O)];$
$\qquad\qquad\qquad Fm_4 [A''' \longrightarrow (A'''' \wedge O)]$

8.11. The semiotic square

8.11.1. Narrative analysis may be illuminated further by the use of the semiotic square. Western music is often built from contrasting or complementary themes; yet a mere binary distinction is often not enough to explain all the workings of a complex piece. Each of the themes may have a 'negative', so that as well as contraries there are contradictories. The two themes may be called *actant* and *antactant*, their opposites *negactant* and *negantactant* (Tarasti 1984, 61 n. 17).

Narrative analysis is particularly appropriate for enigmatic pieces that checkmate traditional methods. Chopin's *Polonaise-Fantaisie*, Op 61, is described by Gerald Abraham as 'a hard nut to crack'. Its opening is certainly enigmatic enough; with a key signature of A flat major, a brisk call-to-action of two chords in an inverted-dotted rhythm, the first a tonic minor chord, the second a chord of C flat major, leads to a wide-ranging arpeggio with added notes, *senza misura*, spanning the whole registral space.

Figure 8.35

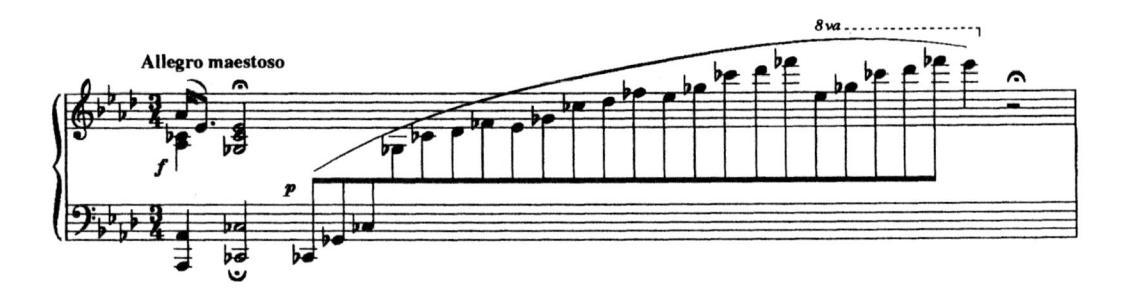

Of these two gestures, the first is vaguely intelligible; it is a kind of distanced version of the typical 'polonaise' rhythm, resembling, for example, the beginning of the more famous A major Polonaise, Op 40 no 1, where the key is unclouded and the dotted rhythm is straightforward. It is, at least, a vigorous 'in-thrust' *(enfoncement)* suitable for the beginning of a piece in polonaise style; its 'distancing' signifies, perhaps, that this is a 'polonaise-fantaisie'. At least, its vigorous 'enfoncement' and dotted rhythm will continue to be an important seme. The polonaise element, however distanced, must be an actant in this piece.

But what of the long arpeggio? Elsewhere, Chopin begins pieces with an exploration of the registral space - in the G minor Ballade, for example - but here there is a feeling of strangeness that suggests something more profound.

8.11.2. At bar 24 there appears the main theme of this piece; 'at last,' we cry, ' the protagonist, the hero-subject enters the scene' (62). Tiny fanfares in the tenor register signify that this is indeed a 'polonaise', and there are touches of dotted rhythm. But nothing could be further in spirit from the thrusting character of the opening *('enfoncement')*; the theme is *mezza voce*, vacillating between B flat and C, apparently seeking the tonic, which it gains only temporarily at bar 27; a sequence takes the music immediately to B flat minor, where the cadence, of course, leads to the inconclusive B flat with which the theme began. This passage is soft, melodic, lyrical, unassertive; a 'non-polonaise'. It is, perhaps, the 'negactant', the negative form of the opening in-thrust.

Figure 8.36

[musical notation: mezza voce, p]

8.11.3. It is to be suspected that the arpeggio is one of the four terms of the semiotic square of this piece. But which? Let us first place the opening 'in-thrust'. It is in itself not a true polonaise gesture, for reasons already stated; it is a 'polonaise-fantaisie', a sort of poetic contrary to the virile and martial polonaise rhythm. It is, therefore, s_2, the contrary or *antactant*.

The main theme, perversely, is the negative of this; identifiable as a polonaise only by the most tenuous traces, it is soft and lyrical, 'in a certain manner the negation of the negation'. This provides $\overline{s_2}$, not the negactant but the *negantactant*.

The arpeggio scarcely qualifies as s_1, the logical contrary of the 'in-thrust'. Provisionally, we must assume that it is the negative form of s_1, that is, $\overline{s_1}$, the negactant. Only the main term, the actant, is now missing from the semiotic square; it is something in the nature of a 'rise' (*montée*) or 'elevation'.

Figure 8.37

$$s_1 \qquad s_2 \text{ 'enfoncement'}$$

main theme $\overline{s_2} \qquad \overline{s_1}$ arpeggio

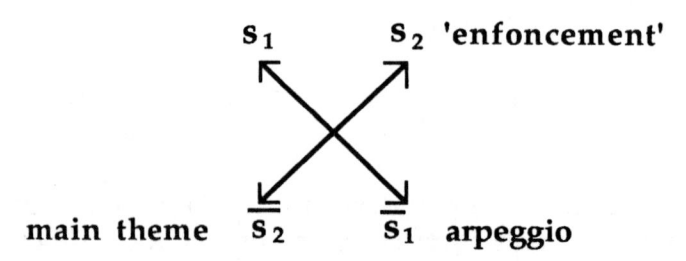

8.11.4. The impotence of traditional analysis, faced with a structure in which the main theme is 'the negation of a negation' and in which the principal actant is systematically held back from the expository passages, is easy to understand. The two actants continue to appear in conflict or in dialogue. In the central nocturne-like section (bar 152) the vacillating major second of the main theme is accompanied by undulating arpeggios in the bass. It is a passage of 'being' (*être*) rather than action; 'the actant and the negactant are not in conflict one with the other, but sing a conciliating duet'.

Figure 8.38

Recapitulation does not bring a solution to the problematics of this musical structure. The *pianissimo* reference to the opening at bar 214 is no more than a nostalgic hint, and even the triumphant reappearance of the main theme, with a bass in triplet octaves, at bar 242 cannot explain the many traits of 'elevation', rising arpeggios with added notes, which have intruded at various points. Nevertheless, this passage is the ultimate 'enfoncement', a victorious climax for the contrary actant.

Figure 8.39

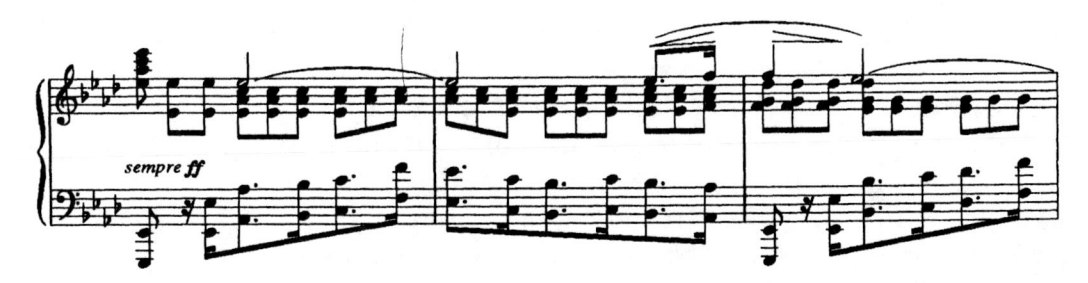

The passage which follows (bar 254; Figure 8.39), rather strangely, presents the theme of the 'nocturne' in its opposite modality; it is now a motive of 'doing', of virile action. Above all, the undulating bass arpeggios now appear in *fortissimo* dotted rhythms, the epitome of an equestrian polonaise. 'Now the negactant truly receives sovereignty over the actant'.

As the piece draws to a close, the arpeggio figure swamps the whole texture, matching the extreme registral *débrayage* of the opening unmeasured arpeggios, but now storming in thunderous double octaves. This figure 'escapes from its subject position in the bass to become the veritable actant, the principal subject, rather than its initial role of helper or opponent'. It becomes clear that this is 'a modalised variation of the motive of an arpeggio with added notes describing the "elevation"... that is to say, the term s_1 of the semiotic square only manifests itself now as a kind of reply to the problematics of the fundamental narrative programme of the complete work'(72).

Figure 8.40

8.12. Markedness theory

8.12.1. As an epilogue to this discussion of narrative grammar, the work of Robert Hatten on markedness theory may be mentioned. It was remarked in passing that opposed terms can sometimes be distinguished on the axis marked/unmarked. Thus, in the opposition *being/seeming*, *being* may be the marked term since it carries the marker *truth*. Hatten's work is partly dependent on Greimas, as well as bearing some relation to the theory of intonation. Its immediate source is the theory of linguistic markedness of Michael Shapiro (*The Sense of Grammar: Language as Semeiotic*, Bloomington 1983).

In the simplest form of markedness, one term in a binary opposition is marked, the other unmarked (Figure 8.41a). In most cases, however, the marked term covers a smaller semantic space than the unmarked. For example, in the case of the present and past tenses, the past is marked because the present can imply 'pastness' as well as 'presentness', but the past can never signify 'presentness'. The marked term is more specific; it 'conveys a narrower range of expressive content'. It is, perhaps, a comparatively significant event in a universe of lesser significance (Figure 8.41b).

Figure 8.41

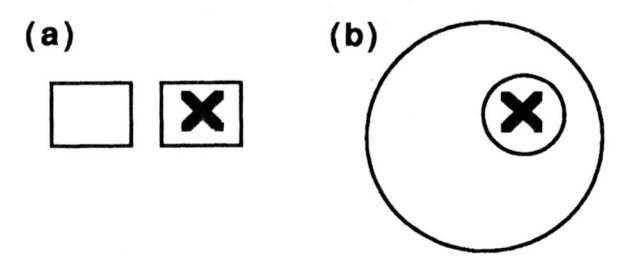

In the music of the eighteenth and nineteenth centuries the minor mode is marked, the major unmarked. The major occurs much more often than the minor, and consequently has many possible expressions, 'from the pastoral to the *galanterie*, and from the singing style to the comic *buffo*' (Hatten 1988, 5). The minor, however, always has some implication of 'tragicness', and for this reason Romantic critics tended to find extramusical content especially in works in minor keys (Mozart's D minor Piano Concerto and Beethoven's Fifth Symphony).

Figure 8.42

Markedness is tellingly illustrated when a musical figure, recurrent in a particular work, is suddenly presented with some conspicuous alteration. The new version of the figure seems to possess an especial depth of significance. In Beethoven's *Waldstein* Sonata, the initial statement ends with a descending arpeggio of C minor, and this figure often recurs (Figure 8.42a). In the recapitulation the last note is raised to A flat; this unaccountable 'accident' seems a dramatic and ironic gesture of extraordinary pregnancy. This is the marked form (Figure 8.42b).

8.12.2. If musical figures and features are distinguished in this way then a new kind of analysis may be envisaged, based on *markers* (correlations with content) rather than *labels* (technical descriptions). Indeed, expressive analysis and technical analysis are complementary, for the moments of high significance (the most marked events) often do not coincide with points of structural importance (themes, reprises); 'the hierarchy of dramatic relevance or salience may not be congruent with the hierarchy of a purely syntactic analysis of a work' (Hatten 1987a, 209).

The significance of a marked event is related to the context, like the sememe in Greimasian theory. Every work has its own dramatic schema, the 'dramatic accounting of a spiritual journey' (Hatten 1988, 10), called an *expressive genre*. For example, Beethoven's works, which often begin tragically, follow different trajectories, ending in victory (Fifth Symphony), in confirmed tragedy ('Appassionata'), or serene transcendence (op 111 and other late works). There may also be *intertextual* links; a passage of falling diatonic intervals in the second subject of the slow movement of the Sonata, Op 106, suggests the idea of tragic resignation, and this is confirmed when similar figures begin the song 'Resignation' and are used for the words 'Dona nobis pacem' in the *Missa Solemnis* (1988, 13-14).

At their greatest extent, intertextual links become cultural units; that is to say, a certain gesture or manner acquires a fixed signification for a whole musical style. Thus, loud fanfares suggest a heroic mood; a musette-like pedal point evokes a pastoral atmosphere. At this point Hatten's ideas recall the 'topics' of Agawu, and indeed the intonation theory of Asafiev, though he does not stress the *popular* aspect of style retention. The content of these established correlations is consistent and can be expressed extramusically; since an extramusical link appears to be constant, these significations are not, strictly speaking, metaphorical. It was asserted by Nelson Goodman (1968) that expressive correlations to works of art ('the music is sad') are always metaphorical. But there seems no difference in identifying established cultural content in a musical gesture, from recognizing the 'meaning' of a linguistic morpheme. In a sense, therefore, the tragic referent of the minor mode in Romantic music is a *literal* meaning. The category *metaphorical* should be reserved for more fanciful or programmatic descriptions, like

Beethoven's finding in the slow movement of his Quartet, Op 18 no 1, *'les derniers soupirs* of Romeo and Juliet in the tomb' (Hatten 1991, 4).

8.12.3. A particular type of marked event is termed a *trope*. In rhetoric this term denotes a word or expression used in a sense other than the literal (as in metonymy or syndecdoche). For Hatten, the trope gains significance by contradicting stylistic expectations. For example, a piece may start with a gesture of closure (as does Beethoven's First Symphony). This kind of contradiction is not the same as contrast; Mozart's 'Jupiter' Symphony begins with two figures in oppositional contrast, but these are heard as a single theme.

The appearance of the pastoral mood in an eighteenth-century musette would not be an example of troping, though it is clearly a significant cultural unit. At the start of the finale of Beethoven's Op 101 Sonata, however, the recurrence of pastoral material from the first movement is a marked event because it conflicts with stylistic expectation. The loud imitative passage that follows, *geschwind und mit Entschlossenheit*, is equally unexpected; its expressive contrast (it is both 'fanfare-like' and 'learned') generates a meaningful syntagm - not just a structural syntagm, like the 'Jupiter' opening. Both moods, the *pastoral* and the *fanfare/learned*, are tropes; together they make a syntactic expression which is, perhaps, a 'narrative utterance' realising a structural relation on the deep level. And indeed, Hatten interprets the passage with a single opposition (active vs. passive) and reduces it finally to a single complex term ('a pastorally inflected victory', 1991, 12).

Contradiction of expectation as a stylistic marker is not confined to beginnings. It may occur during the course of a movement. Certain locations in sonata form are commonly unmarked and low in expressive content. For example, the end of the transition, before the second group, is often a passage of featureless cadence-prolongation. In the slow movement of Beethoven's Op 106 Sonata, there occurs at this point an extraordinary chromatic passage in which the dominant note is quitted in the bass (bar 41 in Figure 8.43) for a contour that rises twice to B but droops away to G sharp and beyond, scarcely touching the dominant, A, again until just before the second group (in fact, at bar 44). This 'drooping' contour can be illustrated from several works of Beethoven; it seems to mean 'yielding' or 'submission'. Instead of an unmarked passage, low in significance, a highly suggestive trope is embedded in the movement at this point.

Figure 8.43

[musical score, measures 40–44]

8.13. The formal nature of semantic analysis

8.13.1. It may be thought that the structuralist approach invalidates referentialism. This is not necessarily the case provided the referential level is handled formally, and this is the essence of structural semantics.

The 'analysis of the neutral level' is able to present a comprehensive inventory of musical features from which individual analyses are shown to be selections. Performers, too, stress some features rather than others; the interpretative complexion of the analyst or the performer can thus be plotted.

The analyses of structural semantics have a similar generalising function. If the emotional trajectory of a work is described in abstract terms by the use of a metalanguage based on narrative grammar, interpretations written in more evocative terms may be classified.

8.13.2. Liszt's description of Chopin's *Polonaise-Fantaisie*, for example, is peculiarly illuminated by Tarasti's analysis of this piece.

> One by one, all the phases of passion are traced: charming deceptions of coquetterie; the touch of imperceptible leanings; capricious garlands sketched by fantasy; the mortal depressions of wilting joys which die as they are born, flowers of mourning, like black roses which bring sadness with the very scent of their petals, that fall from the frail stalks with the least breeze;... pleasures without past or future, enraptured with chance meetings; illusions, inexplicable tastes, enticing us to adventure... (from *Chopin*, quoted by Tarasti, 1984, 67).

The analysis showed that musical syntagms are almost always of mixed modality. The dotted rhythm of the polonaise genre, for example, often appears in languid or lyrical contexts, and the heroic 'elevation' motive takes on its true evocation only at the end. Passages of 'vouloir' regularly lead to unfulfilment or part fulfilment; much of the piece is occupied with nostalgic reminiscence or anticipation.

These features, systematically described by Tarasti, are Liszt's 'deceptions', 'wilting joys', 'chance meetings', 'pleasures without past or future'. The structural analyst does not mean to expose or replace the intuitive accounts of interpretative writers. On the contrary, his purpose is to reassure; idiosyncratic commentators like Liszt were not talking about nothing at all, but were expressing in poetic terms a real insight.

8.13.3. The topical analysts would say this view blesses introversive semiosis but disqualifies extroversive. Yet even the most rigorous of these, Kofi Agawu, admits that the 'interpretation' of topics is, finally, not essential.

> We need to acknowledge the inadequacy of topics as ontological signs, and replace that formulation with structuralist notions of arbitrary signs, for it seems clear that even those listeners for whom the referential elements are real and substantive would agree that the individual gestures derive their importance less from their paradigmatic or associative properties than from their syntagmatic or temporal ones (Agawu 1991, 117).

And finally, let us admit that there is room for a 'dirty' view of musical semantics, as well as the intellectual purity of the structuralist approach. Indeed, reference and narrative may be demanded by historical conscience; this was how the composers meant it, and how contemporaries heard it. But there is no signifying without structure, which is where semiotics has its true home.

9

THE THEORY OF INTONATION

9.1. *The music of speech*

9.1.1. I exclaim, 'Get off.'
My words have a slight degree of denotative or literal meaning, which can be derived from reading them on the page. But in fact most of the expression is conveyed by the intonation of my voice. If my pitch and dynamic level are high, the tempo rapid and each word is stressed, I am probably giving an urgent and angry command to an inferior: perhaps instructing a small boy to cease climbing on my car. If my tempo is slow, only the second word is stressed, the pitch sinks about a fifth and the second word is much longer than the first, then I am merely chiding: perhaps telling my lover to cease her affectionate caresses, in which case I may really mean, 'Please continue.'

9.1.2. The speech-tunes that convey these meanings are not peculiar to me. Everyone understands these combinations of high and low pitch, rising and falling intervals because to some degree they are universal in the language and culture, like the phonological aspect of the language itself; intonation is not, however, rule-bound. There is no 'grammar of intonation' (Karbusicky 1986, 165).
And all of these intonational features, stress, pitch, tempo, timbre, syllable duration, are *musical* features (linguists would call them 'suprasegmental'). It should be noticed that none of them are of any interest apart from their expressive meaning. It is fruitless to study pitch-variations in speech as some kind of abstract pattern; these variations are expressive and must be examined as such.

9..2. *Asafiev's* Musical Form as Process

9.2.1. The writings of B V Asafiev (1884-1949) have been particularly influential in Eastern Europe. Reading his *Musical Form as Process* (Asafiev 1976), with its vague, speculative ideas and its windy style, comes as a shock after the intellectual crispness of Hjelmslev and Nattiez. His approach, however, has important theoretical consequences, and his views are resolutely interpretative and semantic (though Asafiev himself repudiated the term 'musical semantics'). He has been called a 'pre-semiotic' writer by some; for Nigel Osborne he is a 'proto-sémiologiste' (Osborne 1986, 220).

9.2.2. For Asafiev all the aspects mentioned above are features of *speech intonation* which is distinct from musical intonation. However, music has its origin in speech intonation, like two branches springing from the same trunk; here Asafiev follows Hegel. 'Music takes its origin from a voice touched with a lively emotion. Intonation, its manifestation, begins from a tension. The act of speaking is a tension which betrays, through its trace in muscular effort, an order of the brain, the presence of a consciousness. Music responds to the same series of influences that pass through the voice' (Osborne 1986, 217).

Asafiev writes a speculative history in which music, beginning as speech intonation, serves next as the declamation of verse, its rhythm dependent on verse prosody, its pitch indeterminate but retaining the instinct of an expressive speaker. In this style there is an 'inevitable combination of word and tone'. But the rhythm and pitch-contour of expressive speech had to be modified in order for musical intonation to be born.

Speech rhythm was adapted, first to the rhythm of dance, which can be heard in medieval *laudi*, and finally to the rhythm of breathing; the periodicity of language is much more irregular and fragmentary than the long, regular, arched periods of breathing which are the basis of song.

9.2.3. Speech is a continuous glissando without precise definition of pitches. But certain speech intonations became habitual and their pitches recognized: the *intervallic* principle came into being. Intervals acquired their own figurative value, apart from the content of the words. Though there is a 'condition of tonal tension' which governs both speech and poetry, there now arose a new phenomenon, 'of which verbal speech had no need...the *interval*, the precise *determinant* of the emotionally meaningful quality of intonation' (Asafiev 1976, 931).

> The interval makes it possible to isolate and neutralise music, dissociating it from the voice. But the operation brings only a qualified

> success, in that the interval cannot entirely replace intonation (Osborne 1986, 217).

The expressive value of intervals was based on their 'ponderability', their 'degree of surmountability by the voice'; it is harder to sing a ninth than a second, harder to sing a tritone than a perfect fourth. The fourth and fifth are the normal extremes of an emotionally heightened speaking voice, so these became the first recognized intervals and modes resulted from filling them in with extra notes. Thus, the most primitive forms of music are built on tetrachords.

Eventually *melos* came into being, a type of intonation based on metrical rhythm (rather than speech rhythm) and on the intervallic principle. Its communicative quality was dependent only on musical figurativeness; it did not need verbal content. It could thus be transferred to instruments. Its vocal origin was ever the basis of its expressiveness, however, and people might compliment a violinist for his 'singing' tone. Melos only became fully independent of speech-content - it only became *melody* - in Italy in the seventeenth and eighteenth centuries.

The intervallic principle also made possible another kind of musical independence. The intonation of a religious text might be surrounded with 'musically free intonations'; polyphony came into being and eventually harmony, through the perfection of the principle of voice-leading.

Music, now fully independent, is wholly free of verbal content. In the case of speech, on the other hand, the intonation is not entirely necessary for communication: 'words may be spoken without intoning their *quality*, their true meaning'. For this reason, words retain some of their expressiveness even when they are read silently. Music has no denotative or literal meaning and so *must* be intoned. 'Music is always intonational, or otherwise it is inaudible' (1976, 631). Thus a written score is in no way music.

9.2.4. The figurativeness of music is something which develops socially within a whole community, in a dialectical relation to musical works. All aspects of intonation - intervals, melodic figures, harmonies, timbre, forms - are worked out by the whole society and represent a universal competence. 'The people, the culture, and the historical epoch define the stages of intonation, and through intonation are determined both the means of musical expression, and the selection and interconnection of musical elements'. Important pitches and formal moments become 'knots' joined by 'arches' - intervals or longer sections producing the musical motive which is 'an expression of figurative thinking'.

Certain intervals are 'characteristic for a given epoch'. The fourth was the most important interval of the French Revolutionary period; two fourths begin the *Marseillaise*. The sixth typified the Romantic period, the augmented fourth was seminal for the Russian 'Five'. The meaning of an interval depends on period and culture; the *Marseillaise* fourths and the fourth which forms the basis of Don Juan's theme in Dargomizhsky's *The Stone Guest* are, in effect, different intervals because their expressions are different.

The last two centuries (before the writing of *Musical Form as Process* in 1942) have been characterized by a single musical mode: the mode of the *leading note*. The dynamic quality of the leading note, its generation of tension, prolongation and 'dominantness', have led to a style characterised by development and scale-oriented melody. The tritone appeared as a derivative of the leading note, and with it the chromatic semitone. There are, however, three kinds of semitone: the note of chromatic coloration, the scale degree, and the leading note, all with different meanings.

The creative mastery of large forms by prominent composers is not questioned. The people, however, do not listen primarily to large forms; they hear and memorize short fragments - often at cadences - which 'enter into oral tradition as *living intonations*... Beyond the compositions themselves lies the world of music as the activity of the mass public consciousness, from little more than sound interjections, at times simply rhythmic intonations, and from characteristic, universally loved melodic figures, to more developed melodic shoots and harmonic turns...'

Thus develops a 'vocabulary of intonations'. understood by a particular society. This is not a vulgar misapprehension of music. Haydn and Mozart, for example, understood and used the vocabulary of their time. It is up to the composer to make a valuable statement within the language of his society; otherwise the cynical exploitation of familiar intonations for cheap appeal merely leads to a 'consumer's jumble'.

It is vital that good music be performed. However great the work of music, its salient traits cannot enter into the public consciousness if the work is not performed. 'Music which is not heard is not included in the auditory memory of the people... and consequently, it is not in the storehouse of intonations which are generally accepted by society, by the environment, by the epoch, and of course by the [ruling] class...' (translator's insertion).

The comprehension of music can only begin with the familiar. 'Each listener... begins an auditory acquaintance with a composition new to him through recognition and comparison as to whether there are elements in it of intonations familiar to his consciousness.' No work can be wholly new, or it would be wholly incomprehensible.

Unfortunately, intonations lose their expressiveness with over-use. 'The vital content of the intonations of a given music are exhausted... in this process of exhaustion there remains less and less of the music [as an expressive medium]... till it is no longer heard; its content and spirit are gone.' Eventually this leads to an *intonational crisis* in which familiar devices are given new meanings and new intonations are discovered. These crises reflect periods of social change. For instance, the dissolution of feudal society in the eighteenth century produced an intonational crisis that was resolved by Beethoven. His music embodied the ethical idealism of the democratic classes. As an example of his re-evaluation of traditional devices we may take the *tonic*. Previously a mere 'formal resolution of dissonances, a state of rest', it becomes for Beethoven 'the sphere of affirmation, of firm conviction'.

9.2.5. Music is *an art of intoned meaning*. Like the intonation of speech, musical intonation is important only because of its expressiveness, not as an abstract pattern. While many meanings can be traced for a given composition or extract, interpretation is not necessarily a guarantee of meaning. Musical melody reflects a kind of melody of thought. Asafiev sees thought as 'melodic, tuneful, fluid, conditioned by a kind of mental breathing and rhythm, appearing as "mental intoning"'. This elusive idea comes remarkably close to the views of Gestalt psychologists.

Music analysis, then, should concern itself primarily with the expressive level of music. Schenkerism, the neutral level, generative analysis would all have seemed equally sterile to Asafiev. Intonation theory is focussed on meaning. It is the most radically *semantic* theory discussed in this book.

9.2.6. Certain important consequences may be drawn.

The whole society - the 'people' - is seen as the generator and repository of musical style. While musical greatness is respected, there is no corresponding contempt for folk, rural or popular styles.

Clearly an ignorance of popular music would disqualify a musicologist as an analyst of serious compositions. This goes against the *Wertästhetik* of the nineteenth century, the view of aesthetics as hammer of triviality and guardian of profundity.

Since the significance of music depends on cultural and social norms, intonation theory is universally valid for ethnic musics. The study of written scores by Western scholars is also legitimate, however; the score, like the intonation, is a cultural object and records many intonational aspects. None of the concepts of Asafiev - interval, melos, intonational vocabulary, exhaustion, crisis - is inherently limited to Western music; ethnic music may equally be seen as relating to a vocabulary of intonations in the public consciousness.

The various dictionary meanings of the word 'intonation' are all embraced by Asafiev's term. The intoning of liturgical texts is clearly a form of expressive intonation. Even the notion of pitch-precision, the kind of intonation sought by string players, is a vital part of 'intonation'; ordinary people hear music with extraordinary precision and are quite able to discern when a performance, in any style, is out of tune. 'The public ear hears with displeasure the smallest falsity, the smallest digression from pure tuning.'

9.3. Intonation in popular song

9.3.1. It is not surprising that Asafiev's theories have proved especially fruitful in the field of popular music. Vladimir Zak (1979 and 1982), in his work on Russian popular songs, has demonstrated the process of *re-intoning*. In a changed social situation a musical form has to be intoned differently in addressing new listeners. The new intonation, called the 'address of the form', causes a shift in the meaning; but something of the original meaning is bound to be retained.

A brief cadential figure of four notes occurs often in nineteenth-century music, always in lyrical circumstances. It is illustrated from Tchaikovsky's *Francesa da Rimini* (Figure 9.1a). This phrase appears in the works of Schumann, Mendelssohn, Chopin, Liszt and Wagner, and recalls especially the *Agnus Dei* from Verdi's *Requiem*.

In Russian love songs this figure often expresses 'intonations of entreaty, complaint or distress', for example in 'Zkazhi, zachem' ('Say why') (Figure 9.1b). Sometimes, however, it is re-intoned in heroic marches. 'This does not result in complete suppression of the original character. On the contrary, it undoubtedly leads to the austere march sounding more lyrical.' The example is a phrase from the march 'Friendship is all' by V Muradeli (Figure 9.1c).

Figure 9.1

(a)

(b)

TY IZ - MO - NI - LA MNA TAK ZHES - TO - KO
['You have betrayed me so cruelly...']

(c) *Tempo di marcia*

NA MOS - KOV - SKOM MIR - NOU FES - TI - VA - LE
['We made friends at the Moscow festival.']

Asafiev, it will be recalled, considered the fourth to be a characterising interval of the French Revolutionary period, shown most obviously in the opening phrase of the *Marseillaise* (Figure 8.2a). This formula (two fourths divided by a second) became very common in Russian opera, and appears in patriotic songs like 'The Red banner'. However, it is also adapted to slow tempi; the popular composer V Solv'ev-Sedoy employs it in a lyrical song with a heroic theme, the 'Soldiers' song', but also in a nostalgic waltz, 'Igrai, mor bayan'. 'The hard intonational core of these lyrical compositions is directly traceable to the melodic turns originating in the songs of struggle' (Figure 9.2b and c).

9.3.2. These fragments drawn from the intonational vocabulary are sometimes hidden within a tune, discernible only when inessential notes have been subtracted. The *Marseillaise* motive, for example, is reflected in the popular song 'Build up the fires', if the stressed notes are extrapolated (Figure 9.3a). The pattern of accented notes is called the 'line of latent mode' (LLM). Surprisingly often, the LLM of popular songs - and indeed of all lyric melody - turns out to be pentatonic in character. The pentatonic flavour may be an important feature of the intonation, with its own burden of

The Theory of Intonation

meaning. The major pentatonic mode, for example (the mode on *doh*), carries a suggestion of light: 'images of bright sunshine or of moonlit countryside, of spring blossoming or of an early morning awakening'. This is illustrated by the folksong 'When night is vanquished' as well as the Serenade from Khrennikov's orchestral suite to *Much Ado about Nothing* (Figure 9.3b and c).

Figure 9.2

(a) Al-lons en-fants de la pat-ri-e

(b) SKA-ZHU MO-EY MA-TE-RI, DE-TYAM SKA-ZHU...
['Tell my mother, tell my kids...']

(c) *Facilmente*
SDA-LA-KOY YA ZAS-TA-VY
['I came from afar...']

Figure 9.3

(a)

(b) *Vigoroso*

(c) Khrennikov, Serenade
Allegro no troppo

[The leaves are stirring slightly, the silvery moonlight is sweet;
No one is going to see us, the passionate lovers of the night.]

Other pentatonic LLMs have different evocations. The *soh*-mode, for example, imports a solemn atmosphere to Dunaevsky's 'Song of the Motherland', the signature tune of Soviet radio (Figure 9.4).

The LLM may also play its part on the syntagmatic level. There is often an intonational contrast between the verse and the refrain of a song; the structural passage from verse to refrain marks also a semantic passage so that the refrain is an answer or a solution to the problems of the verse. This feature is discussed at greater length below, in connection with Western popular music. In Zak's example (Figure 9.5), the song 'In a sunlit glade' by Solov'ev-Sedoy, the LLM of the verse is in the pentatonic *lah*-mode, which has a minor sound. Its inventory of pitches (A-C-D-E-G) excludes F. The refrain then begins strongly on F, declaring the independence of its LLM.

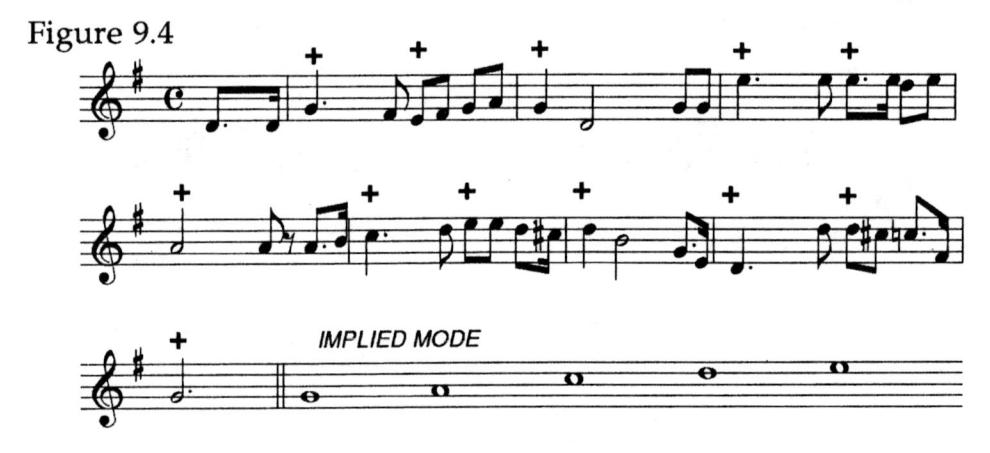

Figure 9.4

A similar progression may even occur within the same section of a song, to mark a climax or emotional crux in the words. The revolutionary hymn 'March on comrades, and be brave' is based on an ahemitonic mode, like the other tunes cited above: in this case the *doh*-mode, which in the key of C excludes F and B. As the words prefigure the successful outcome of the revolutionary struggle ('We will fight our way through to freedom') the tune breaks out of the mode, its final phrase being constructed on the very cadential tritone which is impossible in pentatony. Zak calls this a 'colour explosion' (Figure 9.6).

Figure 9.5

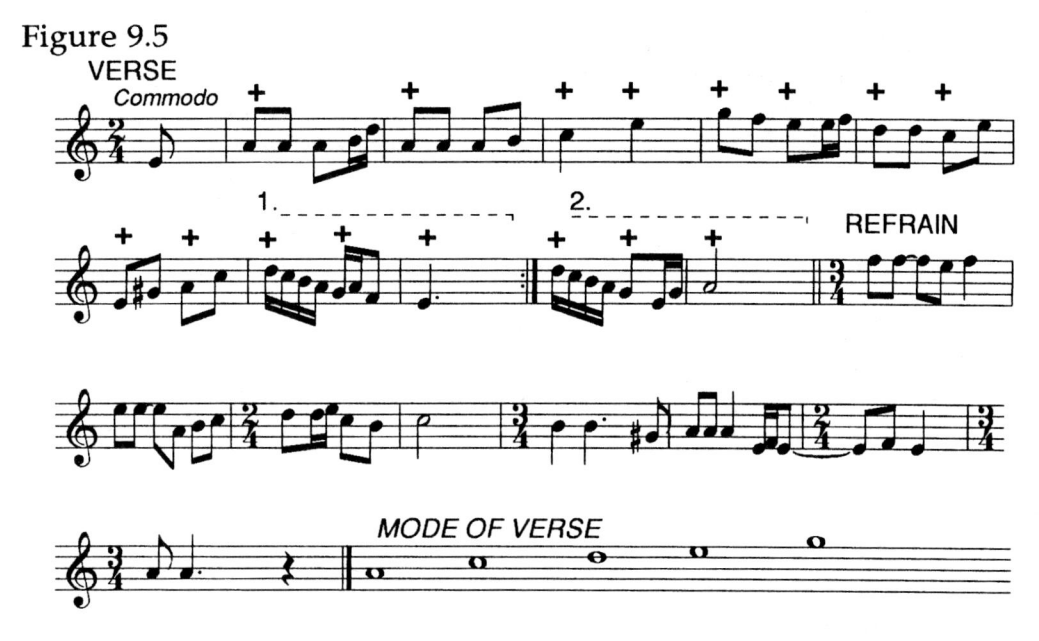

[Musical notation: VERSE, Commodo, with 1. and 2. endings, REFRAIN, and MODE OF VERSE]

9.3.3. The popularity of a song guarantees that it will be sung by many people in many different circumstances. Sometimes there will be re-intonation caused by the temperament of the singers. When one sings a familiar song, according to Asafiev, one presents 'one's own ideas, views, tastes, habits or simply one's own emotional disposition' (quoted by Zak 1982, 108). People are especially fond of lyric intonations and often introduce these into songs of different character. For example, the lyric formula quoted above (Figure 9.1a) is often heard when Dunaevsky's Sports March is sung, in place of the simpler original (Figure 9.7).

Figure 9.6

[Musical notation: Tempo di marcia, with MODE OF TUNE and LAST PHRASE]

['March on, comrades, and be brave! May struggle give us courage. We will fight our way through to freedom.']

Figure 9.7

Dunaevsky, Sports March

Popular variant

The common people, remarks Zak, are 'romantic at heart and always eager to live'. However, nuances much more subtle than this may be expressed when an individual singer performs a familiar song.

9.4. Two Scottish singers

9.4.1. The individual idioms of folk singers have been noted often by researchers. The concept of intonation is demonstrated vividly when the same song is sung by two singers with personal connections. Jeannie Robertson was a Scottish traveller or 'tinker', a member of a vagrant group who have preserved much of Scotland's ancient folksong. Her daughter, Lizzie Higgins, settled down in Aberdeen as a fish-filleter. The singing of both women has been recorded and carefully transcribed, and it shows that while Jeannie's style was comparatively direct, Lizzie, though she learnt all the material from her mother, sings in a more highly ornamented style. In Jeannie's singing you were more aware of the 'address of the form'.

> Jeannie conjures up a picture of the campfire with an audience, probably small but always responsive and inspiring the singer to sway them in the style that moves them most (Munro 1970, 178).

Lizzie's style is very different. The voice timbres are quite distinct: 'Lizzie's has a husky element to it, very expressive and attractive, with a strength and steadfastness which contains hardly a trace of vibrato.' Her more elaborate ornamentation shows the influence of bagpipe music, 'in particular the playing of her father, the piper Donald Higgins, to whom she has listened from her earliest years'. In addition, 'her comparative lack of dynamic variation and her freedom from vibrato may be attributable to the strong influence of pipe-music'.

Here is the first phrase of the ballad 'Edward' ('Son David'), first in the simplified form provided by Bronson (1959-1966), then as sung by Jeannie, then by Lizzie. Jeannie Robertson's version is from Gower and Porter (1970), Lizzie Higgins's from Munro (1970).

Asafiev would hear in the daughter's singing the settled worker, no longer vagrant; the child of two famous performers; the Aberdonian; as well as the different personal expression of the words of the song, just as we can derive much information about a speaker from the intonation of his speech.

Figure 9.8

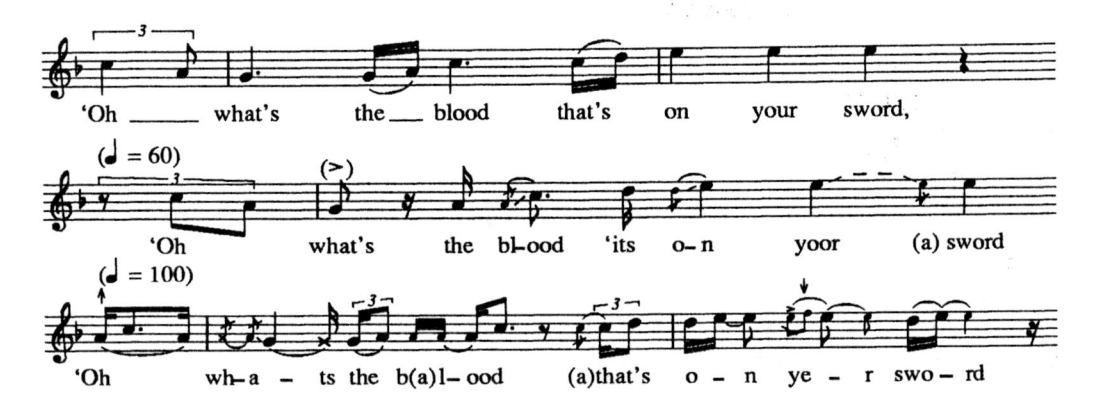

9.5. Kojak and Abba

9.5.1. The remarkable analyses of popular music by Philip Tagg are not expressed in the language of intonation theory, though the author admits that it 'easily lends itself to application in the realm of popular music since it embraces all levels of musical expression and perception from onomatopoeic programmatic signals to complex formal constructions without... placing them on either overt or occult scales of aesthetic value judgement' (Tagg 1979, 42). Tagg's work is similar in many respects to Zak's, however, and illustrates especially clearly the dependence of musical expression on the vocabulary of intonations stored within a cultural group. He admits that his ideas have 'much in common with the holistic character of Intonation theory'. Without saying so, he regards music as 'intoned idea', and devotes himself to discovering the meanings which have generated musical forms. Like Asafiev he refuses to link two musical features which, though formally the same, have different meanings: 'Just as no one would presume the same morpheme to mean the same thing in two different languages..., it would be absurd to presume that a B flat 13 chord "means" the same in the language of nineteenth-century operetta and in bebop jazz' (1979, 75).

Traditional analysis, preoccupied with form, can contribute little on its own. 'Instead of opposing extrageneric... and congeneric... approaches' (the terms are Wilson Coker's; see above, p. 205) we should treat them as complementary; analysis must be 'based on a thorough study of the dialectical relations between the musical structure, its conception, production, transmission, and reception, and its social meaning, uses, and functions' (Tagg 1987, 285).

To this clearly intonational spirit Tagg joins an avowedly semiotic technique. He describes his field as the 'semiotics of popular music' (Tagg 1987) and identifies his method as 'hermeneutic-semiological' (Tagg 1982, 47). Above all, his metalanguage is largely drawn from linguistics, and he revives Charles Seeger's idea of the *museme*, the musical morpheme (see Chapter 3, above).

For this reason, Tagg is of especial importance in the field of music semiotics: otherwise, the whole tradition of intonation theory is only 'proto-semiotic'.

9.5.2. The *logical*, and thus abstract, basis of Seeger's museme is neither discussed nor acknowledged by Tagg, for the later writer's museme is clearly a carrier of semantic content. Nevertheless, he accepts Seeger's definition of the museme.

> A unit of three components - three tone beats - can constitute two progressions and meet the requirements for a complete, independent unit of music-logical form or mood in both direction and extension. Both variance and invariance can be exhibited in each of the four simple functions. It can be regarded as binary and holomorphic - a musical morpheme or museme (Seeger 1960, 239).

It will be recalled that Seeger considered two events necessary for a unit of musical signification; since two pitches (or rhythms, tempi and so on) are needed for a single event, the smallest number of units that can make up a museme is three (above, pp. 74-80).

Tagg adds that the progression from silence to sound at the beginning of a phrase may go towards a museme, so that the first two notes of a phrase may suffice. He replaces Seeger's various types of museme with three classes only: *melodic, accompanying* and *contrasting*. It is apparent that Tagg's segmentation is based on pertinence and meaning; Seeger's approach remained obscure, and it would be hard to apply his methods, except to music already fragmentary by nature. Tagg isolates and interprets musemes by a process called 'inter-objective comparison' (IOC), which means looking for similar patterns in other music of related traditions.

9.5.3. He analyses the theme from *Kojak* (a television series about an American detective). This is played by four horns in unison, accompanied by strings, synthesizer and electric bass. The initial gesture is a horn 'whoop', an upward octave portamento. The theme itself begins with a similar 'whoop' at a lower pitch (Figure 9.9a). Since this is the first motive in the theme, the two notes may count as a museme, the progression from silence to sound being its first element (Figure 9.9b).

Figure 9.9 (© 1973, 1975 by Duchess Music Corporation. All rights controlled and administered by MCA Music Publishing, a division of MCA Inc.)

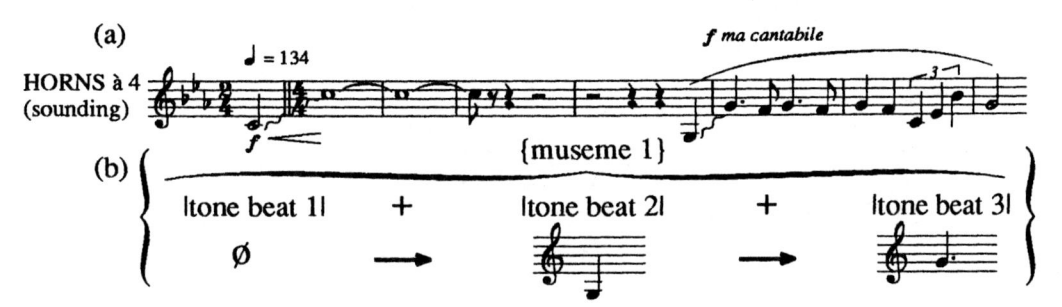

The timbre of the horn is the first aspect to be discussed. While brass instruments 'have traditionally been connected with male-dominated areas of activity, such as war, marching, parades... and their inherent affective sensations of bravery, danger, threat, energy and excitement', the horn has been 'less commonly used in military circumstances' and has been associated more specifically with 'hunting and postage' (Tagg 1979, 125). The horn's traditional connection is with 'men on horseback galloping through woods and fields, hard on the heels of hounds in pursuit of game... or riding "post-haste" along country lanes'. Horn calls thus evoke 'speed, excitement and energy'. Some of these old calls have been preserved; they often leap upwards to a strong beat in the manner of the *Kojak* tune, though not usually by so much as an octave; fifths are more common, as in the English post horn signal 'Clear the road' (Figure 9.10a).

The horn leap of a fifth (tonic to dominant) is well-established in the literature. The television series *How the West was Won*, with its 'strong, fair-minded, fair-haired, outdoor pioneering hero' had a theme tune beginning with a rising fifth played by unison horns (Figure 9.10b). Mark Trail, 'preserver of wild-life, guardian of the forest', the hero of an advertising feature for Kellogg's Pep Breakfast, was introduced by a theme played on Wurlitzer organ (imitating horns) which incorporated the same interval (Figure 9.10c).

Figure 9.10

Heroes of classical music often express themselves in rising fifths: we list the horn-like call of the Flying Dutchman (Figure 9.10d), Siegfried's horn call (Figure 9.10e), and the theme of the hero

Siegfried (Figure 9.10f; the latter two from the *Ring*). Strauss depicts his 'hero's life' *(Ein Heldenleben)* with a selection of intervals: first the familiar fifth, than a fourth and two sevenths (Figure 9.10g).

The 'whoop' which rises an octave is just as common. The American radio series *Gunsmoke* features 'Mat Dillon, US Marshal - the first man they look for and the last one they [the baddies] want to meet'. The theme music is at Figure 9.11a. The 'Saint' - the 'Robin Hood of modern crime' and hero of a radio series - is also introduced by an octave leap on horn (Figure 9.11b).

Various heroes of the classical literature are characterized by octave leaps from dominant to dominant, the second note usually on the strong beat. We may cite Strauss's Don Juan whose theme is played on horns (Figure 9.11c), and Liszt's Tasso, with a similar figure on strings (Figure 9.11d). Sibelius's Kullervo (in the movement entitled 'Kullervo goes to battle') is characterized by a similar octave leap, though this time the lower note is on the strong beat (Figure 9.11e).

Figure 9.11

This list of 'reveille signals preparing the viewer and listener for heroic action' could be made very much longer. The common elements seem to be (1) a call to action (to the hero), (2) a call to attention (to the listener), (3) male heroism, energy and excitement.

Related musical figures of this kind are called IOCM (inter-objective comparison material). They undoubtedly illustrate the 'vocabulary of intonations' envisaged by Asafiev. These are the short fragments which lie in the public consciousness as 'living intonations'. Both Tagg and Asafiev would maintain that the rising octaves in all these themes are essentially the same interval, while a rising octave in a different context may be quite a different interval because its signification is not the same. In Harold Arlen's 'Over the rainbow', for example (Figure 9.11f), the steady downward continuation 'seems to "negate" the lift upwards and outwards, gradually falling back to the initially low starting point on the tonic' (Tagg 1979, 131).

Consequently, it does not threaten Tagg's position to cite octave leaps which have nothing to do with heroism. These figures are merely illustrations of different paradigms; they are different musemes, which, though homophones of the 'heroic call to action', have quite separate meanings.

An examination of all the musemes in the melody and accompaniment of the 'A' section of the *Kojak* theme suggests that it portrays 'something individual and male... which may be characterized as strong, energetic, virile, heroic, calm, confident, martial... and which is both called and calls to attention and to action upwards and outwards. He is thrown into relief by, stands out against, is a dominant part of and moves in harmony with an environment which may be characterized as modern, full of general, constant, bustling, nervous, luminous, pleasant activity and excitement, nervous, unrestful, energetic and agitated but tinged with a pleasant shimmer in which the somewhat aggressive energy and modernity of a North American metropolis and its subculture may be distinguished as an important part' (Tagg 1979, 147).

9.5.4. Abba's hit recording 'Fernando' has alternating verses and choruses which are different in character. A musematic analysis will thus have to draw important syntagmatic conclusions; and indeed the syntagmatic level of analysis is important in other ways.

The song is apparently about a woman who has fought alongside her companion Fernando in a freedom fight in South America. In the verse she mentions 'drums and sounds of bugle calls' and 'the roar of guns and cannons'; 'We were young and full of life and none of us prepared to die.' These ominous concrete references disappear in the chorus which has an atmosphere of pleasant nostalgia.

> There was something in the air that night, the stars were bright, Fernando.
> They were shining there for you and me, for liberty, Fernando.
> Though we never thought that we could lose, there's no regrets:
> If I had to do the same again, I would, my friend, Fernando.

The musical settings of verse and chorus are sharply distinguished. It will be noticed that the exact location of the war for liberty is left unstated, apart from the hispanic name 'Fernando' and a mention of the Rio Grande (which could mean Brazil, Argentina, Mexico or the USA). However, the piece begins with an introduction played by two descant recorders in thirds, with a very characteristic figure (Figure 9.12a).

Figure 9.12

The distinctly hispanic evocation of this motive ('museme 1a') may be demonstrated by citing various items of 'mood music' from the *Selected Sound Recorded Music Library Catalogue*, where the evocation of the music is clearly specified. For example, *Spanish Autumn*, a piece for recorder and alto flute, is meant to evoke 'Spain, South America, dancing, people' (Figure 9.12b). Another piece called *Cordigliera* (Figure 9.12c) depicts 'carnival, festivity in the valley' (the Italian spelling is presumably a mistake).

These examples have tempi much quicker than the introduction to 'Fernando', however. Another mood-music collection, produced in Italy by Campi, contains a piece called *Exotic Flute* ('impression... journey over exotic landscape' - see Figure 9.12d). This is not only slower but is pentatonic like the 'Fernando' figure. In addition the accompaniment takes the form of strummed chords on *charangas*, small South American guitars made from armadillo shell. The accompaniment in 'Fernando' includes strummed guitar chords. The solo part here (Figure 9.12d) is played on a *quena*, an Andean flute which is somewhat like a recorder in timbre. The instrumentation places this piece firmly in the Andes.

This recalls Simon and Garfunkel's cover version of Los Incas' 'El Condor pasa', which is slow and pentatonic and accompanied by charangas. The evocation of the 'Fernando' introduction becomes clear: 'exotic environment, probably Andean-Indian, with a rural view large enough to see and experience the passing of a condor overhead' (Tagg 1981, 6).

All of this provides a backdrop for the female vocalist, whose verse, with its irregular periodicity in the text, is delivered in a fervent quasi-recitative, a very unusual conception in popular music. However, she is placed centre front in the stereo panorama; 'any possible individuals... in the musical environment (e.g. the quenas) are positioned out in the panning periphery rather like the picturesque poverty of Indian peasants or slum-dwellers placed as suitable backcloth to the pretty European model posing in the latest poncho outfit, in front of an adobe shack on the front of a glossy magazine'. The open, melancholy, beautiful Andean environment is retained throughout the verse.

The chorus is heralded by a change of rhythmic character. In place of rubato, irregular periodicity, charangas and bells there are regular Afro-American rhythms in a soft-disco beat with a continuous bass on electric guitar. The melody of this section, however, is built around a museme that repeatedly spans a tritone and thus takes up a position in the intonational vocabulary (Figure 9.13a).

Figure 9.13

(a) There was some-thing in the air that night, the stars were bright

(b) (Written by Hakan Tollesson)

(c) So ist die Lieb'! So ist die Lieb'!

(d)

(e) It's now or nev-er, come hold me tight, kiss me my dar-ling,

(f) You nev-er close your eyes an-y more when you kiss my lips

(g) If I had to do the same a-gain, I would, my friend, Fer-nan-do.

*(Written by B. Anderson, B. Ulvaeus and S. Anderson.)

At first hearing, this motive might seem merely cadential; but the natural move to a cadence is avoided and the figure is repeated. Apparently, the tritone figure that moves to a cadence is a different museme. It is illustrated from the popular Swedish song 'Skepp son mötas i natten' (Figure 9.13b).

Motives which span tritones and which come at the beginnings of phrases, and moreover are repeated, have something to do with a yearning sadness. This is the sentiment expressed in Wolf's 'Nimmersatte Liebe' (Figure 9.13c). The tritones in the oboe obbligato the the tenor aria 'Ich will bei meinem Jesu wachten' in the *St Matthew Passion* are similarly non-cadential, and are again expressive of a sad longing: 'I want to watch over my Jesus' (Figure 9.13d).

If Abba were thinking of a similar motive which is to be found in 'O Sole mio', they would probably have recalled the song in the sentimental contrafactum sung by Elvis Presley, 'It's now or never' (Figure 9.13e). Presley's sadness was caused by an imminent parting. The Righteous Brothers in 'You've lost that loving feeling' lament the departure of love itself. Their melodic figure is identical to that in 'Fernando' (Figure 9.13f).

It might be thought that the young woman in 'Fernando' was suffering a genuine sadness, perhaps for the loss of Fernando, perhaps for the unsuccessful rebellion and for the predicament of the people of Peru, Chile, Colombia or any other South American state. This interpretation is ruled out for syntagmatic reasons. It has been shown that the tritone figure carries no special burden of meaning when it is merely cadential. The initial emotional charge of this museme is dispelled, therefore, when the figure recurs at the end of the chorus and leads at once to a cadence (Figure 9.13g), as in 'Skepp son mötas i natten'. 'This means that, whereas the words say, "If I had to go back and fight for freedom in Latin America, I would", the music expresses the affective attitude "I may be longing for something here at home but I'm really quite content with things as they are"' (Tagg 1982, 60).

9.6. *The piano music of Liszt*

9.6.1. Intonation theorists find plenty of connections between popular music and classical music. Both depend on intonations that are rooted in society. Classical composers, however, are able to sort them into types, and create for them a context and a possibility of development and change.

> According to the materialist tradition of music aesthetics, intonation is determined by the 'sonorous images' of music that characterize a given social setting, a human attitude or type of conduct or indeed a situation. Intonation indicates the musical formulae and the types of particular sonorities which transmit precise significations of social and human types...
> Composers of strong personality concentrate and condense the characteristic events of the musical consciousness of surrounding society into types, uniting them into different genres and structures for the purpose of an artistic creation. (Jozsef Ujfalussy, in *Zeneesztetika* ['Music aesthetics'] from *Bevezetes a marxista-leninista agazati esztetikaba* ['Introduction to

Marxist-Leninist aesthetics'], Budapest, 1978, quoted in Grabócz, 1986, 28-29).

Neither Ujfalussy nor Asafiev meant to belittle the classical composer's important role in shaping a musical culture. But like the popular composer, he has to take his materials from the established intonations of society.

9.6.2. The Hungarian Marta Grabócz applies Ujfalussy's principles to the piano music of Liszt. She considers that the intonational 'types' that form Liszt's material were inherited largely from Beethoven and from Italian and French opera. They appear most obviously in his themes, announced at the beginning of each piece, and they fall into two groups, the pastoral and the heroic, the latter connected with the 'rescue' operas of the French Revolutionary period (Grabócz 1986, 28). Liszt remained for a long period the only member of the 'young Romantics' to perpetuate the revolutionary-humanistic intonations which had been first put into instrumental music by Beethoven. In the Hungarian composer, however, these social and public ideals are converted into individual and inward terms; they become (in the composer's words) the sentiments of 'an exceptional individual' (according to his essay on Berlioz's *Harold Symphony*, quoted by Grabócz, 1986, 31). Liszt's epic spirit centres on the solitary Romantic hero rather than the victorious group.

9.6.3 These intonational types are divided into twelve groups. Each group contains themes of much variety, and Grabócz goes to considerable lengths to describe the many ramifications. Brief examples will show the method and content of her study. The taxonomy is as follows:

> (i) Quick themes of an *appassionato* character. Although Liszt applies all kinds of novel keyboard techniques to these, they reveal their ancestry in Beethoven's movements of an agitated, *ostinato* cast. For example, the passage marked *presto agitato assai* in the *Sonata Après une lecture de Dante* (Figure 9.14) may be compared with the opening of the 'Waldstein' Sonata (the Liszt example furnished by Grabocz, the Beethoven comparison mine).
> (ii) Scherzo themes, much enriched by the virtuosic innovations which betoken Liszt's indebtedness to Paganini. The character is diatonic, in dance measures, with trills and

figurations in semiquavers and demisemiquavers. An example is given from *Feux follets* (Figure 9.15).

Figure 9.14

Figure 9.15

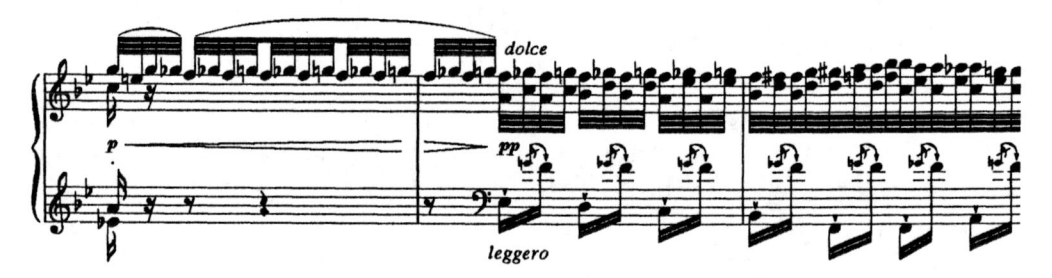

(iii) March tunes. The triumphant revolutionary march in a major key is comparatively rare; it is marked by swaggering dotted rhythms. There is an example in the middle section of *Orage* (marked *meno allegro*).

Much more common is the funeral march. Grabócz considers that this type is a symbol of national mourning, the lament of a people fighting for independence; Liszt tells us *Funerailles* was written in memory of the defeat of the 1848 independence movement in Hungary, and the same reference is made in the inscription to the middle section of *La Notte*. Often there is a suggestion of Hungarian traditional music; the introduction to the *Grand solo de concert* has a melody resembling the *verbunkos* recruiting dance.

The heritage of Beethoven and French opera becomes clear, however, in the section actually entitled 'Marcia funebre' in the *Grand solo,* where the addition of acciaccatura flourishes in the left hand recalls the slow movement of the *Eroica* Symphony (Figure 9.16).

Figure 9.16

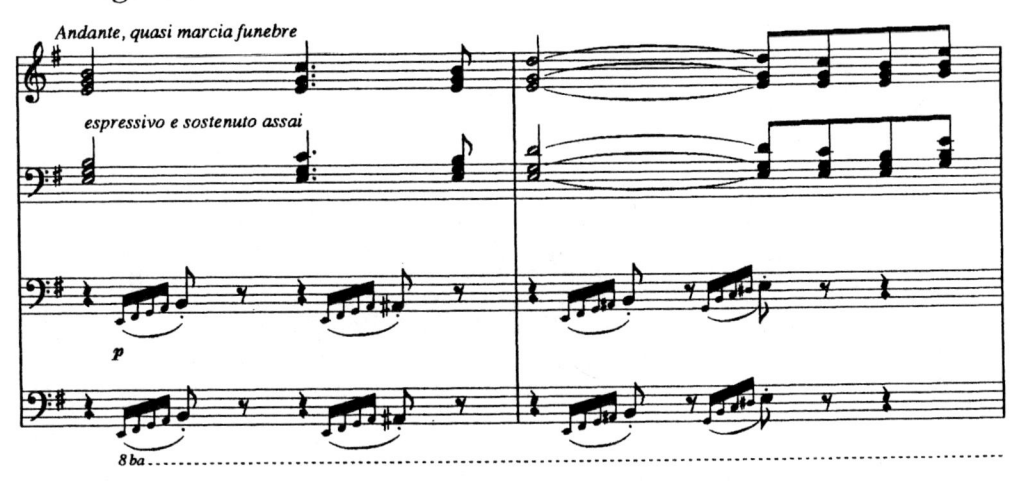

(iv) Pastoral themes. These are calm, with a broadly arching contour and an undulating, regular accompaniment. Typically they are in the major mode, stressing the interval of a fifth. The archetype is the opening melody of *Au lac de Wallenstadt* (Figure 9.17).

Figure 9.17

(v) *Religioso* themes. These come in two varieties; firstly, themes of pastoral character to which a devotional reference is attributed by title, epigraph or instruction in the score. The theme of the fourth *Consolation*, for example, is marked 'cantabile con divozione'.

The other type is characterized by a strongly marked pentatonic contour, with a homophonic accompaniment. The commonest associations in the title or epigraph are the ideas of 'faith' or 'benediction'. In *Invocation*, such a theme appears to illustrate the text 'Elevez-vous, voix de mon âme' (Figure 9.18).

Figure 9.18

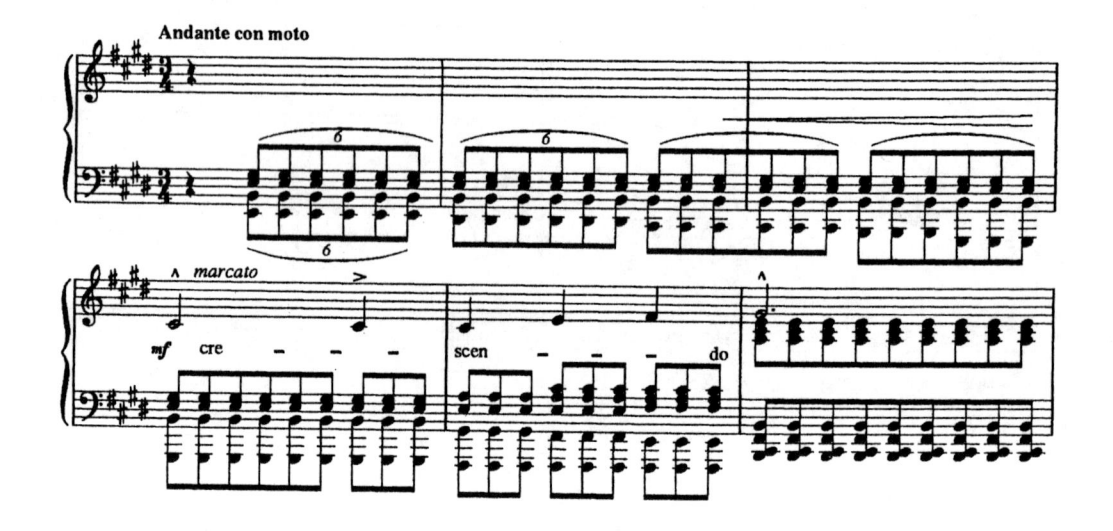

[musical score: Andante con moto, marked marcato, mf crescendo]

(vi) Themes based on folk music. Some are real folk material, others ape the style with parallel thirds and sixths and figures based on augmented fourths.

(vii) The large class of heroic themes, which are musically very varied. Their background lies in French opera, and they are described by Bence Szabolcsi (in *A melòdia története* ['History of melody'], Budapest 1950) during his discussion of the operas of Spontini and Méhul: 'Here we have before our eyes in germ all that will later be realised by Romanticism in the form of a stirring, gesturing and agitated melodic line. The atmospheric background of these melodies is nearly always heroic, warlike and full of pathos. The very essence of the melody is tension, movement, dash, leaping, or - rarely however - exhaustion; the swelling, heaping and flooding character is always present... It is evident here that the most generalized sentiment or leaning of the century, buried deep in its being, has been embodied: the rhetorical gesture and allusion, the heroic perspective and action' (quoted by Grabócz, 1986, 44).

The theatrical nature of this type of theme leads to its becoming the principal actor in the instrumental drama, subject to changes of character like the hero of an epic play or an Entwicklungsroman. Much of Grabócz's study involves the application of Greimas's narrative theory; the functioning of the heroic theme as a dramatic protagonist is an important part of her argument.

The first of her examples, the theme of *Lyon*, I have compared with the duet 'Quand l'amitié seconde mon courage' from Spontini's *La Vestale* (Figure 9.19).

Figure 9.19

(viii) The Italian *bel canto* theme. There are only four examples in Liszt's piano music; one of these is the passage marked *adagio dolente* in the character piece *Le mal du pays*.

(ix) More commonly, the contrast with the opening heroic theme is provided by a melody of declamatory *bel canto* character, derived from French-Italian opera. This is another large category. The gestural world of such tunes, tending towards pathetic exclamations, is less bound to the four-line structure of the heroic theme.

Again it is Szabolcsi who characterizes these melodies; they are connected with Rossini's adoption of the French style, which produced a kind of pathos that expressed itself in 'boastful' *(hâbleux)* declamation. It evinces 'the "speaking" [*parlant*] opening, in a clear rhythm, with various tragic, pathetic or religious turns of phrase; a planned intensification that appears without slowing, careful and transparent symmetry (possibly with question/answer patterns in sequences); a high climax reached gradually and, to end, an impressive cadence, almost always using a figure of rhetorical extension and formulaic schema' (Szabolcsi, *op. cit.*, quoted by Grabócz, 1986, 48).

These long themes need to be illustrated with a complete example, which is impossible here. The whole 79 bars of *Sonetto 104 del Petrarca* represent a melody of this type, rising to a majestic climax and falling away into quietude. Figure 9.20 shows the opening of the main section, virtually a setting of Petrarch's line, 'Pace non trovo, e non ho da far guerra'.

Figure 9.20

As principal themes, these are found above all in the pieces written to illustrate Italian and Swiss impressions, like the Petrarch sonnets and *Les cloches de Genève*. Their especial duty as secondary themes is illustrated not only by character pieces like *Bénédiction de Dieu*, but also by music without programmatic content, where they may be either new ideas (in the Ballade in B minor, for instance) or reworkings of the original heroic theme (in the Sonata in B minor at bar 125).

(x) The lament, often marked *lagrimoso, dolente, con duolo, lugubre, lamento,* or in the original version of *Vallée d'Obermann* 'avec un profond sentiment de tristesse'. This was unquestionably 'inherited from a traditional intonation', Grabócz says (p. 53). The most striking example is *Il lamento* from the *Trois études de concert.*

(xi) Instrumental recitative. Quite apart from those themes which match the prosody of a written epigraph (like the *Sonetto 104 del Petrarca,* mentioned above), there are passages which suggest a speaking voice, yet are given no text. In some cases (*Sposalizio; St François d'Assise, la prédication aux oiseaux*) it is easy to imagine the character who speaks. In others (the *Grand solo de concert,* for example) a recitative passage suggests a hidden dramatic plot in a work of pure instrumental music.

(xii) Associative/symbolic themes. This is the only type not dependent on a traditional intonation, and arises from visual, motor and gestural iconism. It is described by Ujfalussy in a chapter entitled 'The direct relation between the musical image and certain phenomena of reality' from *A valòsàg zenei képe* ('The musical image of reality', quoted by Grabócz, 1986, 62). The reflection of reality is not necessarily a simple process; it depends on 'a special logical order which does not directly reflect the spatio-temporal order of the world, but embraces and transports this order into a system of significations with the aid of more abstract generalizations'. Thus, the representation of bells in *Les cloches de Genève* (Figure 9.21a) is an obvious piece of musical realism. But when the inscription 'Vivre en travaillant; vivre... ou mourir', above the character piece *Lyon,* appears in the form of an instrumental recitative, the heroic character of the first utterance and the ominous reference of the second are symbolized by a musical expression that is at first a bright major third, then a mournful diminished seventh (Figure 9.21b). The symbolic force of these intervals can, in fact, be seen as a traditional intonation connected with eighteenth-century *Figurenlehre,* though Grabócz does not suggest this; the falling diminished seventh has a similar function in

Bach's chorale prelude *Durch Adams Fall* from the *Orgelbüchlein*.

Figure 9.21

9.6.4 It comes as no surprise to learn that Liszt's intonations derive from Beethoven, French Revolutionary opera and Italian *bel canto*. Grabócz does not present these ideas as anything novel; nor does she attempt to prove the connections by quoting examples from Spontini, Méhul and Lesueur, since her primary concern is to establish a typology of Liszt's intonations. I have added from time to time a comparison with earlier music. For her, the intonational basis of all musical invention is axiomatic, and in any case her work is based on the theoretical exposés of Ujfalussy and Szabolcsi. She would find Tagg's lengthy citings of 'Inter-Objective Comparison Material' profoundly redundant. Her study is important because she shows how intonation can be used for dramatic and programmatic purposes. Different intonations, connected with sociological functions, theatrical situations, traditions of word-setting, can be adopted in an instrumental composition to illustrate a title or epigraph and to suggest a dramatic plot; even works without evocative titles may seem to portray a hero's tragic destiny through the language of intonation.

9.7. The art of intoned meaning

9.7.1. The duty of the analyst, according to the intonational tradition, is to seek out the intoned meaning. To consider as identical two musical features which have the same notes, as all analysts - including the practitioners of 'semiotic' analysis - have always done, is merely naive. The true identity of a musical figure can only be approached through its signification, to ascertain which one must consult the intonational vocabulary of a society and an epoch. Intonations, in Asafiev's sense, are not merely the short 'musemes' illustrated by Tagg. Anything can be an intonation, from the merest fragment of accompanying texture to whole sections or movements: anything that can carry an ascertainable semantic message. And intonations may group themselves into large categories or types. We should ask of a musical item, not 'has it formal and syntactic unity?' but 'does it express a single coherent meaning?' By this means, the intonational unity of a Liszt Hungarian Rhapsody, or a keyboard Fantasia by C P E Bach, may at last become clear.

10

DECONSTRUCTION AND ALLEGORY

10.1 Deconstruction and Différance

10.1.1. The newest theory to influence literary criticism - the outstanding idea of the eighties - has been the notion of deconstruction. This differs from Saussurean linguistics and structuralism in having twin roots, on one side in structuralism itself (which, along with everything else, it *deconstructs*) and on the other in philosophy, especially that of Nietzsche and Heidegger. Linguistics has a practical side; its status as theory (rather than speculative philosophy) is always recalled by the fact that the theory is regularly put into practice. Of course, it has philosophical components. But no linguist ever wanted to claim that his ideas promoted a different view of the world (a different *metaphysical* view) or a criticism of logic and epistemology (a new theory of knowledge).

Linguistics, then, together with the various semiotic fields including the semiotics of music, is primarily a field of theory rather than of philosophy. But deconstruction is largely a philosophical movement and launches us on wider and more dubious seas.

10.1.2. Jacques Derrida, the originator of this movement, was led to consider the relation of speech and writing by his reading of Rousseau's *Essay on the Origin of Languages*. Like Plato in the *Phaedrus*, Rousseau deplores the parasitism of writing, which is language in the absence of a speaker. If language brings people together in an act of communication, how can there be language on the pages of a book that lies unread in a library? Speech is a direct representation of the thoughts of the speaker; its meaning is manifestly present. But writing is a representation of a representation. It is a 'supplement' to speech, sinister and elusive, an unreliable counterfeit.

This idea of the primacy of speech survived into modern linguistics. Saussure, too, maintains that 'language and writing are two systems of signs; the second exists for the sole purpose of representing the first. The linguistic object is not both the written and the spoken forms of words; the spoken forms alone constitute the object. But the spoken word is so intimately bound to its written image that the latter manages to usurp the main role. People attach even more importance to the written image of a vocal sign than to the sign itself... This illusion, which has always existed, is reflected in many of the notions that are currently bandied about on the subject of language' (Saussure 1974, 23-24).

This traditional attitude can be criticized in two ways. First, the 'thought' of the speaker which is supposed to be the present meaning of a spoken sign is, in fact, itself part of the linguistic circle. The sign is identified by its difference from other signs (its paradigmatic difference); similarly, the thought is characterized by its differences from other thoughts, and sign and thought are inextricably bound together. It is normal to say that the sign is a sign of the thought, but equally, the thought is a sign of the sign; in phonology *bat* is opposed to *pat*, but somehow also *high* is opposed to *low* because of some relationship in semantics, that is, in the realm of thought. In all its forms, language is a system of differences; linguistic meanings - 'thoughts' - are just as much part of this differential web as the words themselves. What is the importance, then, of the presence of a speaker? Present or not, he is subject to the structures of language and thought.

Secondly, the relation of speech and writing is much more complicated than is implied in terms like 'representation' and 'dependence'. The purely formal differentiation of linguistic units is shown much more clearly in writing than speech; Saussure himself cites the letter *t* as an example of a paradigm, identifiable in the many different forms produced by the handwriting styles of different persons.

> Values in writing function only through reciprocal opposition within a fixed system that consists of a set number of letters... Since the graphic sign is arbitrary, its form matters little or rather matters only within the limitations imposed by the system (Saussure 1974, 120).

There are very obvious ways in which the written language displays features that are only *implicit* in speech. Paradigmatic equivalence of phonemes - the equivalence of clear l and dark l in English, for example - is shown by writing them with the same letter; this could not be known from the spoken language, unless a native informant were consulted. The feature called 'strong juncture', an important point of division which causes a change in many syntagmatic rules, is usually shown in writing by placing a space between words; in speech, the division between words is not always audible.

Apparently, the kind of pattern we associate with language, with its divisions of words and its principles of differentiation, is more clearly shown in writing than in speech. In fact, when we speak we employ and assume a kind of hyper-speech which is something more like writing - an 'archi-writing', *archi-écriture*, of which both speech and writing are dependent forms.

The privileged position given to speech, therefore, must be motivated by some extraneous prejudice. It is the purpose of deconstruction to unearth this attitude, and thus to pose a radical critique of the whole of Western thought.

10.1.3. Behind language, the Western tradition seems to imply, there is something pure, full, original, essential, eternal. Derrida calls this *presence*. In any opposition - writing/speech, language/thought, culture/nature, expression/content - one term is hierarchically superior to the other because it is nearer to present reality. 'Presence' seems to be opposed to 'absence', as the present speaker is opposed to the silent book; but the present is also opposed to the past and the future. Surely the point about time is that the present is uniquely real, the past just a remembered present and the future an anticipated one.

But again, since time implies movement, there can be no present without past and future; the presentness of an event makes sense only in opposition to the past and the future, for its outstanding characteristic is its being-in-movement. If this were not so, movement and stillness would be undistinguishable and a moving train would, at every present moment, be stationary. A single note from the middle of Mozart's 'Jupiter' Symphony is of its own account not a part of the symphony; it is nothing at all without its musical context. The present, therefore, cannot be given primacy over the past and the future. It is entirely dependent on them for all its characteristics.

10.1.4. Philosophy has sought the *original* as well as the essential; Rousseau's essay was about the *origin* of languages. Just as the sign is meant to point to something not dependent on itself, so it is meant to lead back to something absolutely first and simple. But again, any attempt to find a simple and undifferentiated origin leads to the discovery of more and more differences.

> We find only nonoriginary origins. If a cave man is successfully to inaugurate language by making a special grunt to signify 'food,' we must suppose that the grunt is already distinguished from other grunts and that the world has already been divided into the categories 'food' and 'non-food" (Culler 1982, 96).

10.1.5. If there is not some present 'thing' which language signifies, then what is going on in language and thought? Saussure laid the foundations of deconstructionist ideas when he made his famous statement that 'in language there are only differences'.

> Even more important: a difference generally implies positive terms between which the difference is set up; but in language there are only differences *without positive terms* (Saussure 1974, 120).

It is as though I am given an I.O.U. in place of the money which I am owed. The I.O.U. has to do in place of the money, for the moment at least. The return of the money is *deferred*; it is awaited and hoped for, but for the moment I have only its sign.

The linguistic sign, and the thought that constitutes its meaning, are both deferrals of the real and original presence that I have learnt to seek. For this reason, Derrida respells the French word *différence* as 'différance'; the new spelling refers to the double meaning of the French verb *différer*, which can mean 'to defer' as well as 'to differ'. This witty gambit also has the advantage of creating an expression that can only be recognized in writing (in which the speaker is absent), since *différence* and *différance* are pronounced alike. The favoured home of *différance* is in the written language, not the spoken. And since written language was formerly regarded as no more than a shadow, the speaker being absent, the new word seems to gravitate towards absence instead of presence. It is not merely another expression with its own content, but a strategy, an intrusion into language of the very thing that language cannot capture. Yet, it is not therefore the principle of language, or the secret of language's origin. Even if language is dependent on the principle of differentiation, *différance* cannot be identified with this principle, for it lies behind it and beyond it. It is the 'non-full, non-simple, structured and differentiating origin of differences', and its action is not logical but "play"' (Derrida 1982, 11). Any attempt to capture it in conceptual or logical terms is bound to be doomed, because such terms are based on structured differentiation and thus on *différance* itself. 'Deconstruction does not consist in passing from one concept to another, but in overturning and displacing a conceptual order, as well as the nonconceptual order with which the conceptual order is articulated' (Derrida 1982, 329).

10.1.6. Deconstruction reveals, not the 'true' meaning of a word, text or concept, but the 'space' which makes it possible for signifier and signified to separate. Hierarchical preferences are renounced, because it is always possible to show that the dependent or marginal term in the opposition - the 'supplement', using Rousseau's word for writing as subordinated to speech - is an essential condition for the dominant member. Thus, there are no signifieds without signifiers; the idea of a 'world' that exists with all its characteristics before language comes along to describe it, is untenable. There are no meanings without texts; no nature without culture; no causes without effects; no objects without representations.

As a natural result of this, every text contains subtexts with the seeds of its own subversion. Rousseau, for example, demonstrates unwittingly that speech depends on a set of principles that are best revealed in writing, in spite of his intention to proclaim the parasitism of writing on speech. Saussure similarly wants to favour speech, but the consequence of his principle of difference 'without real terms' is to undermine the true reason for such favour, which was related to the 'presence' of the speaker and thus, apparently, of his meaning. The characteristic mission of deconstructive criticism is 'the careful teasing out of warring forces of signification within the text' (Barbara Johnson, quoted in Culler, 1982, 213). The text's inner subversion of itself is a sign of the play of différance.

10.2. Deconstructive criticism

10.2.1. The world of literary criticism has been profoundly affected by deconstructive theories, especially in America. Derrida himself has written critical accounts of certain texts, by Mallarmé, Genet, Shelley and others. But his criticisms are not always classically deconstructive; the definitive applications to criticism are found in the works of others, in literary theorists like Michael Riffaterre and progressive critics like Barbara Johnson (for a useful list of their works, with brief abstracts, see Culler's bibliography: Culler 1982, 293 and 299).

10.2.2. The first casualty of deconstruction is the idea of *organic unity*. The American Paul de Man, who is second to Derrida as an expounder of deconstructive theory, refers to 'the intent at totality of the interpretive process' (de Man 1971, 31) which arises from the artistic 'frame', the fact that the artwork, whether literary, visual or musical, has traditionally been surrounded by a physical or imaginary boundary which turns it into a microcosm with its own rules and logic.

The idea of the artistic frame depends on the division *inside/outside*. This is deconstructed by Derrida in *La Verité en Peinture*. By excluding the outside as outside, we make it necessary to the definition of the inside; the frame is absolutely essential to the artwork, but it also makes the artwork dependent on the world that surrounds the frame, a world that is physical, intellectual and imaginative.

The trivial consequence of this is that the work will contain traces of the cultural and historical world that gave it birth. But Derrida means much more than this. The world of criticism and metalanguage is, of course, outside the frame, but it is also 'folded in', as, for example, the external world is folded inside the body through its orifices. The vagina and the intestines are as much part of the external physical world as a tidal inlet is part of the sea; and similarly the critical metalanguage penetrates into the work itself. It is not merely a view through a long lens.

Hence, the critic looks for confirmation of his judgements in traces of metalinguistic material in the work itself; for example, the analyst of Beethoven's early string quartets, Op 18, may find the category of 'second subject' apparently written into the music with some intention of being aurally isolated, confirming the descriptions of writers like Georg Joseph Vogler (in the *Mannheimer Tonschule*, 1778) and Francesco Galeazzi *(Elementi teorico-pratici di musica,* 1791).

The completeness of the artwork is, therefore, dependent on a lack. Its very intelligibility depends on a flow and counterflow across the frame; there is no understanding without a consideration of what the work is not. It is not its historical and cultural background, but neither is it its criticism or metalanguage; yet without these it cannot be understood, and since a text can only function in the encounter with a reader, there can be no text without the outside.

Consequently, all texts contain traces of what they lack; there can be no text wholly complete in itself, and thus we shall always find elements that are not conducive to unity because they are parts of the outside 'folded in'.

Does this mean that the concept of organic unity is to be abandoned? By no means. It is, of course, part of the critical metalanguage that is outside-yet-inside the artwork, outside the frame yet folded in. It is profoundly true of a Brahms symphony that it embodies formal unity. Yet every symphony of Brahms has traces of the lack, evidence of its habitation of a world outside its frame. The brief brass chorale in the introduction to the Finale of the First Symphony is just the most obvious of these.

10.2.3. If the critic is to look for traces of the hinterland beyond the frame - disunifying and destabilizing features, details that fail to confirm the hierarchies and principles on which the best analysis may depend - then his attention will be drawn to the apparently unimportant. 'Deconstruction involves attention to the marginal' (Culler 1982, 215).

As has already been seen, apparently marginal features of the text may by signs of subtexts which subvert the declared meaning. Thus, Saussure's passing reference to writing as the best exemplification of linguistic differentiation is the trace of a subtext; deconstruction reveals that his subordination of writing to speech constitutes also a recognition of writing as essentially involved with speech.

There are further, more fundamental reasons for seeking the marginal. The interpretation of a text can only proceed with reference to a context; that is, the world outside the frame is necessary to give significance to what is inside. It is traditionally supposed that this context is *limited* in certain ways. For example, you cannot transplant a work of the eighteenth century into a twentieth-century context, or speak of contextual meanings that the author clearly did not intend.

But in fact, every limitation of context is really an extension of context. 'Any attempt to codify context can always be grafted onto the context it sought to describe, yielding a new context which escapes the previous formulation' (Culler 1982, 124). The context has become, not merely every possible context within which the text may be read, but every possible context plus someone's principle of limitation of that context. I may now interpret the text by talking about the limitation, as well as the text itself.

Much 'historical interpretation' of texts, including musical ones, has in fact been talk about the limitations. For example, Elaine

Sisman's description of Haydn's music in terms of Heinrich Christoph Koch's *Versuch einer Anleitung zur Composition* of 1787 (Sisman 1982) is a demonstration of the validity of Koch's models as well as a survey of their relevance to Haydn. Such an essay does not prevent me from considering Haydn in terms foreign to Koch, in Schenkerian terms perhaps, though it may suggest that such consideration is a 'supplement' to the true historical method, and therefore dangerous. But such dangerous supplements also turn out to be necessary to the definition of the 'legitimate' interpretation, and thus, in a different way, 'legitimate'. This is a theme that runs through deconstructive thinking.

In any case, Haydn's musical methods may have been partly unconscious. Derrida writes wittily about the act of signing a document (in the essay 'Signature event context' in *Margins of Philosophy*). The effect of my signature is to give my written utterance the force of speech, as though it had been uttered by me in the present moment, as though it had the privileged meaning of 'presence'. Thus, a present moment is perpetuated; it becomes 'a past now, which will remain a future now, and therefore ... a now in general' (Derrida 1982, 328). All that I 'really' mean is privileged in an interpretation of the utterance. Yet the signature is itself detached from the present moment, being a paradigm which I imitate every time I sign. It is possible for a signature to be placed on a document that has not been read, or to be photo-lithographed and printed, or even forged. In what respect, then, is the content of the utterance 'really' meant by the signatory? It is 'as though' meant, since I intend it to mean that the utterance is meant, even if I may have no idea of the content of the utterance.

Suppose, then, that Haydn's 'signature' - that is, the identity of Haydn's music as the product of a particular composer in a particular historical period - may guarantee all kinds of items of content that Haydn, or his contemporaries, never dreamt of?

This kind of view recalls the 'New Criticism' of T S Eliot and Ezra Pound, the view that an author's intentions are irrelevant because the critic should be concerned with the integrity of the text. But Derrida would go further than this; the composer's intentions - and any other material of which contemporary composers and listeners may have been aware - are themselves 'a particular textual product or effect, distilled by critical readings but always exceeded by the text' (Culler 1982, 218). There is no such thing as a text which is wholly limited to the intentions of the author or the horizons of its age. This was made clear in the discussion of Rousseau, whose clearly stated intention was to show the superiority of speech to writing, but who nevertheless obliquely reflected the fundamentality of writing.

10.2.4. The outstanding danger in a critical methodology based on intention and historical limitation is that major works may be interpreted, and thus circumscribed, in terms of simpler, lesser works. By observing the forms of Mozart's keyboard sonatas and the piano sonatas of Beethoven's Op 2 and Op 10, it is possible to show the 'essential' features of some of Beethoven's later sonatas like the 'Waldstein' and the 'Hammerklavier'. To do so is to submit to a historical narrative that excludes surprise. A great work of music always escapes the limitations of 'historical' criticism. But in order to find its routes of escape, the critic must pay attention to the inessential.

10.2.5. Traditional metaphysics and epistemology have always privileged one of the terms in each opposition; speech is preferred to writing, nature to culture, presence to absence. In the field of aesthetics, the preference has been for forms of signification that revealed the 'essential'. Thus, *symbolism* has been preferred to *allegory*, *metaphor* to *metonymy*. In each of these oppositions, the first term is considered motivated, organic, the second arbitrary, mechanical.

Thus, music is a symbol of affective life (Langer); music is a metaphor of the stress and release of emotion (Ferguson). In each case music does more than merely point to feeling as its object; it typifies, exemplifies, clarifies feeling by presenting its essential qualities. The connection with feeling is motivated rather than accidental.

Criticism, too, is considered to have a metaphoric relation to its text. The critic seeks, not simply a fugitive gloss on the text, but a penetration into its central principles; and thus, ultimately, he imagines that there is a final, objective criticism which is the best judgement on the text. Thus, writers on criticism struggled with the fact that our writings imply an objectivity and finality in criticism, and yet we revise our views endlessly and constantly disagree. Music analysis is a pertinent case; there is, surely, a right analysis of each musical work, yet new analyses are continually being written for familiar pieces. If analysis is metaphorical - if it penetrates into the essence of the piece - then how can there be more than one right analysis?

10.2.6. The opposite of metaphor is *metonymy*. This is the figure of speech in which an idea is indicated by some object or quality only accidentally related to it. The most trivial examples are the use of 'head' to mean the whole animal ('two hundred head of cattle') or of 'wood' to meaning something made from wood, such as a barrel of wine or a ball used in the game of bowls. There is no suggestion of touching on the essential quality of the object; there is merely some simple, non-motivated relation between the object and the metonymic term.

In his essays on rhetorical figures, Paul de Man shows that every trope has a literal meaning as well as a figurative one. If this were not the case there would be no separation of the idea and its figurative representation. Yet literature plays just as much with the accidental, unmotivated aspects of the figure as it does with the strictly metaphorical ones; and consequently it deconstructs itself.

10.2.7. W B Yeats's poem 'Among school children' ends with the line, 'How can we know the dancer from the dance?' This is usually considered to be a kind of trope called *rhetorical question*, in which the literal meaning - a real enquiry - hides a true meaning which is not a question at all, but an assertion: 'We cannot know the dancer from the dance.' Since the poet is concerned with fundamental matters in this piece - the unity of form and experience, of creator and creation, of sign and meaning - the exact meaning of this line is of some importance.

But suppose the line were literally a question? The reader who had lost touch with the separation of form and experience, of sign and meaning, would be in deep epistemological trouble. It is this very separation that makes it possible to talk sense. If the sight of the dancer threatened to deprive the onlooker of this essential distinction the question might become urgent and desperate: 'Please tell me, how can I know the dancer from the dance?' (de Man 1979, 11-12). Now, the theme of the whole poem is no longer the illusion of wholeness presented by watching the dancer, a conventional idea, but the neurasthenia of epistemological collapse. A Romantic warmth has been replaced by a very contemporary anxiety; the poem has been subverted, or to put it more precisely, has subverted itself.

Thus, deconstructive criticism proceeds by restoring literal meanings to figurative expressions, generally finding that 'it is not necessarily the literal reading which is simpler than the figurative one' (de Man 1979, 11), but on the contrary that the literal meaning brings to light unsuspected and unnerving truths. This leads to a discovery that literary works are constructed just as much by the unmotivated and accidental branching of literal meanings, as by the insightful dialogue of figurative ones - that is, metonymically as well as metaphorically.

10.2.8. The *locus classicus* of this kind of metonymic construction is Proust. In *Swann's Way* there is a cook, Françoise, expert in her work but given to persecuting her kitchenmaid. So exemplary is the cook, and inefficient the kitchenmaid, that Proust even contrasts them as 'truth' and 'error'. The maid often leaves and has to be replaced, but nevertheless the writer thinks of her as one person, an emblem of servitude and suffering. One of these kitchenmaids was pregnant; Swann himself used to refer to her as 'Giotto's Charity', because her way of carrying the weight of her pregnancy resembled the weighty surcoat of Giotto's allegorical frescoes in Padua.

Presumably, Swann singled out Giotto's figure of Charity (rather than any of the other Giotto figures) because of some accidental facial resemblance to this particular kitchenmaid. However, the narrator of the story sees another quality in common; the kitchenmaid seemed to have no understanding of her pregnancy, just as the figure of Charity performs an action (holding out her hand with some object in it) of which she appears to have no understanding. Whence comes this metaphorical comparison? It is the construct of a 'reader', in this case the Proustian narrator (because the 'reading' is part of the fiction of the novel; this novel is unusual in being written in the first person, yet informing us that the narrator is not the same person as the author). Such readings constitute the activity of the real reader, too. Thus, literary meaning is drawn by the reader out of the writer's metonymies. At base, then, Proust's novel is an 'allegory of reading'.

But there is more: the curious gesture of Giotto's Charity is to hold out in her left hand something resembling a heart. 'She stretches her incandescent heart towards God or, better, she hands it over to him, as a cook would hand a corkscrew through a window of her basement to someone who asks for it at street-level'(quoted by de Man, 1979, 75). At first reading this seems a metaphorical remark; the narrator wishes 'merely to stress the homely quality of the gesture'. But in so doing, he reminds us of the kitchenmaid's persecutor, the cook Françoise. This seems to be a serious misfunction; the figure of Charity is meant to stand for the kitchenmaid, not the cook. In any case, charity is the last quality that could be attributed to Françoise. There is a metonymic residue in this reference; de Man feels that it is, in fact, an essay on the conflict between metaphoric and metonymic meaning, and the final collision of Françoise and the kitchenmaid in the same figure reflects the everlasting conflict of literal and figurative meaning, a conflict as blind and endless as that of the cook and her maid.

You cannot make a metaphor without such metonymic residues. If Achilles is called a lion, his strength is referred to, but there are residues in the regions of bestiality, cruelty, hairiness and so on. De Man believes that literature is built around the metonymies, just as much as the metaphors, and that the relation of literature to life, previously considered metaphoric, is more profoundly metonymic. If music is a symbol of affective life, then it must also - and maybe first of all - be an allegory. It has 'literal' meanings which lead in unexpected directions.

10.3. Some errors

10.3.1. Since the term 'deconstruction' has become fashionable and is often used loosely, it will be worthwhile to list a few false meanings.

It does not mean 'analyse, dismantle into component parts', a connotation often attributed. A recent book on music, for example, comments:

> The pianist has to 'deconstruct' the musical text into its essential components so that he can then organize his motor actions round the resulting abstract scheme.

This writer does not, presumably, mean that the 'essential components' are conflicting poles of a deconstructed opposition or that the pianist's disassembly of the music unearths an inner subversion.

10.3.2. The deconstructive approach is sometimes imagined to constitute a search for principles of differentiation. But of course, a principle of differentiation would be already differentiated; it would be in opposition to a principle of non-differentiation. *Différance* comes before all differentiation and is in play throughout differentiation. Differences, therefore, are not produced by the play of *différance*, but by the forces of variation, development, continuity.

In an article on Brahms's Intermezzo, Op 118 No 2, Robert Snarrenberg describes the denaturing of gestures of beginning and ending so that the expectations of the listener are frustrated (Snarrenberg 1987). His description of the piece is subtle and penetrating, but he assumes that the changes in 'meaning' of the opening melodic gesture demonstrate the play of *différance*. As Robert Samuels points out (Samuels 1989b), Snarrenberg treats *différance* as a concept or critical tool; this is 'to fall into the very trap that the term sets out to designate'. Snarrenberg is happy to use much of the Derridean terminology, which he consistently misunderstands. The unexpected outcome of movements towards apparent goals is said to 'subvert my expectations of patterned continuations'; yet this cannot be subversion in Derrida's sense, for the force that moves the music to behave unexpectedly is a differentiated force, of course, something very like the idea of probability which forms the basis of Leonard Meyer's theories in *Emotion and Meaning in Music*. Later, the original meaning of the opening gesture is said to be held 'under erasure', Derrida's word for an idea that is present in its own denial, like a word that has been crossed out but remains legible. It is all a terrible warning to those critics who love fashionable terminology.

10.4. Deconstruction and music theory

10.4.1. So far, the deconstruction movement has intruded only into the margins of music theory. Nevertheless, its proponents argue that music is peculiarly suitable to demonstrate the deconstructive principle.

Music signifies by means of some signifying code, and analysis also refers to code in interpreting music. But no code is originary; there is no single code which is the key to the work, nor is there a code which explains all other codes. The branching of terms within a code may itself be governed by some code or codes, and the apparent power of a code to 'explain' a piece may in fact be subverted when the listener realises that the code is itself part of the surface material governed by other codes. Any interpretation of the music must, therefore, remain 'open'; analysis loses its claim to metaphoric and symbolic status. No analysis reveals the 'true' nature of the music.

But this does not mean that analysis is impossible, or that all analyses are of equal validity or irrelevance. An analysis is the analyst's track through the unending codes that permit the music to be heard as a structure. Placed metonymically alongside the music, it represents an encounter between music and listener that suggestively opens the space between signifier and signified and invites the third person, who is both reader and listener, to embark on structuration.

Music, in fact, is especially well-equipped to prompt this kind of deconstructive analysis, because unlike literature it does not seem to make unequivocal assertions. 'Music is allegorical through and through,' remarks Christopher Norris, 'since its significance can never be grasped once and for all in an act of fulfilled, self-present perception' (1989, 341). In addition, the holding of text and subtext in simultaneous balance, which is characteristic of literature and philosophy, is replaced in music by the successive presentation of contradictions: music is 'the diachronic version of the pattern of non-coincidence within the moment' (de Man 1971, 129).)

10.4.2. We should therefore expect that music will deconstruct itself in a more obvious way than literature or philosophy. R J Samuels, in a paper read to the Royal Musical Association in 1989, refers to 'generic codes' in the interpretation of the Scherzo of Mahler's Sixth Symphony. These are characterized by certain forms of rhythmic and intervallic movement; they are called *Charakteren* by Adorno and are much the same as the expressive 'topics' mentioned by Kofi Agawu in his study of Classical music (see above, p. 226). This piece - and much more of Mahler's output - refers to the topics of *Ländler* and march.

The opening bars of the Scherzo seem, at first hearing, to be one of those rustic Ländler typified by the second movement of the Second Symphony. But there is something unnatural and perverse about these bars; Adorno finds the movement 'asphyxiating' (quoted by Samuels, 1989a, 14). The traditional dance texture of melody and accompaniment is replaced with an unrelenting linear texture that is not so much counterpoint - simultaneous melodic lines which relate to each other - as a bony succession of repetitive fragments and static pitches.

A closer examination reveals certain distortions of the Ländler character in the areas of rhythm and melodic motive. Ländler phrases begin with upbeats; this movement presents at the outset a repeated upbeat figure on a kettledrum tuned to A, each upbeat marked with a *sforzato*, combined with repeated As played *martellato* by the lower strings, without any upbeat, the *sforzati* on the first beat of each bar. Some kind of deconstructive effort is exerted from the very start, it would seem.

Samuels makes an inventory of the rhythmic configurations of every bar in the first 32 bars. This leads to two conclusions: first, there is little or no interrelation or development of the figures, which remain isolated in their contrasting identities. Second, there is a distinction between rhythms typical of the Ländler and other rhythms. Constantin Floros, in his book on Mahler, lists the definitive rhythms of the Ländler, referring to Mahler's compositions and to popular types. Broadly speaking, the rhythms of bars 2-5 of the Scherzo conform to these definitive types, except for the lurching unequal values in the violins.

Figure 10.1

At bar 15, however, there are rhythms which distance the piece from its Ländler character, notable a swooping anacrusis in demisemiquavers and a long trill on the first beat.

Figure 10.2

In spite of the triple metre, these motives refer to another genre, that of *march*, as is seen by comparison with the first movement, which is a classic Mahlerian march (Figure 10.3). The lack of rhythmic development, and the predominance of Ländler rhythms, suggest that this section of the music signifies more through the dance-code than the symphonic code. However, the Ländler code is mixed almost from the start with the march code. Even in the opening bars (Figure 10.1) the lurching unequal rhythm is related to the march rhythms of the first movement.

Figure 10.3

Furthermore, the intrusion of march motives seems to arrest the harmonic momentum; in passages of harmonic mobility like bars 7-10 and 21-31 the rhythms are mainly Ländler-like, while the static bars (10-20) introduce march figures.

> This suggests a reversal of generic character: the Ländler, a repeating dance-form, gives forward motion; while the march, essentially a generic type of progressing, is made static (Samuels, 1989, 20).

Is this mixing and denaturing of generic codes a sign of the unification of movements of the symphony, by introducing into the Scherzo characteristics of the other two movements? That is, may the generic codes be controlled fundamentally by the symphonic code? Or is there a wish to situate the music in the space between two generic codes?

The latter possibility is hinted at by the Trio sections, marked 'altväterisch'. This instruction seems enigmatic; according to Paul Banks it refers to a Bavarian dance form. There are Ländler-like rhythms in this section, but here and there an extra beat is added to the bar, giving a moment of true march rhythm. Is the Trio a Ländler or a march? It stumbles midway between these codes like an old codger, an *Altvater*.

Figure 10.4

If our analysis of the Scherzo is allegorical - suggesting, not an originary code but an infinite regression of codes - then the Trio is an allegory, too. 'The analysis reflects allegorically on the piece, and the Trio reflects allegorically on the Scherzo.'

10.5. The myth of unity

10.5.1. Derrida writes that 'metaphysics imposes the necessity of its own critique' (quoted by Alastair Williams, 1989, 191). Adorno felt that art, also, calls for a radical investigation of its own contradictions; in this respect, as in so many others, the Viennese master was in advance of his time.

> Philosophy says what art cannot say, although it is art alone which is able to say it: by not saying it... the unresolved antagonisms of reality appear in art in the guise of immanent problems of artistic form (quoted by Williams, 1989, 193).

Somewhere written within art, then, is the very deconstruction which philosophy seeks. The true art analysis would uncover contradictions rather than pursue unities.

This is especially true when art has taken on board the contradictions of society; and this is pre-eminently the case with nineteenth-century music. The philosophers of the period became preoccupied with aesthetics because art seemed to offer a reconciliation of the conflicting pressures of society. Nor was this purely an abstract need; political goals like independence, and cognitive needs like individualism, were pulling society apart. Art was the favoured area for the bringing together of centrifugal forces into imaginative unity (this paraphrases Alan Street, 1989).

The artist was called upon to 'provide the focus necessary to hold together an apparently miscellaneous content' (Kathleen Wheeler, quoted by Street, 82). The idea of the genius flourished; the heroic task of the Romantic artist was to master the paradox of centrifugal inspiration in a centripetal economic structure. Thus, the predominant myth was organic unity, whereby the artist brought together disparate ingredients into an illusion of synthesis and gave a pledge of wholeness to a society that was fragmenting.

10.5.2. As a result, music theorists became attached to the notion of organic unity, with a fierce tenacity that survives almost unchecked. All the prominent authorities, different though they are in other ways, build their systems around a demonstration of unity and base assessments of value on this consideration. Marx, Riemann, Schenker, Schoenberg, Reti, more recently Boulez and Allen Forte, at some level or other assume that works of music are unified, by style, interval-pattern, motive, rhythm or in more global ways.

The work is seen as a reified, finite, hypostatized entity. This is, admittedly, an appropriate way of envisaging the music of the German/Austrian tradition, as Alan Street remarks; for this corpus was produced mainly to sanctify the myth in question. It is less suitable for other musics - newer music, aleatory music, ancient music, ethnic music - and indeed is inadequate even for the study of German Romantic music, for it fails to illuminate the inner contradictions.

Consequently, analysis is hijacked by the organic lobby. Instead of offering an objective structuration of music, it 'exists for the purpose of demonstrating organicism, and organicism exists for the purpose of validating a certain body of works of art' (Kerman, 1980/1, 315).

10.5.3. Here and there an analyst brings to light a trace of music's self-deconstruction. Even D F Tovey, more devoted than most analysts to the idea of organic growth, denied that symphonic works grew out of their themes; these were surface features, uniquely definitive of the works that bore them, but in no way determining the structure (summarized by Bent, 1987, 55). Arnold Whittall, assessing the received view that Berg's Violin Concerto demonstrates a miraculous reconciliation between serial technique and fragments of tonal material, decides that, on the contrary, it proves their irreconcileability (quoted by Street, 1989, 97).

10.6 *The implications of deconstruction*

10.6.1. The deconstructive analyst concentrates on the *signifier* in order to find surprising and untidy connections which lead to new insights. In metonymy, the connection of two terms is 'nowhere but in the signifier' (Lacan, quoted by Ayrey, 1991). In metaphor there is a 'sliding' across from the plane of the signifier to that of the signified; as soon as you have crossed the boundary you are in the country of interpretation and *parti-pris*, your analysis has begun to harden.

Once again, music is cited as the *locus classicus* of human expression because it is 'all signifier'. Like Schopenhauer and Langer, De Man and Norris anticipate that music will provide the ideal example of allegory and the subversion of meaning because its business is constantly to evade translation and interpretation, to turn metaphor into metonymy. So musical connections - thematic, rhythmic, harmonic details - are pre-eminently metonymic features. When a theme is identified by playing its first two notes or adapting its rhythm to a new contour, there is an example of 'part for whole', the rhetorical device of *synecdoche*, a kind of metonymy. Within itself, music is incapable of producing metaphoric connections; it is all signifier and all metonymy, the real deconstructive art.

Older hopes that music would prove the key to everything have remained dreams, and the new hope will probably have the same fate. However, it is probably true to say that post-structuralism is more amenable to music than was structuralism itself; the strain involved in the application of structuralist linguistic theories to music has been apparent from time to time in the present work. But how is music to be illuminated by deconstructive theory, except in trivial ways?

10.6.2. Craig Ayrey suggests that an important mission is the deconstruction of the 'dogmatic allegories' of music analysis. This does not mean merely *comparative analysis*, a recent preoccupation, for the comparison of analyses does not demonstrate the inner subversion of each analysis. Nor does it mean a sort of vague interpretation 'without rules', a mere abandonment of interpretative strategies in order to approach every work *ad hoc*. The unmasking of the 'myth of organic unity', for example, does not eliminate the myth from the field of formal discussion; it is no less relevant to the music in which it is infolded.

10.6.3. Probably the most important consequence is the call to examine the untidy, the irrelevant and the marginal. Like Proust's long novel, music is full of cooks with corkscrews. Samuels illustrates this in his study of Mahler's Sixth Symphony. This may lead to a kind of 'gapology' (Gushee, quoted by Nattiez, quoted by Ayrey, 1991,9), a science of lacunae or analysis of the bits we cannot comprehend.

Instead of seizing on the fragments that support our view of the piece - the instances of thematic unity, the traits of stylistic coherence, the topics of extra-musical meaning - we must observe the spaces between them, which means not only the syntagmatic spaces but also the aspects of construction that seem to evade our motivated analysis.

10.6.4. Yet the gaps are not only in the music. There are spaces between the analyses, too; finally, the rigorously systematic programme of structuralism leads us, not to the promised land of objective truth, but the the acceptance of plurality. No listener to music can fully inhabit the land of Tovey, Schenker or Nattiez. He lives in the space that surrounds them, where he may from time to time pitch his own camp.

Attend to mythology, then, but not only to mythology. Attend to analysis, but attend to many analysts and to none. Observe the salient parts of the musical work, but not only the salient; search also in the gloomiest clefts and crannies.

11

EPILOGUE

Some of the proponents of deconstructive theory, especially those who write in an ugly and self-important bratspeak, give the impression that it thumbs its nose at all its predecessors and makes fools of us all. Neither Derrida nor De Man would take this view; their attitude is not the humanistic obeisance to individual intuition disavowed in Chapter 1, but a declaration of the non-final and non-originary character of every analysis. It would be a fatal mistake to think that they release the musicologist from the requirement of scientific precision. The dogs of 'intuitive' analysis will always bark at the doors and must be repulsed with the same energy.

The present work has been full of excursions into scientific musicology. Still, they are no more than individual excursions; it may be, as Jean-Jacques Nattiez once suggested in conversation, that semiotics is more of an approach and a style than a unified theory. The positivistic attitude of paradigmatic analysis has little in common, apparently, with the florid speculation of intonation theory or the inspired ingenuity of structural semantics. Nevertheless, there is something about semiotic investigation and linguistics-based studies which distinguishes them from the critical heuristics of writers like Kretzschmar, D F Tovey and Charles Rosen.

In semiotics, the principles of analysis and criticism are explicit and the application of these principles is systematic and public. All dialogue with heuristic criticism is dialogue with the man; any dissent from a semiotic finding must engage either at the top or at the bottom of the theoretical edifice, either with the principles themselves (which ought to be *appropriate*, in Hjelmslev's language) or with the item-to-item details of their use. The conclusions of traditional heuristics carry no more authority than does their maker and their standing is that of a personal reputation and charisma. Semiotic writers are mostly unspectacular people: Nattiez, Karbusicky, Tarasti, Hatten and Tagg have the air of patient and honest practitioners, the smell of the workshop rather than the pulpit. They do not invite you to submit to their great erudition but merely to acknowledge their small and scrupulous experimental results. Their style is rationalistic and scientific, without rhetoric or conceit. For purple passages, you have to go to heuristic writers.

But there are also specific features of methodology that perhaps characterise the semiologist. Saussure's distinctions of synchronic from diachronic, and paradigm from syntagm, lie behind most semiotic thought. Certain traditional procedures (for example, Schenkerian graphic analysis) are diachronic and syntagmatic, concerned with the temporal continuum of music and the texture of successive events in a syntactic structure. Other traditional approaches (the isolation of Wagnerian *Leitmotive* or Réti's search for basic motives in a large work or series of works) are paradigmatic, searching through the whole discourse for recurrent items which can then be grouped taxonomically. It is unfair to disparage a syntagmatic method for ignoring the paradigm; for example, to complain that a Schenker graph underplays the effect of musical reprise. Even the shrewd Eugene Narmour does not wholly avoid this error; he complains that a synchronic system is 'untenable' because 'an important part of music has to do with diachronic meaning' (Narmour 1977, 209). Of course, a synchronic or paradigmatic system would depend on its diachronic realization.

The contrary mistake is to find Wagner essentially formless on the strength of a *Leitmotiv*-based analysis. Alfred Lorenz's monumental syntagmatic study *(Das Geheimnis der Form bei Richard Wagner)* is an attempt to redress this, but the work has not been popular. Deryck Cooke's paradigmatic study *The Language of Music* may perhaps be defended as an explicitly and exclusively synchronic approach. It is irrelevant to complain, as have some critics, that Cooke makes nothing of the ongoing development of musical ideas in time.

In spite of the views of Wilson Coker and Eduard Hanslick, semiotics seems to base itself on a non-autonomous view of music. To the question, what is to be expressed by the expression-plane of music? Hanslick makes the reply: 'musical ideas.' This is Coker's 'congeneric' view of musical meaning, which has had much currency in studies of Western classical music. But if music is a sign, then its meaning must be 'simply human', in Greimas's words. This is not to say, of course, that its meaning is referential; merely that the process of music is embedded in other processes, logical, natural and perceptual. Musical coming-before and coming-after, augmentation and diminution, inversion and retrogression, development, hastening and delaying, similarity and difference, linearity and spatiality, success and frustration, are not different from the dynamic processes of the observed world. The return of a musical phrase, of the words 'Ich grolle nicht' (in Schumann's famous song), of a sad thought in the mind of the singer, and even of the lover himself to plead with his beloved, are similar processes semiotically related. There has never been a gesture that was 'purely musical'.

However, semiotics is also committed to a non-realistic view of meaning. If every gesture has some signification, this signification is not necessarily a reference to some actual or imaginary state of affairs. 'There are only differences, without real terms.' Semiotic structures reflect semantic structures (though they are not replicas of each other, as Hjelmslev insists). They do not reflect real structures, whatever these are. The referential use of language, in Jakobson's sense, makes it easy to imagine that words merely describe things and events. But things and events are features of semantic structures, just as much in referential language as in emotive or conative language; there are no 'real' things, except in some abstract ontological sense that has nothing to do with structural studies. Viewed in this light, the semantic dimension of music is obvious. Music does not 'mean' emotions or natural sounds, but its very nature is grounded in common qualities with other structures. Without these it would not be 'pure music', but simply non-semiotic phenomenon, like the sighing of the wind.

It is sometimes objected that semiotics, claiming that music resembles language, obscures the fact that language is a medium of ordinary communication while music is an 'art' (Narmour, for example, makes this complaint). Music is never used to convey day-to-day information or to make conversation at cocktail parties. Music's uselessness for conveying information is, of course, no proof that it is non-semiotic. Some semiotic processes are designed to conceal information (the subliminal symbolism of advertising, described by Roland Barthes) or quite apart from any information that might be conveyed (digital computer languages, or Umberto Eco's 'Watergate model'); Barthes also shows how syntagm and paradigm are at work in dress and food, without any clear 'meaning'.

As for music's 'artistic' status, this is clearly not a semiotic issue, but has to do with metaphysical and ontological matters. The special standing of artistic semioses derives from their moral and spiritual content which has the power to ennoble or degrade, and which requires that we discriminate between good and bad, better and best. But semiotics, like linguistics, is rigorously non-normative, radically rejecting the *Wertästhetik*. Good language and bad language are not concerns of the linguist, and the music semiologist studies at one moment the symphonies of Beethoven, at another moment Russian pop songs, later Indian, Chinese and African music. The aesthetics of idealism arose from a conviction, not that music was meaningful - for the worst music is vilely meaningful, and comparatively meaningless music can be charming - but that certain transcendent qualities, sensual, moral and metaphysical, ought to be expressed in music. A symphony by Walter Piston is 'better' than a Gershwin tune (Henry Pleasants's example in *Serious Music - and All That Jazz*) because it seems to inhabit a higher moral and aesthetic plane. This has nothing to do with signification, and probably nothing to do with music either.

The chief enterprise of music semiotics remains unfulfilled. The complaint of ethnomusicologists, that music analysis was based on a vague and impressionistic metalanguage, was to have been met by a scientific and universal methodology which would make it possible to describe and compare ethnic musics as linguists do with language. But with all the making-explicit of principles and criteria, there has been no single agreed and tested method for the description of music, and writers have still tended to confine themselves to discussion of one musical style only. Only Jay Rahn (1983) seriously tries to lay down a theory for all music, and his results are inconclusive. It is a lamentable failure for our study, and perhaps shows that there is much still to be done.

BIBLIOGRAPHY

Abbreviations:

MS: *Musical Signification, Proceedings of the Second International Congress on Musical Signification, Helsinki, November 1988,* ed. Eero Tarasti, The Hague, Mouton. Publication was imminent at the time of compilation of the present work; items from this collection are therefore dated 1991.

SML: *The Sign in Music and Literature,* ed. Wendy Steiner, Austin, University of Texas Press, 1981.

SOM: *Semiotics of Music,* ed. Eero Tarasti; Special issue of Semiotica, 66, 1/3, 1987.

SW: *The Semiotic Web,* ed. Thomas A Sebeok and Jean Umiker-Sebeok, Amsterdam, etc., Mouton de Gruyter, 1987.

Agawu, V Kofi (1991) *Playing with Signs: a semiotic interpretation of classic music.* Princeton: Princeton University Press

Arom, Simha (1969) Essai d'une notation des monodies à des fins d'analyse. *Revue de Musicologie,* 55/2, 172-216

Asafiev, Boris V (1976-1942) *B V Asafiev's Musical Form as Process,* translation and commentary by James Robert Tull, Dissertation, Ohio State University

Avison, Charles (1752) *An Essay on Musical Expression,* London: Davis

Ayrey, Craig (1991) Diversity and method: some prospects for the 1990s. Unpublished paper read at the City University, London

Baroni, Mario and Jacoboni, Carlo (1978) *Proposal for a Grammar of Melody: the Bach Chorales,* Montreal: University of Montreal

Barry, Kevin (1987) *Language, Music and the Sign: a study in aesthetics, poetics and poetic practice from Collins to Coleridge.* Cambridge: Cambridge University Press

Barthes, Roland (1968) *Elements of Semiology,* translated by A Lavers and Colin Smith. New York, Hill and Wang

Batteux, Charles (1746) *Les Beaux Arts Réduits à un Même Principe,* Paris: Durand

Becker, Judith and Becker, Alton (1979) A Grammar of the musical genre Srepegan. *Journal of Music Theory,* 23/1, 1-44

Bent, Ian (1987) *Analysis* (The New Grove Handbooks in Music), London: Macmillan

Bernstein, Leonard (1976) *The Unanswered Question, Six Talks at Harvard,* Cambridge, Mass.: Harvard University Press

Blacking, John (1971) Towards a theory of musical competence. In *Man: Anthropological Essays presented to O F Raum,* edited by E J De Jager, pp 19-34. Cape Town: Struik

_____(1981) The Problem of "ethnic" perceptions in the semiotics of music. In SML, pp 184-194

_____(1984) What languages do musical grammars describe? In *Musical Grammars and Computer Analysis, Atti del Convegno, Modena, 4-6 ottobre 1982,* Florence: Olschki

Boilès, Charles L (1967) Tepehua thought-song: a case of semantic signalling. *Ethnomusicology,* 11/3, 267-292

_____(1973) Sémiotique de l'ethnomusicologie. *Musique en Jeu,* 13, 34-41

Bright, William (1963) Language and music: areas for co-operation. *Ethnomusicology,* 7/1, 26-32

Bronson, B H, ed (1959-1966) *Traditional Tunes of the Child Ballads.* 3 vols.: Princeton

Brown, Thomas Alan (1968) *The Aesthetics of Robert Schumann.* Westport, Conn.: Greenwood

Chandola, Anoop (1977) *Folk Drumming in the Himalayas: a Linguistic Approach to Music.* New York: AMS Press

Chenoweth, Vida (1966) Song structure of a New Guinea highlands tribe. *Ethnomusicology,* 10/3, 285-297

_____(1969) An Investigation of the singing styles of the Dunas. *Oceania,* 39/3, 218-230

_____(1972) *Melodic Analysis and Perception.* Ukarumpa, Papua New Guinea: Summer Institute of Linguistics

_____and Bee, Darlene (1971) Comparative-generative models of a New Guinea melodic structure. *American Anthropologist,* 73/3, 773-782 (see end of bibliography listing for further entry)

Chomsky, Noam (1965) *Aspects of the Theory of Syntax.* Cambridge, Mass: MIT Press

_____and Halle, M (1968) *The Sound Pattern of English.* New York: Evanston, and London: Harper & Row

Clarke, Eric F (1988) Generative principles in music performance. In *Generative Processes in Music,* edited by John A Sloboda, pp 1-26. Oxford: Clarendon

Coker, Wilson (1972) *Music and Meaning: a Theoretical Introduction to Musical Aesthetics.* New York: Collier-Macmillan

Cook, Nicholas (1990) *Music, Imagination, and Culture.* Oxford: Clarendon

Cooke, Deryck (1959) *The Language of Music.* London, Oxford University Press

Cooper, Robin (1977) Abstract structure and the Indian raga system. *Ethnomusicology*, 21/1, 1-32

Crystal, David (1971) *Linguistics*. Harmondsworth: Penguin

Culler, Jonathan (1975) *Structuralist Poetics*. London: Routledge

_____(1982) *On Deconstruction: theory and criticism after structuralism*. London: Routledge

Dalmonte, Rossana (1987) The Concept of expansion in theories concerning the relationships between music and poetry. In SOM 111-128

Delalande, François (1987) L'analyse des conduites musicales: une étape du programme sémiologique. In SOM, 99-107

Deliège, Célestin (1987) Pour une sémantique selon Rameau. In SOM 239-256

De Man, Paul (1971) *Blindness and Insight: essays in the rhetoric of contemporary criticism*. London: Methuen

_____(1979) *Allegories of Reading: Figural language in Rousseau, Nietzsche, Rilke, and Proust*. New Haven: Yale University Press

Derrida, Jacques (1982) *Margins of Philosophy*, translated by Alan Bass. New York, etc: Harvester Wheatsheaf

Dunsby, Jonathan (1982) A Hitch-hiker's guide to semiotic music analysis. *Music Analysis*, 1/3, 235-242

Dunsby, Jonathan and Whittall, Arnold (1988) *Music Analysis in Theory and Practice*. London: Faber

Eco, Umberto (1979) *A Theory of Semiotics*. Bloomington: Indiana University Press

Ehrenfels, Christian von (1978-1890) Über Gestaltqualitäten. In *Gestalthaftes Sehen*, edited by F Weinhandl. Darmstadt

Engel, Hans (1950) Sinn und Wesen der Musik. *Die Musikforschung*, 3, 204-212

Epperson, Gordon (1967) *The Musical Symbol*. Ames: Iowa State University Press

Feibleman, James K (1960) *An Introduction to Peirce's Philosophy, interpreted as a system*. London: Allen and Unwin

Ferguson, Donald N (1973) *Music as Metaphor: the Elements of Expression*. Westport: Greenwood

Glucksmann, Miriam (1974) *Structuralist Analysis in Contemporary Social Thought: a Comparison of the Theories of Claude Lévi-Strauss and Louis Althusser*. London: Routledge

Goodman, Nelson (1968) *The Languages of Art*. London: OUP

Gower, Herschel, and Porter, James (1970) Jeannie Robertson: the Child ballads. *Scottish Studies*, 14/1, 35-58

Gràbocz, Màrta (1986) *Morphologie des Oeuvres pour Piano de Liszt*. Budapest: MTA Zenetudomànyi Intézet

Granger, Gilles-Gaston (1968) *Essai d'une Philosophie du Style*. Paris: Armand Colin

Greenlee, Douglas (1973) *Peirce's Concept of Sign*. The Hague and Paris: Mouton

Greimas, A J (1966) *Sémantique Structurale, recherche de méthode*. Paris: Larousse

_____(1970) *Du Sens*. Paris: Le Seuil

_____(1983a) *Du Sens II*. Paris: Le Seuil

_____(1983b) *Structural Semantics, an Attempt at a Method*, translated by Daniele McDowell, Ronald Schleifer and Alan Velie. Lincoln: University of Nebraska Press

_____(1987) *On Meaning: selected writings in semiotic theory*, translated by Paul J Perron and Frank H Collins. London, Pinter

Guertin, Marcelle (1981) Différence et similitude dans les préludes pour piano de Debussy. *Revue de Musique des Universités Canadiennes (Montreal)*, 2, 56-83

Gurney, Edmund (1880) *The Power of Sound.* London: Smith, Elder.

Hanslick, Eduard (1891) *The Beautiful in Music,* translated by Gustav Cohen. London and New York: Novello (photographic reprint, New York: Da Capo, 1974).

Harris, James (1765) A Discourse on music, painting, and poetry. In *Three Treatises,* 2nd edn. London: Nourse

Harris, Zellig S (1951) *Methods in Structural Linguistics.* Chicago: University of Chicago Press

Harweg, Roland (1968) Language and music, an immanent and sign theoretic approach: some preliminary remarks. *Foundations of Language,* 4, 270-281

Hatten, Robert S (1987a) Aspects of dramatic closure in Beethoven: a semiotic perspective on music analysis via strategies of dramatic conflict. In SOM, 197-210

_____(1987b) Style, motivation and markedness. In SW, 408-429

_____(1988) The Role of expression in musical understanding. Unpublished paper read to the International Musicological Symposium, Melbourne

_____(1991) The Troping of meaning in music. In MS

Hawkes, Terence (1977) *Structuralism and Semiotics.* London: Methuen

Hervey, Sandor (1982) *Semiotic Perspectives.* London Allen & Unwin

Hjelmslev, Louis (1961) *Prolegomena to a Theory of Language*, translated by Francis J Whitfield. Madison: University of Wisconsin Press

Imberty, Michel (1973) Introduction à une sémantique musicale de la musique vocale. *International Review of the Aesthetics and Sociology of Music*, 4/2, 175-196

Jakobson, Roman (1960) Closing statement: linguistics and poetics. In *Style in Language*, edited by Thomas A Sebeok, pp 350-377. Cambridge, Mass: MIT Press, 350-377

_____(1963) *Essais de Linguistique Générale*. Paris: Minuit

_____(1978) *Six Lectures on Sound and Meaning*, translated by J Mepham. Hassocks: Harvester

Jankélévitch, Vladimir (1983-1961) *La Musique et l'Ineffable*. Paris

Kaeppler, Adrienne L (1972) Method and theory in analyzing dance structure with an analysis of Tongan dance. *Ethnomusicology*, 16/2, 173-217

Karbusicky, Vladimir (1983) The Experience of the indexical sign: Jakobson and the semiotic phonology of Leos Janacek. *American Journal of Semiotics*, 2/3, 35-58

_____(1986) *Grundriss der musikalischen Semantik*. Darmstadt: Wissenschaftliche Buchgesellschaft

_____(1987a) The Index sign in music. In SOM, 23-35

_____(1987b) 'Signification' in music: a metaphor? in SW, 430-444

Keiler, Allan R (1977) The Syntax of prolongation, part 1. *In Theory Only*, 3, 3-27

_____(1978) Bernstein's The Unanswered Question and the problem of musical competence. *Musical Quarterly*, 64, 195-222

_____(1981) Two views of musical semiotics. Some properties of the design and syntax of tonal music. In SML, 151-168

Kerman, Joseph (1980/1) How we got into analysis, and how to get out. *Critical Inquiry*, 7

Kivy, Peter (1980) *The Corded Shell: Reflections on Musical Expression*. Princeton: Princeton University Press

Kretzschmar, Hermann (1887) *Führer durch den Concertsaal*. Leipzig

Langer, Susanne (1942) *Philosophy in a New Key*. Cambridge, Mass.: Harvard University Press

_____(1953) *Feeling and Form*. London: Routledge

Lavignac, Albert (1897) *Le Voyage Artistique à Bayreuth*. Paris: Delagrave

Le Huray, Peter, and Day, James (1981) *Music and Aesthetics in the Eighteenth and Early-Nineteenth Centuries*. Cambridge: Cambridge University Press

Lerdahl, Fred, and Jackendoff, Ray (1983) *A Generative Theory of Tonal Music*. Cambridge, Mass.: MIT Press

Lévi-Strauss, Claude (1968) *Structural Anthropology*, translated by Claire Jacobson and Brooke Grundfest Schoepf. Harmondsworth: Penguin

_____(1970) *The Raw and the Cooked: Introduction to a Science of Mythology, I*, translated by John and Doreen Weightman. London: Cape

_____(1981) *The Naked Man: Introduction to a Science of Mythology, 4*, translated by John and Doreen Weightman. London: Cape

Levy, Morton, 1975 On the problem of defining musical units. In *Actes du Premier Congrès International de Sémiotique Musicale, Belgrad, 17-21 Octobre 1973*, pp 135-149. Pesaro: Centro di iniziativo culturale

Lidov, David (1975) *On Musical Phrase*. Montreal: University of Montreal

_____(1979) Structure and function in musical repetition. *Journal of the Canadian Association of University Schools of Music*, 8/1, 1979, 1-32

_____(1981) The Allegretto of Beethoven's Seventh. *American Journal of Semiotics*, 1/1-2, 141-166

Lippman, Edward A, ed. (1986) *Musical Aesthetics: a Historical Reader, vol. 1, 'From Antiquity to the Eighteenth Century'*. New York: Pendragon

Locke, John (1964) *An Essay Concerning Human Understanding*, edited by A D Woozley. London: Fontana/Collins

Lyons, John (1963) *Structural Semantics, an Analysis of Part of the Vocabulary of Plato*. Oxford: Blackwell

Mâche, François-Bernard (1969) Langage et musique. *La Nouvelle Revue Française*, 17/196, 586-594

_____(1971) Méthodes linguistiques et musicologie. *Musique en Jeu*, 5, 75-91

McLeod, Norma (1971) The Semantic parameter in music: the blanket rite of the lower Kutenai. *Yearbook for Inter-American Musical Research*, 7, 83-101

Malinowski, Bronislaw (1932) *The Sexual Life of Savages*, 3rd edn. London: Routledge

Mann, William (1964) *Das Rheingold; Die Walküre; Siegfried; Götterdämmerung*, libretto translations. London: Friends of Covent Garden Royal Opera House.

Molino, Jean (1975) Fait musical et sémiologie de la musique. *Musique en Jeu*, 17, 37-61

Monelle, Raymond (1968) Notes on Bartók's fourth Quartet. *The Music Review*, 29/2, 123-129

_____(1970) Bartók's imagination in the later quartets. *The Music Review*, 31/1, 70-81

_____(1989) Music notation and the poetic foot. *Comparative Literature*, 41/3, 252-269

_____(1991a) Music and semantics. In MS

_____(1991b) Structural semantics and instrumental music. *Music Analysis*, 10/1-2, 73-88

_____(1991c) Music and the Peircean trichotomies. *International Review of the Aesthetics and Sociology of Music*, 22, 99-108

Morin, Elisabeth (1979) *Essai de Stylistique Comparée*. Montreal: University of Montreal

Morris, Charles (1946) *Signs, Language and Behaviour*. New York: Prentice-Hall

Morris, David (1989) A Semiotic investigation of Messiaen's "Abîme des Oiseaux". *Music Analysis*, 8/1-2, 125-158

Munro, Ailie (1970) Lizzie Higgins and the oral transmission of ten Child ballads. *Scottish Studies*, 14/2, 155-175

Nattiez, Jean-Jacques (1972) La Linguistique, voie nouvelle pour l'analyse musicale? *Cahiers Canadiens de Musique*, 4, 101-115.

_____(1975) *Fondements d'une Sémiologie de la Musique*. Paris: Union Générale d'Editions

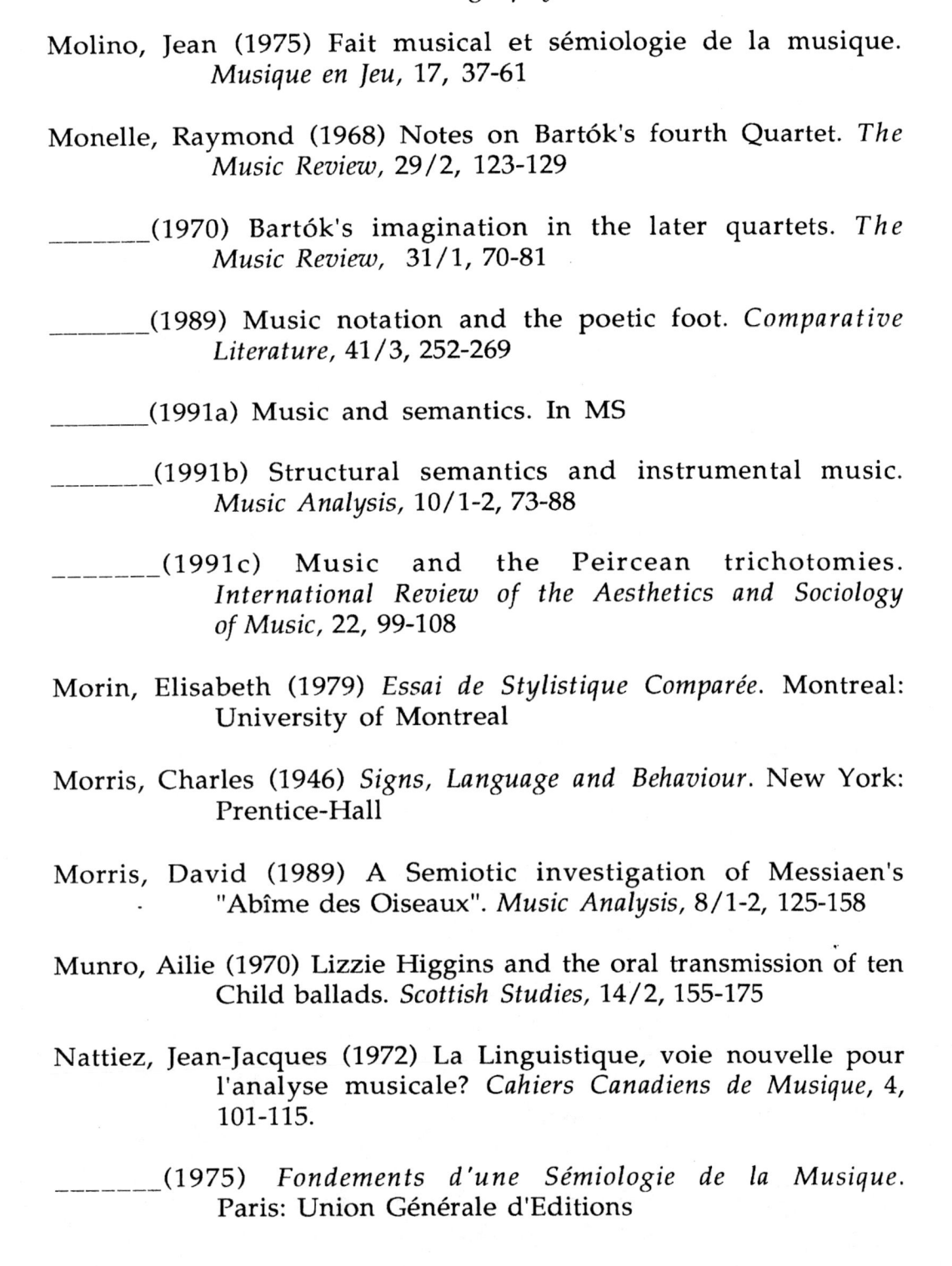

_____(1982) Varèse's *Density 21.5:* a study in semiological analysis, translated by Anna Barry. *Music Analysis,* 1/3, 243-340

_____(1987a) *Musicologie Générale et Sémiologie.* Paris: Bourgois

_____(1987b) Sémiologie des jeux vocaux Inuit. In SOM, 259-278

Narmour, Eugene (1977) *Beyond Schenkerism, the need for alternatives in music analysis.* Chicago: University of Chicago Press

Naud, Gilles (1975) Aperçus d'une analyse sémiologique de *Nomos Alpha. Musique en Jeu,* 17, 63-72

Nettl, Bruno (1958) Some linguistic approaches to musical analysis. *Journal of the International Folk Music Council,* 10, 37-41

Neubauer, John (1986) *The Emancipation of Music from Language.* New Haven and London: Yale University Press

Newcomb, Anthony (1984) Once more "Between absolute and programme music": Schumann's Second Symphony. *19th Century Music,* 7/3, 233-250

Newman, Ernest (1949) *The Wagner Operas,* vol. 1. New York: Knopf. Reprinted: Harper and Row, 1983

Norris, Christopher (1989) Utopian deconstruction: Ernst Bloch, Paul de Man and the politics of music. In *Music and the Politics of Culture,* edited by C Norris, pp 305-347. London: Lawrence and Wishart

Noske, Frits (1977) *The Signifier and the Signified, Studies in the Operas of Mozart and Verdi.* The Hague: Nijhoff

Nylund, Heikki (1983) Syntactic structures of North Indian ragas. *The World of Music,* 25/2, 45-57

Osborne, Nigel (1986) La Forme musicale comme processus. *International Review of the Aesthetics and Sociology of Music*, 17/2, 215-222

Osmond-Smith, David (1972) The Iconic process in musical communication. *VS, Quaderni di Studi Semiotici*, 31-42

_____(1975) L'iconisme formel: pour une typologie des transformations musicales. *Semiotica*, 15/1, 33-47

Peirce, Charles Sanders (1931-1958) *Collected Papers of Charles Sanders Peirce*, edited by Charles Hartshorne, Paul Weiss and A W Burk, 8 vols. Cambridge, Mass: Harvard University Press

_____(1940) *The Philosophy of Peirce, Selected Writings*, edited by Justus Buchler. London: Kegan Paul

Perlman, Alan M, and Greenblatt, Daniel (1981) Miles Davis meets Noam Chomsky: some observations on jazz improvisation and language structure. In SML, 169-183

Piaget, Jean (1971) *Structuralism*, translated by Chaninah Maschler. London: Routledge

Popper, Karl R (1959) *The Logic of Scientific Discovery*. London: Hutchinson

Powers, Harold S (1976) The Structure of musical meaning: a view from Banaras. *Perspectives of New Music*, 14/2 - 15/1, 308-334

Propp, Vladimir (1958) *Morphology of the Folktale*. Bloomington: Indiana Research Centre in Anthropology

Rahn, Jay (1983) *A Theory for All Music. Problems and Solutions in the analysis of non-Western forms*. Toronto: University of Toronto Press

Réti, Rudolph (1962) *The Thematic Process in Music*. New York: Macmillan

_____(1967) *Thematic Patterns in the Sonatas of Beethoven*, edited by Deryck Cooke. London: Faber

Rouget, Gilbert, and Schwarz, Jean (1970) Transcrire ou décrire? Chant soudanais et chant fuégien. In *Echanges et Communications: Mélanges Offerts à Claude Lévi-Strauss*, vol. 1, edited by J Pouillon and P Maranda, pp 677-706. The Hague, Mouton

Ruwet, Nicolas (1962) Note sur les duplications dans l'oeuvre de Claude Debussy. *Revue Belge de Musicologie*, 16. Reissued in *Langage, Musique, Poésie*, pp 70-99 (see below)

_____(1966) Méthodes d'analyse en musicologie. *Revue Belge de Musicologie*, 20, 65-90

_____(1967a) Musicology and linguistics. *International Social Science Journal*, 19/1, 79-87

_____(1967b) Quelques remarques sur le rôle de la répétition dans la syntaxe musicale. In *To Honour Roman Jakobson*, pp 1693-1703. The Hague: Mouton

_____(1972) *Langage, Musique, Poésie*. Paris, Le Seuil

_____(1975) Théorie et méthodes dans les études musicales. *Musique en Jeu*, 17, 11-35

Samuels, R J (1989a) Deconstruction/reconstruction: some recent theory and music analysis. Revised form of unpublished paper delivered to the Royal Musical Association, November 1989

_____(1989b) Derrida and Snarrenberg. *In Theory Only*, 11/1-2, 45-58

Saussure, Ferdinand de (1974) *Course in General Linguistics*, edited by Charles Bally and Albert Sechehaye, translated by Wade Baskin. Glasgow: Collins

Schneider, Reinhard (1980) *Semiotik der Musik: Darstellung und Kritik*. Munich: Fink

Schoenberg, Arnold (1950) *Style and Idea*. New York: Philosophical Library

Sebag, Lucien (1964) *Marxisme et Structuralisme*. Paris: Payot

Seeger, Charles (1960) On the moods of a music logic. *Journal of the American Musicological Society*, 13, 224-261

Singer, Alice (1974) The Metrical structure of Macedonian dance. *Ethnomusicology*, 18/3, 379-404

Sisman, Elaine (1982) Small and expanded forms: Koch's model and Haydn's music. *The Musical Quarterly*, 68, 444-475

Sloboda, John A (1985) *The Musical Mind: the Cognitive Psychology of Music*. Oxford: Clarendon

Snarrenberg, Robert (1987) The play of Différance: Brahms's Intermezzo, Op 118 No 2. *In Theory Only*, 10/3, 1-25

Stefani, Gino (1974) Progetto semiotico di una musicologia sistematica. *International Review of the Aesthetics and Sociology of Music*, 5/2, 277-289

_____(1976) *Introduzione alla Semiotica della Musica*. Palermo: Sellerio

Steiner, George (1989) *Real Presences*. London: Faber

Stoianova, Ivanka (1987) On isotopies and disengagers in music. In SW, 460-467

Street, Alan (1989) Superior myths, dogmatic allegories: the resistance to musical unity. *Music Analysis*, 8/1-2, 77-123

Sundberg, J, and Lindblom, B (1976) Generative theories in language and music descriptions. *Cognition*, 4, 99-122

Sychra, Antonin (1973) Le Chanson folklorique du point de vue sémiologique. *Musique en Jeu*, 10, 12-33

Tagg, Philip (1979) *Kojak, 50 Seconds of Television Music. Toward the Analysis of Affect in Popular Music*. Studies from the Department of Musicology, Göteborg, no. 2

_____(1981) *Fernando the Flute: the analysis of affect in Abba's Fernando which sold over 10,000,000 copies and has been heard by over 100,000,000 listeners*. Stencilled paper from Gothenburg University Musicology Department

_____(1982) Analyzing popular music: theory, method and practice. *Popular Music*, 2, 37-67

_____ (1987) Musicology and the semiotics of popular music. In SOM, 279-298

Tarasti, Eero (1979) *Myth and Music, a semiotic approach to the aesthetics of myth in music, especially that of Wagner, Sibelius and Stravinsky*. Paris, etc.: Mouton.

_____(1984) Pour une narratologie de Chopin. *International Review of the Aesthetics and Sociology of Music*, 15/1, 53-75

_____(1985) Music as sign and process. In *Analytica: studies in the description and analysis of music, in honour of Ingmar Bengtsson, 2 March 1985*, pp 97-115. Stockholm: Royal Swedish Academy of Music

_____(1987) Some Peircean and Greimasian concepts as applied to music. In SW, 445-459

_____(1989) L'Analyse Sémiotique d'une Prélude de Debussy ('...La Terrasse des Audiences du Clair de Lune'). Unpublished typescript

_____(1991) Après un rêve - l'analyse sémiotique d'une mélodie de Gabriel Fauré. In MS

Thibaut, Anton Friedrich Justus (1861-1826) *Ueber Reinheit der Tonkunst*. Heidelberg: Mohr

Ullmann, Stephen (1963) *Principles of Semantics*. Oxford: Blackwell

Webb, Daniel (1769) *Observations on the Correspondence between Poetry and Music*. London: Dodsley

Williams, Alastair (1989) Music as immanent critique: stasis and development in the music of Ligeti. In *Music and the Politics of Culture*, ed. C Norris, London, Lawrence and Wishart

Winograd, Terry (1968) Linguistics and the computer analysis of tonal harmony. *Journal of Music Theory*, 12/1, 2-49

Zak, Vladimir (1979) *On the Melodies of the Popular Song* (in Russian). Moscow

_____(1982) Asaf'ev's theory of intonation and the analysis of popular song. *Popular Music*, 2, 91-111

Chenoweth, Vida (1979) The Usrufas and their Music. *SIR Museum of Anthropology, Publication 5*, Dallas

INDEX OF PERSONS

ABBA, 285, 290-4
Abbate, Carolyn 121-2
Abraham, Gerald 264
Adorno, Theodor W 317, 320
Agawu, Kofi 226-232, 270, 273
Althusser, Louis 125
D'Alembert, Jean le Rond 5
Arlen, Harold 290
Arom, Sinha 87
Asafiev, Boris 12-13, 30, 213, 226, 270, 274-9, 280, 283, 285 290, 295, 303
Avison, Charles 2-3
Ayrey, Craig 321-2

Babbitt, Milton 115
Bach, C P E 4, 18, 303
Bach, J S 16, 122, 137, 154, 243, 302
Banks, Paul 319
Baroni, Mario 154-5
Barry, Anna 90
Barry, Kevin 20
Bartha, D 66
Barthes, Roland 25, 326
Bartòk, Bela 210, 218, 260
Bath, Hubert 207
Batteux, Charles 3, 200, 208, 216
Beattie, James 156
Becker, Judith and Alton 180-187
Bee, Darlene 177-180

Beethoven, Ludwig van 61, 66, 69, 124, 130, 140, 196, 207, 210, 213, 218, 221-32, 269-71, 278, 295, 297, 302, 309, 312, 327
Bell, Clive 8-9
Bengtsson, Ingmar 31
Bent, Ian 123, 227, 321
Berg, Alban 321
Berlioz, Hector 207, 221-3, 225, 295
Bernanos, Georges 244
Bernstein, Leonard 127-131
Birdwhistell, Ray L 163
Blacking, John 93, 155-8, 191-2
Bloomfield, Leonard 40, 47, 193
Boilès, Charles 187-8, 190
Boulez, Pierre 94-5, 320
Brahms, Johannes 66, 96, 114, 124, 130-1, 310, 315
Bréal, Michel 26
Brémond, Claude 247
Bright, William 28, 162
Byron, George Gordon, Lord 217

Cavanagh, Beverly 93
Chandola, Anoop 28, 165-7
Chenoweth, Vida 63, 65, 122, 177-80, 193

Chomsky, Noam 29, 46-51, 57, 127, 131-2, 135-6, 145, 149, 154-6, 158-61, 192
Chopin, Frédéric 68, 220, 264-8, 272-3, 279
Clarke, Eric F 127
Coker, Wilson 204-6, 286, 325
Coltrane, John 134
Constable, John 201
Cook, Nicholas 91
Cooke, Deryck 1, 11-13, 19, 24, 227, 325
Cooper, Robin 67, 170, 172-5
Crystal, David 47, 50
Culler, Jonathan 247, 307-8, 310-11

Dalmonte, Rossana 31
Dargomizhsky, Alexander S 277
Debost, Michel 114
Debussy, Claude 12, 67, 69-74, 100-8, 115-20, 122, 206, 260-4
Delalande, François 114
Deliège, Célestin 13-14, 31, 114, 214
Delius, Frederick 206
Delvaux, André 98
Derrida, Jacques 19-20, 304, 306-9, 311, 316, 320, 324
Descartes, René 212
Dickens, Charles 218
Du Bos, Charles 211
Dunaevsky, Isaak 282-3
Dürer, Albrecht 202
Durkheim, Emile 24

Eco, Umberto 15, 17, 19, 31, 200-2, 206-8, 210-11, 326
Ehrenfels, Christian von 213
Einstein, Albert 126
Elgar, Edward 79

Eliot, T S 311
Engel, Hans 213
Epperson, Gordon 9

Faltin, Peter 31
Feibleman, James K 200
Ferguson, Donald 198, 312
Fétis, François J 124
Fink, Gottfried W 220
Finscher, Ludwig 221
Floros, Constantin 318
Forte, Allen 123, 320
Freud, Sigmund 56, 125

Galeazzi, Francesco 124, 309
Garfunkel, Art 292
Gazzelloni, Severino 114
Genet, Jean 308
Gershwin, George 69, 327
Gilson, Etienne 90, 214, 216
Glinka, Mikhail I 253
Gluck, Carl W von 59
Glucksmann, Miriam 23, 122, 125-6
Gombrich, Ernest 201
Goodman, Nelson 270
Gottfried of Strassburg 242
Gottschald, Ernst 221
Gower, Herschel 285
Grabócz, Márta 226, 258, 295-303
Granger, Gilles-Gaston 194, 197, 215
Greenblatt, Daniel 134
Greenlee, Douglas 194, 196
Greimas, Algirdas J 30, 233, 235, 237-8, 244-50, 252-3, 259-60, 262-3, 268, 299, 325
Guertin, Marcelle 116, 118-20, 124
Gümbel, Martin 115
Gurney, Edmund 212

Halbreich, H 115
Halle, Morris 149, 161
Handel, Georg F 12, 132, 206
Hanslick, Eduard 9-12, 200, 212, 325
Harris, James 2
Harris, Zellig S 41-43, 47, 65, 83, 87, 127, 193
Harweg, Roland 14
Hatten, Robert 31, 268-71, 324
Haydn, F Joseph 87, 226-32, 277, 311
Hegel, G W F 6-7, 123, 275
Heidegger, M 304
Heinichen, J J 123
Herder, Johannes G 5, 212
Herrick, Robert 217
Hervey, Sandor 25
Higgins, Donald 284
Higgins, Lizzie 284-5
Hjelmslev, Louis 15, 29, 43-6, 50, 90, 108, 126, 146, 238, 275, 324, 326
Hoffman, E T A 6-7
Hornbostel, Erich von 167
Husserl, Edmund 23, 58
Husson, R 168

Imberty, Michel 211

Jackendoff, Ray 25, 30, 135-46, 152, 157-8, 244
Jacoboni, Carlo 154-5
Janácek, Leos 187
Jakobson, Roman 16-17, 37, 46, 53, 70, 74, 326
Jevons, W S 75
Jiránek, Jaroslav 30
Johnson, Barbara 308
Jolivet, Hilda 114
Jolle, André 254-5
Joplin, Scott 68

Kaeppler, Adrienne 28, 163-4, 193
Kant, Immanuel 123
Karbusicky, Vladimir 14, 16, 26-7, 31, 187, 203, 220, 211-13, 216, 274, 324
Katchen, Julius 98
Keiler, Allan R 93, 131-4, 138, 158-60
Keller, Hans 18
Kerman, Joseph 321
Khrennikov, Tikhon N 218
Kivy, Peter 5
Klein, Walter 98
Koch, Heinrich C 311
Kretzschmar, Hermann 91, 213, 324
Lacan, Jules 321
Lambert, J H 26
Lang, P H 66
Lange, Konrad von 217
Langer, Susanne K 1, 7-9, 212-13, 216-17, 219, 312, 321
Lavignac, Albert 241
Lehrdal, Fred 25, 30, 135-146, 152, 157-8, 244
Lesueur, Jean F 302
Lévi-Strauss, Claude 13, 30, 34, 38, 53-5, 57, 80-83, 125, 172, 223, 251-2, 256
Lidov, David 66-9, 74, 83, 90, 116, 221-6
Lindblom, B 149, 153, 155, 158, 161, 180
Liszt, Franz 22, 253, 258, 272-3, 279, 294-303
Locke, John 13-14, 26
Lomax, Alan 123
Lorenz, Alfred 257, 325
Lyons, John 15, 174-5, 233

Mâche, François-Bernard 14, 61, 95, 162
Mahler, Gustav 317-18, 322
Mallarmé, Stéphane 308
Malinowsky, Bronislaw 53
de Man, Paul 20-1, 309, 313-15, 317, 321, 324
Mann, William 253
Marx, Adolf B 123-4, 320
Marx, Karl 56, 125
Mattheson, Johann 26, 123, 212, 227
McLeod, Norma 21-2, 190, 192
Méhul, Etienne N 298, 302
Mendelssohn, Felix 279
Messiaen, Olivier 94, 115-16
Meyer, Leonard 67, 123, 260, 316
Molino, Jean 25, 90-1
Morellet, André 2
Morris, Charles 203-5
Morris, David 115
Mozart, W A 12, 60, 66, 87, 94, 129, 139, 143, 154, 226-32, 269, 271, 277, 306, 312
Munro, Ailie 285
Muradeli, Vano 280

Narmour, Eugene 123, 325-6
Nattiez, Jean-Jacques 22, 25-7, 29, 61, 65, 69, 80, 83, 87-8, 90-6, 99-101, 108-15, 120-7, 158, 162, 193, 214, 216, 275, 322-3
Naud, Gilles 115
Nettl, Bruno 28, 60, 162
Neubauer, John 3, 5, 19-20, 203
Newcomb, Anthony 220-1, 226
Newman, Ernest 236, 241
Nietzsche, Friedrich 304
Norris, Christopher 23, 123, 317, 321

Noske, Frits 31
Nylund, Heikki 169-72, 174

Osborne, Nigel 275-6
Osmond-Smith, David 116, 205-9, 214

Paganini, Niccolo 295
Parker, De Witt 205
Parker, Charles 134
Peirce, C S 5, 25-6, 30, 193-201, 203-5, 220, 212-13, 216, 219
Perlman, Alan J 134
Piaget, Jean 56-58, 169, 172
Pike, Kenneth 38, 63, 65, 83
Piston, Walter 327
Plato 304
Pleasants, Henry 327
Popper, Karl R 126
Porter, James 285
Pound, Ezra 311
Powers, Harold 169, 174-7, 233
Presley, Elvis 294
Prieto, Luis 17
Propp, Vladimir 247-8, 251-2, 258
Proust, Marcel 314, 322
Prout, Ebenezer 60
Purcell, Henry 213

Radcliffe-Brown, A R 54
Rahn, Jay 327
Rameau, Jean-Philippe 21, 38
Rastier, F 238
Ratner, Leonard 227, 230
Ravel, Maurice 30, 223, 251
Réti, Rudolf 51, 90, 124, 157, 244, 320, 325
Riemann, Hugo 67, 90, 124, 320
Riffaterre, Michel 308
Righteous Brothers, The 294
Robertson, Jeannie 284-5

Rosen, Charles 324
Rossini, Gioacchino 299
Rouget, Gilbert 83, 167-9, 242
Rousseau, Jean-Jacques 3-5, 19-20, 212, 304, 306, 308, 311
Rubinstein, Anton 220
Ruwet, Nicolas 29, 43, 31, 67, 70, 74, 80, 83-5, 87, 90, 94-6, 98, 100-1, 109, 116, 124, 127, 158

Said, Edward 228
Saint-Saens, Camille 16
Samuels, Robert 316-9
Sapir, Edward 39-40, 193
de Saussure, Ferdinand 10, 13, 24-6, 32-4, 39, 42, 50, 53, 58, 89, 125, 156, 199, 304-5, 307-8, 310, 325
Schaeffner, André 69-70
Schenker, Heinrich 30, 51, 88, 90, 120, 123, 134, 136, 157, 161, 229, 244, 311, 320, 323, 325
Schering, Arnold 124
Schiller, Johann C F 217
Schilling, Gustav 220
Schneider, Reinhard 31
Schoenberg, Arnold 66, 70, 87, 123, 320
Schopenhauer, Arthur 5-6, 321
Schubert, Franz 12, 122, 221
Schumann, Robert 60, 212, 220-1, 226, 279, 326
Sebag, Lucien 23-4
Seeger, Anthony 252
Seeger, Charles 12, 38, 59, 75-80, 286-7
Shapiro, Michael 268
Shelley, Percy B 308
Sibelius, Jean 252
Simon, Paul 292

Singer, Alice 165
Siohan, R 214
Sisman, Elaine 311
Sloboda, John A 153
Smetana, Bedrich 16, 252
Snarrenberg, Robert 315-6
Spontini, 298-9, 302
Stefani, Gino 1, 29
Steiner, George 22
Stoianova, Ivanka 30
Strauss, Richard 253
Stravinsky, Igor 12, 94-5, 198, 207, 252
Street, Alan 320-1
Sundberg, J 149, 153-5, 158, 161, 180
Sychra, Antonin 191
Szabolcsi, Bence 298-300, 302

Tagg, Philip 12-13, 38, 214, 285-94, 302-3, 324
Tarasti, Eero 27, 30, 216, 219, 251-64, 272-3, 324
Tchaikovsky, P I 253, 279
Tegnér, Alice 149, 153, 158
Tenney, James 109
Thakur, Omkarnath 176
Thibaut, Anton F 6
Toch, Ernst 205-6
Tolstoy, Leo 212
Tovey, D F 122, 321, 323-4
Trubetzkoy, N 35, 53

Ujfalussy, Jozsef 30, 294-5, 301-2

Valéry, Paul 90
Varèse, Edgard 61, 95, 108-15, 162
Verdi, Giuseppe 12, 279
Vivier, Odile 115
Vogler, Georg J 309

de Vries, Jan 255
Vuillermoz, Emile 122

Wackenroder, W H 6
Wagner, Richard 12, 236-42,
    247-58, 279, 325
Warburton, Annie O 122
Webb, Daniel 4, 9, 11, 12
Welby, Victoria, Lady 26, 216
Wheeler, Kathleen 320
Whitehead, Alfred N 7
Whittall, Arnold 321
Williams, Alastair 320
Winograd, Terry 146, 237
Wittgenstein, Ludwig 113
Wolff, Christian 212

Xenakis, Iannis 115-16, 243

Yeats, W B 313

Zak, Vladimir 30, 279-84
Zoller, Karlheinz 114

Printed in the United Kingdom
by Lightning Source UK Ltd.
101080UKS00001B/31-56